Hitler Confronts England

Denn wir fahren, denn wir fahren,
Denn wir fahren gegen Engelland, Engelland, Ahoi!

Walter Ansel

HITLER CONFRONTS ENGLAND

Duke University Press
Durham, N. C.   1960

Cambridge University Press, London, N.W. 1, England
Library of Congress Catalog Card Number 60-12513
Printed in the United States of America
by the Seeman Printery, Durham, N. C.

To my friend Charles Dodson Barrett.

In the late twenties and early thirties the United States Marine Corps tired of rehashing the glories of land campaigning in World War I and began a return to its true role on the sea.

A number of the Corps' deeper thinkers and students identified the scope and depth of this role with the development of Landing Power. In the forefront stood Major Charles D. Barrett (the late Major General Charles D. Barrett, USMC), who was then serving at the Marine Corps Schools, Quantico, Virginia.

There he pioneered a rediscovery of Landing Thought, inspired his colleagues, and labored unceasingly to transfer that thought to paper as amphibious doctrine. How true and farsighted his thinking was, World War II proved.

This book is a contribution to the understanding of the doctrines Charlie Barrett enunciated.

This book was published with the
assistance of funds from a
grant to the Duke University
Press by the Ford Foundation
and from the income from the
P. Huber Hanes Fund.

Preface

Fact and fancy are often at odds in men's minds, and in their hearts. Of the two, fantasy often becomes the more important to history. The fantasy of a leader for instance, or of a particular professional group, or even of a whole people, sometimes explains events that would otherwise remain inexplicable.

In the summer of 1940 the world was convinced that Adolf Hitler would invade England. The public mind pictured him as ready with well laid plans and numberless planes and craft to hop the Channel and take over. In Britain men fed these imaginings with a rereading of Erskine Childers' tale, *The Riddle of the Sands,* and hardened their fantasy of invasion into conviction. An equal conviction that he could be denied the opportunity led eventually to Hitler's downfall. This book concerns itself with the incredible beginnings of that fall.

Not that I suspected this was so; the truth of it developed as the story of Hitler's efforts to subdue Britain unfolded. It thereupon became necessary to ascertain why Hitler had turned the general conviction back to a fantasy.

An outline of the story began to form for me in 1952 through study of the official German records as a Forrestal Fellow of the U.S. Naval Academy. So briefed but unconvinced, I proceeded to Europe and during the course of the following year discussed and rediscussed Invasion England with many 1940 participants. One source led to another so that in all eighty-nine officers directly concerned were consulted and queried on the meaning of the records, plus a greater number of ex-soldiers, sailors, and airmen. The fact and feeling of the 1940 scene began to fill out, and proofing could be undertaken against published works on the episode and its background. A common difficulty became manifest in assessing both the verbal and written judgments.

Both sources, it seemed, tended to endow the actors of the 1940 scene with the omniscience of our post knowledge; that is, the actors were granted a breadth of knowledge and a keenness of judgment equal to that afforded by our current perspective and knowledge of the outcome. Yet at the time of decision in 1940 such powers were not at all at the command of the harried deciders.

Naturally the actors lack much pertinent information that history later possesses, and also, they misinterpret information that is on hand. Worst of all, the actors frequently respond, not to the logic history expects, but to the urges of a local or highly personalized concept. The situation might well be shot through with emotion, with fantasy and perverse preconditioning. Even if this were not the case, even if all the factors for logical decision were before the deciders, their limited human powers of assimilation and judgment could spark logical reaction to only a fraction of the data.

The new amphibious command ships demonstrated this fact during each landing operation they directed. This ship-type evolved in the course of development of today's landing doctrines. She is a ship designed to receive, process, and present all the information that modern communicating devices, radar, and observation gadgets can bring in. On this wonder ship the army, air, and naval commanders were to embark and there together were to decide and conduct the operation out of the new fullness and centralization of intelligence. But the wealth of data and its manifold displays at times became so great and the technology of its presentation so complex as to impede rather than speed action. At times decisions were retarded by too much intelligence; odd bits of information were presented so emphatically that they became magnified out of proportion. Of course the scheme was a step forward; many items were accelerated. But many basic items still escaped attention and they always will. Most often the operations proceed as destined by the forethought and feeling that each commander had put into his preparations.

Thus, war decisions like all others are subject to the feelings and the past of the individual decider. It may well be that the logical and indisputable story that perspective encourages is a story that the reconstruction of the events must sometimes reject. One gets a scent of this in trying to reconstruct the progression of Adolf Hitler's war decisions. There were factors inside of him that counted heavily. They demand a valuing if we are to get at the root of things. This is all the more the case in an attempt to reconstruct his invasion of England.

In reconstructing the invasion project my approach was to try to make myself a part of it in talk to officers and men, in visiting the scenes of their labors in Germany, in the Low Countries, and in France, and then in carrying their high expectations cross-Channel to test them visually and mentally against the natural and man-made defenses of England's shores. Many pertinent lights came from conversations in England, but in the main this report stems from German advices. The job turned out to be a stimulating and heartening adventure all around. My endeavors were met with kindly interest and helpfulness. They were rebuffed in only two instances. New friendships were founded.

In Germany special thanks are due:
Kapitän zur See Heinz Assmann
Kapitän zur See Heinrich Bartels
General der Infantrie Günther Blumentritt
General der Flieger Paul Deichmann
Generalleutnant Gerhard Feierabend
General der Flieger Hellmuth Felmy
Kapitän Kurt Freiwald
Generaloberst Franz Halder
Generalleutnant Adolf Heusinger
Vizeadmiral Hellmuth Heye
General der Infantrie Rudolf Hofman
General der Pioniere Alfred Jacob
Kapitän zur See Wolf Junge
Generalfeldmarschall Albert Kesselring
Generalmajor Hans Kissel
Dr. Karl Klee, whose own work on the planning for the invasion of
    England has recently been published in Germany
Dr. Justus Koch
Kapitän zur See Erich Lehmann
Konteradmiral Werner Lindenau
General der Artillerie Herbert Loch

Generalmajor Bernhard von Lossberg
Generalfeldmarschall Erhard Milch
Konteradmiral Wilhelm Mössel
Dr. Karl Georg Pfleiderer
Konteradmiral Karl Jesko von Puttkamer
Kapitän zur See Hans Jürgen Reinicke
General der Infantrie Friedrich Edgar Röhricht
Vizeadmiral Friedrich Ruge
Generalleutnant Josef Schmid
Admiral Otto Schniewind
Vizeadmiral Erich Schulte-Mönting
Kapitän zur See Alfred Schulze-Hinrichs
General der Flieger Hans Seidemann
Herr Fritz W. Siebel
General der Infantrie Georg von Sodenstern
General der Flieger Wilhelm Speidel
Dr. Heinrich Uhlig
Konteradmiral Gerhard Wagner
General Walter Warlimont
Vizeadmiral Eberhard Weichold
Oberst Wilhelm Willemer
General Josef Windisch
Dr. Ernst Wörmann

In England opportunity offered for a fleeting discussion of Hitler with Mr. Alan Bullock at Oxford, and a lengthier general talk while a guest of Mr. E. H. Hinsley at Cambridge. Mr. Brian Melland and Mr. Ronald Wheatley, of the Historical Branch Cabinet Office, offered a helpful comparison of notes, as did Commander R. M. Saunders of the Admiralty Historical section. Mr. Wheatley's account of German invasion planning was published in England in 1958. Meanwhile, Mr. Peter Fleming's book had treated the question of invasion from the English viewpoint.

Dr. Albert Plesman at the Hague was most kind in granting a free discussion of his 1940 peace efforts and access to his documentary record thereof. Later I was able to go into this episode further with Dr. Heinrich Uhlig of Munich, who had also worked over the record.

Many friends at home also helped me prepare the manuscript. Some of them serve on the staff of the U.S. Naval Academy. Foremost has been my guide, counsellor and friend Associate Professor

William H. Russell. He has sat alongside, editing, focusing, advising, often restraining, but never losing his sage equanimity. Dr. Robert W. Daly has given generously of his wide understanding of writing and publishing. Mrs. S. P. Fullinwider of the Naval Academy Library has encouraged the writing with many pertinent suggestions. Dr. Rocco M. Paone was instrumental in establishing the fruitful liaison with the Office of Military History in Washington. Dr. Ford K. Brown of St. Johns College first pointed up the importance of reporting Hitler's trouble over England and has supplied an abiding interest.

In Washington, General Orlando Ward, Chief of Military History, gave the first real spur to the project with suggestions as to sources, and by opening the facilities of his office at home and abroad. In the Washington office General Paul M. Robinett, Head of Special Studies, and his staff aided me in finding and winnowing out materials. Mr. Detmar Finke was especially helpful.

General Ward introduced me to the Historical Division USAREUR in Karlsruhe under Colonel Wilbur S. Nye. He took us in as shipmate and provided a base of operation with friendly guidance and opportunity for meeting German officers. My project could not have got far without this kindly hospitality.

The office of Naval History in Washington accorded facility for the study of the German naval records. The trail led to Bremerhaven and Heidelberg where the hospitality of Rear Admiral H. E. Orem, Commander U.S. Naval Forces Germany, and Captain John G. McClaughry in Bremerhaven, made possible the pursuit of the German Navy's side of the story through documents and consultation with German officers. Our friends Commander M. F. Hathaway and Lieutenant Commander A. A. Steinbeck eased the way in Bremerhaven, where they were stationed. Also in that port Herr Klaus Dieter Schack helped with the identification of landing craft types and in the preparation of charts and diagrams.

And finally, the present Director of Naval History, Rear Admiral E. M. Eller, has been kind enough to read the manuscript and offer useful suggestions.

A man's family is bound to suffer from the tyranny of his preoccupation with writing. In this regard my wife has cheerfully borne with much more than a normal share of toil and trouble, for she had on her hands a sailor unused to the compromises of shore life and unskilled in the task he had set himself. The work took such an interminable, tortured time. Our daughter, Mrs. Carvel Blair, caught the brunt of the drudgery. While running her own household in Alexandria she managed to beat out the first manuscript copy on her portable. Moreover, as she typed, she read more than mere words and thus became one of our more partial boosters.

It has been a pleasure to think back over the course the manuscript has come and to remember a host of contributors. I hope they share my feelings. Not nearly all can be mentioned nor their generosity adequately described. To all of them I remain grateful.

Annapolis, June 1958   WALTER ANSEL

P.S.

A word is yet due on the use of German ranks and American equivalents. The mention of an officer's rank made trouble: he was of a certain rank at the time of the event, he advanced in rank during the course of the story, and still later when I talked with him he might have held yet another rank. Some German ranks have no counterparts with us, in other instances the ranks are not exactly equivalent. On first mention of an officer I have tried to name him by the rank with which his name has been generally associated. As the tale goes along the German rank of the moment is used, and later his rank in retirement. Wherever an American equivalent may clarify an officer's position, this is used.   W.A.

Contents

Illustrations

Maps and Diagrams

Photographs

Hitler Confronts England

1. *The Time and Setting*

Wunschkonzert

Professor Herms Niel was a German band leader of the war, a popular one, and still is today. He was in good form on that fine July Sunday afternoon in 1940 while officiating with his band at a request radio concert in the splendid broadcast auditorium of the State Radio Building in Berlin. The crowds promenading through the city's many gardens were sympathetic and the beer excellent; Nazi Germany, taking its ease for the moment, looked about expansively and wondered, "What next?"

Life had improved vastly over the dreary past winter of war. It seemed almost like peace. Besides beer there was now coffee—from France, to be sure—and the ladies were again wearing silk hose. The Wehrmacht Wunschkonzerte were request programs broadcasted each Sunday afternoon from Dr. Goebbels' magnificent Grossdeutscher Sender. Goebbels and his assistant, Gödecke, had instituted the programs on the previous New Year's Eve.[1] They liked to speak of the bond thus established between the home folk and their soldiers, of soldiers hovering about field and barrackroom loudspeakers awaiting the Wunschkonzert when they might have been off on liberty. The tie with home held them.

[1] Joseph Goebbels, *Die Zeit ohne Beispiel* (Munich, 1941). This booklet is a collection of Goebbels' speeches of 1939-1941, published by the Nazi party Zentral Verlag. The speech in point commemorated the 50th Wunschkonzert.

On this Sunday Niel at once struck the mood at home and in
the field with singular understanding. He played a well-known composition, which had for a time been restricted in use, Löns's[2] World
War I sailor ballad, "Denn wir fahren gegen Engelland." Goebbels
had withheld it against the time when England should become the primary target. This time had come.

> Heute wollen wir ein Liedlein singen,
> Trinken wollen wir den kühlen Wein,
> Und die Gläser sollen dazu klingen,
> Denn es muss, es muss geschieden sein.

> Gib mir deine Hand, deine weisse Hand,
> Leb wohl, mein Schatz, leb wohl, mein Schatz,
> Leb wohl, Lebe wohl,
> Denn wir fahren, denn wir fahren,
> Denn wir fahren gegen Engelland, Engelland, Ahoi.

To superb professional skill, Niel added patriotic fervor. The
audience at home and in the field approved instantly. He played an
encore and then another. "What about England?" Niel had the
answer. His catchy tune with its march tempo raised the sought-for
battle cry of action: "On to England!"

Inaction there had been aplenty; despite the apparent cheerful air
of confidence, people had begun to wonder. Nothing real had happened since the fall of France. Then, the play-by-play broadcast of

[2] Herms Niel, whose true name is Hermann Nielebock, was conductor of the
stupendous Reich's Labor Service Band. He and his march tempo compositions
enjoyed great popularity; his 100-piece band became an indispensable property for
every Nazi spectacle. He was referred to as Professor Herms Niel. Hermann Löns
was better known as Germany's beloved *Heide-Dichter* (poet of the heaths) than
as the author of the "Engellandlied." It is said he composed the words while a
guest in a German Navy mess during August 1914. Löns fell before Reims on 26
September 1914 shortly after composing the song. Friedrich Eberle set them to
music. In World War I and later the song counted as a cheering messroom ballad
that belonged exclusively to the German Navy. For World War II Niel set the
words to his own tune. To have the song blatted about with this new melody did
not sit well with the German Navy. A free translation of the Löns ballad goes:

> Today a ditty we'll be singing,
> Drinking too, the cool, cool, wine,
> And the glasses they'll be ringing,
> For it's parting, tender parting, that is mine.

> Give me your hand my love,
> Your pale, pale hand,
> Farewell my love, farewell,
> For we're sailing, yes we're sailing,
> 'Gainst England we are sailing
> In the morning.

the signing of the armistice at Compiègne had stirred everyone with thoughts of peace; the war of 1914-1918 had been rewon, there was no other reason for continuing. Peace pervaded the air, and the Germans gave themselves over to a prolonged festival in its honor. "When will peace break out?" became the popular quip of the street. And so time passed in high hopes and happy anticipation.

Late in June the Führer had departed from his headquarters near Rocroi on the Franco-Belgian border for a tour of the West Front with old comrades of the First War. He wanted to give the British a little time to come around; it was just that they did not realize that the war in the West was over. He visited Paris and ordered his generals to organize a gigantic victory parade. Units therefor were designated from the armed forces, and the troops set about polishing and readying their equipment in the odd moments they could spare from taking in the sights and multiphotographing that fabulous city. The French shared the sentiments of peace, as did the Continent in general. The festival rolled along unhindered.

On 6 July 1940 Hitler made his triumphal entry into Berlin amid all the fanfare, pomp, and circumstance the Party could marshal. But contrary to Berlin's expectations, London made no overture toward peace. The Führer postponed his expected speech before the Reichstag and retired abruptly to Berchtesgaden. Ten puzzling days passed without a sign of anything but defiance from London. At length it became impossible to delay longer. Hitler called the Reichstag into extraordinary session for the 19th of July 1940, and there, in re-enactment of Party pageantry and splendor, he delivered himself of an accounting of the war in the West, extolled the virtues of German soldiery, promoted the deserving leaders, and in the end brought out a thin and disappointing tender of peace toward Britain. A few days later the *Völkischer Beobachter,* house organ of the Nazi Party, carried the headline: "ENGLAND HAS CHOSEN WAR."[3] The carnival was over; it had, in fact, been in doldrums for some days.

It was in rescue from these very doldrums that Niel with his "Engellandlied" had been able to release the popular feeling. Goebbels adopted the song as the signature number for all public announcements of action against Britain. The *Sondermeldung* (special announcement) of the radio alert system had become an institution in German life. Introduced in April during the Norwegian

---

[3] *Völkischer Beobachter* (Munich), Wednesday, 24 July 1940.

campaign, the system carried the people of Germany through the stunning successes of the western campaign, virtually as active participants alongside their men at the front.   Hans Fritzsche, the alert's chief exponent, put it thus: "None of us will ever forget how millions and millions of Germans . . . were all warned in one and the same second when the trumpets announced a new deed of glory . . . ."[4]

The Germans were indeed rallied and made one as at no other time in those tense moments of communion.   Here was a device suited as nothing else to their genius for pride and high aspiration. They responded eagerly to re-emphasis on the England problem. *"Achtung! Achtung! Sondermeldung."* All other transmission ceased, trumpets sounded the quickening bars from Liszt's "Les Preludes."

An announcer read the stirring news, and then, in resounding march-off tempo, came the signature, *"Denn wir fahren, denn wir fahren, denn wir fahren gegen Engelland!"* Out it boomed from each of the 15,657,000 radio sets spread over the length and breadth of the land whenever the Navy or Luftwaffe scored.   It never failed to produce an extra hush and pause; England was always news.   There were other war chants, all from the facile baton of Herms Niel, the "Frankreichlied," the "Afrikalied," one for each of the widely separated theaters of war.   The "Engellandlied" alone survived while the others receded into obscurity.   It expressed, after all, the one answer for deciding the war, as popular Germany understood better than its leadership; the one answer Hitler never found.

The renewed confidence and burgeoning hopes of Germany were well founded in the summer of 1940.   The accomplished fact was there.   In forty-three days German legions had knocked out France, chased the British from the Continent, and now stood on the shore of the Channel flexing muscles and acting like a new race of amphibians. If it was not to be peace, what could be more logical than invasion?

The far shore of the Channel, the distant shores of America, and those throughout the world, all shared the tension—even near panic— implicit in the question.

[4] Ernst Kris and Hans Speier, *German Radio Propaganda, Report on Home Broadcasts during the War* (London, 1944), p. 59.

The turn of events since those fateful July days of twenty years ago has been so great that it is hard to recapture their pain and anxiety or to realize what momentous happenings were underway. Epochal changes were in the making, changes in all that existed in memory as "every day" and normal. World communities were being obliterated. New and offensive neighbors had moved in; new signposts pointed to strange destinations. The old way of life seemed in grave peril; truly uneasy, ominous days, those summer days of 1940.

Poet Churchill understood their import thoroughly and felt it in his soul. Already on 18 June he had given Hitler and, for that matter, all the world its cue: ". . . Hitler knows he will have to break us in these islands or lose the war. If we stand up to him all Europe can be free and the life of the world can move forward into the broad sunlight, but if we fail then the whole world, including the United States, and all that we have known and cared for will sink into the abyss of a new dark age . . . . The whole fury and might of the enemy must very soon be turned on us . . . ." Britain struggled in desperation to bring order out of her confused defenses. Her army beaten and disorganized; equipment, tanks, and munitions strewn along the coast of France; her beach defense works pitifully inadequate—rarely had she been so vulnerable. No memory could recall a disaster so sudden in its impact or so overwhelming and far reaching in its portent. Embattled Britain rallied to Churchill's call: "Let us do our duty and so bear ourselves that if the British Commonwealth and Empire lasts for a thousand years men will say, 'This was their finest hour.' "[5]

Sternstunden der Menschheit! (star-fated hours of mankind) prescient and moving; the hour had struck, but spellbinder Hitler could summon up no magic that would deal with it. Had perhaps the dynamics of events outrun his planning? Bemused and baffled he fretted at his mountain retreat where he was wont to withdraw for thinking himself clear. He was attempting to rationalize a practical military problem into one of politics.

Invasion! Ah, but there's a strong word, a rousing word of peculiar and special significance when coupled with England. For an invasion had made her a nation, and successive threats had kept her one and made her great. As she had to Hitler's predecessors, England was posing the age-old problem of insular security, an island freehold anchored close off Europe with a wide choice of action for

[5] Statement by Winston Churchill in the House of Commons, 18 June 1940, *Times,* Weekly Edition (London), 19 June 1940.

or against any mainland operator. To deprive her of this freedom
had been the constant object of each rising Continental strategist.
Now was Hitler's turn at the wheel. Where he would steer became the
gripping question of the day.

What Hitler in truth intended and what he and his machine did
to resolve the problem of England is to this day not clear. We know
an invasion operation *Sea Lion* was set up and fully mounted
in the Channel ports during the summer of 1940. It never came off;
Sea Lion remained a land beast. The reason why has ever since challenged the understanding of laymen and professionals alike. How did
the Germans really think to deal with England? It will be our business
in this study to examine and attempt to clarify the record, principally
from German sources. It will require an examination of Hitler, and
his systems, and the development of German policy and strategy. We
shall review the record of intentions, actions, and events expressed
in official and personal documents. On them we shall bring the
light or shadow of recollections, opinions, and assertions of participants as afforded by direct consultation or as revealed in their writing.

Sea Lion, that forerunner of amphibious operations of the war,
we shall trace from conception in 1939 and birth in the serenity of
anticipated peace after France, through the uncertainties of growth
during the air war to an ignominious end on his native shore. Above
all we shall endeavor to keep attune to the humor, disposition, and
comprehension of those portentous days.

2. Hitleriana

Attitudes Toward England

The attitude toward Britain that Hitler exemplified in the summer of 1940 had long been an authentic part of him and his *Weltanschauung*.

For all time, the thinking of Germans about England has savored more of the political arena than of the battlefield. Striking a workable balance between persuasion and coercion, a business that could so easily be gauged and applied toward European land neighbors, grew fuzzy and unsure when projected over the Channel to include England. On the Continent it was a simple estimate of how much bargaining power to leave the opponent, while against the island kingdom the proposition could barely get beyond the wish to induce bargaining in the first place, to say nothing about portions of a bargain. The Germans hated and admired their British kinsmen, reviled and revered them, but also feared them. The feelings were a mixture of awe and envy, awe inspired by Britain's world empire and vexation at her aloofness and disdain but also respect for the lordliness and social graces she took for granted. Where to draw the line of violence against such a people grew into a fateful dilemma for the landbound Germans, and all the more for their Führer.

Austrian Hitler suffered from the curious anglomania more deeply than ordinary Germans. A casual incident of 1942 typically illustrated his malady.   He had been indisposed, and it was necessary to render reports in his private quarters.   General Halder, the Chief of the Army General Staff, came on him there unawares one day and found him bending over an illustrated London magazine in deep abstraction.   The fine ladies and gentlemen on the page before him typified the way in which he felt the English gentry lived.   Hitler was staring at it in fixed wonderment.   Without greeting he came toward Halder, poking the paper before him, and exclaimed, "That we have to make war on such personages!   Isn't that a pity?"   There are innumerable like anecdotes, bits of table talk and unguarded expressions bearing out the fact of a superspecial place for Britons in the mind and feeling of Adolf Hitler.

Both stories and feeling carried back to World War I when he first met Englishmen in the flesh during the brisk fighting around Ypres.   The first bullet or shell fragment that makes one dive for cover possesses singular power for hammering home a lasting impression.   A British bullet fired by a British soldier had done this for Adolf Hitler, and that observant and sensitive young man never forgot the bullet nor the steadfast Tommies behind it.   He noted their pride. They gave no quarter nor wanted any.   How different these British were from the childish cartoons used by the German press at home to deride them.[1]

Whence sprang this *Herrenvolk,* and what gave them their pride? They had something to uphold, something to fight for.   Was this not what Germany lacked and must attain—position and desirability, that is, a dower to encourage recognition or, if skilfully presented, even alliance?   Germany had nothing.   Once she had something to recommend her, such as a solid position on the Continent, would not England be attracted toward closer ties?   *Bündnisfähigkeit,* he decided, must be built up.

In this approximate sequence can Hitler's halting, but surprisingly candid, valuing of Britain be traced in *Mein Kampf* and in the later confirmatory remarks.   Matters of feeling and the spirit arrested his attention and pressed themselves into his eager but limited understanding.   He sought a place for haughty England in his world philosophy, and it was this very problem that he had elaborated in a secret writing begun in 1925.   Rudolf Hess alone was party to it. His secretary heard him cry out to Hess when news of Britain's

[1] Adolf Hitler, *Mein Kampf* (Munich, 1939), pp. 159, 747.   Hereinafter reference to this book will be made by *MK.*

declaration of war broke in on the two of them on 3 September 1939, "Now my whole work falls to pieces. My book has been written in vain."[2] The existence of such a writing he remarked upon at various times. In that same year of its beginning, 1925, the first volume of *Mein Kampf* made its appearance. Therein Hitler treated foreign policy only briefly, yet showed his deep interest and conviction of its crucial importance. To him German pre-World War I policy had been stupid. He had arrived at something better—emphatic concentration on expansion eastward. But, he concluded, "For such a policy . . . there was in Europe only one possible partner: England. Only with England could one, his back being covered, begin the new Germanic expedition [eastward] . . . to win England's acquiescence . . . no sacrifice should have been too great. It meant the renunciation of colonies and sea power, moreover, the sparing of competition to British industry."[3]

Only one Hitlerian political concept became more deeply ingrained than this one of marriage with England; the other, more basic, urge was for space on the Continent. These two drives complemented each other and together comprised the central theme of his personal mythology—Germania astride Europe, in association with world empire, *Grossbritannien*. The marriage was to come first, in his scheme of timing.

All through the early years of his chancellorship, in fact, until the end of 1937, by which time Hitler reckoned his marriage portion sufficient, and he could consider risking a showdown, Adolf plied an outlandish suit toward England. He felt his eligibility keenly, and for good reason. His ship of state he had cleaned up and put in order. When taken over by him in 1933, she was a rusty decrepit wreck, without engine or rudder, manned by a confused and dis-

---

[2] Albert Zoller, *Hitler Privat* (Düsseldorf, 1949), p. 156. This little book reports the penetrating observations of a woman who, as private secretary, saw Hitler almost daily from 1933 to 1945.

[3] *MK*, pp. 153-59, 366, 697-700, 754-56. The ideas expressed in *MK* on Britain endured to be repeated time over by Hitler when deep in Russia during 1941 and 1942. *Hitler's Secret Conversations 1941-1944* (New York, 1953), pp. 11, 13, 42, 76, 154, 194. Rudolf Hess had to reduce much of Hitler's formative thinking to paper. He alone had access to Hitler's unpublished writing on foreign policy. Shortly after parachuting into Scotland in May 1941, he said to British officials: "I can attest that since I have known the Führer, since 1921, he has always spoken of this, an understanding must be brought about between Germany and England . . . . As soon as he was in power he would do this." *Trial of Major War Criminals before the International Military Tribunal, Nuremberg, 14 November 1945—1 October 1946* (42 vols.; Nuremberg, 1947-1949), XL, 280. The record of these trials will hereinafter be abbreviated *IMT*. *Hitler's Secret Conversations 1941-1944* will be abbreviated *SC*.

affected crew. Four years later she shone with a spic and span smartness that betokened faith in herself and devotion to her captain. The prevailing tone was confidence; Germany felt all but ready to go her own way—but hand in hand with England, if she only would.

Hitler's professions, however, had failed to move Britain. Except for the mild self-interest implicit in the London Naval Agreement of 1935, the British had not responded to the courtship. So in late 1937 Hitler turned his thoughts toward achieving his Continental aims without marriage. The end of his persuasion cycle approached. He would go it alone. Courtship cycles analogous to this first one followed one after the other, each moving closer to coercion.[4]

During the summer and fall of 1937 Hitler idled at his mountain retreat in bafflement over British coolness. Envoy von Ribbentrop had gotten nowhere in his grotesque maneuvers at London (one had included an attempt to win over Mr. Churchill). He reported to his Führer and found him inclined to agree that nothing was to be done with England. Hitler sent him on to cultivate Mussolini in Rome while he himself indulged in monologue debates to work a way out of his perplexity. Signs of change multipled. On 5 November 1937 he staged the first warlike briefing conference to push over his political program with top officials. Hitler disclosed his intention to use force in achieving his ends on the Continent, starting with Austria and Czechoslovakia. England, he averred, would not interfere.[5]

The years of courtship and their aftermath exerted an easily distinguishable influence on planning papers of the German armed services. Their papers at first evidenced an absence of war games with Britain in opposition. An interdict amounting to taboo had been laid against such a thought. The taboo was agreeable to the military, for their problem, England, could be shrugged off to the high priests of the political hierarchy. This posture was above all agreeable to the Navy. In their hearts the German sailors could see no solution except Association. The futility raised by Tirpitz still lay heavily upon them. They hailed the 1935 London Agreement as

[4] Sir Neville Henderson, British Ambassador at Berlin, 1937-1939, threaded apart some of the cycles of Hitler's behavior. ". . . in spite of all his professions of a desire for an understanding with Britain, . . . good relations with England only meant, for him, the acquiescence of England in his schemes for the redrawing of the central European map, . . ." Henderson, *Failure of a Mission* (New York, 1940), p. 96; see also pp. 113-19.

[5] The conference record, called the *Hossbach Notes,* is contained in *IMT* doc. 386-PS. The Hitlerian weather at the Berghof (Hitler's mountain chalet 100 miles southeast of Munich) comes from visitors of the period.

a new, and at last solid, foundation for naval policy. It implied to them mutual naval expansion and co-operation with Britain and encouraged other like hopes, which were totally unjustified. The misconceived hopes persisted well into 1938, when the political climate changed radically.

A change of feeling reached the boisterous young Air Force first. Göring stood closer to the Führer and the political scene and could therefore better judge how the wind was blowing. Privately he preferred peace and tranquillity, but after Hitler in February 1938 assumed personal command of the Wehrmacht (Armed Forces) in the stead of disgraced Marshal von Blomberg, Göring found it prudent to alert the Luftwaffe against possible conflict with Britain. General Hellmuth Felmy, the commander of Luftflotte 2 (Airfleet 2), facing England, commenced tests and studies for air war against that island.

Shortly afterward, Hitler encouraged Admiral Raeder, the Commander-in-Chief of the Navy, to step up and expand the Navy's shipbuilding program without regard for the London Agreement. Conflict with Britain thereupon entered Navy planning. The Army, while not concerned directly with England, prepared to hold in the West and act in the East. Hitler pumped hard to get his own spirit up to facing a trial of British strength, though until May 1938 his essays looked more exploratory than purposeful. The ferment worked further during the following summer.

Definite change came about for Hitler immediately after the Munich agreement of September 1938. On 29 September Ulrich von Hassell noted in his journal, "This time he [Hitler] could not freely follow that inspiration he so blindly trusts. The pressure from the outside has become effective. The question is whether recent events produced any sort of inner shock and how this will affect him psychologically." In contrast to an exultant Chamberlain proclaiming "peace for our time" to a jubilant populace, a chagrined Führer sulked in Berlin like a child done out of a promised visit to the circus. He had been robbed of a chance to smash the Czechs. Worst of all, the defeat, for so it counted, came of his own making; he it was who had weakened. He himself had made the resolve to strike, and it was his will that had faltered, his fears that had won out and induced him to write that pusillanimous letter to Chamberlain, bringing him the man of peace, over from England for a last try. Then in betrayal of inspired resolve to "smash" the despised Czechs—a consuming passion defended so fiercely against the "reactionary" German Army[6] all through the summer of 1938—he, Hitler, had given in to a negotiated settlement of a purely Continental matter. The British had no business in it at all. On reflection, instead of a smashing victory, he had only a half-loaf deal with interloping meddlers, and far worse, around about him, the German nation took an un-Nazi delight in the fact that violence had been averted. Hitler was definitely out of sorts with himself; he had failed his own "voice" and someone was going to have to pay. The disagreeable mood persisted.[7]

What was at the root of his trouble, or who was? Who had forced this uncomfortable feeling on him, the Führer? Who had foiled him—in short, who was to blame? These were intimate and important personal questions to Adolf Hitler. Ulrich von Hassell reported a visit by the Führer to the house of his friends, the Hugo Bruckmanns; it was only two weeks after Munich. "He [Hitler] was said to have been human and pleasant. But everything he said clearly indicated that he had not recovered from the intervention of the powers and he would rather have had his war. He was especially annoyed with England—that accounts for the incomprehensibly rude speech at Saarbrücken." Hitler had hit on his culprit: England! She always obstructed the way, always held Germany down; history was full of it; momentarily she displaced the Jews. England was to blame, was to blame for everything: "England is to blame" became a byword that held on thenceforth and through the summer of 1940. So Hitler fumed and fretted against the British after Munich. "I don't give a damn," he shouted over and over, "if it takes ten years, I am going to rub them down."[8]

---

[6] General Jodl testified at Nuremberg (*IMT*, XV, 294) that Hitler was fond of saying: "I have a Reactionary Army, a Christian Navy (sometimes he said, Imperial Navy) and a National Socialist Air Force." *"Christliche Seefahrt"* (Christian seafaring) is a term often jocularly applied to the Navy. It may have stemmed from the days of legitimate (Christian) seafaring as against illegitimate (piratical) seafaring. But by Christian Navy, Hitler probably referred to the Navy's Commander-in-Chief, Admiral Raeder, noted for strong religious beliefs and the strict correctness he required of his officers.

[7] *The von Hassel Diaries, 1938-1944* (New York, 1947), pp. 7, 11, 12. Ulrich von Hassell was dismissed from his post as German Ambassador at Rome in 1937. Later he engaged in undercover operations to stop Hitler. He was executed for complicity in the plot of the 20th of July 1944 to assassinate Hitler. Before the war he was on friendly terms with Sir Neville Henderson, the British Ambassador in Berlin (1937-1939). See also Ernst Freiherr von Weizsäcker, *Erinnerungen* (Munich, 1950), p. 157.

[8] Schmid to Ansel (Germany, 1953). As Göring's Chief of Intelligence and member of his mess and official family, General Schmid took in indications of Hitler's moods and thought from Göring who, events proved, reflected Hitler faith-

It was now to be a beating for the groom, or, even worse, to bring him around. The angry outcries could well inflame a populace and ignite a blaze hard to control. There was no doubt they expressed Hitler's feelings. They marked the end of the first courtship cycle and a definite turn toward proof of eligibility by feats of violence. Some call it *die grosse Wende,* or the "great turning" from bombast to imagined blows, from Hitlerian gospel of association back toward the discredited practices of World War I.

But the aftermath of Munich, even as it crystallized Hitler's thoughts about England, dealt his ego a blow. His private problem became the twofold one of expending the pressure built up against the Czechs and rescuing his self-esteem from the trough of personal cowardice. The urge to smash he would eventually vent on the Poles, and rebuilding his ego, though more complicated, would follow the same route of graphic proof of the might of the German sword (*die Stärke des deutschen Schwerts*). And so he proceeded.

Directions followed to the services most concerned, the Air and the Navy. They occupied themselves more and more with plans of armed conflict with Britain. The Navy launched into the gigantic Z plan for ship-building. Both services tested operational possibilities on the game boards. As these endeavors unrolled they gathered a spurious validity; they appeared genuine and plausible to the people about the Führer and to Hitler himself. In time provisional strategies for war with England were placed on the books, but for years hence.

Years hence or not, the thought of conflict with Britain was basically inadmissible. It signaled abandonment of all that had gone before in preaching and planning and, moreover, in the organization of Hitler's personal mythology. Admiral Raeder braced him on the contradiction after a famed briefing conference before the commanders-in-Chief and top staff members on 23 May 1939. By then Hitler had rationalized through to a considered admission of a possible war with Britain. He parried Raeder with assurance that political measures underway would reduce the chance of conflict there to a bare one per cent. The briefing conference just ended had implied the exact opposite. Actually Hitler was trying to straddle the issue— within, to himself, and without, to his hearers.

---

fully. See also Paul Schmidt, *Hitler's Interpreter* (New York, 1953), pp. 117-20 and Fritz Hesse, *Hitler and the English* (London, 1954), pp. 60, 61.

So prophetic did the minutes of this meeting of 23 May become that the Nuremberg tribunal was impelled to treat them exhaustively. Early in that briefing talk Hitler admitted that his intended attack on Poland could hardly be separated from conflict with the West. He went over immediately to ideas about the "motor" that drove the West, namely Britain. Invasion he made but fleeting reference to, and the chief interest in the reference lies in the fact that invasion had not escaped him, as it seemed to have his service chieftains. It is the only record encountered in which Hitler, before the war, considered a cross-Channel attack by Germany. He spoke of it as a "surprise attack" and all but discarded it because of weather difficulties and the meager chance of achieving surprise. Nevertheless he commended "surprise attack" to the study of his commanders-in-chief as well as a long war by siege, which to him offered greater possibilities. Later Führer Directives of the war and official actions followed these portents with complete fidelity, as we shall see in Hitler's *Memorandum and Guiding Principles for the Conduct of the War in the West* of 9 October 1939 and the related Directives No. 6 and No. 9 (see pp. 40, 45, 46 below). On 23 May 1939 he expressed the gist of siege in a single sentence: "If success comes in occupying Holland and Belgium . . . and also in knocking out France, then the basis for a successful war has been created against England." In other words, a "basis" for reduction by siege, but reduction only provisionally.[9]

The summer of 1939 seethed like the one of the year before. Ribbentrop, now Foreign Minister, and Hitler succeeded in neutralizing Russia and felt that this achievement had had a like effect on Britain. The Führer began his newest England cycle; this was to be

---

[9] There are older hints on the origins of Hitler's thoughts for reducing England. In *MK*, pp. 695, 696, he evaluates France's strong position vis-à-vis England: "In her coast [France] spreads out a long front before the life nerves of the British Kingdom . . . not only do the English life centers provide profitable targets for aircraft and long range artillery but also the traffic lanes of British commerce are laid bare to the effect of submarines." These ideas he expanded to include Belgium and Holland by the time of the 23 May 1939 briefing conference. The record of the conference, called the Schmundt Protocol, has become controversial because the accused at Nuremberg claimed they saw it for the first time at the trials and questioned its authenticity and accuracy. Colonel Schmundt was Hitler's chief adjutant, his devoted disciple, and, according to observers, none too reliable in his talk or writing, which by habit were flavored with alcohol. Nevertheless what he recorded for 23 May 1939 persisted unchallenged in OKW files as minutes of the meeting. His record fits the Hitler pattern; doubtless Schmundt had heard the thoughts expressed so often in Hitlerian monologue that he scarcely needed to attend the conference to put them down. The Schmundt Protocol is *IMT* doc. 079-L.

one of "showing" the English. He fell upon Poland and got his "smash." Hard upon her defeat he steadied momentarily from the Great Turning to test the British reaction. He had demonstrated his capacity and courage to go it alone; perhaps now they could see things his way, but he waited hardly long enough for Britain to reject his tender of settlement before again throwing the wheel over in a turn against her. Officially he put siege on the books for coercing Britain. Yet the old urge was hard to shake.

We suspect that in Hitler's private *Weltanschauung* alliance had faded not one bit. For problem England held the key to all later happenings. The latter-day travail of self-debate and show of Great Turning against Britain had succeeded only in interchanging the positions of the principals of the game. England must henceforth seek him out. But would she? The question bothered him. How he could induce her to, or even force her to, was left as his inner contention. He confronted a fatal dilemma.

If we are to understand what went on during the summer of 1940 while Hitler assayed to solve this problem of England, we need to know more about him; we need to know this man, his selfhood, and the unique spiritual machinery that went into play when he sought to decide, and to act.

Adolf Hitler and Decision

Deep in East Prussia at his headquarters near Rastenburg, Hitler remarked to his messmates at the end of prolonged table talk on the night of 6 January 1942: "It is a great time when an entirely unknown man can set out to conquer a nation, and when after fifteen years of struggle he can, in effect, become the head of his people. I had luck to number some strong personalities among my supporters."[10] A great time to be sure, and evidence of strong personalities! But who was it that saw into the times and realized their needs and opportunities? Who marshaled the strong men and made them effective? Hitler took the answer for granted. There was also a great man at the helm, a man of genius, endowed with a magnetic personality and a mind so profound in its discernment and so complex in its working as to defy all analysis and rational understanding. This was (and in some places still is) the mystical enigma, the Hitler *Mythos*. He had cre-

[10] *SC,* p. 180.

ated and carefully nurtured the legend with the aid of an incomparable propaganda machine. To Germans it came near to being an article of faith during the war years. To Hitler it was equally so; he believed in himself as few men have.

A predestined self was what Hitler believed in, one based in primitive feelings of singular sensitivity. It demanded more than ordinary fleshpots for satisfaction and could drive with frightful force to get its fill. But only when he knew what had to be. When he did not, fears crowded in to bring uncertainty and indecision, or even failure. Finding out what had to be, and how, made the trouble. Signs of this unhappy spiritual make-up led back to Hitler's earliest childhood.

Evidence points to an indulgent mother, set off by a stern and much older father. Mother saw rare talents in her son and promised him high destiny; father exemplified what faith in one's destiny might bring. Alois Hitler had risen from obscurity by his own obdurate will power to recognition in the Austrian customs service. Father and son differed from the earliest days, and each defended his side with an emotional fervor that could only end in rage and hatred. In later life Adolf Hitler was wont to relate in the intimacy of his official family. "I did not love my father . . . and therefore feared him all the more . . . . He flew into rages and struck out right off. My poor mother then always feared he would hurt me." The mother was ever ready with comfort and refuge.

The major conflict turned about Adolf's future career. This career question badgers childhood days of boys in Continental families more than elsewhere. *"Was willst du denn werden?"* is thrown at them as the vital question, and persistently, in order to squeeze out an answer, unhappy though it may be for the boy. In the Hitler family the routine incited a running fight in which the father held that son should follow his own footsteps in the Hapsburg government service, while the son stubbonly maintained he never, "no never would become an official to sit as an unfree man with others like monkeys in a cage." In dictating *Mein Kampf* years later Hitler first used his favorite expression, *unabänderlicher Entschluss* (unalterable resolve), to describe the vehemence of his opposition to his father. The words were to become fateful in German history. He went on to tell how, on being again tested by father to bring the career matter to a head, he came out with it: He wanted to become a painter. The old man in resentful astonishment responded, "Painter? No, as long as I live, never!" And so the matter stood, neither giving in.

The son recounts how he held his counsel, dreamed his dreams, and circumvented the paternal tyranny by sabotaging school work pointed for officialdom. Death came to his rescue and took the father two years later. The boy was free to relax in the encouraging comfort provided by his beloved mother and the unorthdox figments of his own imagination. He had experienced serious conflict with a hostile external force and tasted the compensation offered by fantasy. Also he had learned something of the emotional reserves available for supporting his side of a conflict. External force could be waited out, sometimes outwitted. This pattern, vague as we have it today, has significance. It may indicate the genesis of an odd mental system that he contrived for pondering what he wanted and how to get it.

On the death of his mother the young Hitler moved to Vienna, firm in the resolve "to make something of myself," he assured relatives at parting. He had not given in to his father, but neither had he found himself as a young man. A failure in school, he had learned no trade; he had created nothing, no recognizable destiny outside of fantasy beckoned. Yet to himself as a youth of nineteen the aim remained clear; he would follow the approved route to fame as a painter by way of the National Academy of Art at Vienna. Much later he likened himself to an émigré making his way, forging a destiny, in a foreign land.

For the first time he was on his own, shifting for himself among strangers in a big city, which showed no more inclination to recognize his peculiar talents than had his father. The National Academy rejected him once in 1907 and with finality in 1908. No means of revenge or circumvention came immediately to hand. But as before, he could refuse to give in and wait the business out in belief of a higher destiny. Mere breadwinning was not enough, wrote his friend and companion of this period, August Kubizek. To the world of fancy in which he floated he made the important addition of soliloquy for expression. At odd times the soliloquies broke out in harangues toward his unfeeling companions. Essentially his life remained the same as at home; rejection of steady effort, abnormal interest in the novel and unorthodox for solving all problems, and the concoction of many schemes for achieving fame and fortune.[11]

[11] In 1941 Hitler remarked, "In one respect the climate of want in which I lived left no mark on me. At that [Vienna] time I lived in the palaces of the imagination." *SC*, p. 38. See also Konrad Heiden, *Der Führer* (Boston, 1944), pp. 68, 69, and Alan Bullock, *Hitler* (London, 1952), p. 30. Hitler's companion of early days in Vienna was his friend from home, August Kubizek. His book, *The Young*

Mother was no longer on hand to provide logistics or refuge, and the émigré slipped slowly down the social ladder to the slums. He hit bottom in a flophouse at the end of the first year, and there forsaken, he vagabonded during three years. Body and soul stayed together through the usual dodges of the brotherhood, tempered by efforts at art, odd jobs, chiseling here and there, illustrating advertisements, and selling water-color sketches from his own hand. Between time he submerged himself in the snatch reading of newspapers, political pamphlets, and fragments of obtainable books on those aspects of the world around him that met his demanding interests. His appearance kept pace with his queer action and habits. Heiden reports a picture constructed by one Hanisch, who peddled Hitler's art offerings: "He wore a long coat given him by Neumann and stiff greasy black derby; his matted hair hung down over his collar, his fuzzy beard formed a thick ruff around his chin . . . 'He constituted an apparition such as rarely occurs among Christians.'" Another companion of later Vienna days, Josef Greiner, wrote years afterward: "Fundamentally Hitler was a Sonderling [a separate one, an eccentric]. This was also the first impression that I gained of him." Hitler himself conceded in *Mein Kampf* that his fellows of the asylum for the homeless regarded him as such an eccentric.[12]

The picture looks like defeat of youth, frankly admitted, or, at best, escape. It was probably some of each. Failure was plain in a dilemma as deep as it was wide. The youth had lost the What of his dreams—a career in painting—and floundered in the doldrums of adolescent indecision hoping fortune would strike and bring decision, a purpose in life, yet a purpose with spectacular recognition. Recognition was the consuming passion that kept him going. But recognition in what?

Hitler never admitted the loss of aim, and while he now claimed it lay in the field of architecture, his preoccupation seemed to be sociology and politics. An early bent for politicking came to the fore. The teaming masses of Vienna with their futile parades and rallies, the vagrants around him in the asylum with neither conviction nor

Hitler I Knew (Boston, 1955), recounts a close companionship in Linz and Vienna during their ages 15-19. The following pages are particularly pertinent at this stage of our investigation: pp. 9, 13, 18, 83-97, 116, 139, 146-58, 177, 180.

[12] Heiden, *op. cit.*, p. 68 and also Josef Greiner, *Das Ende des Hitler-Mythos* (Vienna, 1947), pp. 12-18, 40, 135. According to Greiner it was later established that Hitler had lodged in sixteen places in Vienna. Among them were the Obdachslosenasyl (Asylum for Homeless) and the Männerheim (Home for Men).

goal, but most pointedly his own lot, all gave food for thought. He would study the problem out; there must be a comparatively simple answer. It was just that these others were too stupid to see it. Years afterward he said to Hermann Rauschning, the President of the Danzig Senate, "These people cannot think simply. I have the gift of simplification and every thing works itself out." A belief that every problem had its finality and that simplicity was its essence already possessed his undisciplined, unenlightened thinking and learning in the Vienna days. Everything the young Hitler liked (and could understand) stood for good, and everything (and everybody) he disliked or could not comprehend was bad. He called this differentiation, retaining the essential and discarding the unessential.

Hitler elaborated the system devised in Vienna in *Mein Kampf* (pp. 36, 38). His companions of those days tell of an insatiable book-hunger. An individual, Hitler explained, should select his very own topics of interest by feeling, and having rehearsed these well, as he read further, he took in only pieces of information that could raise related feelings and pushed them "like bits of a mosaic" into the image already outlined in his mind. So information became knowledge and built answers to the innumerable problems surrounding the eager student. If in Vienna days the technique had not reached perfection, it was on its way. It used primitive emotion for sharpening and recording impressions, and, thus clarified, the data could be reviewed, polished, and corrected in muttered self-debate. This practice persisted. Fräulein Schröder, his later secretary, tells us that Hitler daily schooled his memory with a drill of mental gymnastics by which, he explained, he grasped the essentials and allowed them to sink in. By wartime the system in Hitler's own opinion had reached machinelike precision. Captain Heinz Assmann, who, from the spring of 1940 on, presented the situation at sea to the Führer in the daily *Lagebesprechung,* recorded that Hitler remarked after hearing a particularly unfavorable naval report: ". . . bear in mind that my brain works in about the same way as a calculating machine. Each officer who makes a presentation here introduces into this calculating machine a small wheel of information. There is formed a certain picture, or a number on each wheel. . . . I press a button and there flashes into my mind the sum of all this information. This is the estimate of that particular day."[13]

[13] Heinz Assmann, "Some Personal Recollections of Adolf Hitler," *U.S. Naval Institute Proceedings,* LXXIX (December, 1953), 1293, and Zoller, *op. cit.,* p. 40.

Pressing mosaic pieces to fill out a picture or theory—but whence came the original image, being made whole? There was but one source, the real or fancied experience of self. Gratifying release came with fitting in a missing piece, and likewise encouragement to further fancy. Things not inimical to self found easy admission, and from there on anything became possible. The novel, unorthodox, revolutionary, pseudosimple, all enjoyed free entry to this council chamber that worked eagerly for simple finality through linkage with the past. The process bordered on what psychologists call free association, albeit an odd fragmentary brand in which the individual practiced on himself. Hitler practiced intensively and got some results.

In his version he eased access to buried emotions and tapped them off into current use. At the Vienna stage he got no further creatively with these hidden reserves than the outlining of a personalized store of plans and theories and solutions for many problems of his world. Yet "he was at odds with that world," said his roommate Kubizek. As in boyhood, he could not bring his creations to action on the outside. When the barriers of the past held fast against his prying, or when no kindred experience to the current problem existed, he was stopped. He either created nothing, the mosaic remaining jumbled, or his creation lay sterile awaiting favorable environment. An impasse of this character obtained during most of the Vienna days. Hitler looked back on that period as the unhappiest of his life, but he rightly named it the most fateful. The ungratifying, frustrating "school of life" hardened the integrity of self and armed him with a philosophy that never more changed. "I obtained there," he said, "the basis for a philosophy of life in general and a system for judging politics in detail which I later only had to fill out in single minor items, and which never left me."

In this manner a diversity of conceits and total solutions grew into set convictions. Hitler learned the power of the spoken word. He prided himself on having acquired a deep understanding of human nature. In the exactitude of the German language the apt expression is *Menschenkenner* (a knower-of-man). But again, introspection raised subjective reactions that told him what he must guard against in others. He quested for their motives and claimed he thus differentiated "aspect" from "inner being"; the truth was he held his fellow man in deep distrust and contempt. Inevitably the quest for motivation led to people in mass and their psychology; ultimate power resided, he came to realize, in the *Volk*. What would move the people? Not the written word, for "the pen deals only in theory . . . the broad mass of the people is, above all, subordinate only to the power of speech." It is apparent that he arrived at this judgment through the effect of the spoken word on himself, even his own words. "The word," he said to his intimates of later days, "builds bridges in unexplored regions." Vienna companion Hanisch reports an occasion when, having attended a motion picture portraying an agitator who roused the populace by speech, "Hitler almost went crazy . . . for days afterwards he spoke of nothing except the power of the spoken word." He had begun to sense that rousing the masses might be his bridge to glory.[14]

The student of life joyously abandoned Vienna for Munich when he found he could manage it in 1913. Joyously, because at last he would be united with the motherland. The ultranationalism of an expatriate was a part of him from childhood and that ardent zeal his youthful loathing for Vienna had fortified into pan-Germanism. If the drifting émigré thus came home on arrival in Munich, he returned decisively to mother and happiness at the outbreak of war in 1914. He was saved. Automatically he rejected any idea of fighting for Austria, the land of his father, and volunteered in a Bavarian regiment to fight for his heart's motherland. As of yore mother (in the guise of the German Army) provided for the body, and ultra-patriotic fancies sustained the soul.

He very early managed a detail to the independent position of regimental staff runner and there rested content. The post is ideally suited for observation, learning, and, on occasion, showing off with daring. A few staff perquisites, plus freedom from watches or regular tasks, are thrown in. The runner is always in on the "know," for he can read the commander's dispatches and squeeze out his innermost thoughts. Both commander and subordinates come under closest scrutiny and judgment of the runner, and so does the next superior command, the division. The runner can even imagine himself in the place of his superior, as this runner from Austria many times did. The job was made for Hitler; there he stayed for the "duration," never missing a trick. In four years of campaigning he got an imprint of World War I land warfare through the division level in all grim detail. But there his picture stopped.

[14] Zoller, *op. cit.,* p. 45; Bullock, *op. cit.,* p. 30; Kubizek, *op. cit.,* pp. 18, 19, 155, 174.

· · If we accept his own account, along with reports of others, we
find this young soldier throughout the war defending an attitude of
do or die for country and, incidentally, growing mightily in self-
esteem.   By habit he kept himself informed, particularly on the subject of politics, which was not too difficult with access to regimental
and division headquarters.   Aplenty to mull over and sort out came
his way.   Questions crowded into the endless periods of waiting.
The familiar role and routine of *Sonderling* returned; apart from his
fellows, he brooded over war problems and now and then, to their
amazement, broke out in ranting diatribes against the unsolved
dangers of Marxism or the small regard of the home front for sacri-
fices at the fighting front.   Special scorn he reserved for the politicos—
"I hated the whole pack of country-betraying bums to the utmost"—
and for the criminally deficient leadership of the masses.   "More often
than once the thought troubled me," he wrote, "that if Providence
had placed me in the propaganda post of these unqualified know-
nothings and do-nothings, destiny would have challenged to a battle
differently . . . . *I was at that time already convinced I could
have succeeded*.   However, I was a nameless one of eight million. . . ."
It was no idle fleeting notion, for seventeen years later Hitler repeated
the identical thought at his headquarters mess table; the pattern of
thought had proved durable.   At the earlier time he noted how propaganda must be directed at emotions, limited to few points and these
forever reiterated, and for this task "the most gifted knower-of-souls
is only just able to qualify."   He meant himself.

He managed to think himself clear on some pet obsessions: the
British and world policy.   There was a place for England, he thought,
and a bigger one for Germany.   Then there was Marxism.   How
could it be rubbed out, or "can one fight a philosophy with raw
violence?"   The painful conclusion emerged that movements of
spiritual foundation can be eradicated only "when the physical
weapons [used against them] are themselves the carrier of a new in-
flaming concept . . . .   Every philosophy fights less for the negative
destruction of the opposition than . . . for the positive pushing through
of its own" cause as a substitute.   Ergo, the crying need was a cross
for the crusade.   Peter was on hand to inveigh against the infidels;
but to what purpose?   The binding cause was lacking.   To this task
of formulating a cause for a movement this newest crusader now
applied himself in earnest.   He recorded his vague decision in these
words:

In the course of the events of the World War, I became confirmed in this opinion through the obvious impossibility of joining battle ruthlessly with Social Democracy directly because of the lack of a movement . . . and more, the first thoughts of entering politics later, now came to me . . . [and] this was the reason for assuring the small circle of my friends, that after the war I wanted to become active as a speaker . . . alongside of my profession [the arts]. I believe I was very earnest about it.[15]

Here the baffled drifter rediscovered his What, a chance for creative work. Observe how he granted the new role equality with the old urge to follow the arts. It was a decided step forward. A fresh role toward recognition had been made eligible alongside the unattainable one of his youth.

Then came the decisive shock—the cataclysmic end of the war, the sellout. Collapse at the top of the Army and in its rear. Bewildering charge and countercharge! What could this not work in the mind of a hyperpatriotic soldier carrying a messianic torch? The disaster was all the more overwhelming for Hitler since it caught him out of touch, in the alien surroundings of a hospital. His account of the shock is mixed, some of it touching and convincing, and the rest pure self-rabble-rousing. The disillusioned soldier approached his more natural role, and as he recounted these events in *Mein Kampf* while reliving them, he unwittingly revealed his approach to his own true role. Discharged from the hospital, Hitler took to the road for Munich. He had resolved to enter politics.

In the familiar surroundings of the big city he found Army indoctrination courses in progress for teaching the horde of drifting troops the responsibility of a new-found citizenship. There he fell in with like-thinking firebrands, aflame with ideas of a new party. At one open-discussion meeting a participant undertook to defend the Jews. Hitler's aroused reply attracted the attention of his superiors; shortly thereafter they appointed him to the post of Training Officer. Thenceforth he could do some indoctrinating on his own. His joy knew no bounds; recognition at last! "No task could make me happier than this one," he rhapsodized. "I began with all zeal and liking . . . now there was opportunity to speak before large audiences; and that, which I had formerly always taken for granted . . . now struck home: *ich konnte 'reden'* [I could speak]." The newly designated Training Officer went happily about the business of winning

[15] *MK*, pp. 187, 188, 192.

former comrades back to the fold of nationalism; he succeeded by the hundreds, even thousands, he wrote.

The future Führer had arrived. Happy days of spellbinding the boyhood gang and the subsequent periods of frustrating introspection drew closer together. Their combining would ultimately form the wellspring from which Hitler derived his powers, great and small, good and bad, throughout his miraculous career. Thus, he found himself. The time was early summer of 1919. We shall call it the Awakening, for from this point the star of Adolf Hitler took its rise. The early self had persisted. It had been a matter of the elements growing into maturity until released by a favorable environment, and postwar Munich supplied it.

The big cosmopolitan city seethed with violence and revolt, with scheming and politicking, but most, with longing for relief. Despair could be read on every face. As Hitler found vocal expression, he recognized his own confused spirit in the faces of the people and in the agitated atmosphere oppressing them. Who could save? Here prodigious self began to come alive with the answer—they must follow him, follow him to redemption. He, personifying their volition, would lead them out of the wilderness. Heiden described the treatment brilliantly (page 106):

With unerring sureness Hitler expressed the speechless panic of the masses . . . . He did not conquer them, he portrayed and represented them. His speeches are the daydreams of this mass soul; they are chaotic, full of contradictions . . . often senseless as dreams are yet charged with a deeper meaning. . . . The speeches begin always with deep pessimism and end in overjoyed redemption . . . often they can be refuted by reason but they follow a far mightier logic of the sub-conscious . . . .

The private technique of free association Hitler had practiced so assiduously on himself he now shared with the masses in a climate of the revival meeting. He acted both preacher and convert. The mutual stimulation hastened one release after another in chain reaction. The joy of it became near unbearable. Fatherland saved and self too! Redemption.

No further need existed for old mother Army. In the budding movement and the exaltation of speechifying, Hitler found both What and How to glory. The first step was to give his impress to the cause and make it all his. He got its message out into the wider public notice of the large beer halls. He reveled in the happiest days of his life. They were the days of *die frühe Kampfzeit* (the early struggle period), and he never wearied of recalling them. From them came his favorite nickname, Wolf, which he happily prefixed to various Führer Headquarter code names during the war, like *Wolf-schanze,* wolf's dugout. But it failed to bring back the *Kampfzeit,* when the light had first struck and sent him storming about, haranguing, organizing, directing goon squads, snapping out devastating decisions. Ah, there was a time! The happiest, the unforgettable. Dragons were on hand in abundance, and he slew them all. His instrument was the spoken word. It brought redemption. Moreover he created. The movement grew, and in his image. The spiritual apparatus of Adolf Hitler consummated its evolution during the *Kampfzeit,* and he rarely thereafter recaptured its élan. From there forward self pursued a set pattern, changing but little.

Hitler changed little, but circumstances did. Inevitably the *Kampfzeit* had to find its counterpoise of failure. It came about through the impatience of the bustling ringleader. He overreached when he attempted a bluff to seize control of the Bavarian provincial government for a march on Berlin. (Had not Mussolini marched on Rome?). The constituted Bavarian officials, after equivocating at first, stood firm. Police lines of Munich held against Hitler's marching column, and at the crackle of rifle fire his role of demiurge collapsed. His strategy was prepared no further than bluff, and when it was called, he threw in the sponge and abandoned the scene in irresolution. Mark it well—the abortive *Putsch* of 9 November 1923.

A succeeding mild prison sentence provided freedom for reflection and recording. At Landsberg prison Hitler commenced to codify his many theories by dictating *Mein Kampf.* A fellow *Putsch* prisoner, Rudolf Hess, who had already reached the status of alter ego, recorded and edited. However this book may be reviled as a hindsight fabrication, an unreadable conglomeration of speeches, slogans, and obsessions, a piece of party propaganda, it is nonetheless authentically Hitler—full of his theories and their testing. One feels he wanted to get them down, and this he did with brutal, boastful candor. Again he assumed the dual role of preacher and convert, convincing and converting and energizing, himself as well as the audience, or reader, as he went. The book presents Hitler's unique spiritual apparatus in operation and therein lies its value.

He lets us in on the secret of decision formulation. On page 552 he eagerly expounds how to confound the opposition at mass meetings:

At that time [it was the Kampfzeit] I learned something in a short time, namely to knock the weapon of retort out of the opponent's hand myself at the outset . . . . Two years later I was a master at this art. It was important to clarify before each speech the probable form of the objections that could be expected and then to take these and pick them apart in one's speech . . . . Thus a listener [and the speaker] was won over more easily by advance refutation of his doubts.

This is a highly instructive guide to Hitlerian estimating toward decision. He proceeded to elucidate at length two favorite themes that bore on the process, the drill of speech composition and the virtue of will power. Sensing opposition came instinctively to his animal nature; he could smell hostility or danger far off. So armed, his speech composition sharpened a vague concept already in mind toward a course of action, while will power lent energy for devastating execution. He struck down the daggers of opposition and raised up in his mind's eye a vision of grand exhilarating action; he rehearsed and re-rehearsed it. The formula succeeded marvelously to deflate Red hecklers of the mass meeting and street brawl, but for Hitler it quickly took on universal application. It became the framework of all his dialectical thinking.[16]

How wonderful, and how fearless! The young politician outwitted and forestalled the pictured foe at each turn; his spirits rose in pace, stroke on stroke. Emotional reserves worked up, not alone to discomfort the enemy, but of greater importance, to buttress self in a decision of finality, or what did for one. The play came alive as the monologuing Hitler lay about him, fairly acting out forthcoming events. He felt all their pain and tumult, all their triumph and acclaim. And in his chosen field of politics he got results, speechifying his way to national and then international recognition. He threw his adversaries off balance, played one against the other, while keeping his own choice of action wide open. A good measure of ex-

---

[16] Many a watch officer aboard ship has practiced a similar drill to school himself in keeping his ship safe and to while away the empty hours of his watch. He thinks out his action to counter every conceivable casualty that might endanger his ship and her crew—man-overboard, rudder jammed, engine failure, torpedo to starboard, aircraft astern, and so on. So prepared, he feels on top of his job and in command of his ship. But useful as the drill is to meet local emergencies, it is basically defensive in character and can be overdone if applied universally. It is not the born fighter's formula.

pediency and straddle always figured strongly. So ran this man's conditioning prior to the war. It was a political conditioning based on oratory and machination and operated without fear of mortal ending, as is sometimes the case in war. Later, when the offensive going got rough, fear showed as one of his most potent motors.

As Hitler, after release from Landsberg prison toward the end of 1924, reconstituted the Party and gradually climbed to national prominence, his concepts changed but little; his methods he kept within the law. Some refinement of tactic and polishing of approach followed naturally, as did the addition of a little more craft, persuasion, and dealing. There were few fireworks; nothing much got done in Hitler's spiritual world. The time was reminiscent of Vienna until the unrest of the world depression gave his rabble-rousing an appeal. He managed to hold the Party together by the drive of faith in himself. It never wavered and was transmitted to his followers. In the sharp political bargaining that preceded the fateful day of his accession—30 January 1933—Hitler's intransigent all-or-nothing against all offers of governmental participation won the day. The day was commemorated in the later Nazi years as the dawn of a new era by the name of *Machtergreifung* (the seizure of power).

Some of the Party stalwarts had become disaffected in the struggle of achieving national power. The trouble reached a climax in 1934 and was surmounted by an inspirational blood purge that eliminated not only Party dissidents but a good many others as well. Hitler had now achieved supremacy as the volition and "possessor of all competence" in Germany. "His will transcended fact," and he was free to devote more of his energies to the international field. This task he eagerly took in hand.

But on what had he settled as the ultimate goal or as role for himself? In the beginning the goal was simple recognition, first as artist-painter, then artist-builder, politician, founder of a movement, and finally, as Messiah-Führer, the absolute. There is good reason to believe that long before the war Hitler had arrived at the simple absolute truth: that it was he, his spirit, his cause that deserved to be put above all else. In the dreadful cold winter of his first war reverse (January 1942) he came out with it to his companions at mess. The unvarnished truth was, he said, that if the German nation was not willing to expend itself for self-preservation (meaning his preservation), then it deserved nothing better than extinction.[17]   Not motherland, country, people, or even Party, but Adolph Hitler, as expressed in the Führer *Mythos,* was the godhead for whom no sacrifice was too great.   The goal and role were synonymous: Germania (if she could hold through) supreme in the heartland of Europe with Adolf Hitler at her head.

War was implicit in such a concept.   In Hitler's mind it would be a continental affair after the manner of another great liberator, Frederick II of Prussia; only this modern leader would carry the cause to completion.   He had need of formula or pattern, and the older leader, who had likewise suffered in childhood, supplied it.   Frederick became Hitler's beau ideal, and to him he turned more and more as his international maneuvering drew war nearer.

By war's advent Hitler's theories and solutions constituted a basic library of stock guides, almost plans, on which he could draw as his spirit and circumstances demanded. . In the sense of "courses of action," his concepts were more firmly organized, integrant with self, than with most men.   Those that he completely admitted we have called his personal mythology; they included all that betokened security, faith in himself, and mastery over a glorious destiny.   They needed less prodding for asserting themselves than plans and ideas more remote from his person, or those brought in from the outside. His own feeling of the times determined whether or not action was indicated.   The process of deciding and implementing pursued the now perfected inspirational pattern.   "If an idea is not yet mature," he said to Rauschning in 1933, "then there is only one thing to do: have patience, wait, try again, wait again.   In the subconscious the work goes on . . . unless I have the inner incorruptible conviction: *this is the solution,* I do nothing . . . .   But if the voice speaks, then I know the time has come to act."[18]   This was self calling on its base for ideas and setting about to review them in unending monologue in the hope of raising the holy voice of inspiration.   During the war the restless drill usually went on in the presence of an adjutant, deep

[17] The remark is given in Dr. Henry Picker's record of *Hitlers Tischgespraeche im Führerhauptquartier 1941-42* (Bonn, 1951), p. 202.   Hitler had been talking of the responsibility of a leader to a cause and of the devotion of a people.   Then he used a pet phrase to express his view, *"Ich bin auch hier eiskalt"* (in this I'm cold as ice) and went on, ". . . if the German nation is not ready to commit itself to its self preservation, good!   Then it should pass away."   See also Heinz Assmann, *op. cit.,* p. 1294.

[18] Hermann Rauschning, *The Voice of Destruction* (New York, 1940), pp. 181, 182.

into the night according to the old routine of speech composition. Words were encouraged to "build bridges in the unknown."

Yet there was a difference now; this was war! Little time was on hand for the creative idea to mature and, as it matured, gather momentum for execution. War demanded more than arousing a following with oratory, or, as he was wont to say, "putting the creative urges under tensions." He really had only himself left on whom tensions could be imposed, and logic had to be produced as well as elation. And in a certain odd measure, logic was forthcoming, though it emerged by a route quite different from that of the military. He intensified his system of self-debate. In that drill he thought aloud in rough draft, von Puttkamer, his naval aide, explained, allowing the words to pour forth in a flood to be banked up, corrected, crossed out, and redrafted, all vocally. It was the only way to make thought come. The subject might be dropped for a while and resurrected in a new version for rephrasing, polishing, and rubbing down to barebone essentials. Thus, as the drill proceeded, the weakness of this or that point came to light and was countered or corrected exactly as the cries of the Red hecklers long ago. Every conceivable objection was ferreted out and turned not so much by logic, as by feeling, and the logic primitive feeling could stimulate. By the time the job was done it took on the compelling assurance of simple and primitive reason. What is more, it had gathered drive as it moved toward conclusion. The voice, when it spoke, had given entrance to the storechambers of the inner self whence energies spilled out to convert the concept into compulsion. There resulted an impeccable decision surrounded by a great charge of spiritual drive, ready to do execution. Rauschning described the process as screwing up courage "to put up a bold front."[19] It was all of this—a bold face to defend self—and more too. These fronts could hold fast, or become dynamic and offensive, much as the fronts in weather do.

Indeed, the turbulent Hitlerian spirit suggests the vagaries and irresponsible violence of weather and its expressive language. There we find warm and cold air charges contending for mastery of the heavens. They vie to and fro, and they tense and sharpen their boundaries into specific fronts as the struggle goes along. A bend

[19] Rauschning's description appears on his p. 261. My use of the term "drive" could be confused with the psychological term and usage in which it carries the connotation of a hunger or need, as sex drive. By drive here is meant rather the spiritual force Hitler could marshal to cause the filling of a need, that is, his get-what-I-want force of personality.

occurs in one of them and develops gradually into a wave of motion. Comes a trigger in the shape of extra energy (or inspiration), and the disturbance breaks loose as a fullfledged tempest of action along an advancing front. Frontal storms sweep over the earth with seeming definiteness of purpose—often with destructive fury—only to subside again into the uncertain equilibrium of normality. Their diversity, size, and violence are as uncertain as were Hitler's actions, yet they conform to pattern, and he did too. According to contemporary observers, he invariably approached a problem with the fretful to-and-fro activity of the frontal disturbance. A front could work up from the charged ideas already on hand in his mythology; whether he reached decision and triggered off a storm of action depended on the voice and the drive he and voice together succeeded in imparting to the front. He might get a whole sweep of violent thunderstorms, a narrow vicious single-aim tornado (energized by spite), or only a mild extratropical cyclone. Again the disturbance might prove counterfeit, caused by a false front that had served as a screen and then fizzled out. In some cases he simply was incapable of working up a genuine front, no matter how hard he tried.

As with most humans, Adolf Hitler's elemental problem had to do with knowing what he wanted and how he would get it. Where he became remarkable was that when he did know, he was able to surpass most men in the spiritual force he could loose toward attaining it. This faculty was among his most arresting manifestations. In the ideal situation he worked up a front of decision and charged it with the aggressive but redeeming conviction of *unabänderlicher Entschluss* from the past. Expression came as a wave of stormy compulsion that flowed out from him on his surroundings, gathering momentum as it descended, until it was irresistible. Barriers fell before the vigor of his words. Many traditional impossibilities were overrun pell-mell; things got done, not alone in the small matters of the moment, but in the highest level of the war's conduct. A note of urgency habitually pervaded the atmosphere. The press of time became a consuming passion when Hitler drove for action; he used it as his strongest lever in briefing sessions that were so characteristic of frontal activity. Time must be capitalized; only a short span remained to him. Attack in time before the enemy is ready; all action must be timely. The Drive of Front, spurring for timeliness, can be reckoned as one of the strongest influences in the German conduct of the war. Its absence in any war project made itself felt very quickly.

Undoubtedly it blotted out for Hitler and his contemporaries the more common intervals of irresolution.

Doldrums of indecision multiplied as the problem of England came closer. Not all situations responded to frontal treatment; indeed, optimum conditions had to prevail both within Hitler and on the outside if a true front was to develop. Moreover, true front meant sudden change, rapid movement, action! Many situations were devoid of any such characteristics or the possibility of their development. In these cases Hitler was in trouble. Then pressures would continue in fretful equilibrium (as in the summer of 1937); only weak frontal activity developed or perhaps none at all. The savor of snap decisions out of the blue, on which the *Mythos* subsisted, was a phony rising from a frontal attitude maintained in daily life and the rare occasions when a true front did evolve. The blitz into Poland was such a one, and from its close, the whipping up for attack in the West, and the actual attack during a few short days, exhibited all the characteristics of genuine frontal activity. But then when the first violent blasts had spent themselves and no time was available for successive front-building, fear and indecision came markedly to the fore—as in the *Putsch* of 9 November 1923. "The spirit of decision," Hitler said in the bitter winter of 1941, "does not mean acting at all costs, but consists simply in not hesitating when an inner conviction commands one to act . . . ."

Would the inner voice speak for him before England?

3. *Genesis of Invasion England*

Nightingales—May 1940

Whenever Grand Admiral Erich Raeder, the Commander-in-Chief of the German Navy, wanted to get the gospel word straight from the prophet, he requested a conference with his Supreme Commander, Adolf Hitler, *unter vier Augen* (under four eyes), as the expression for privacy runs in the German naval records. Such was the case on 21 May 1940 at lovely Felsennest, the Führer's simple woodland headquarters in the Eifel Rhineland country just twenty miles west of Remagen bridge. Raeder had come to report and take a reading on the Hitlerian weather, as he did from time to time, usually once a month, sometimes twice. It was close to midday, a fine spring day and a special one, for on the previous evening General Guderian's tankmen had finished their crashing drive to separate the British from the French. Guderian had reached the Channel coast in the vicinity of Abbeville. At Felsennest, that nest on a rock, the air quivered with suppressed exultation.

Admiral Raeder got quickly over the routine matters on his agenda: the situation in Norway; resumption of the Atlantic sub-marine war; tentative plans for battleship operations; extension of North Sea mining. He touched on the improbability of enemy land-ing operations on the Continent and then advanced gingerly into the unknown: What was the Führer's estimate as to the prospective length of the war? The question was pertinent to the Navy's submarine

training program. Should school boats be withheld from war operations for training personnel of an expanded submarine arm? In a
long war that arm might yet become decisive. The Naval Operations
Office, Raeder declared, inclined toward the long-war view. "The
Führer," the war diary of the Naval Operations Office recorded, "goes
along with this [long-war] interpretation and expresses his intention,
after the close of the main operations against France, to permit the
shifting of the center of gravity to the submarine and JU 88 [heavy
dive bomber] program for the conduct of the war against *England*."[1]
At this gratifying agreement Raeder asked for further discussion
"under four eyes," and Generals Keitel and Jodl, Hitler's conference
advisers, and Commander von Puttkamer, the Führer's naval aide,
withdrew.

While the conference thus continued in private, Admiral Raeder's
aide, Lieutenant Commander Freiwald, waited outside on a bench
that flanked the closed door of Hitler's office. His friend Major von
Below joined him to pass the time of day; there was plenty of world-
shaking news to talk over. Even the birds in the fresh May foliage
felt the excitement: Was the war over? How about the British? The
two young men were barely launched in these pleasant speculations
when the closed door burst open and brought them to attention. Out
stepped the Führer, radiating good will in some final words to Raeder.
Then, noting the two aides, he bade them sit down and went about
settling himself between them in comradely fashion. "Isn't everything just fine? What a glorious countryside!" exulted the happy
Führer. "This morning for the first time in twenty years I heard
again the trill of the nightingales." His happiness brimmed over.
Evidently that easy mood had ruled the discussion "under four eyes."
Raeder and aide made their adieus and departed.[2]

As usual the methodical Raeder handwrote his Führer Conference notes while he and his aide rode back to the Naval Headquarters
on Tirpitzufer, Berlin. On arrival Raeder turned the notes over to
Lieutenant Commander Heinz Assmann for editing and entry into the
war diary of the Seekriegsleitung, the Naval Operations Office. Often

---

[1] Kriegstagebuch Seekriegsleitung, 1. Abteilung, Teil A, Heft 9, vom 1. Mai—31.
Mai 1940 (War Diary, Naval Operations Office, . . . 1-31 May 1940), pp. 211, 212
(MS, Office of Naval History, Navy Department, Washington, D.C.). Seekriegs-
leitung is abbreviated Skl. Its War Diary will be referred to as W.D. Skl.

[2] Detailed to me by Captain Kurt Freiwald (Heidelberg, July 1953). He served
Raeder as personal aide (the Germans use the military designation adjutant) during
a good part of the war. Colonel Nikolaus von Below served as air adjutant to Hitler
up to almost the end in the Berlin bunker in 1945.

Raeder gives the impression of writing for history. The notes invariably portray him as putting the best face on things and the best foot forward for his Navy. On the private discussion of 21 May 1940, Assmann recorded that Raeder had raised the possibility of a later need for a landing attack on England, which subject, he averred, had been included in the deliberations of the Naval Operations Office ever since the end of 1939. Further, he urged the necessity for the Army to clarify its ideas on the composition of landing divisions and, first of all, on what an overseas movement might demand. This somewhat critical eye the Chief of the Navy cast on the Army arrests attention. He seemed ready to reflect on OKH, as the Army high command was called.

OKH, Skl, OKW—initial abbreviations for commands, offices, and agencies proliferated among the Germans even more generally than with us. The senior service, the Army (das Heer), was commanded from a headquarters called OKH, Oberkommando des Heeres (High Command of the Army). Similarly, the Navy and the Air Force had their top commands: OKM, Oberkommando der Kriegsmarine, and OKL, Oberkommando der Luftwaffe. Over the services and their commanders-in-chief stood the Führer as Supreme Commander. For his headquarters he had put together a unique staff apparatus to furnish information and work up papers implementing his decisions. Directives were drafted, and there was some informatory planning, but no command functions were exercised except through Hitler himself, although the organization called itself High Command Armed Forces, Oberkommando der Wehrmacht, or OKW. General Wilhelm Kietel presided as senior adviser under the title of Chef OKW. He contented himself by and large with ministering to Hitler's wishes through the efforts of the members of his complex staff organisms, leaving war operational matters to General Alfred Jodl.

OKW was not, in practice, what may be thought from its title, that is, it was not a joint command nor even a co-ordinating agency among the services. Quite the opposite. Often interservice differences were accentuated through OKW instead of smoothed. It in no sense constituted a joined command of the combat arms that could function with decision. Rather it did the staff drudgery required to give effect to Hitler's ideas. Army officers controlled. To the Luftwaffe this made no difference because of Göring's personal position close to the Führer, but for the Navy, it meant swimming against the tide much of the time. There were six main OKW divisions: Operations; In-

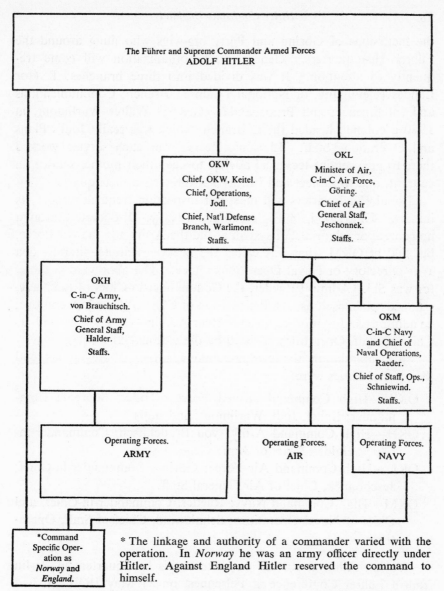

The Führer and Supreme Commander Armed Forces
ADOLF HITLER

OKW

Chief, OKW, Keitel.

Chief, Operations, Jodl.

Chief, Nat'l Defense Branch, Warlimont.

Staffs.

OKL

Minister of Air, C-in-C Air Force, Göring.

Chief of Air General Staff, Jeschonnek.

Staffs.

OKH

C-in-C Army, von Brauchitsch.

Chief of Army General Staff, Halder.

Staffs.

OKM

C-in-C Navy and Chief of Naval Operations, Raeder.

Chief of Staff, Ops., Schniewind.

Staffs.

Operating Forces.
ARMY

Operating Forces.
AIR

Operating Forces.
NAVY

*Command Specific Operation as *Norway* and *England*.

* The linkage and authority of a commander varied with the operation. In *Norway* he was an army officer directly under Hitler. Against England Hitler reserved the command to himself.

Operational Command linkages, German war machine, 1940.
The size and position of each block is an indicator of its weight and power in the war machine.

telligence; Economy and Armament; General; Central; and Legal. From the beginning Keitel confined his interest to such nonoperational activities as Economy, Manpower, and the like. Jodl, acting in the role of day-to-day counselor to the Führer in military action, became Chief of Operations. Exception in the counseling must be made for the incursions of Göring and Party big-wigs who hung around the Führer Headquarters. General Jodl's organization will come frequently to attention. It was divided into three branches: L (for Landesverteidigung, or National Defense) Branch; Communications and Intelligence; and Propaganda. General Walter Warlimont, in 1940 a colonel, headed the L Branch, which was really Jodl's Plans and Operations Staff. Liaison officers from each service worked there to give service technical advice, to keep their mother service au courant, and to protect and further her interests at headquarters.[3]

Naval Headquarters will meet our inspection frequently too. Its initials, OKM, stood for High Command Navy. It operated through no general or admiral staff system as did the Army and the Air Force, but had at OKM what was called the Seekriegsleitung, literally Sea War Directory or Naval Operations Office. The abbreviation therefor was Skl. Admiral Raeder, the Commander-in-Chief of the Navy, retained for himself as well the position of Chief of Naval Operations; he administered that office through Rear Admiral Otto Schniewind, as Chief of Staff, Operations, assisted by the various Skl sections.

In recapitulation, the leading commands, their abbreviations, and their personalities were:

OKW—High Command Armed Forces: Hitler, Supreme Commander; Keitel, Jodl, Warlimont, and staffs.

OKH—High Command Army: von Brauchitsch, Commander-in-Chief; Halder, Chief of Army General Staff.

OKL—High Command Air Force: Göring, Commander-in-Chief; Jeschonnek, Chief of Air General Staff.

OKM—High Command Navy: Raeder, Commander-in-Chief, and Chief of Naval Operations; Schniewind, Chief of Staff, Operations.

We left Admiral Raeder en route to his headquarters in Berlin from a Führer Conference at Felsennest on 21 May 1940. It had been a gratifying session, which could not be said of his every contact with Hitler. Raeder recorded nothing in his conference notes about the Führer's reaction to the trial balloon on invasion, but remarked to Freiwald later that the reaction had been noncommittal, almost

[3] No single command agency for the planning and conduct of war, as implied by the English term "German General Staff," existed. The Army and the Air Force each had their general staffs; the Navy had no counterpart. The Army was the senior service, and since the general staff had originated and become influential there, German reference to "the General Staff" normally meant the Army General Staff.

The German High Command. Seated, Göring, Hitler; standing, General Jodl, General von Brauchitsch, Admiral Raeder, General Keitel. *(Courtesy Rear Admiral von Puttkamer)*

Admiral Raeder confers with Hitler on 21 May 1940, at Felsennest. In the course of this meeting Raeder first broached Invasion England to Hitler. General Keitel is on Admiral Raeder's right. *(Courtesy Rear Admiral von Puttkamer)*

indifferent. England? The Führer was not worried; although it would be wise to prepare for a long war, he expected England to come around. There would be peace. Here was good news for Raeder—the Führer's own wish for peace and the probability of his efforts in that direction. Thus the Navy would be sprung from an impossible war situation. The Admiral's chief fear, and what impelled him to explore landing thoughts with Hitler at all, had been that orders to invade England might issue suddenly and catch him short. He was glad to find his worries unfounded. In the private conference of 21 May, Hitler gave no indication that he was at all interested in invasion or that he even remotely entertained any such ideas. His interest was nightingales.

The weather? For the Navy, it promised fair.

First Thoughts of Landing in England—November 1939

Admiral Raeder stretched things a bit to Hitler when he represented the Navy as having forehandedly kept landing ideas under scrutiny since the end of 1939; the matter had never been so clear cut.

Undoubtedly Raeder himself had by habit turned over in his mind the thought of invasion, but the record of deliberations, mentioned to Hitler, had months before sunk into the lower recesses of the Skl files, unwanted and forgotten. The record was unwanted in more ways than one, for among German officers, Army and Navy alike (Air Force officers scarcely recognized the idea), there exists a singular aversion for association with the early studies about invading England or with their propagation. Some taint attaches thereto. In conversation the Army still blames the late 1939 invasion heresy on the Navy, and the Navy returns the compliment. Time and again officers have stressed to me that landing ideas just did not exist before the war, and they seem loath to admit any personal connection with the genesis of such ideas after war broke out. The attitude may arise from a wish to refute the British propaganda that accused Germans of unlimited plans of conquest; it may be related to the Nuremberg emphasis on that ambiguous crime, planning aggression; it may stem from the early Hitlerian taboo against war with England. At all events, the aversion so complicated any investigation to establish the origins of the first landing thoughts and to trace their evolution that one wonders the more what could be back of it all. For when one contemplates the climate of those times today, it seems that such invasion planning should have been an inevitable professional interest.

In any case, it is to Admiral Raeder's professional credit that he raised the landing question in November 1939 and not alone because of its obvious relevance. The engrossment of Hitler and the Army leadership in differences over launching a land campaign into France blinded them to a consideration of what might follow and blacked out all thought of amphibious operations. Except with Raeder, long-range strategical thinking faded from the highest level. Conflict arose between Führer and Army from a drive, deep in Hitler's personal make-up, to take the offensive in the West. Even while still in Poland, as early as 20 September, he alerted his immediate staff to it, and once back in Berlin he made haste to press his intention home to the service chiefs. They were given scant opportunity to present their views. On 10 October he summoned the Commander-in-Chief of the Army and the Chief of the Army General Staff to the shining new Reichskanzlei to acquaint them with his views in detail. He had learned to brace the services separately, and the Army became his first target.

At 1100 on that day, Hitler read to Generaloberst Walther von Brauchitsch and General Franz Halder, a personally prepared evaluation of the war, dated 9 October, and prescribed guides for continuing by attack in the West. He wanted a shattering blow there to knock out the Allies while Germany still held ascendancy. From bases seized in France and the Low Countries, he declared, siege could be laid against England by air and sea. But this last came out as a sort of afterthought; paramount was another smashing land victory on the Continent. This very day Hitler had implemented this firm intention with the issue of Führer "Directive No. 6, for the Conduct of the War." The stated ultimate purpose was "to defeat as large parts as possible of the French field Army along with allies fighting at her side, and at the same time gain as much ground as possible in Holland, Belgium and northern France as a base for successful air and sea warfare against England and as a wide outpost belt for the vitally important [German] Ruhr area."[4] Thus expressed as an action decision, Hitler's intention collided head on with high Army thought favoring a defensive posture toward the West. Having sensed this passive tendency, Hitler aimed to quash it by seizing the initiative with a specific plan for

---

[4] Hitler's *Memorandum and Guiding Principles for the Conduct of the War in the West, IMT* doc. 052-L. Führer Directive No. 6 is *IMT* doc. 062-C.

a western offensive. The result was a prolonged wrangle that climaxed in a major trial of strength. Hitler won on 23 November 1939. On that day he lectured the refractory Army "Tops" on the power of his resolve and promised: "I will shrink from nothing and will destroy everyone who opposes me."[5] Opposition wavered; the soldiers yielded to the vigor of his resolute language. Attack in the West it would be!

Such being the case, the probable tasks falling to the Navy came naturally under examination. At 1700 of the same day, 10 October, Hitler conferred with Admiral Raeder, but said nothing of his memorandum, which did not reach Raeder until the twelfth.[6] Possible uses of the ports on the English Channel bobbed up repeatedly at Führer Conferences, sometimes at Hitler's instance, rarely at Raeder's. In these brushes the Navy stuck steadfastly to the seizure of the whole French side of the Channel as a naval requirement; no mere half loaf of Dutch and Belgian harbors, which others might turn on the Navy as an excuse for violating Lowland neutrality. No, that would not suffice for the siege of England by sea. And so at this conference of 10 October Admiral Raeder explained that the Belgian coast would be of no use for U-boat war; on the other hand, bases in Norway, he thought, would be most useful.

The Navy had settled on siege as the only workable solution to the perplexing problem of Britain and just at this time in late 1939 was waging a staff campaign at headquarters to gain the backing of a specific Führer directive for its siege plans.

Naval Headquarters in Berlin adjoined the quietly winding Spree at Tirpitzufer, a setting that reflected the calm efficiency of the place. There each day at 1100 a select group met in Admiral Raeder's austere office to report on the day's events and dispatch its business. Raeder, short of stature but long of head, presided at one end of the table; opposite, at the other end, sat Kapitän Schulte-Mönting, his confidant and personal Chief of Staff. On Raeder's right was Kapitän Gerhard Wagner, who customarily handled the discussion papers and charts; next to him came Kapitän Kurt Fricke, Wagner's im-

---

[5] *IMT* doc. 789-PS. This lecture, delivered 23 November 1939, climaxed the fight. Earlier on 5 November an irreparable break with von Brauchitsch had occurred. Hitler, in a fury over the Commander-in-Chief's maladroit explanations for not wishing to undertake the West Offensive, broke off the discussion. Von Brauchitsch departed a beaten man.

[6] When Göring, the Commander-in-Chief of the Air Force, received Hitler's personally prepared memorandum is unclear; customarily, in the close relationship existing between Hitler and Göring, he would have been first to have knowledge of it, or to discuss it and offer suggestions at private meetings with the Führer.

mediate superior in the planning and conduct of operations. Konteradmiral Schniewind, the Chief of Staff, Operations, sat at Raeder's
left. Scattered in the few remaining places, or in chairs nearby, sat
the younger "work horses," among them Kapitän Heinz Assmann,
stylist for papers and keeper of the war diary, and Kapitän Hans
Jürgen Reinicke of Operations. The various technical and supply
bureaus sent representatives according to the matter under deliberation. This select group came to be called *der kleine Kreis,* the little,
or inner, circle. It looked at all, discussed some, pondered many,
and settled most of the things naval in the war for Germany. But
debate was not strong suit with the methodically studious head of the
organization. Admiral Raeder was no negotiator; he preferred to
work from papers and prepared drafts susceptible of editing and correction or rejection. He seemed always prepared for the next move.

The very hue and cry over a West offensive, its pressure and
tension, which the Navy had largely escaped, and queries about the
use of the Channel ports, all penetrated the professional conscience of
Admiral Raeder. He possessed, as Admiral Schniewind explained,
the guilty conscience of the good staff officer over sins of omission.
Worry about things left undone plagued him in the wakeful watches
of the night. His Navy must not be caught short. He would turn
to his bedside memo pad and note this or that for checking on the
morrow. At the close of a Führer Conference on 10 November
1939, Hitler asked him pointedly "if particular wishes on the part
of the Navy existed with respect to bases on the Dutch-Belgian coast."
Raeder was prepared with a negative answer, explaining that such
bases would be useless to submarines because they lay within the zone
of British coastal action. Occupying Belgian and northern French
harbors had importance only in so far as it might force British troop
transports farther south toward the open sea where submarines could
attack. On the day following this conference the formal decision to
occupy all of Holland fell at Führer Headquarters and was embodied
in a new directive of 14 November. It directed the Navy to assist the
Army in seizure of the Dutch coastal islands. The prospect of such
combined action together with speculation on landing in Norway,
brewing at about the same time, apparently proved too much for
Raeder's conscience. His mind carried the actions through to success
for the Army and saw German troops standing on the shore opposite
England. Then came nagging questions: What next? How to meet
the challege of the Channel? At the meeting of the inner circle on

15 November 1939 he directed according to its War Diary, that Skl examine "the possibility of troop landings in England should the future progress of the war make the problem come up." It is the earliest record of German invasion thought of World War II.[7]

No clear recollection remains in the memory of the members of the inner circle of any discussion surrounding Raeder's direction. Unquestionably discussion there had been, for such instructions are not given right out of hand. In a speech at the Naval Headquarters Building in Kiel ten months later Raeder, speaking about Invasion, said that landing attack first occurred to him during November 1939 in connection with conjecture about occupying Norway. He characterized the vagrant idea as seeming mad (*verrückt*), the risks prohibitive. Yet he admitted talking about it with his Naval Group Commander West, who would have been the man closest to the problem and whom he visited on 6 November 1939. Group Commander West reacted by proposing to block the Channel with mines at the Narrows, as the British had done in World War I, and then to land in force on the English shore. It is highly probable that Admiral Raeder brought these ideas forward in Skl. It is certain that he mentioned the matter to Fricke, the alert head of Plans and Operations under Schniewind, and that Fricke instructed his assistant, Reinicke, to prepare an invasion study.

In the short space of five days Reinicke, a relatively junior assistant, produced a paper that reduced the complex question of invading England to twelve and one-half typewritten pages. It shows all the earmarks of a good-riddance job, disposal that would pacify the Old Man, who at times got farfetched notions into his head. There is, however, strong interest for us in this writing and in a companion paper drafted by the Army in OKH near the same time. These two papers constituted in World War II the first formal high-level consideration of large-scale amphibious operations. They set the pattern and colored all further German thinking about Invasion England.

Obviously convinced in advance of the impossibility of invasion, Reinicke built a case against it. But he began hopefully by speaking

[7] *Führer Conferences on Matters Dealing with the German Navy, 1939-1945* (hereinafter to be abbreviated *FC*) (7 vols. in 9; Navy Department, Washington, D.C., 1947), 1939, p. 36 reports on the pertinent parts of the conference of 10 November 1939 with Hitler. The Jodl diary fixes the decision on occupation of Holland. The entry for 11 November 1939 notes this fact. It is given in "Quellen zur neusten Geschichte, III," *Die Welt als Geschichte*, XII (1952), 286.

of strength newly acquired by an inferior sea power in a coastal zone through the modern developments of the mine, submarine, coastal artillery, and aircraft. With these weapons the inferior power could dispute command of the sea along its coast. In typical Army terminology, the Germans had dubbed this zone the Küstenvorfeld (the field before the coast, that is, the coastal glacis). One German naval officer who was instrumental in bringing these ideas into current use has explained that such terminology was the only means of making the matter clear to the Army-dominated thinking of the times. Yet, curiously, the Reinicke study did not grant that the new accession of power enhanced the amphibious capability of the inferior German Navy. Instead, it merely recognized that mine, submarine, and plane strengthened British defensive capacity against invasion. Hostile air reconnaissance in the coastal zone, continued Reinicke, had eliminated all thought of surprise. Air would be able to vector the defending coastal forces onto the approaching transport fleet and sink it. Accordingly, even under the protection of a superior fleet, the landing of large troop masses on a hostile shore in the old style would no longer be practicable. In sum, he visualized that four preliminary actions had to be undertaken before troops landed on an enemy coast: (1) Eliminate or seal off enemy naval combat forces from the landing and approach areas; (2) Knock out opposing air power; (3) Destroy all enemy naval power in the coastal zone; (4) Neutralize any submarine threat to the landing fleet. These four tenets grew into the stupefying prerequisites of landing thought.

Moreover, landing in England raised questions of finality scarcely dreamed of. For instance, satisfying all prerequisites would mean that Britain was on the point of collapse, thus making landing and occupation pointless. Under such circumstances, why bother with landing attack at all? This appeared to wind up the case. But Reinicke went on to do a job of it by stressing several advantages falling to the defenders and fresh difficulties for the attacker. He treated the project as a movement over an extensive sea area from German home ports and thereby made it a transport problem. He quickly dismissed the Channel ports for assembly and loading as being oversensitive to enemy counteraction. German home ports or those in the Lowlands looked safer. As for good landing areas in England, the study found few. The east coast between the Tyne and the Thames was offered as the best of a poor selection. All in all, a dark and forbidding picture emerged from this unschooled theorizing.

The gloom could be relieved only by shifting to the Navy's private war of siege by sea. Reinicke ended with a weak concession that landing, given the prerequisites, might incline the British toward peace. Though some progress toward fulfilment of the landing prerequisites might come about in the course of the war, specific actions to that end were not to take precedence over opportunities to damage the enemy. The conduct of the war against Britain required first the cutting off of her imports, which demanded the sealing of her ports. The fact that harbor areas might some distant day become bridgeheads for a landing was not to lead to sparing them for this purpose. Establishment of a bridgehead would in any case have to be done by airborne troops. Thus the whole line of reasoning neatly pushed the bridgehead business over to the Army and the Air Force. Reinicke wrapped up the unwelcome deliberations in the following concluding words: "In time when forces on the West front should be released through the defeat of the enemy there, or by stabilization of the front, a *large scale landing over the North Sea under the prerequisites given would appear as a possible means of forcing readiness for peace.*"

The end phrase, "readiness for peace," is worthy of special note. In German it reads, *"Friedensbereitschaft."* Continental opponents evoked from the Germans expressions of forcible action, like *Zerschlagen,* or beat to pieces. But toward Britain the feeling differed markedly. *Friedensbereitschaft* implied something political, something short of surrender by Britain. It carried a sense of dealing and negotiating, that is, a willingness to talk, after a spate of not too desperate fighting. In other words, German measures against Britain wound around a central theme of a deal rather than conquest.

Clearly the Navy labored under a predisposition against landing operations, a field strange and foreign to its ken and one that could only interfere with the favored theory of siege, already worked out carefully and just on the point of validation in its own Führer Directive. This paper, which was Führer Directive No. 9, gave exhaustive instructions for the preparation of concentrated action against the British economy by air and sea. A Navy-inspired work, which culminated much staff campaigning, it was issued on 29 November 1939, not alone to please the Navy but also to get Göring and his Luftwaffe to co-operate against Britain. So General Warlimont, whose business was the preparation of directives in OKW, explained the matter. Two closely related Führer papers, already noticed, preceded this one, in October: Hitler's own *Memorandum and Guiding Principles for the Conduct of the War in the West*; and "Directive No. 6, for the Conduct of the War." The former (from Hitler's own hand) built a case of great urgency for an immediate knockout blow in the West, while the latter implemented such action. The second-thought purpose, according to Directive No. 6, was to conquer as large an area as possible in Holland, Belgium, and northern France to serve as a base for air and sea warfare against Britain. Directive No. 9 followed then, under Navy-sponsored pressure, to implement preparatory work for operations that would be undertaken when Directive No. 6 had been fulfilled. The three documents together expressed provisionally the "official" Hitlerian war plan against Britain. Hitler's "private" plan was a far different thing. Neither the trilogy nor Hitler's own scheme gave the slightest hint of invasion.

Such a fanciful business, this idea of landing attack! The negative Navy attitude encouraged a tendency to fight the problem, instead of exploring what could be done. If ever, November of 1939 was the pivotal period for visualizing confrontation of England cross-Channel and bringing that picture into focus. Erich Raeder tried hard, almost alone, to do that, but his heart was not in it; his faith rested in siege. Yet, in order to prepare for any imaginable contingency and, above all, for any win-the-war-at-one-stroke notion that might strike the Führer, Raeder had ordered the study. He got what he wanted—a negative answer, after admittedly superficial treatment. Raeder's conscience was thus eased, while the unique moment for developing landing thought and supporting it with landing material slipped by all but unnoticed, and without action.

Whether questions from the Navy on landing stimulated interest in the Army or whether General Walther von Brauchitsch, the Army Commander-in-Chief, suffered like Raeder from a guilty conscience is not clear. The landing question did arise in OKH despite the fact that the Army, in the fall of 1939, was enmeshed in practical problems far removed from landing in England. World War I and its trenches still cast a long shadow. At one point during November Admiral Schniewind, the Navy Chief of Staff for Operations, suggested to General Halder, the Chief of the Army General Staff, that the Navy wanted the whole French side of the Channel right to the Atlantic, not as a base for invading England, but as a gateway toward blue water. The General, taken aback, replied, "Well my dear Admiral, do you want a Thirty Years' War?" Heaven forbid! The bogey of a long war, the *Sturm und Drang* of Hitler for attack in the West—and now the Navy wanting the moon! It was too much. And, as for rumored landing ideas, they were just fantastically theoretical. So thought the Chief of the Army General Staff.

The Navy had, however, delivered its landing study to Führer Headquarters (OKW) nonetheless. General Jodl recorded its arrival in his diary on 1 December 1939 in these apathetic words: "Landing Operation England, study of Commander in Chief Navy, pass to 'L.' "[8] The L, remember, stood for Landesverteidigung (National Defense Branch), Jodl's working staff under Warlimont. From that office the wild Navy idea could have filtered down to the Army at OKH. It is known that OKH also received a copy of the Navy work, directly, and thought very little of such loose play with Army troop organizations by sailor novices. Whatever spurred the soldiers to landing thought, on 13 December 1939 a paper sent to the other services solicited help on a study of invasion possibilities. It opened with a remarkable sentence: "The Commander-in-Chief [of the Army] has ordered examination of the possibilities of landing in England. The results are to be set forth in a study designated *Nordwest*. Collaboration is requested on the following points . . . ." The head of the Army Operations Section in OKH, Colonel Heinrich von Stülpnagel, signed the paper. In the heading he named Major Stieff, his youngest assistant, as co-ordinator.

The resulting explorations fared poorly indeed, but its authors even worse. Stülpnagel and Stieff were party to the conspiracy to overthrow Hitler that culminated on 20 July 1944 and paid with their lives.

A preamble like Stülpnagel's introduction to *Nordwest* was abnormal for a job on which the Army General Staff expected to do something. In staff language, as interpreted to this reporter, the opening sentence meant: "The General Staff is averse to discussing such plans at this time; however, the Commander-in-Chief has ordered it and for this reason some thoughts on our requirements from the Navy and the Air are given in the following paragraphs." Further, designating the youngest officer of Operations as monitor, plus the unusual step of identifying him by name, was so far out of line that it rendered the project suspect. No one wanted anything to do with the crazy thing.

[8] See page 56 of the diary of Generalmajor Alfred Jodl, given in "Quellen zur neusten Geschichte, III," *Die Welt als Geschichte*, XIII (1953), 61. Hereinafter references to General Jodl's daily notes will be taken from *IMT* doc. 1809-PS.

In contrast to the Navy's worried speculating about this and that hazard, "Stülpnagel's effort jumped happily, and with refreshing directness, into the business of producing a plan to do something. The simple purpose was to take London. No impending doom scowled from the waterline, the beach was swiftly hurdled in a bound, and the earnest task of coming to grips with the land fight entered upon. Seaway, tide, and weather belonged to someone else. The assault, to be launched from Low Country ports, would direct its main effort at the east coast of England between the Wash and the Thames. The creation of a beachhead in the Lowestoft-Great Yarmouth region came first through the landing of a reinforced infantry division and one airborne division in the ports and other forces on the flanks. Northward a diversionary operation was to insure enemy dispersion. A straightforward listing of the Navy task included: closing the Straits of Dover; neutralizing enemy naval action; mine clearance; transport assembly; loading and operation; and the two most important items, providing special landing craft and supporting the landings with naval gunfire. This list is practical and well considered. Other questions raised were: Considering the Navy ship-building plans, would it be practicable to neutralize the Royal Navy while moving across the North Sea? How much time would be required for outfitting ships and readying landing craft? How much time was needed for mounting the assault and for the approach over the sea? What season of the year would be best in view of the Luftwaffe tasks? These questions pinpointed dire Navy weaknesses.

The demands on the Luftwaffe, the questions and responses they evoked, paralleled those on the Navy: control of the air; cover and support during the approach; the beach assault; and subsequent field operations. When could the Luftwaffe be ready? Could supply be carried out by air? Were there important air prerequisite conditions? Commander-in-Chief of the Air Force, Generalfeldmarschall Hermann Wilhelm Göring in a single-page letter signed by a staff officer, turned these preposterous conjectures back without bothering about the demands. His concluding paragraph reflected a negative view even stronger than that of the Navy study: ". . . a combined operation having the objective of landing in England must be rejected. It could only be the final act of an already victorious war against England as otherwise the preconditions for success of a combined operation would not be met." Here Göring expressed a view that became standard.

Navy replied more carefully, but with even less enthusiasm. Each question raised was checked off in utter seriousness and the Army General Staff reminded of many omissions and misconceptions. For good measure Skl appended a copy of the Reinicke study to back up Navy objections. Points worthy of particular note on the Navy listing were: a time estimate of well over a year for preparation of floating landing material; insistence on prior elimination of all opposing naval forces; immense shipping requirements; and finally, a cautionary restatement of vast superiority at sea enjoyed by Britain. To consider it practicable, reasoned the Skl, for the German Navy to render the Royal Navy helpless during the approach to landing, while the originally inferior German sea forces still remained fit for executing a landing attack of tremendous scale and complexity, had to be designated as fallacious and untenable.

So ended the first sallies into the mysteries of amphibious warfare. We say *first,* advisedly, because the small previous intellectual or material work on this subject had left no lasting impression, either on the Kaiser's armed forces or on those of National Socialism. In October 1917 the transport and landing of Army forces against the Ösel Islands, guarding the Gulf of Riga, furnished the sole amphibious operational experience of consequence. The records reveal little interest in doctrine for joint action in the new Wehrmacht. One joint communication training exercise of minor proportions during 1937 furnished a lonely example of operating together. Thus the Navy study and the Army plan of late 1939 broke new ground; but they failed signally to stimulate strategical thinking toward solving the problem of England. These twin studies, Navy and Army, became linked under an odious name—*Studie Nordwest*—to which, after the war, neither service would own any connection.

The unhappy end of von Stülpnagel and Stieff, and obvious concomitants, may explain the odium. The unthreading of that complex has no place here, but a judgment on the validity of the work and its influence on later amphibious thought is pertinent. Both works were so weak in amphibious planning that they seemed counterfeit. They cannot be accepted as bona fide German efforts to explore this new and truly complex problem. Both evidence haste, superficiality, and preconceived solutions. The ulterior motive on the Navy side was frank riddance, and there it succeeded until the day German troops stood on the shores of the Channel in June 1940. The Army motive was less apparent, but the result worked out the same. More important, orphan that *Nordwest* became, its thinking nevertheless exerted definitive influence on invasion planning of the summer of 1940. First, it blocked the Channel sector from timely consideration as an area for a shore-to-shore invasion movement. Instead, it confirmed the Navy in ship-to-shore (transport) concepts, thus limiting further Navy responsibility to the mere provision of transport space for so many bodies, rather than fighting an assault force across water against a hostile shore. Second, command structure, as well as its involved ramifications in joint action, was ignored. But worst of all, the landing thought became bound round to the point of stupefaction with the hopeless prerequisites of absolute air, sea, and beach superiority. As a result, doubt prevailed in both Navy and Air about the basic validity of any invasion thought at all. If Britain were that far gone, invasion would be superfluous.

Nor did *Nordwest* strike fire in Führer Headquarters. From that quarter, we have only Jodl's diary entry while processing the Navy's paper and a recollection by the naval liaison officer in the planning staff of the scant attention paid to it in OKW.[9] There is no evidence that Hitler learned of the work on Invasion England during late 1939; he had long before turned over some ideas of that sort and had, in fact, directed attention to them during a conference with his top military leaders on 23 May 1939. But how differently did things turn out. In November 1939 Hitler found himself deeply mired in details of the impending attack on France. From the perspective of time, the question of where he expected this attack to lead rises automatically. Would Hitler end up on the Channel, surrounded by a victorious host, with no place to go? Yet, arrival on the Channel was clear enough in his mind's eye, because to him it meant control of the Continent and menace toward Britain. It was the pressure of his own momentum, and the inevitable challenge of his posture that escaped him. Here stood Hitler late in 1939, at the point of no return, beating the drums for a charge that had to reach the Channel or fail. Thence a void. The thing had not been thought through in 1914-1915 nor was it thought through in 1939-1940.

A firm invasion plan, presumed by many Britons, did not exist.

---

[9] The naval liaison officer on the OKW planning staff of the time, Lieutenant Commander Wolf Junge, has told me that he recalls the arrival of the Navy study and the early submergence of the subject. It was he who supplied Reinicke in Skl with Army troop and equipment data for the Navy study (Germany, March 1953).

4. Preliminary Actions

Norway, the Navy's War—April, May 1940

Just as the fight between Hitler and the Army leaders inhibited long-range thinking in OKH, so did the urge toward blue water draw the Navy to another overseas project of a much more plausible character, the seizure of Norway. Such a prospect had been bruited about Skl since early October. Here was a genuine Navy project.

The German Navy became Norway-minded between the wars through the writings of Vice Admiral Wolfgang Wegener, a witness to the unhappy demise of the Kaiser's Navy. Writing from retirement in the mid-twenties about ideas he had already expressed during the preceding war, Wegener analyzed the misconceptions of naval thought and its subjection to the narrow continentalism of German strategy. He preached that the fleet must get free of the German Bight and shake the defensive role von Tirpitz had cast for it. It must contest for the sea lanes of the Atlantic. As an area on which to base such operations, Wegener could suggest only Norway, in the hope of gaining exits leading to the Atlantic.[1]

Tirpitz had pursued a curious course of reasoning that produced an anomaly called the *Risikogedanke* (the risk concept). It assumed that the British were by tradition bound to seek out and bring any

[1] Wolfgang Wegener, Vizeadmiral A.D., *Die Seestrategie des Weltkrieges* (Berlin, 1929 and 1941).

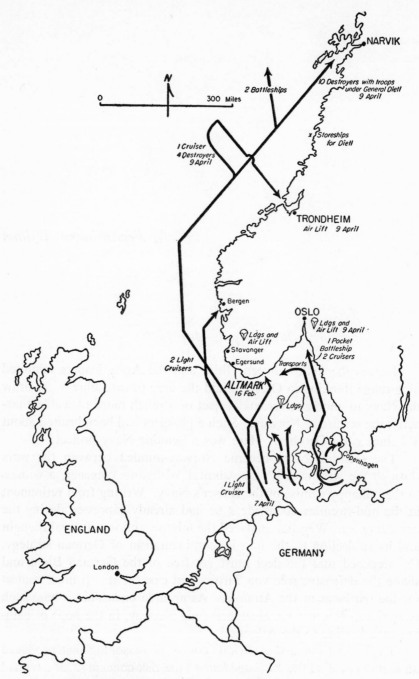

Operation Norway: Setting, events and personalities.

German Navy interest in the strategical significance of Norway worked up through the fall of 1939. Hitler was kept informed by Admiral Raeder,

enemy fleet to decisive battle. He would, reasoned Tirpitz, build a fleet specially fitted to fight in the German Bight, where, if sought out, the Germans would be superior. The risk of battle would thus become prohibitive to the British, and they would face an impossible war. Ergo, there could be no war. When the British failed to conform to his reasoning by going to war and simply neutralizing his fleet with a distant blockade, the whole *Risiko* concept tumbled. The Germans had built a costly, short-radius fleet to no purpose, which foundered in futility on the dismal bottom of Scapa Flow, sunk by its own hands. Futility remained the eternal problem of the German sailor.

German sailors suffered the same handicap that earlier hemmed the Dutch. It was a case of geography. The British Isles outflanked the North Sea and cut off its short Dutch-German shore from the blue water of world oceans.

This blue-water problem Wegener wanted to solve, and he ran head on into the old Tirpitz school, which still stubbornly clung to its bridge, or what was left of it. Admirals Ingehol, Zenker, and Erich Raeder, a rising officer who had served as Hipper's Chief of Staff in

---

C-in-C German Navy. Russian attack of Finland, late November, warmed interest in Norway. After hearing Quisling from Norway, Hitler on 14 December ordered a staff study, *Studie Nord,* on Norway.

On *27 January 1940* Hitler converted *Studie Nord* into an operation plan, *Weserübung.*

On *16 February* Captain P. L. Vian RN in HMS *Cossack* forcibly removed 300 British seamen prisoners from the German supply ship *Altmark* in Norwegian waters. The incident angered Hitler; he decided to occupy Norway.

On *1 March Weserübung* directive was issued, services commenced preparations. On 2 April Hitler ordered *Weserübung* attack for 9 April.

7 April naval movements began; 9 April attacks on Denmark and Norway commenced under the operational control of General Nikolaus von Falkenhorst commanding XXI Group of special Army units.

10 and *13 April* British naval forces attacked German destroyers in Narvik. All ten German destroyers were lost; Dietl, commanding Army forces who had landed from the destroyers was believed cut off. Hitler became wrought up. British landed north of Narvik, 13-14 April.

On *17 April* Hitler directed Keitel to telegraph Dietl to intern in Sweden. Message not sent through staff intervention in OKW.

By *27 April* German situation Norway stabilized except that Narvik remained in dispute until early June. On 10 June occupation Norway a fact.

the battle cruisers, all took up the cudgels to defend Tirpitz and brand Wegener a heretic. Officially his writings became taboo. Nevertheless they left their mark, especially on the youngsters who were hungry for a new gospel. Two of Wegener's sons were among them. Norway, with its possible strategic significance, came to represent more than just a pleasant region for cadet practice cruises; using northern bases for access to the oceans became a subject of wardroom discussion. All of this went into the Navy's Norway conditioning.

More important, Hitler was exposed to Norway thinking, and from two quarters, naval and political. His long-time naval aide was familiar with the Wegener thesis and recalls vaguely that long before the war he furnished the Führer a copy of Wegener's little book.[2] Hitler's other Norway exposure came from the Party's foreign-policy chief, Alfred Rosenberg. He had long pursued an interest in Scandinavia. During the summer of 1939, while events worked toward a climax, he submitted reports of his Norway findings to Hitler and fashioned a liaison of sorts with Norwegians. Thereby, later in 1939, Quisling sought out Rosenberg as first contact for entree to Hitler. Rosenberg referred him to Raeder.

Since the war's outbreak Admiral Raeder had been receiving disquieting intelligence of British plans for moving into Norway. Private letters from Admiral Carls, the German naval commander for the Scandinavian region, heightened these suspicions, and argued the significance of Norway in German hands. Raeder respected Carls' strategical thinking, and it appears that the rekindled thought of outlets via Norwegian bases began to appeal to him more than formerly. He directed his Naval Operations Office to examine the question. The thought was not strange to Skl either; a gameboard maneuver at Oberhof during the preceding February (1939) had considered northern bases, but with a much stronger German fleet projected for the years 1943-1945 under the so-called Z ship-building program. The year was still 1939, the expanded fleet was not on hand, and therefore on 9 October an Skl report counseled caution. From notes of this report, a separate report from his Chief of Submarines, and his own

---

[2] Konteradmiral Karl Jesko von Puttkamer served as naval adjutant to the Führer from 1935 to 1938 and from the outbreak of the war in 1939 to 1945. It was his business to maintain Hitler's interest in things Navy; he has told me of his efforts in this direction and believes it probable that he furnished Hitler a copy of the Wegener treatise.

reaction to the exchanges with Carls, Raeder reported to Hitler at the end of the Führer Conference of 10 October.[3]

The conference took place early in Hitler's drive for a shattering blow at the western powers. In his memorandum of the time he had declared himself for an immediate offensive into France. Scandinavia he mentioned only to remark that these countries would doubtless remain neutral. Now came the studious Commander-in-Chief of the Navy with another prognosis: There was danger that the British might outflank the Continental position from Norway. The advantages of getting there first were plain. The uncomfortable possibility turned out something of a coup for the Admiral. He had raised a strategical probability not thought of first by the Führer. Raeder wrote later, "The significance of the Norway problem was immediately perceived by the Führer; he asked me to leave the notes and explained he wished to go into the question." The long-headed chief of the navy was impressing Hitler, and not long afterward the Führer said as much in the tirade of 23 November, while roundly berating the Army leadership.

Nothing further happened for about a month. Hitler pursued his wrangle with the Army over the commencement of a western offensive. It ended, as noted above, in a reading of the riot act. He hinted at defeatism and promised to eradicate it with all ruthlessness. In his journal General Halder recorded 23 November as a "Day of Crisis." In sharp contrast, Raeder and his Navy had been highly complimented by the Führer.[4]

[3] *IMT*, XIV, 86-88; XXXIV, 281. See also Karl Jesko von Puttkamer, *Die Unheimliche See* (Vienna, 1952), pp. 29, 30; and *FC*, 1939, pp. 13, 14. The greatly expanded Z ship-building program came into being at the close of 1938 when Hitler was particularly annoyed with Britain. We notice this instance as the great turning against Britain. The German naval records reveal that the commander of the submarines, Dönitz, submitted a report on 9 October 1939 on the selection of Norwegian bases for submarines. It becomes clear that the primary stimulation of a Norway operation rose first from interest in bases leading to blue water.

[4] Admiral Raeder took pains to apprise his assistants of the Führer's praise and to support fully the Führer's strategy in the West. In an estimate prepared for conference of his section Heads on 25 November 1939 Raeder reviewed the European scene and concluded:

"*Conclusions:* At present there is definite military superiority on the part of Germany. Germany has no military obligations in the East. For the first time in fifty years a war on one front is possible.

If Germany takes a defensive attitude, her situation will gradually deteriorate not only from the military point of view but also in foreign policy. *Victory* can be achieved by offensive action alone.

"*Decision:* By means of offensive action in the West and an advance into the area of the French *Channel coast, we must seek to obtain favorable strategic bases* for an offensive war against Britain by *submarine, mine, and plane.* By

At the end of November a new departure drew attention north-ward. The Russian attack on Finland disturbed all Scandinavia and greatly intensified the situation for Germany; the thought of British aid to the Finns via Norway brought practical realities to the fore. Admiral Raeder kept close to the pulse of events and continued his weighing of factors. By 12 December he was able to report the result of interchanges with Quisling and to review extensively for Hitler the pros and cons of occupation. The project began to assume personal meaning for Raeder. In no circumstance must Norway fall to the British; he suggested that OKW be permitted to explore an occupation, after the Führer had checked Quisling. Hitler received Quisling, and thereafter, on 14 December, he instructed General Jodl to have a small staff group examine the Norway possibilities. The work undertaken by this group received the name of *Studie Nord*.

Though he appeared to assimilate the various contingencies, these new and eccentric ideas struck no natural chord with Hitler. The thought of reaching overseas, said his naval aide, was alien and un-comfortable to him. It lay outside his orbit and he put off coming to grips with the question. The first draft report of *Studie Nord* lay untouched while he continued to bend his effort toward triggering a West offensive against France. When at length this enterprise proved impracticable, through a combination of poor weather and the chance revelation of German attack plans, Hitler had to give in to a pro-tracted postponement there. Thus freed, he busied himself more di-rectly with Norway. On 27 January 1940 he ordered *Studie Nord* converted into a regular operation plan under the code name *Weserübung* (Weser Exercise) by an expanded combined staff di-rectly under himself. His interest still lagged far behind its customary vigor and drive in such scheming. Among the combat services, the Navy led, especially her Commander-in-Chief, with marked energy and concern. The other two services, Army and Air, had been de-ployed for the western attack and could only regard talk of the digression northward as a nuisance. Indeed, Hitler did not want them in on it.

---

extending the north German front to the West, the *Ruhr*—the "Achilles heel" of the armament industry, can be defended. Neutrality questions are irrelevant in case of victory.

"The Führer expresses his special appreciation of German naval warfare."

FC, 1939, p. 44. Thus Raeder echoed the thoughts of Hitler as given in the memorandum of 9 October 1939.

The Navy record shows that Raeder and his operations staff differed on Norway. His wish for seizure prevailed through British help. The staff, from the beginning on the tepid side, depreciated the imminence of British interference and, in view of the great naval risks involved, counseled abiding by Norwegian neutrality. Raeder, on the other hand, feared the British might move in, keep Germany from establishing northern naval bases, and deny her Scandinavian supplies. However, he cautiously acceded to the staff view. Within him several influences appear to have been at work. Against the traditionally rich Army and the glamorous new Luftwaffe, it was not easy to contrive distinction for his Navy in this, so far, purely Continental war. Things seemed destined to remain so. Could he but break the Navy out of its geographic prison, something might get done on the sea. A Norway operation offered a chance! It was nothing else but natural for the Navy to pursue this ancient sailor aspiration; the official records reflect the theme throughout, but leave decision hanging. At this point the British obliged with a thrust into Norwegian territorial waters that dissolved all doubt for Raeder and staff, and for their Führer.

Shortly before midnight on 16 February 1940, Captain P. L. Vian, R.N., commanding H.M.S. *Cossack*, felt his ship's way into dark Joessing Fjord on the southwest tip of Norway. Far in he found his quarry close to an ice floe skirting the steep shore. She was the German naval auxiliary *Altmark*, homeward bound from supplying the pocket battleship *Graf Spee* in the South Atlantic. She carried as prisoners 303 seamen whom the *Graf Spee* had taken out of British merchant prizes. Vian's job was to take them away from her. He ran his destroyer alongside; there was bumping and maneuvering. Kapitän Heinrich Dau of the *Altmark* endeavored to force the *Cossack* against the shore, but she cleared and managed to get a twenty-man boarding party over. The scuffle on the *Altmark* was short and to the point. Seven Germans were shot, several more wounded. The *Cossack* embarked the freed prisoners and headed for England. This incident, which took place in the presence of the two Norwegian torpedo boats, *Skarv* and *Kjell*, well within Norwegian territorial waters, sharpened belief of impending British intervention. An outraged Hitler read of the skirmish in Berlin the following day; he questioned the weak resistance offered by the *Altmark* and lashed out at high-handed British tactic. It was intolerable. General Jodl remarked in his journal on 19 February, "Führer unpleasantly disturbed over the behavior of *Graf Spee* people on the *Altmark*. No resistance, no British casualties. Führer presses hard for preparations on *Weserübung*. Get steamers outfitted. Get units told off. He wants to talk to working staff."[5] Two days later the Führer in person instructed General Nikolaus von Falkenhorst, the newly designated commander for *Norway*, about his own wishes in the operation. The *Cossack* action had crystallized things for Hitler.

On 1 March 1940 the formal *Weserübung* directive was issued, and the three services commenced physical preparations.[6] On 2 April Hitler ordered that the operation be launched at dawn 9 April. Thence the reduction of Norway, the first genuine attempt of the Germans to break from their geographic prison, ran its well-known course. Striking through Denmark, and directly at Norway by sea, the Germans quickly seized key points. This amazing forerunner of attack in the West had claim to a number of distinctions. It startled the world with Hitlerian blitz technique on an expanded scale, hitting within as well as without; it exposed opposing sea forces for the first time to shore-based air attack; it tested the extension of combat arms overseas in co-ordinate action. But in none of these interesting departures were the disclosures as revealing and meaningful as in the spiritual peculiarities of Adolf Hitler, which came to the surface during the operation.

Weserübung was the sole operation undertaken by the Germans that Hitler did not himself conceive and develop from the beginning. The spark of all previous Nazi plans and projects, as far back as his political awakening in 1919, had come out of him and succeeded because of him. A history of complete dependence on self-generated inspiration of this character impeded the acceptance of differing ideas from without, unless Hitler could rediscover a counterpart urge from the deeps of personal experience to build upon. He never succeeded in doing this for Norway, never was able to devise a true role for himself in this discomforting adventure. As contemporaries put it, the thing just did not "lay right with him"; he could not feel at home with it. He gained the opposite of confidence in operations projected overseas. His conduct of *Weserübung* showed as much, which one striking episode demonstrates.

[5] Walther Hubatsch, *Die deutsche Besetzung von Dänemark und Norwegen 1940* (Göttingen, 1952), p. 381.
[6] *Weserübung* directive is given in Hubatsch, *op. cit.*, pp. 425-27.

The ore port of Narvik, far up on the north coast of Norway, figured importantly from the very beginning in all of the planning for *Weserübung*. To make it secure and thereby insure a flow of ores to Germany, was, in fact, belatedly advanced as one of the compelling arguments for undertaking the operation at all. But taking Narvik would entail sending a combat team some 300 miles northeastward on its own, far out of practicable supporting range. Supply posed the major problem. Accordingly, by plan, three storeships, disguised as ordinary merchantmen (but actually loaded with munitions and supplies), were to be dispatched ahead of the combat team. This team of 2,000 mountain troops under Major-General Edward Dietl embarked in 10 destroyers to overtake the storeships at high speed. So, Narvik would be entered and taken.

Hitler took a special and personal interest in the expedition, for it ran the greatest hazards and promised high profit. Besides, Dietl, like some Bavarians, enjoyed special favor with the Führer, who had known the General for a long time and liked him. Beyond that, the troops came from the nativeland, Austria's own mountains. The expedition got underway on schedule and progressed smoothly as planned. Hitler was nervous about it. Jodl could show his Supreme Commander the advance of the storeships and the overhauling destroyers on his daily situation plot. Dietl entered Narvik and quickly took over, but he found no storeships carrying his artillery awaiting him. The machinery and fuel situation of the destroyers was critical. Also, contrary to intelligence advices, Narvik possessed no coastal guns for driving off expected British counteraction. When this bad news, together with rumors of attacks by British naval forces, reached the Reichskanzlei in Berlin, Hitler was beside himself. Lieutenant Colonel Bernhard von Lossberg, the Army liaison officer, remarked, "In the Reichs Chancellory during these days there was the devil to pay," and Jodl, who took the brunt of the abuse, characterized the uproar as something "fürchterlich." The campaign was but four days old; in Hitler's facile imagination the whole project was already wrecked. He showed signs of giving up.[7]

It developed that the positions plotted for the storeships on the charts shown Hitler were not verified positions but merely those esti-

[7] Bernhard von Lossberg, *Im Wehrmachtführungsstab* (Hamburg, 1950), pp. 66-69. General von Lossberg was the Army representative in the Warlimont staff in OKW. We discussed the above and related actions with him during 1953 in Germany. For Jodl comment, see *IMT*, XXVIII, 420.

mated in OKW from day to day according to plan. Since radio silence precluded confirmation, there could be no absolute assurance of correct plotting. Here was Hitler's first exposure to the uncertainties of operating over the sea. The incurable impairment to his direct control took him aback. Thereafter a naval officer had the direct responsibility for informing him on the situation at sea.

The true mettle of Adolf Hitler revealed itself. Fantastic schemes immediately took wing for bringing relief to Dietl, who was fancied in the worst possible straits. Reinforcement by airdrop and submarine was prepared; evacuation by seaplanes and a score of other measures appeared, crying all hands to the pumps. Not to be outdone, Göring bounced in with a scheme to dispatch a superliner like the *Europa* or *Bremen* with a division or so of troops aboard. That would be sure to hang one on the Navy. By 13 April the last of the ten German destroyers at Narvik (one-half of all there were) succumbed to Royal Navy action, and an assembly of British ships was on the point of landing troops in the area. Hitler could stand it no longer. On 17 April without consulting Jodl, the operations adviser, he directed the more pliable Keitel to draft an unbelievable message to Dietl. It ordered him to clear out of Narvik toward the Swedish border for internment. In the end no such transmission was made. Dietl's situation improved momentarily, and Hitler got over his fright. Not so his staff. The exhibition augured no good for the further conduct of the war. A fair-weather sailor stood at the helm.

Indeed, this helmsman, beset by fears of the worst, showed trouble in making up his mind. He fidgeted about and seemed often on the point of throwing over the whole enterprise. Close observers say not once, but time and again, that at no period during the war, in far more critical circumstances on land, did Hitler exhibit concern and nervousness, yes, even fright, so plainly as during the early days of *Weserübung*. At the root may have been mere ignorance of the sea coupled with animal fear. We find these spectacles in practice explaining themselves more fully through the idiosyncrasies of the Hitlerian decision–action machinery. He himself spoke truly when during *Norway* he cried in anguish, "If I could have seen in advance that the storeships might not arrive, then I would never have arrived at the decision for this undertaking." There in actuality was the German Führer's weak suit, decision-making, and doubly so in *Norway,* because he had not conceived the project. It was not his.[8]

Weserübung abounded in tempests until early May, when the scene shifted to the more salubrious climate of Felsennest and the great West offensive. "What a lovely place Felsennest was!" exulted the happy Führer in restrospect. "The birds in the morning, the view over the road by which the columns were going up the line. Over our heads the squadrons of aircraft. There I knew what I was doing."[9] He was glad of release to his own true field—mighty land operations; he had had his fill of sea adventures. Perhaps he had also had his fill of being pitted against the British alone.

We have called *Norway* the Navy's war, and, in feeling, that it was, as *Japan* became the U.S. Navy's Blue Water war. But the German sailing turned out far from easy in this master stroke, which Raeder hoped would bring spiritual and operational freedom, once and for all. Crisis followed crisis, one day of anxiety after another— over Narvik, over homing the precious heavy ships, over placating the Führer and contending against Göring. Losses were grave, and they would tell later. At the close of the undertaking the surface fleet approached operational paralysis; there remained fit for action just one major ship, the heavy cruiser *Hipper.* In lesser vessels only two light cruisers, six destroyers, and an assortment of small craft were combat ready. What could one hope to do against the might of Britain, bases or no, with this ill-assorted remnant Navy? Yet despite this dark look of things, the Commander-in-Chief of the Navy was content. From the onset of the operation he had maintained a serenity that spoke for a deep confidence in this, his own handiwork. He arrived in his office at 0500 on the morning the ships were expected to enter combat waters. His Flag Lieutenant went in to ask what could be done for the Chief; to the younger officer's amazement, he found the old gentleman completely at ease, absorbed in a novel. For the first (and only) time he had ordered his ships into a finish fight. There would be no avoiding of superior enemy forces. The supreme

[8] The Narvik episode and the message to Dietl are almost as famed as Dunkirk and the halt order to the German tanks. Both have been discussed with German officer participants. On the Dietl incident, the accounts given in the sources are in substantial agreement and are borne out by German official records. Heinz Assmann, *op. cit.,* p. 1292. Hubatsch, *op. cit.,* pp. 189, 395. Von Puttkamer, *op. cit.,* p. 35. Helmuth Greiner, *Die Oberste Wehrmachtführung* (Wiesbaden, 1951), p. 85 (Herr Greiner acted as diarist for the L section of OKW). Jodl diary, *IMT,* XXVIII, 420.

[9] *SC,* p. 59.

moment had arrived!   Scapa Flow would be expiated, his Navy would
acquit itself with honor.   And it did, at heavy cost.

It is impossible to overstress the power of Raeder's yearning to
erase the stain of 1918 mutiny and defeatism from the Navy scutch-
eon.   The hunger of it fortified his resolve to stand or fall by the
blue-water test he had instigated.   So may the spirit have urged action.
Yet Raeder hoped for still greater recompense.   At *Norway's* close
he exclaimed in a paean of praise to his Navy, "The portal to the
ocean has been broken open!"   By widening the base of operation,
Raeder argued, he had dispersed the enemy and multiplied opportunities for his favorite strategy, *Handelskrieg* (merchant shipping warfare) and siege.   One can wonder what good an open portal was to a
paralytic and gravely inferior Navy, if indeed any portal was open.
The value of each remaining major ship, all but one under extensive
repairs, had risen immeasurably; each irreplaceable unit had now
become a great treasure.   The profit of *Norway* proved illusory.
The extended base line overstretched meager German naval resources
and left a smaller number of combatant ships just as securely bottled
up as they had been in the German Bight.[10]

"Old Sailors Never Die" nor does their propensity for wanting to
settle matters single-handed at sea.   Should not the amazing German
success in this combined operation have encouraged them to think of
going further with combined operations, perhaps even against mighty
Britain?   Little evidence comes to hand of any such reaction on the
German side.   It remained for the British to take the initiative in
propagating this line of thought.

Invasion scare was on in Britain.   During debate over British
failure to stop occupation of Norway, a member of the House of
Commons remarked that, though the Royal Navy appeared equal to
saving Britain from starvation by keeping some sea lanes open, it did
not seem up to preventing Invasion; if the Navy could not cut off a
landing in Norway, it was conceivable a German descent on Lincoln-
shire and the Wash could not be stopped either[11]—Britons commenced
to wonder uneasily about sea power against air power and whether

---

[10] Admiral Raeder's World War II advocacy of *Handelskrieg* did not agree completely with his own published writings of the early twenties on this subject.   Apparently he accommodated his views to the new situation, as he had his early opposition to Wegener's suggestions about Norway.

[11] See the Speech by Colonel Josiah Clement Wedgwood, member of Newcastle
under Lyme, Tuesday, 7 May 1940, as given in the *House of Commons Official
Report of Sessions 1940*.

under Luftwaffe wings Invasion England had not become relatively easy.

The Germans allowed British opinion to mold their own. The diarist of the German Naval Operations Office took instant note of the invasion observations in Parliament and entered them in the journal of Skl for 8 May 1940. Also on that day he entered at the top of a list accounting for the British failure, "An overestimation [on the part of the British] of the power of sea command in a coastal defense zone [*Küstenvorfeld*] controlled by the Luftwaffe" from shore. Earlier, on 4 May, the diarist, while musing on the question of plane versus ship, had recorded that "the operation of heavy combat forces in the coastal zone . . . especially within reach of Stukas [dive-bombers] would subject the naval units committed to the gravest dangers, representing a risk that England would hardly take upon herself." Norway fell because the Germans maintained an Army supply line across the Skagerrak; the British had not ventured to commit heavy ships to the task of severing this line. Winston Churchill, First Lord of the Admiralty, said on 8 May 1940 in the House of Commons: "But immense enemy air strength made this method [cutting of sea supply lines in the Skagerrak] far too costly to be adopted . . . losses inflicted from the air would very soon constitute a naval disaster."

A spark of interest in Invasion and related subjects had been kindled but, of all things, by the British! This ironic turn recurred not once but time after time, until it became the peculiar history of publicity about Invasion England 1940 to have British uneasiness take the lead. The Germans printed news stories from England and other foreign sources, perhaps to work up pressure at home. Only in one particular was there divergence. For deception purposes, they had advertised the preparations for *Norway* as pointed toward the east coast of England.[12] The canard took. Goebbels' propaganda machinery made the most of it; Herms Niel's ditty, "Wir Fahren Gegen Engelland," was added to the *Sondermeldung* (special announcement) routine of reports from the fighting forces. The German public waxed more and more England-conscious, and its invasion spirit far outstripped official feeling and, perhaps, official intent.

To what extent the entries of the Skl diarist were his own or those of life-thinking associates, is hard to fix.[13] It is certain that any Skl

---

[12] In the representative *Völkischer Beobachter* (Munich edition), the discussion was lively and free. For data on radio broadcasts in the same vein see analysis

landing thought generated by the Norway operation led to no practical result; and no waterfront application of the few lessons learned
came about. If anything, the German Navy attitude—that its role
in overseas expedition was simple transport, moving so many bodies
en masse overseas—grew stronger.

On the question of improving interservice relations, which was
Norway's greatest opportunity, strife rather than concord resulted.
One might have expected some gropings toward a solution of this
problem, which has not been fully resolved to this day. The Germans were the first in the war to encounter the complexities of combined operating overseas. But alert and intelligent though they are,
they failed to register lasting progress. Recognize the command
problem they did, and they tried to resolve it by a Führer instruction
of 14 March 1940 that prescribed reasonable lines for exercising
command. Personalities high up, however, counted too heavily.
Human frailty of the Führer and contending henchmen alike inhibited
real progress. The pseudo Commander of *Norway,* General von
Falkenhorst, stood directly responsible to Hitler; for major air and
naval support he depended on requests to the respective commanders-
in-chief. The Army High Command, as such, did not participate at
all. Amongst themselves the fighters of all three services within their
own purview achieved a high degree of teamwork initially, both in
planning and acting. Urgent need and common danger carried the
day. The three arms labored and fought as one; things had to get

---

by Ernst Kris and Hans Speier, *German Radio Propaganda,* pp. 301, 302, 388.
Foreign date lines were used exclusively.

[13] So many times in questioning German records participants have said, "Oh, that
was only the idea of some staff duty officer who had to make some record." Of
course, this can sometimes be the case; it will vary with the individual and the
circumstance. The diarist here was Heinz Assmann. He kept superior records of
German naval events and the thought surrounding them. This reporter has seen
none better. We met in December 1952 and talked of his work in Skl and later in
OKW, of his *Kriegstagebuch* (the war diary of Skl), and of the invasion thought
expressed therein. He and a number of the younger zealots favored landing ideas.
More important, so did their immediate superior, Admiral (to be) Fricke. He
had told Reinicke to get on with the 1939 study on landing in England. Fricke
was a dynamo who could dilate for two or three hours on strategical plans that
would win the war—late into the evening. Then he would close with admonition
to the listening assistant to bring in a smooth write-up of the subjects discussed by
eight in the morning. While contemporaries found Fricke hard to get along with,
the younger people were for their strong man of vision and drive. The opinions
expressed in the diary received notice while circulating through the customary
channels: first to Wagner, the senior assistant in operations; to Fricke (the head of
operations); and then on to Admiral Schniewind, the Operations Chief of Staff,
before going to Commander-in-Chief Raeder for final perusal and approval.

done with what was at hand. This perfectly natural development is borne out in combat experience the world over. At the outset one makes common cause. As time and action wear on, the early perils recede, common cause begins to wane, and inherent differences reappear. With the Germans, passionate personal jealousies at the top accelerated this retrogression.

On the whole, teachings from the *Norway* experience were of greater profit to the British than the Germans. Friction threatened to break into open warfare at several points, notably between Raeder and Göring. Göring indulged in a vicious type of backbiting, by making a habit of frequent dashes to the Führer with reports of poor Navy performance and suggestions for improvement. One officer underlined the tactic by quoting him as follows: "It is hard for the Luftwaffe to do everything, but if the Navy, who started this can't do its job, I will do it, Mein Führer!" Observers thought Hitler saw through him and that he must have been aware of the faulty command relationship. He did nothing about setting it aright. There was good reason, for a sound command system might have impaired the tight and unencumbered control Hitler required for himself. His know-better system brooked no dissent, which he always smelled a mile off. Consequently, even though the Germans ofttimes perceived the lessons of experience, they were blocked from applying them by this inflexible Hitlerian barrier. Experience could profit then but little. On the British side, no such barrier existed; experience paid off handsomely.[14]

Thus *Norway* signaled something of a warning to Britain. The action there approached its end about the time that the main event in the West for the British reached its climax in the Dunkirk pocket. Both events provided lights for what was to follow in the summer of 1940. We return to Felsennest to pick up the Dunkirk story.

Dunkirk Prologue—May 1940

To most Americans Cap Gris Nez has meant cold water, grease, and gasping Channel swimmers. Few have stopped to think that Calais nearby once held seat in England's Parliament or that ancient

[14] Jodl diary, *IMT*, XXVIII, 400-30, gives a terse but telling account of the development of the *Norway* operation under the handicap of Hitlerian command structure.

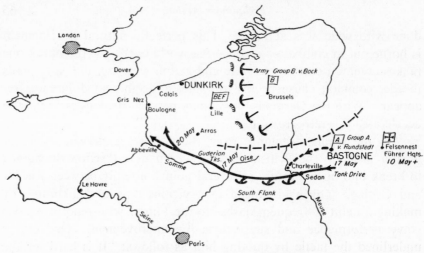

Dunkirk prologue: 10-20 May 1940.

10 May: German Army Groups A (von Rundstedt) and B (von Bock) attack in the West, Group B through the Lowlands and A through the Ardennes Forest.

The Guderian XIX Armored Corps (von Kleist group under 4th Army of Army Group A) forces the Meuse at Sedan and drives westward through the Allied lines.

17 May: Guderian tanks cross the Oise and continue northwestward. Breakthrough a fact. Hitler at Felsennest is faced with a "great decision." Should he keep on? He grows uneasy over his lengthening southern flank and fumes to reinforce it rather than drive on. In the afternoon of the day he motors forward to Bastogne to consult von Rundstedt. He seems to find von Rundstedt in agreement on slowing the armor; hints that Britain would make peace now anyway.

20 May: The armored forces nevertheless press on, reaching the English Channel waters near Abbeville on the Somme.

Hitler is jubilant. Peace is at hand.

Dunkirk along the coast to the northeast once served as an outpost for Cromwell's Ironsides. Ironsides or Channel swim, it is all one, for there in the Narrows off Dover lies the shortest distance between England and Europe; and thus for English action on the Continent or Continental design on England, the region has been one of crisis in history.

Here, before Dunkirk, Hitler's self found its peculiar play and left us a murky vignette of Hitleriana. His inertia-overcoming drive unleashed the action on that momentous tenth of May in 1940. Who does not recall how his jubilant words broke in on our consciousness far across the Atlantic? The fortune of the German nation for a thousand years rode with this venture, he shouted as his legions hopped off. And away they went with astounding celerity and apparent smooth efficiency. For him, to follow the campaign's progress from beautiful Felsennest developed into a marvelously elating experience. To watch the maps, to feel a part of the fight, yes, even to direct it! What more could a lance corporal want? Just as Hitler hoped, success piled on success; but just as in Norway, pressures mounted. He commenced to apply the brakes; he could not refrain from nervous meddling.

Renewed tensions built up between the Führer and Army leadership at OKH. Guderian and his tanks of the Kleist Group, as promised, had forced the Meuse at Sedan in record time; thence they drove a wedge westward through the Allied lines. A breakthrough perhaps, but as the wedge lengthened, its vulnerable south flank troubled Hitler. Fears crowded in on him to urge caution. He flailed about Führer Headquarters, getting support forward, preparing defense toward the South, and slowing Guderian's drive. This was 16-17 May. General Jodl confided to his notebook, "Führer presses hard for the release of all armored and motorized units from Army Group B [on the north] to Group A [in the center], and for the speedy follow-up of strong reserves . . . ." Jodl made a significant closing entry indicating that Field Marshal Göring spent two and a half hours in conference with the Supreme Commander—significant because Göring always managed to be on hand at the crucial juncture, throwing his counsel this way or that, often volunteering to do the upcoming job himself when all else failed. It could be counted certain that something was afoot. The breakthrough was fact. On the seventeenth the Führer decided to go up front for a sounding at the headquarters of Generaloberst Karl Rudolph Gerd von Rundstedt. Rundstedt commanded Army Group A, including the Kleist group, of which Guderian, commanding XIX Armored Corps was a part.

For the forenoon of that day of 17 May General Halder's journal confirmed an atmosphere of tension: "A great decision must be taken now!" he wrote. Should a prong also sweep southwest toward Compiègne and Paris to complement the stroke northwest toward the Channel? So had General Erich von Manstein, former Chief of General Staff to von Rundstedt, advocated from late 1939 on. He aimed at Continental decision in one grand operation: force the Meuse at Sedan and cut the Allies asunder; trap the British against the coast by driving a wedge west and northwest toward the Channel, and under that shock sweep southwest from the botton of the wedge to gather in the bulk of the French armies. While OKH from the first had opposed the plan, Hitler on his own gradually formulated similar ideas, with special emphasis on trapping the British, possibly because of the political connotations, to catch which politician Hitler always cocked an ear. As late as 1955 von Manstein expressed doubt that Hitler ever took unto himself the risk of the second stroke, to sweep southwest as well. Breakthrough, followed by consolidation; then possibly a dash to the Channel—these appeared to be the ideas uppermost in Hitler's thinking, as revealed in word and action. Rather than "great decision," he preferred to temporize.[15]

[15] Generalfeldmarschall Erich von Manstein gives his estimate of Hitler's grasp of the plan on page 122 of his *Verlorene Siege* (Bonn, 1955). His story of the development of the plan appears on pages 103-32. The records bear it out substantially. The records also show the long, tortuous course (October 1939 to March 1940) the plan took until finally adopted. Hitler himself in October mentioned cutting off the Anglo-French armies in the north and directed that the possibility be included. He would therefore have been receptive to like suggestions, which Rundstedt's headquarters sent to OKH, but which that office did not favor and, of course, was loath to pass on to Hitler. Not until February 1940 was Hitler directly exposed to the complete conception, and that by von Manstein personally. By this time OKH itself had come along. The plan was issued in an OKH *Aufmarsch Anweisung* (assembly directive for attack) of 24 February 1940 and was thereafter tested in extensive game board exercises. It was apparently also outlined in a Führer Directive No. 10, for Hitler refers to its sense in his Directive No. 11 of 14 May 1940. It runs, "This situation and the rapid forcing of the Meuse by Army Group A have created the first prerequisites for achieving a grand success in the sense of Directive No. 10 through a push northwest with concentrated strong forces north of the Aisne . . . ." The genius stroke of diverging sweeps, one to the northwest and the other to the southwest, it seems was not fully expressed, nor is there evidence that these sweeps were played through on the board to complete encirclement. Rather, in conferences succeeding the games, the initial breakthrough, followed by a dash to the Channel, gained emphasis over the rest of the plan. At Führer conferences on 15 and 16 March, General Halder recorded: "(1) Decision reserved on further moves after crossing of Meuse. (2) He [Hitler] reckons with the possibility the French and British might adopt a passive attitude in the face of our invasion. This belief, he feels justified by the difficulty of prompt communication between the political and military authority. (3) He plays with the idea that a mild bleeding of the enemy forces will suffice to break their will to resist" (*War Journal of Franz Halder*, Lissance translation, III, 125, hereinafter referred to as *Halder Journal*). Thus Hitler seems to have become predisposed to "hesitate and re-estimate" after the breakthrough, although Guderian, in the same conference, hammered home to him his intention to dash for the Channel. See Heinz Guderian, *Erinnerungen eines Soldaten* (Heidelberg, 1951), p. 82. We should note Guderian's added comment on the resulting execution: "Also in the resulting events I received no order that went beyond the gaining of the bridgehead over the Meuse. I arrived independently at all the decisions up to arrival on the Atlantic at Abbeville. Superior command in the main exercised restraining influence on my operations." The records bear this out amply. Guderian commanded XIX Armored Corps of the Kleist group.

But this was no time to temporize, according to the leaders at OKH. When General Halder speculated on "great decision," armored and motorized units already poured through the breach, and his thought must have revolved around utilizing that offensive momentum to the southwest as well as toward the Channel. He urged forward the forces on the fighting front in telephone exchanges with head-quarters of both Army Groups A and B, while the Commander-in-Chief, von Brauchitsch, repaired to OKW to placate the Führer. The General had little luck there. At noon he returned with a dis-couraging picture for his Chief of Staff, Halder, who sketched it in his journal. "Noon, ObdH [C-in-C Army] with Führer; apparently little mutual understanding. The Führer stresses he sees the main danger threatening from the south. . . . For that reason infantry di-visions should be moved up at the earliest for the security of the south flank. . . . ObdH discusses matter with Rundstedt, to whom the Führer plans to run up during the afternoon [of 17 May] . . . ."[16]

While Hitler visited General von Bock of Army Group B (op-erating on the north flank in the Lowlands) but once, and that late in the game, he favored Army Group A with visits on three occasions, 17 and 24 May and 2 June. It is entirely probable that he singled out von Rundstedt of Group A for this attention because of need for a sympathetic climate against OKH. For Rundstedt and staff had likewise been at odds with OKH over Manstein's plan to breach the Allied lines at Sedan and then cut to the Channel. After Hitler had adapted the plan to some of his own thinking during February 1940, it became his very own brain child and, of course, his absorbing in-terest. With the operation underway, however, he manifested symp-toms reminiscent of the explosion over Dietl and Narvik during *Norway*. But Dietl at Narvik had been far away, unreachable, where-as Rundstedt held forth at Bastogne, but a scant two hours' distance by car.

Bastogne, that battered crossing of many roads, became memo-rable to Americans almost five years later when the immortal word

---

[16] See *Halder Journal*, IV, 16. General Halder painstakingly recorded the events of the war as they came to his notice and in particular the events affecting OKH and his thoughts and work connected therewith. This is a most valuable source not alone for its recording but also for the insight furnished into the char-acters and the atmosphere surrounding them and their actions. Since the English translation (Lissance) is more readily available here, this is cited. The citations have been compared and adjusted where necessary to the German edition, as, in some instances, the sense suffered in translation.

"nuts" issued from the lips of General McAuliffe in the Battle of the Bulge. Rundstedt was destined to command the Germans then, too, and his forces would be pressing likewise to exploit a breakthrough. On the earlier occasion of our interest, success came swiftly, for he established his headquarters at Bastogne in the course of the first few days of the 1940 campaign. The Führer arrived there by car in the mid-afternoon of 17 May and was closeted immediately with von Rundstedt, his Chief of Staff, General Georg von Sodenstern, and his Chief of Operations, Colonel Günther Blumentritt.

The war diary of Army Group A depended for accounting of the meeting on General von Sodenstern, who by habit kept precise personal notes. The diary recounts that the Army Group Commander presented the situation, stressing the sensitiveness of his south flank, and the measures he had in prospect for dealing with the circumstance.

The Führer agrees fully [ran the diary] with the estimate and approves the measures thus far taken. He nevertheless underlines especially the significance that the south flank has, not only for the operations of the whole Army, but also politically and psychologically. Under no circumstances must a set-back occur at this moment anywhere, a set-back that would give a fateful rise [in spirit] to our adversaries, not alone to the military, but above all, also to their political leadership. Thus the decision, for the moment rests not so much in the rapid forward push to the Channel but much more . . . in the speediest establishment of absolutely reliable *defensive* readiness on the Aisne . . . and later on the Somme . . . . Toward this purpose all measures are to be directed even if time is lost temporarily in the push toward the West [and the Channel].[17]

Group A command, the diary further reveals, interpreted these words as a Führer decision and immediately translated them into orders.

There was no obscurity here. Hitler clearly wanted the drive slowed and welcomed the evidence of agreement from Group A. However, to safeguard the initiative and momentum already built up in still another field seemed also to be in his mind. He gave specific indication that psycho-political considerations lay at the bottom of his thinking. In this area Hitler lost his auditors completely.

To the astonished incredulity of the soldiery, he discoursed at length on psychological and political effects. At first they sat listening appreciatively to his fulsome praise of their achievements, but the

[17] Kriegstagebuch West, Teil II der Heeresgruppe A, 17 Mai 1940 (War Diary, West, Part II of Army Group A, 17 May 1940. *MS*, Office of Chief of Military History, Department of the Army, Washington).

ensuing turn to politics and the virtues of Britain struck them with amazement. It would seem that Hitler's mood gave free rein to his fancy. General von Sodenstern quoted him as saying that his "policy demanded a smooth and victorious run-off of the operation," and continued, "In this connection Hitler thereupon developed to us his idea that England, once destructively beaten in north France, will be ready to come to terms on the basis of [her] power at sea against the power [of Germany] on the Continent. This astonished us very much because we had judged the British otherwise." General Blumentritt added some pinpointing details from Hitler's lecture: England was just as necessary on earth as the Catholic church. At times she had used hard means to build up her empire, but where planing is done, shavings must fly. In six weeks there would be peace, and he would make a gentleman's agreement with England.[18]

Here were soldiers locked in mortal combat with a devilish foe who sought extermination for them and their Fatherland. So had Hitler, Goebbels, and Company advertised Britain in crescendo since the end of 1938. She was the root of all evil and must be overthrown. Now suddenly the author of Armageddon belies his own battle cries with intimation of virtue in the devil and hints of a go-easy policy. From the professional military angle, belief that the British might conform ran counter to all experience. Hitler's gibberish mystified his Group A audience and thereby led inevitably to individual speculation on peace. On reflection, there could be something to it, provided his political demands remained within reason. Ideas of peace were certainly not unwelcome to most Germans—peace at last on a stable German basis. How disingenuous—yet this talk made an indelible impression on the minds of Hitler's listeners. We can wonder why this man, who rarely confided to anyone, mentioned settlement. As was usually the case, he reckoned on getting something over. But what? He may have wanted to cozen these Army leaders whose sympathy against OKH could be useful; he may have wished to encourage his own hopes for association with England. He scored on all these counts, for so ran the effect of his words on his astounded, but also bewildered, listeners, but in no sense did his words whet hostility against Britain or against her imperiled Expeditionary Force (BEF) in Flanders.

[18] Von Sodenstern to Ansel (Germany, March 1953, and in correspondence, 1954). Blumentritt to Ansel by correspondence (Germany, 1953, and January 1955).

Riddle *Dunkirk* began on 17 May 1940. That memorable day gave instructive evidence of Hitler's first reaction to success in the West and of his conditioned intentions toward Britain. The date 17 May 1940 marked the genesis of Halt Order to the German tanks that presaged, in turn, the beginning of German failure against Britain.[19]

An incredible order of things is thus presented; an order regulated in great part by personal predilection, animosity, and incurable duplicity. Between the Supreme Commander and his spearhead there existed a covert liaison founded on vague confidences. He paid little attention to Army Group B, the other Army group engaged, or to its commander, General Fedor von Bock. His forces had been rolling up the Lowlands toward the eastern rim of the Dunkirk trap, but they were in no position to spring the trap, as was Group A. Against the top Army leadership in OKH (von Brauchitsch and Halder) Hitler stood in vindictive antagonism. The Navy hardly came into his consciousness at all, but Air, through Göring, was close at hand so that interchanges took place constantly in a mutually agreeable arrangement. By this means the Air General Staff became almost a part of Führer Headquarters and thus shared its servile atmosphere of belief in the Hitlerian magic. These were the queer signs of the unnatural climate pervading upper German command levels when the campaign to usher in a millennium was but a week old.

Dunkirk and Problem England

The engines of war rolled on oblivious to their background and with a swiftness that left the world aghast. Hitler said at Bastogne, "All the world hearkens!" and he spoke truly. Where would it end? Guderian and Hans Reinhardt of the XXXXI corps pushed their tanks over the Oise tributaries and drove for the Channel. Forward elements reached Abbeville, then Montreuil, and turned north along the Channel coast. Guderian's tanks ringed Boulogne and Calais

[19] The visit of Hitler to Army Group A on 17 May 1940 has been neglected. General Blumentritt's photograph of Hitler's arrival by car at Bastogne fixed it and also recalled memories for him. It has not been difficult to sort out the data among the three Hitler visits to the Group A command, although he repeated talk on related matters. Clues from the Group A war diary have helped to rearrange for Hitler's listeners the sequence of his utterances. For example, the war diary entry of political and psychological factors, mentioned by Hitler, revived memory of his elaboration about these factors on 17 May.

and pursued their way along the coast northeastward to cut off the BEF, the French First Army, remnants of the Seventh, and the Belgian Army from the coast. By 23 May Guderian's northernmost column rested before Gravelines on the Aa Canal, a scant twelve miles west of Dunkirk, the last primary Channel port of escape open to the BEF. That force still fought deep inland about Lille, some forty-two miles southeast. The Germans before Gravelines were thus closer to Dunkirk by thirty miles than most of the British. German forces of Army Group B were pressing frontally from the east. The gratifying picture etched its outlines on this fair May evening as the reports from the front permeated the top commands and found excited expression in the war diaries. Realization that the last act of a thrilling drama approached shows in those recordings. It was anticipated that the all-but-trapped BEF would be annihilated in a grand *Kesselschlacht,* or those unfortunates in the kettle could give up![20]

Indeed, Hitler had already become convinced of some such denouement three days earlier (20 May) when word first arrived that Guderian stood on the Channel near Abbeville. General Jodl's memo book of day-to-day business at OKW carried an entry for the end of that day: "Führer is beside himself with joy . . . busies himself with the peace treaty . . . . Initial negotiations in the forest of the Compiègne as in 1918. British can at any time have a separate peace after return of colonies . . . ."

Things were turning out exactly as he had hoped, and as the Führer had said at Bastogne on the 17th. Present evidence indicates that by 23 May the elation at Führer Headquarters outran all others; symptoms of grand finale appeared. The last act of the war might be at hand! OKW hurried its routine of medal-distribution in order that all the deserving might be included.

Hermann Göring, First Huntsman of the Reich, played the outdoor man in war as well as in peace. When his rail headquarters stopped at a siding, as now at Polch, he by habit ordered a thick round table set up outdoors under the trees as his workbench. There he lolled on the late afternoon of 23 May, attended by the Chief of the Air General Staff, General Jeschonnek, and his Chief of Intelli-

---

[20] General Von Bock (Army Group B) was pushing strongly on the eastern rim of the kettle through Belgium. His forces were heavily engaged frontally and stood no chance of gaining a decisive position in the enemy's rear as readily and quickly as the forces of von Rundstedt at Gravelines on the coast.

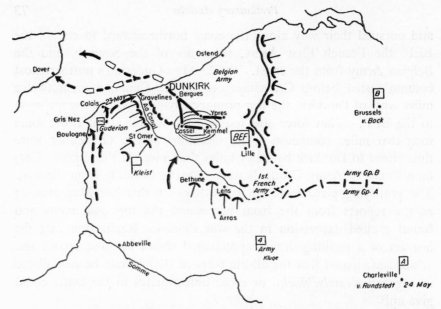

Dunkirk and Problem England: Situation 24-26 May.

By *23 May*, having reached the English Channel German tank forces (von Rundstedt) turn north and northeast and follow the coast to Gravelines on the Aa Canal, 12 miles from Dunkirk, the principal supply port for the BEF. Army Group B pushes against a failing Belgian army from the east but is still 50 miles from Dunkirk. Thus the BEF with Headquarters near Lille, far south, stands in danger of being cut off from its main port by the western German forces under von Rundstedt.

Göring perceives the situation as a special task for his Luftwaffe. He obtains Hitler's telephonic approval to reduce the BEF by air attack alone. Tanks on the Aa are to halt.

24 May: Hitler again visits von Rundstedt at Charleville on 24 May 1940. He finds him amenable to halting the tanks and instigates an order to that affect. He then first learns of a von Brauchitsch (C-in-C Army) plan to shift the forces on the Aa to von Bock's command. Meanwhile von Brauchitsch visits von Bock and confirms the shift. Hitler returns to Felsennest, summons von Brauchitsch, has him countermand the shift, and reiterates the tank halt order.

25, 26 May: German commanders on the fighting front in the west along the Aa clamor for release. Bock in the east joins in to recommend their release. But Tank Halt order stands. The British commence evacuation by sea through Dunkirk under redoubled Luftwaffe attack in misty weather.

27 May-4 June: Hitler releases forces by degrees while the British fight their way out and save the bulk of the BEF through Dunkirk.

gence, Colonel Josef Schmid; and there news arrived of the closing situation in Flanders. The tanks advancing from the West along the coast, the reports indicated, would soon have the British cut off from the sea. According to his Intelligence Officer, Göring reacted in a flash. His heavy hand thumped down on the table: "This is a special job for the Luftwaffe! I must speak to the Führer at once. Get a line through by phone!" In the ensuing conversation Göring urged upon Hitler the unique talents of his force for dealing with this special task. If the Führer would only assign the task to him as an exclusive operation, he could give positive assurance that he would deal with the remnant of encircled enemy. All he needed was a free field of action. Let the tanks in the West draw back to give the planes a free target.

Hitler hesitated hardly longer than Göring; he approved the plan out of hand. The trapped British and French were to be finished off from the air. Schmid heard Jeschonnek and Jodl quickly settle the details over the telephone, including the withdrawal of certain army mobile units on the western rim of Dunkirk and the exact time the Air Force would initiate action.[21]

For capricious amateur tampering these astounding doings would be hard to match. Of course it is entirely possible that Hitler and Göring had had this brew cooked up for some days. Yet, think of it! The decisive actions of the campaign are at issue; they are decided far from the spot, apparently out of whole cloth, without benefit of professional advice, unless we include Jodl and Keitel, and without notice to the Army, the Command most concerned. But what about the Army?

Army leadership had delayed overlong about firming-up plans for the final act of the drama. The soldiers, in fact, faced up reluctantly to eventualities that might decide the campaign or perhaps even the whole war. They seem to have entertained a hope that operational developments would of themselves push the direction of things naturally toward their own headquarters. There is little evidence that OKH preparatory planning projected the campaign much beyond the

---

[21] Generalleutnant Josef Schmid discussed this important incident in exhaustive detail with this reporter, verbally during 1953 and in correspondence during 1954. The setting, the circumstances, the characters, the actions have been reviewed, checked, and reduced to paper. General Bodenschatz, Göring's ear at Führer Headquarters, has corroborated the course of the Göring-Hitler exchanges. See, to the same effect, Generalfeldmarschall Albert Kesselring, *Soldat bis zum letzten Tag* (Bonn, 1953), pp. 77, 78.

Meuse breakthrough and initial exploitation by *Operieren*.[22] All
well and good if the operating remained in soldier hands, but there
was the Hitler factor to be reckoned with. In the circumstance it
must have been clear that the Supreme Commander would have to
be satisfied. The Army Command vacillated, tried to evade and
placate him at the same time in the hope that developments might
decide, but succeeded only in compounding the troubles.

It becomes apparent that Hitler was far ahead with well-organized
ideas for disposing of the BEF. He certainly had the ingredients for
quick decision ready at hand for the Göring proposition, and snap
decision without prior self-debate was altogether out of character for
him. Contrary to his publicity, he often disclosed a grave lack of
operational resource. In *Norway* we saw him act the typical D
Day operator who panics soon after the excitement of hop-off has
subsided and from there on requires a deal of screwing up for each
trivial issue. We can take it that Hitler's responses to showdown
with the British on the field of battle had long since been conditioned
in a definite direction. When that moment of showdown arrived
before Dunkirk, the circumstances fitted his own older imagery,
and to these influences he had to conform. A sort of hit-and-run
complex took over. He backed off from trial by physical combat in
favor of pelting the British with stones from afar.

The closing Dunkirk pocket had of course forced questions at
OKH. Some ideas found casual expression as early as 17 May, when
opportunity offered, amidst the strife and tumult with the Führer.
Incessant conflict there abated meanwhile not one whit. A sharp
encounter occurred on the eighteenth when it appeared to Hitler
that measures discussed with von Rundstedt about re-enforcing the
south flank of his wedge were being obstructed by OKH. He summoned von Brauchitsch and Halder and dressed them down. According to Jodl "they were commanded in severest terms to take the
necessary measures forthwith." Professionally we sense a rising drive

---

[22] See footnote 15 of this chapter for the course of early planning. The German
teaching recognizes a field of war conduct between those pillars tactic and strategy,
designated *Operieren*. It grew out of the Moltke tradition when slow and undependable communications favored the initiative of the subordinate on the scene.
Strongly offensive in spirit, it embraced all actions taken by a field commander after
leaving his starting point in order to achieve the desired objective. Between the two
points he was permitted virtually unlimited initiative in operating. The Germans
sometimes seemed to go overboard in this practice, that is to say, they came near de-
pending on the subordinate's *Operieren* to develop the objective. Even a prescribed
objective could grow fuzzy and gradually fade; especially so with Hitler around.

General Erich von Manstein, Chief of Staff Army Group A (von Rundstedt) prior to attack in the West. *(Courtesy General Günther Blumentritt)*

Bastogne, 17 May 1940. Hitler arrives at Army Group A Headquarters (von Rundstedt) to discuss progress of drive into France. *(Courtesy General Blumentritt)*

The Führer discusses operations with von Rundstedt.
(Courtesy Rear Admiral von Puttkamer)

General Georg von Sodenstern, COS Army Group A. *(Courtesy General Günther Blumentritt)*

Colonel Günther Blumentritt, Operations Ar Group A. *(Courtesy General Blumentritt)*

of jealousy on Hitler's part to guard his own undisputed control as crisis neared. In the forenoon of the twentieth he personally gave von Brauchitsch direction for the next task, which Jodl recorded: "Destruction of the enemy north of the Somme and the gaining of the [Channel] coast." By that time von Brauchitsch seemed clear in his own mind on the final phase. For he had confided his ideas to von Bock, whom he had visited at Group B headquarters on the previous day, the nineteenth. In his personal journal General von Bock quoted his visitor as saying that Group B must transfer all uncommitted forces toward the tender south flank of Army Group A, adding that in compensation the 4th Army of Group A, including the armored spearhead, "would eventually turn northwest and thereupon be placed under the [B] Army Group."[23]

There is no record of von Brauchitsch mentioning his solution to Hitler until the twenty-second and then only casually. Although General Halder's record of the seventeenth indicates he favored somewhat the same arrangement at that early day, by the twenty-third he opposed the Brauchitsch scheme because it attempted a radical shift in command organization at a crucial moment. Nevertheless he had the staff draw up the implementing order directed by von Brauchitsch. It was withheld from issue. Brauchitsch had also found Hitler unenthusiastic during the conference on the twenty-second. Together these objections, extending as they did into the Army Commander-in-Chief's own staff, may have raised misgivings and thereby delayed facing up to issuance. No operational reason existed for putting off an order of decisive consequence; on the contrary, approaching climax reared in plain sight. Yet, no action—until the very last moment—and then, to the surprise of both Army Group Commands, the order came out from OKH, prefaced by short notice on the telephone at midnight of 23-24 May. All signs of haste accompanied the transmission. The only credible inference is that something was being pushed over. Trouble developed soon, not from the group commanders and not from the enemy, but from Hitler, with whom OKH had failed to clear the radical departure.[24]

[23] Kriegstagebuch des Generalfeldmarschall Fedor Von Bock, 1939-1945 (hereinafter called Von Bock Diary), entries for 19 May 1940. The 4th Army would later have included Kleist's armored group, of which Guderian's (dashing) XIX Tank Corps and Reinhardt's XXXXI were a part.

[24] That the climactic nature of the situation was thoroughly appreciated by both Army group commands and that both were taken aback by the precipitate, although already belated, orders become clear from the official war diary of Group B and that of Group A. The more pertinent passages are translated below. Army Group

A great prize was at stake. Staff opinion in OKH accepted unified command for the final phase, but under the Commander-in-Chief, instead of under either group commander. Brauchitsch seemed unwilling to assume responsibility for direct command of such proportion, and thereby, as Halder noted, "he forfeits of course also the honor of success." Was this the prize all were contending for? Glory! There is good reason to believe that a prime component of the stew working up was the intense personal rivalry for the glory of victory, within the hierarchy—Hitler included.

Besides Hitler, Brauchitsch and Göring are directly suspect. Of the latter's maneuver by telephone we know. It is conceivable that von Brauchitsch got wind of that scheming through his agents at court. The evidence justifies an inference that in order to preserve the job and its honor for the Army, the Commander-in-Chief of the Army attempted to forestall Göring by setting the first moves of the final action into motion. Such assumption is authenticated by the haste with which he backtracked when discovered, and by other well-established bits. In the morning (24 May) von Brauchitsch visited von Bock again, discussed the ordered shift in detail, and confided his hopes of a smooth runoff. The confidence is reminiscent of Hitler at von Rundstedt's headquarters early in the play. What a curious twist! Two were playing the same game; the Army's Commander-in-Chief favored one field commander with special attention, while the Supreme Commander cozened the other.

The blow fell on the twenty-fourth, when Hitler learned from Rundstedt of the Brauchitsch order during the second Führer visit

---

B, 24 May 1945: "An order noticed in advance by phone from Army Command comes in, by which the 4th Army, including both groups of mobile units who are executing the breakthrough to the Channel, is to be placed under Army Group B Command for the purpose of 'assuring unity of command in the last act of the encircling battle.' This corresponds in every way to the view [this] Group Command has represented for days . . . ." Army Group A, 23 May 1940: "At 2400 hours comes an order of OKH already announced by Colonel von Greiffenberg by phone over a bad connection that places the 4th Army under Army Group B for 'the last act of the encircling battle.' . . . The new organization is to take effect at 2000 hours the twenty-fourth of May. The Chief of the General Staff of the Army Group expresses to the Chief of the Operations Section, Colonel Greiffenberg, during the mentioned phone talk, that he could not regard the prospective change in command organization at this time as a happy one. The answer of Colonel von Greiffenberg was understood by Lieutenant General von Sodenstern . . . that cognizance of this view was taken, but a change [in the order] was not to be expected. The Chief of the General Staff [Army Group A] placed his estimate of the current situation in writing to serve as support for raising objections at OKH the following day and ordered them [the objections] entered in the files."

to Group A headquarters, now moved forward to Charleville in France. Again only the top people were present.

At 1130 [said the Group A war diary] the Führer arrived and had himself briefed on the situation by the Group Commander. He concurs fully and completely with the concept that eastward of Arras *infantry* must attack, the *mobile troops,* on the other hand, may be checked on the attained line Lens-Bethune-Aire-St. Omer-Gravelines [the Aa Canal Line] in order to bag the enemy being pressed by Army Group B. He underlines this by emphasizing that it is in any case necessary to husband the armored forces for the coming operations and that further constriction of the pocket area would only result in highly undesirable restriction of the activity of the Air Force.

On the spot, at 1245, orders went out to the 4th Army, which controlled the tanks on the Aa, giving effect to the Führer's views, and in his name.[25] There went Halt Order without a quiver, but then came the bombshell. The diary continued with a temperate recital of its arrival: "Upon being asked by the Führer about further command arrangements, Generaloberst von Rundstedt reports that in the evening of the day, 2000 hours, the OKH ordered reorganization between B and A would come into force."

Hitler and Jodl showed surprise. Sensing a detonation of the first order, Colonel Blumentritt telephoned OKH to advise his opposite, Colonel von Greiffenberg, of an impending blast from the Führer. At this word Brauchitsch and Halder got busy countermanding their order by telephone. Things could scarcely have turned out better for Adolf Hitler. He had the troublesome Commander-in-Chief of the Army just where he wanted him, on the personal defensive. We stand before notorious Tank Halt Order and can see its author feeding with gusto on welcome emotional stimulants, the worst of all, a burning spite against von Brauchitsch. The Hitlerian rancor could now demand redress.

[25] General von Bock of Army Group B wrote in his personal diary after the von Brauchitsch visit of the twenty-fourth: "Just as Brauchitsch had departed, I learn through liaison officer Groeben, dispatched to 4th Army , . . . [that] an order of Führer's has come in at 4th Army according to which the armored forces are *not* to push farther forward! They are apparently being spared for later tasks. This can have a very unpleasant effect on the final stages of the battle in progress with me! I orient Brauchitsch by telephone . . . . Two hours thereafter . . . comes the order from von Brauchitsch, that I am '*not yet*' today to take 4th Army under my command; he is reserving for himself control over the time for the shift of command! The reason I do not know. *25th May*—order comes that the command-take-over of 4th Army is not only postponed but *is cancelled.* The reason I have not learned today either."

We are interested in this man's attitude toward England and in particular the reason he kept his tanks from cutting off Britain's Expeditionary Force. In order to sort out the pertinent kernels, let us see from what understanding each side, that is, Hitler as against von Rundstedt, spoke at Charleville on 24 May.

General von Rundstedt had OKH orders in hand to separate the 4th Army with its armor from his command at the end of the day. He assumed the Führer knew this and, as his reference to Army Group B showed, his report and proposed actions were framed in that context. Conceivably Rundstedt's feeling ran to satisfaction over a job well done by his group, a sentiment borne out by members of his staff; he would release the 4th Army and its armor, which he planned to hold in check anyhow, to von Bock, who could then have his turn at shouldering the main effort. Of a special task for the Luftwaffe, Rundstedt was totally ignorant, such demarche being still privy to Hitler and Göring. But there was another influence; a week previously, during the Führer's visit of the seventeenth, Rundstedt had been exposed to Hitlerian thoughts of quick settlement and peace with Britain. Those ideas offered additional background for his own reasoning.

By queer coincidence this picture drawn by Rundstedt fitted Hitler's own perfectly, though he lacked knowledge of Group B's new task of finishing off the BEF. For him the Luftwaffe filled that job. The two concepts, Hitler's and Rundstedt's, thus appeared to coincide, though for widely divergent reasons; and having been fortified to this extent, Hitler needed only the emotional spur of Brauchitsch's noxious order to harden his own wishes into headstrong personal resolve. Holding back the tanks became his foremost wish.

General Blumentritt's recounting of the incident, written to this reporter in January 1955, offers important aid in this sorting out. Said he:

The Commander of Army Group A very calmly and unsuspectingly presents the situation on the basis of OKH's new order. He was under the impression Hitler had been informed thereof. It struck me during the presentation that General Jodl was surprised, for he looked over at me questioningly and silently shook his head. Also Hitler's face took on surprise and he turned questioningly toward Jodl, who shook his head. Now for the first time we realized that Hitler and Jodl still did not know of the change of tanks and command organization. But Hitler did not fly into a rage and controlled himself in the presence of Commander Army Group A. On the contrary he emphasized the husbanding of armor and called to mind the great tasks yet before the tank forces. This fitted the thought of Generaloberst von Rundstedt completely. When Hitler had departed the headquarters I received instructions to call Colonel von Greiffenberg immediately and orient him on the visit and on the "astonishment" of Hitler.

Where then did the matter stand on the battlefront at Hitler's hurried departure for his own headquarters? Could Rundstedt rest content, equally satisfied with turnover to Army Group B or now to the Luftwaffe? This posture appears to be the one he chose. A certain fluidity normally rules operational dispositions; they cannot be hard and fast. A wide disparity existed between Rundstedt's provisional order that the tanks *may* be checked and Hitler's hard-and-fast *shall* be checked. According to Group A's Chief of Staff, General von Sodenstern, the Command meant only to check the war machine with motor running, ready to jump into forward gear the moment the situation warranted, as indeed it later did. Hitler, on the other hand, wanted the motor cut off in a full stop to clear the way for air action, and for private reasons quite beyond the ken of the soldiers. General von Sodenstern wrote in a letter of late 1954: "Hitler declared most emphatically that he would dispose of 'the rest' (namely the encircling battle) with the Air Force. Therefore it was positively unwelcome to him for the kettle to be compressed further on the ground since that would only restrict the air action." In the following days the effect of this exposure to Hitleriana by Group A Command became manifest. Its direction fell less sure, less purposeful. Confusion entered between Group A's contingent plan of checking advance and Hitlers' new departure of air action. Who could tell, the soldiers had license to think; perhaps Air could bring quick decision and peace! Hitler's performance on the twenty-fourth ran true to the pattern initiated for his auditors of the seventeenth. He had succeeded in befogging the battlefield atmosphere.

As for invading England! How foreign to Hitler's pattern of preference for psychopolitical effect was so conclusive an action. In the agitated climate of gaining the Channel at Abbeville three days earlier, 21 May, Admiral Raeder, Commander-in-Chief of the Navy, had taken his first sounding of Hitler's invasion England feeling. The empty reaction of the Führer on that day endured; and now on the twenty-fourth his head was filling with a curious concoction of air show and "politicking" to bulldoze the British into talking.[26]

[26] We have spoken of Hitler's varying moods at the conferences with Rundstedt

One thing was sure, Brauchitsch was a rascal. The Führer's
companions on the plane trip of the twenty-fourth to Charleville were
Jodl; Schmundt, the Chief Adjutant; and Engel, the Army Adjutant.
On the return flight there was time and opportunity for unlimbered
talk. Between the lines of Jodl's diary notes, satisfaction tinged with
anger can be read in his record of Hitler's feeling. Like his Führer,
Jodl convicted von Brauchitsch as the following recording shows:

[The Führer] is very happy over the measures of the Army Group (A),
which coincide complete with his ideas. He learned to his surprise that
OKH, without informing the Führer or OKW, placed the 4th Army and
a number of following Divisions under Group B. Führer is very indignant
and holds this arrangement not only militarily but also psychologically
wrong. C-in-C Army is ordered to report. New loyalty crisis particularly
as Fieldmarshal [Göring] vouchsafed earlier that an [additional] order from
OKH in no way reinforces Army Group B but requires it to release
needed reserves. Therefore in the evening a new order goes out, (a)
not to push forward to the east over the line Sandez–St. Omer–Gravelines. Aside from this every change in the assignment of armies to commands is to be subject to the approval of the Führer.

So Jodl, too, managed to relate the question of halting the tanks to
Brauchitsch's crime.

We note Jodl's mention of a new loyalty crisis between Hitler and
von Brauchitsch. The expression is *Vertrauenskrise*. It carries the
literal signification of crisis involving loss of confidence in a subordinate, but in general usage by Hitler's officers its meaning went further
than the superior's dissatisfaction with a subordinate; it included also
questions of personal loyalty of a subordinate who proposed to step
down from office. The expression appears frequently in the German
records, where it evidences the travail of officers between professional
conscience and allegiance to Adolf Hitler.

---

and hinted that his temper offered corroboration to the pattern we are picking out.
At Bastogne on the seventeenth he beamed success; felt so good he tarried for a bite
of lunch. His words kept pace with his expansive mood; he was able to paint an
astonishing picture for the soldiers. Three days later when Guderian's drive reached
Abbeville, he joyously made plans for peace, had them all packaged for Jodl's note
and entry. The next day, the twenty-first, von Etzdorf of the Foreign Office told
General Halder, "We are seeking to arrive at an understanding with Britain on the
basis of a division of the world." On the twenty-third Hitler approved Göring's
plan. On the twenty-fourth at Charleville Hitler quickly showed annoyance at
Rundstedt's surprising information of a change in allocation of forces between Groups
A and B through unapproved orders of OKH. He showed restrained dissatisfaction
and left abruptly to get after von Brauchitsch. He was in no mood to dilate on
British virtues. He was closemouthed, whereas his expansive mood on the seventeenth had encouraged release of thoughts that underlay his attitude toward the
British. He looked forward to a deal with them.

Dissatisfaction broke out at once among Jodl's own people in OKW over the halt order. It vitiated plans already underway. Both planner Warlimont and his Army assistant, von Lossberg, registered objection. The latter braced Jodl and, having failed to move him, delivered himself also to Keitel. The exchanges became a rerun of the Dietl episode in *Norway*, but this time Jodl as well as Keitel took Hitler's side. The answers already sounded a parroting note heard in a byword of the period. "The War is won; it needs only to be ended." As for the tanks, declared Keitel, they would be sure to get mired in the marshy ground of Flanders; Göring had hold of the job all right and would complete the encirclement on the sea side from the air. With like arguments Jodl fended off Warlimont, who had just presented Führer Directive No. 13 covering "the further conduct of the operation" for approval. It was obvious that the halt order corrupted the sense and vigor of the directive, which contained no suggestion of halting ground forces while air pursued a special task. The directive, on the contrary, assigned priority to the ground force objective of destroying the surrounded Allies and added: "In this connection the Air Force is to break all resistance of the encircled parts of the enemy, to prevent the escape of the British Force over the Channel and to secure the south flank Army Group A . . . ." These words were plain and made sense. Yet words on paper can be twisted or even ignored by the originator. What Hitler formally directed (and disseminated) often came out far removed from what his actions showed he in truth intended.

Warlimont's instructions for drawing up directives came from Jodl, often after a *Lagebesprechung* (situation conference) with the Führer. Such a conference took place late on the twenty-third after Göring's "special task" telephone conversation with the Führer. Having acceded to Göring, Hitler needed reasons for holding back the tanks. In the conference he mentioned the tanks and gave marshy terrain in Flanders as ground for keeping them out. It sounds like an excuse, contrived to justify a course already determined upon.[27]

[27] Dr. Hans Meier-Welcker, "Der Entschluss zum Anhalten der deutschen Panzertruppen in Flandern, 1940," *Vierteljahrshefte fuer Zeitgeschichte*, II (July, 1954), 288. Footnote 53 states that evidence of May 1954 from Generalleutenant Engel, Hitler's Army aide in 1940, establishes the conference of the twenty-third and the discussion of halting the tanks because of marshy terrain. Engel, however, believed Hitler had not made up his mind fully prior to arrival at Group A headquarters on the twenty-fourth. Dr. Meier-Welcker makes a first-class analytical study of the episode. He makes small allowances for Hitler's predilections and discounts involvement of political motives, to the exclusion of military matters in Hitler's decision.

Keitel and Jodl, party to the Göring arrangement, supported Hitler, but apparently without notice to directive-writer Warlimont, who must have recognized at once that the sense of the directive he had been preparing was being stretched, if not entirely vitiated. His objection, however, proved fruitless. In so far as concerned the fighting in Flanders, Directive No. 13 served as a sort of cover plan of official character to hide the private design of Hitler and Göring. Shifty duality of this character was part and parcel of the Hitlerian personal system.

Hitler got what he wanted. His design is discernible in the routine of his visits to von Rundstedt. It is remarkable how closely the drill of these visits agree. A crucial decision impended before each; Hitler took counsel of Göring to the exclusion of OKH, and followed with enlistment of von Rundstedt. Then came a quarrel with OKH, fanned into major proportion and capped by forced Army compliance, in a display of sheer emotion. On the visit of 24 May an unexpected break came his way. He caught von Brauchitsch red-handed in a stratagem to thwart him and quickly turned this to account. The Führer's outraged feelings demanded redress, not only in the cancellation of the offending Brauchitsch order, but, under that tumult, in the issuance of a new order, altogether unrelated, to stop the tanks. That had been the point all along. In such wise Hitler struck to consolidate his undisputed control over the final act. He ran OKH off the stage, placed the lead role in the hands of his stooge Göring, and neutralized interference up front through liaison with von Rundstedt. Now on the evening of 24 May a wide but secure choice lay open to him, tyro captain of war and politics. He had the thing made, and to his own order.

On the fighting front along the Aa the absurd stop order made no sense whatever, and no wonder! Six mobile divisions, four of them armored, stood dead in their tracks along its banks by the evening of 24 May. Additional forces were closing rapidly. No opposition of consequence showed on the opposite shore. Why they should not press on was incomprehensible to the movement-conscious tankmen; complaint and dismay filled their records. What could the staffers back there at desks be thinking? Charleville and Felsennest lay 150 miles to the rear in woodland fastness, remote from this open terrain and its engaging picture. The soldiers could see for themselves, and the long-range eyes of their suporting flyers of the VIII Fliegerkorps (under another von Richthofen) offered vivid confirmation. Eagerly they gathered in the details of the picture before them: a vast expanse of watery lowland, crisscrossed by canals, but also by dikes and some roads. Far on the left the spires of Dunkirk punctured the sky, and beyond shone the blue-gray water of the Channel. Away on the right toward the south rose the low Kemmel hills, forming the sole natural defensive position in sight. The British were heavily engaged still farther south around Lille. Connecting the hills around Kemmel and the port of Dunkirk ran a solitary road, or so it appeared, the twenty-six-mile lifeline of the BEF. Surely it should be severed and its port terminal on the Channel taken. The setup was one to dream about. But what was this *Lumperei* one heard? Word filtered down that Dunkirk and the almost trapped BEF were to be left to the Luftwaffe. It was simply unbelievable!

All through the twenty-fifth and twenty-sixth the most exigent representations for release flowed up the Army chain of command without effect. Hitler equivocated and Rundstedt stood emasculated. Had the halt order belonged to soldier Rundstedt alone, it is inconceivable that his professional sense could have denied the urging of his men up forward. At length von Kleist, the tank group commander, and his Chief of Staff Zeitzler joined the charge, though earlier they had felt content with Halt Order. They now applied to comrade of the Air von Richthofen for intercession on high. General von Richthofen agreed to call his close friend Jeschonnek at Air Headquarters in an effort to get the true picture before Hitler via Göring. Richthofen spoke directly to Jeschonnek while his own Chief of Staff, Lieutenant Colonel Seidemann, monitored the conversation on another telephone for the record. The latter commented on the exchange as follows: "Richthofen wanted through Jeschonnek and Göring to bring home to the Führer this singular opportunity to strike the British destructively. Jeschonnek replied among other things, 'The Führer wants to spare the British a humiliating defeat.' These words I myself heard while listening on the telephone." The efforts proved of no avail. Halt Order stood.[28]

[28] General Hans Seidemann related the above incident to me in 1953 and confirmed the facts at length by letter in 1954. As to the feeling of the soldiers, the records reveal that the closer the command stood to the enemy, the more anxious it was to press on. From General Hans Reinhardt, commanding the XXXXI Korps near the south end of the Aa, to General Heinz Guderian on the Channel in the north, the cry had been from first to last for pressing on. Their group commander, von Kleist, and his next superior at this time, von Kluge, of the 4th Army, were more cautious and initially were satisfied to halt on the Aa. Later, by the twenty-fifth, both took up the cudgels for release. Dr. Meier-Welcker, *op, cit.*, pp. 276-78, 281-84, 289 makes this clear. See also Guderian, *op. cit.*, pp. 104-106.

Driving hard on the far side of the Dunkirk pocket, General von Bock echoed the pleas of the soldiers and flyers on the near (western) side. He wrote in his diary:

26th May. In the morning I call up Brauchitsch . . . . He asks about the situation. I report that gradually fatigue signs are showing up among the troops . . . . Brauchitsch thinks the troops should have rest. I explain that *now* there can't be any thought of this. Urgently wanted however was the continuation of heavy, frontal attacks of the Army Groups, that the II Corps (4th Army) and the armored forces attack farther in the direction in which they were committed! Brauchitsch replies: "Unfortunately the armored forces have been held back for today!" *To this I say that I regard the seizure at Dunkirk as absolutely necessary, otherwise the English might transport out of Dunkirk what they please, right under our noses.* Brauchitsch agrees that he wants to try to push through the attack of the armored forces onto Dunkirk. I say once more that this was urgently needed!

Bock foresaw what in fact happened.

As so often when Hitler faced the British, it took their initiative to break the jam. They commenced action that ran contrary to his rules by starting to pull back over the Channel. Though such outcome had scarcely entered the wishful thinking of the Hitler camp, a stream of Channel shipping confirmed that mass troop movements were underway. During the course of the twenty-sixth a marked change came gradually over OKW and, in smaller measure, over the Führer. Were the hostages slipping through his fingers? Hitler shifted his ground. Shortly after noon he authorized forces west of Dunkirk to advance, but only for the limited purpose of interdicting sea traffic with artillery fire. The armored force in the center, headed for Ypres, he permitted to be placed under Army Group B, but not the northern force on the coast. General von Bock had something to say about this peculiar division. He wrote late on the twenty-sixth:

Toward evening comes a new order. The tanks may finally again attack. Their middle shock-group, which is ordered to take the general direction toward Ypres, is placed under me . . . . The northernmost group [on the coast], curiously again not [so placed]! It is not to take Dunkirk, instead only to seal it off! *That is a most serious error*—and [some] one has probably been concerned that I might correct it! . . .

. . . In talk by my Ia [Operations officer] with the 4th Army [Command] it responds to the shift under my command only half heartedly. Since Kluge [4th Army] is not stupid, and since our previous association has been completely happy, this does not make sense.

The Luftwaffe likewise redoubled its efforts to seal Dunkirk off, and someone at OKW even remembered to call Navy for action on the sea side.

Nothing of moment was accomplished, and Hitler did not seem to care. It was too late! The fateful moment had passed; for not only had the momentum of the play petered out, but on top came mist and rain for days to dampen ardor and hinder Luftwaffe efforts. In the midst of the hurrah a new adversary from cross-Channel entered the ring and instantly made a deep dent in German air pride and thought. Spitfires in their debut performance lashed out against the German flyers. The Luftwaffe recoiled in realization that no longer was the air all German. Neither were the Channel waters, teeming with shipping in the smoke and mist down below. Hitler gave in haltingly to other steps for plugging the kettle's leaks, unhurried and with no show of concern. There was no table-pounding, no *musts* or *must nots*, no frantic direct orders by telephone to stop the British evacuation. He left things to his subordinates, and never once during the belated forward movement did he seize the Führer initiative in his familiar insistent fashion.[29]

It makes one wonder what could be at the bottom of the foolish show. One day Hitler showed a strong feeling for letting the Britons go, and the next he switched to sealing them off. Why the change, or was it in fact a change? Probably not. The truth is, the thing was never so clear-cut as we are tempted to make it with full knowledge of the outcome. We tend to twist together factors only indirectly related. Sparing Britain humiliating defeat in Flanders did not mean letting the BEF escape to England. By no means. Hitler proved it by trying to hinder evacuation by ship when this became clear. His thinking might have harked back to World War I brushes with Tom-

[29] No contemporary observation that I have found reports any Hitlerian displeasure at British escape. On the contrary, on more than one occasion he expressed relief and satisfaction over being rid of the British. Rear-Admiral von Puttkamer, his naval adjutant, noted this peculiar reaction and related it to this reporter in positive terms. The Germans had only vague notions of the magnitude of the evacuation. Hitler's personal valet quotes Hitler as saying, while surveying the wreckage of Dunkirk, "It is always good to let a broken army return home to show the civilian population what a beating they have had." His private formula for breaking British morale, and thus encouraging settlement, consistently included, almost banked on, the effect of a sharp punch in the nose. So he admonished his Army leaders during the fall of 1939, while preparing attack on the West; and again in March 1940, when those plans were complete; and he still stuck to that formula for bringing Britain around in table talk of 1941 and 1942 as he pushed into Russia. But then he was thinking of what had to come next—final settlement with Britain.

mies. How he enjoyed recounting them to his official family! According to his naval adjutant he was convinced the Britons in Flanders would stand to the last man, and a pullback by sea hardly crossed his mind. If he could contain the BEF without pushing to annihilation, he would at once render it harmless and gain a dangerous political club. He strove to hurdle the logical operational objective—destruction of the enemy military force—and pass directly to politics. There he left the hardheaded logic of military men for the dreams that lay at the root of the strange performance.

The soldier aim was to trap the BEF and at the same time chew it up in detail as the trap shrank. Tactically the two actions had to go hand in hand, and, once touched off, the melee of pure violence could not halt until the job was done. The British were to be cut to pieces in a welter of failing communications, command, and cohesion. The soldiers' scheme thus left no room for a grand final stand that might offer opportunity for parley.

But parley was Hitler's aim. Where Britain was concerned he invariably thought to persuade rather than to conquer, and only in that light can we explain his uneven maneuver before Dunkirk. It is probable that with Göring he had decided that his overwhelming air power already had the lid securely on the kettle. Göring assured him he would keep the contents of the kettle boiling until the agony of it became unbearable. A doomed British Expeditionary Force, or what was left of one! What if some few did escape to spread dismay at home! Hitler was easily capable of turning the anguish of such scenes to political capital with noble proffer of general settlement. What government could have withstood the play? Happily, that test never came. The plot, if so it ran, was much too cunning. Nonetheless it was basic to Hitlerian aspirations. His words and actions admit only negotiation as the central theme. Secure in that delusion Hitler watched unperturbed while evacuation proceeded during a full week of brutal infighting.[30]

[30] On 30 May General von Bock wrote: "At Dunkirk the Englishman continues to shove off also from the open coast! If we finally arrive there, he will be gone! Holding up the armored forces by the topmost leadership works out as a serious mistake! We continue attack. The fighting is hard, the Englishman is tough as leather and my divisions are pooped out [ausgepumpt] . . . ." On the day previous he had visited Charleville and quoted von Rundstedt as having remarked, in connection with the feeble activity of armored forces before Dunkirk, "I was conerned that the weak Kleist (armored) troops might be overrun by the retreating British." Von Bock found himself unable to credit this excuse. He seemed to suspect an unholy alliance between Rundstedt and Hitler (Von Bock Diary).

From 27 May on through its last bitter days and then into June of 1940 the grim battle raged about Dunkirk. The Royal Navy on the twenty-seventh set into motion its hastily contrived water retreat, called *Dynamo*. Hundreds of boats, large and small, of varied uses —pleasure and work, yachting and fishing—tugs, steamers, destroyers, minecraft and other combat types all joined in a grand scramble toward France. Troops came off by the hundreds. The courageous, the miraculous, the impossible was accomplished many times over, yet in the end it proved to be fierce resistance at each step backward by the British soldiery that carried the day. By 4 June it was all over! The mass of the BEF to the number of 224,320 British troops, plus a good many French, had made good their escape to England—for a fight on another day. How joyously did all Britain acclaim them and sigh in relief.

Dunkirk, that seaport bastion of many years and many wars, lay in unrecognizable ruin. Of its 30,000 citizens only a scant 300 remained to stare sullenly as the jubilant Germans rubber-necked at the deluxe booty left behind. What a rout! Göring made the tour to gape and gloat, abetted by an eager staff. Had not the Luftwaffe done it—chased John Bull out? Mountains of equipment still stood in issue piles; the street and waterfront litter, abandoned trucks, guns, dunnage bags, mess gear, maps, and papers, all attested the haste and confusion of departure. We may be sure Göring's gratifying view of it lost nothing in the telling to his Führer. Hitler, too, had his look and reportedly expressed quiet satisfaction. For him peace and settlement beckoned in the offing. Goebbels filled out that feeling in news advices, so that to Germans generally Dunkirk came to mean decision over Britain for a time. Comprehension of its true measure as a major German military failure penetrated only much later, and then hardly in its true perspective.

The fact of the moment was, however, that there stood Hitler on the Channel, his "race to the sea" won. What would he do with it? Would it impel him toward Invasion? This seductive field of speculation we leave to further examination of the events of the summer. Viewed professionally, as a curtain-raiser for Invasion England, *Dunkirk* was a fiasco. Suffice at this point to note that Hitler relinquished physical contact with his most dangerous foe on the field of battle at the crucial moment, and thereby he loosened his grip on the operational initiative and likewise the political. This became the eventual result of Tank Halt Order; little matter that its author, Adolf Hitler, intended a far different result through the imposition of Göring's air power. They jointly bear the onus for this flagrant blunder in warmaking. They gambled that priceless military advantage, the operational initiative on the ground, for dubious psychopolitical effect, and they lost. Barring invasion, from here on policy had to remain a question of waiting for an opening from Britain.

To Britain this bout with Hitler had been a near thing. But she had rent the German cloak of invincibility. Her troops had fought their way out of the very jaws of the Nazi war monster; and now they were home. Understanding of the reality of the English Channel dawned in England anew and swelled a wave of pride and confidence in English ability to keep it so. Now the citizenry could gird happily for trial in earnest, publishing to the world a vow to fight to the end. Britain might never have risen to the lofty heights of that fateful summer of 1940 but for *Dunkirk* to show the way. This became the essential meaning of the episode.[31]

[31] The Dunkirk story told herein is full of Germans and Britons. The French played a bitter and equally heroic part. Jacques Mordal, who was present as a naval medical officer, tells the French story most effectively in his book with Admiral Auphan, *The French Navy in World War II* (Washington, D.C.: U.S. Naval Institute, 1959). Many of the lights of that writing we have been unable to include.

5. *June Too Soon!*[1]

Compiègne

Now it was June. The British were happily welcoming their BEF home. While there still was a France, the cause might, after all, not be forever lost. Weygand was fashioning a new defense line in France, and a reconstituted BEF would take station in it. And then, at 0500 on 5 June, the storm broke anew cross-Channel. The German war machine jumped into high gear and crashed southwest from the Somme and the Aisne for yet another breakthrough in the region of Rouen on the Seine. France's desperate Premier, Reynaud, made his agonized appeal to President Roosevelt for "clouds of planes." Britain considered removal of her government to Canada. The decision in the field fell on 10 June when the Weygand line crumbled at both ends. France came tumbling down. By the fourteenth, German troops were entering Paris.

General Fedor von Bock, whose Army Group B had led off in the final thrust, ordered up his liaison plane at dawn on that memo-

---

[1] "June too soon" is the first line of the seaman's typhoon warning jingle; it continues:

> "July standby,
> August you must!
> September remember,
> October all over."

rable Friday, 14 June 1940. He had the pilot set him down on Le
Bourget airdrome so that he might welcome the first of his troops into
Paris. The van of the 9th Division was just then on the point of
passing. He greeted the marching column and hurried on ahead into
the city to Place de la Concorde, where he took the salute of the
9th, then that of the 8th and 28th Divisions at Arc de Triomphe.
The Germans in Paris! It was simply unbelievable to him, and likewise to the French general who came to report as representative of
the Commandant of Paris. But there the troops were, marching by,
all in order. It must be so; von Bock took time out. He went to
pay another conqueror his due in a visit to the tomb of Napoleon, and
from there delightedly to the Ritz for lunch. In his personal diary
he reported an extremely good lunch. How could it have been otherwise for this able soldier living the dreams of a lifetime? The Germans in Paris! He repaired contented to his new headquarters at
Compiègne.

Within a week Hitler and Company would appear at Compiègne
to avenge the German capitulation of 1918. Events pressed swiftly
to that conclusion. Feelers for an armistice from the French government under Marshal Pétain arrived at Führer Headquarters at Bruly
le Pêche on 17 June. This Belgian village stood on the French border
near Rocroi. Staff members occupied the village houses, school,
and church; a barracks building did for the Führer. In a flashback
to the Kampfzeit, he had named this new location *Wolfsschlucht*
(Wolf's Lair). On the forenoon of this day, 17 June 1940, he was
out under the old trees near his quarters in conversation with Army
advisers. A woman secretary has recorded the scene that followed
upon delivery of the armistice message. She tells how the news shook
Hitler to the roots. He gave his shanks a slap and went into a wild jig
of joy. Fräulein Schröder, the secretary, could think of nothing like
it except St. Vitus's dance. This was one of two occasions when she
saw Hitler utterly carried away. The staff gaped in sheepish wonderment. Only Keitel seemed equal to the moment. He made a little
speech and hailed Hitler as the greatest Field Commander of all
time—*der grösste Feldherr aller Zeiten*.[2]

[2] Zoller, *op. cit.*, pp. 85, 141. Keitel was probably the first to bring the Feldherr
appellation into prominence. Göring followed suit in like terms, and the press
brought it into public use. Some of the professional military shortened it, as time
went on, into an uncomplimentary nickname: *GRÖFAZ–GRÖ*(sste) *F*(eldherr)
A(ller) *Z*(eiten).

Spring of 1940 at OKH. *(above)* General Franz Halder, Chief of the Army General Staff, and *(below)* the Operations Section: left to right, von Greiffenberg, von Stülpnagel, Winter, Heusinger, Stieff. *(Courtesy Colonel Wilhelm Willemer)*

Dunkirk Beach, June 1940. *(Courtesy Captain Heinrich Bartels)*

Hitler followed by Göring leaving the Armistice coach of 1918 and 1940, Compiègne, 22 June 1940. The statue of Marshal Foch stands at the extreme left.

Arrangements for meeting the French immediately took shape under Keitel's hand at the behest of a happy Führer, whose thoughts ranged ahead to general settlement and peace. Göring, the man of peace, would have ideas; and Mussolini, who had joined the war just a week before, must be drawn in. Hitler's own ideas on setting, procedure, and terms were already well firmed up. He would confront the French in the identical railway coach of 1918, but, aside from this humiliation, the armistice delegation was to be treated considerately. He desired "not to insult so brave an opponent," and the world would see that a former lance corporal knew "how to act." A gigantic parade would be held in Paris; it might be the parade of peace. The staff quickly settled all details and embodied them in a directive. Already, on the day Paris fell, the Führer formally authorized the demobilization of forty Army divisions. Certainly, peace was in the air! Mussolini was bound to be saddened, for he needed more time to establish claims. This was precisely the matter on which Hitler wanted to set him straight—the claims to be included in the armistice terms. The German Foreign Minister, von Ribbentrop, on hand in his field office at nearby Dinant, arranged a meeting with the Italians for the following day, 18 June, in Munich.[3]

Enroute to this new Munich Hitler met Göring at Rhine Main airdrome. It may have been another of those rare moments when the Führer let go. The two old comrades locked each other in joyous embrace. The war is finished, exulted Hitler; "I will come to an understanding with England." Göring, no less moved, agreed. "Now at last," he beamed, "there will be peace."[4]

Peace was the theme that also prevailed on arrival at Munich. Not alone that, Hitler astounded Axis partner Mussolini, like the generals at Bastogne, by observing that the British Empire was "after all, a force for order in the world," and he wondered if it would be a good thing to destroy it. Both Dr. Paul Schmidt, serving as Hitler's interpreter, and Ciano, the Italian Foreign Minister, noted this strange

[3] Joachim von Ribbentrop, after having served as Ambassador at London, became Foreign Minister on 4 February 1938. No friend of the British, he figured as a proponent of war at the earlier Munich of September 1948, whereas Göring had counted there as an advocate of peace The two were avowed enemies in the contest for Hitler's favor. Göring used to order his driver to bump Ribbentrop's car deliberately whenever good opportunity offered.

[4] Told to me by Generalleutnant Josef Schmid (Germany, March 1953). He often accompanied Göring and witnessed the meeting described above. Besides expressing confidence for reaching terms with Britain, Hitler, Schmid said, admitted his own astonishment over the speedy collapse of France.

new mood toward England. To Ciano the contrast was so marked
that he asked Ribbentrop point blank: Was the preference for war or
for peace? "He does not hesitate a moment," Ciano recorded in his
diary, " 'Peace!' He also alludes to vague contacts between London
and Berlin by means of Sweden." A hint of urgency for general
settlement suffused the German talk, Ciano added. The Axis *Brüder*
parted and went about their separate businesses.[5]

The terms pronounced in the melodramatic scene at Compiègne
three days later constituted a Hitlerian straddle, a straddle between
peace and war; not toward France, but beyond her and at her expense,
over the Channel, toward Britain. "The aim of the German demands
is . . . to give Germany security for the further conduct of the war
against England which she has no choice but to continue, and also
to create the conditions for a new peace . . . ." Interpreter Paul
Schmidt read it out in their own tongue to the luckless French sitting
along a table in the ancient railway carriage. War if the British chose
it, but also he proffered peace.[6]

With the general sense thus established, the preamble went into
practical items in a long list of stipulations. Noteworthy was the re-
nouncement of all intention to change the sea-power balance versus
Britain. French naval equipment (for possibly bridging the Channel) was foresworn and put on ice under French jurisdiction, rather
than being sequestered as war booty. In fact, Hitler explicitly
guaranteed that German naval strength would not be augmented at
the expense of the French fleet. German Navy advice offered on
18 June had proposed the contrary, that is, making good *Norway*
losses and otherwise strengthening the inferior position at sea by the
use of French ships. But Hitler rejected this scheme in sharpest terms,
and a like one from partner Mussolini.[7] Hitler reasoned against these
advices, von Puttkamer wrote, that the action proposed could serve

[5] Paul Schmidt, *Hitler's Interpreter* (New York, 1951), pp. 177, 178, as corroborated by *The Ciano Diaries, 1939-1943* (New York, 1946), pp. 265, 266.

[6] Von Weizäcker, *op. cit.*, pp. 292, 298, gives his interpretation of Hitler's terms
at Compiègne. Many other observers agreed with von Weizsäcker that Hitler was
speaking to Britain. Baron Weizsäcker was an old-time diplomat who started a
career in the Navy and after World War I shifted to diplomacy. From 1938-1943 he
served as State Secretary, that is, next under von Ribbentrop, in the German Foreign Office. He was not in sympathy with the Hitler regime, and thought of himself
as an ameliorating influence in his important post.

[7] The Skl paper, dated 18 June, set forth detailed plans for boosting German
naval strength by acquisitions from the French Navy. Von Puttkamer, who had to
represent the Navy's views to Hitler, recalls Hitler's instant rejection (*op. cit.*, pp. 36,
37).

only to drive the French fleet into British hands. Saving the French fleet for German use would not have been easy—in fact, next to impossible. Admiral Darlan exercised a tight control over his close-knit French Navy. It is known that he had alerted the fleet to be ready to abandon home ports as early as 15 June. Moreover, all ships prepared emergency measures for rendering themselves inoperable, if they should fail to get free. Darlan was determined that the ships should not fall to the Germans. A substantial number were in home ports, some important units with the British in Egyptian waters, and another group, containing the newest heavy ships, at Mers el Kebir in Algeria. Even had Hitler made surrender of the ships a condition of cease fire in France, it is doubtful that many would have been taken. It is improbable that he knew of Darlan's preparations. One thing, however, he did know: demand for the fleet would intensify the challenge of war to Britain, and this, he had shown by word and deed, he did not want at all. His thoughts, rather, leaped ahead to a Britain reconciled. He attempted to turn the fact of the French fleet into a vehicle of reassurance to Britain, of her position at sea and of her empire. Hitler was, in truth, again treading the holy ground of marriage. The cycle, begun with the Great Turning in 1938, had reached an end, his ire against Britain appeased. This was Compiègne's significance for this study; in effect, a regenerated gospel of marriage.

So, the armistice terms implied conciliation, but conciliation that could not forego a threat of "or else." Evidently this man thought to bare a heart of gold and yet advertise the power of the initiative he had won. The play failed to get over. He played a grotesque role of magnanimous conqueror to the French and told the British they could have an even better deal for the asking. The hope that they would honor his promise demonstrated how wide of the mark Hitler stood about his personal reputation for evil. He had no comprehension of the loathing and disgust that his name called forth, especially among Englishmen. There were quavering voices among them, but the general public reacted to Compiègne with a hardening against him.

Thus while the proffer of deal failed to dent England one bit, what did get over the Channel from Compiègne, and to all the world, was the signature number that closed the on-the-spot radio reporting of the incredible drama running its course in France on that Saturday afternoon of 22 June 1940. Goebbels and Company had carried all

Germans and the world through the armistice ceremonies. Now at their conclusion he signed off with a smart rendition of "Denn wir fahren, denn wir fahren, denn wir fahren gegen Engelland."

TO THE GERMAN NATION

GERMAN PEOPLE!

In a short six weeks your soldiers have brought an end to the War in the West after an heroic battle against a brave foe.

Their deeds will be entered in history as the most glorious victory of all times.

Humbly we thank the Lord for his blessing.

I order the display of flags throughout the Reich for ten days and the ringing of bells for seven days.

Führer Headquarters, 24 June 1940

ADOLF HITLER

What About England?   The Navy Answer—June 1940

Two views of Britain came into German consciousness by the proceedings at Compiègne, a peace view and a war view. The first, peace, expressed the wishful but unformalized hope of most Germans and the strong expectation, amounting to an obsession, of their Führer. It grew to utterly unreal proportions. We can call it the "private" view. The second was the "official" or planned view, rising from sober professional thinking. Inevitably these men came to grips with realities and had to think: what next? Someone had to keep shop, and the key thinkers in the higher echelons of command did ponder the situation and explore the courses open in this amazing and wholly unvisualized picture before them. What if peace did not come? The Navy led in the soul-searching, having always held that Britain was "the one to beat" and that the job would not be accomplished by land warfare on the Continent. Two recognized courses were already on the books: siege, the "official" plan; and invasion, the discarded *Studie Nordwest*. Siege had been reaffirmed in directives as late as *Dunkirk* time. The announced object of the West offensive had been to gain Channel bases for prosecuting siege. Now there were signs that the slow strangulation of siege fell far short for these bustling dynamic times; something more explosive was called for. To be standing on the Channel coast, confronting England, had forever implied Invasion.

Perhaps Admiral Raeder felt reassured when a month earlier he had retired to the safety of Neptune's hall after the first exploratory talk of invasion with the Führer at Felsennest. Yet the Admiral's conscience and renewed discussion in Skl would not let the invasion thought die. Commander Reinicke reviewed his own study of 1939 along with the Army companion piece, and his boss, Admiral Fricke, took a fresh start in a study of his own titled *Studie England*. Meanwhile, in early June, Fricke instituted an inquiry into the availability of transports and the problem of laying mine barriers to protect them. Invasion appealed to his imaginative thinking, for he saw in it a means of ending the war. From *Dunkirk* time on, he advocated storming over the Channel after the British in any manner of craft at hand and bringing the war home to the English.

His *Studie England* hewed closer to realities than had been done up to this time. It was not a profound strategical evaluation but, rather, a loose collection of operational ideas rising from the demands of a moving and unanticipated situation— a sort of check-off list of items demanding immediate attention, to clear the way for further headwork. The situation was no longer as highly theoretical as in November 1939, when Reinicke and Stieff toyed with landing thought. Now Germans stood on the shore of the Channel and wondered, What next? But even though they had a better grasp on realities, the earlier theoretical studies exerted strong influence. Fricke accepted their prerequisites and added a few of his own. He underlined the imperative need of preliminary air command over the Channel, a fencing-off of the assault area by mine barrages, and the neutralizing of antiparatroop defenses. Also he brought forward more pointedly the practical hazards of weather and tide, and the dimensions of logistic follow-up. Yet with Fricke, as before, the Navy's task centered around so many bodies and transport space for them; he did admit the need for small landing craft and brought the problem of landing on open beaches into consideration. *Studie England* shifted the preferred area of attack from England's east coast to the Channel shore. This strip was designated as Area Red. Across the face of his study Fricke wrote to his assistants: "When cognizance has been taken, we will want to talk over the solutions set forth herein and the further preparations arising out of them." By June he recorded the status of "preliminary work then in hand" on invasion. Apparently it had become a recognized Navy project, though not a popular one, nor one that was widely known.

While Fricke thus sparked invasion, Admiral Raeder obtained fresh reassurance from the Führer on 4 June that the official siege plan stood. At Führer Conference on that day Raeder complained anew that submarine construction suffered for lack of materials and workmen. Göring, heading up war production as well as many other agencies, was still slighting his closest competitor, the Navy. In reply, Hitler reiterated his previous excuse: With France out of the way, the Army's task in the war would end. The Army would be reduced, releasing men and materials to the Luftwaffe and Navy for continuing the war against Britain. On 14 June written instructions from Keitel converted this promise into cash by elaborating the Führer's views and giving them the effect of orders. The official plan accordingly seemed safely fixed.[8]

We have seen that the ill-defined terms of the official plan never got beyond a general concept of siege by sea and by air, with no clear appreciation of the physical proximity of England, should the Germans gain France. France, it had been held, could not be won for years; certainly not before 1943. There was a paucity of imaginative thinking, stemming from World War I; Britain still had the Germans overawed. When faced with a choice between England's conquest and lesser duress, they seemed to turn toward the lesser in default of anything better. It would be siege. Germans generally were fortified subjectively in the efficacy of that choice by a grim and losing tussle of their own with want and hunger during the earlier war. If the day ever came, they would make the English hungry! But how, exactly, had never been worked out. Beginning

---

[8] The war diary of Skl sets forth that during his Führer Conference on 4 June 1940 Admiral Raeder saw an OKW estimate in which it was postulated that the Army's task in the war was near ended. The resulting plans called for industrial resources to be switched to the Navy for submarine construction and to the Air Force for the JU 88 twin-engine dive-bomber program, so that these services might continue the war of siege against Britain. Hitler confirmed this in his talk with Raeder. OKW directive of 14 June advised that the Army was to be reduced to 120 divisions to implement the above. Another source confirms this. General Georg Thomas headed the Office of Defense Economy and Armament (Wehrwirtschafts und Rüstungs Amt). On 7 June 1940 Thomas' records show he received advice from Keitel of OKW that "Führer convinced of early collapse of France, swiftest shift of armament on to fight against England. A bid toward England is apparently to be reckoned on after collapse of France. Army is to retain only 120 Divisions. Great increase of armor. Greatest increase of Air and Submarine . . . ."

soon after the outbreak of World War II, the German Naval Operations Office undertook missionary work on the subject. A lengthy
Skl study, titled "Denkschrift über den verschärften Seekrieg gegen
England," attempted to educate and influence the thinking of the
high leadership. The study did not undertake to evaluate what
had best be done, but built a case for the already accepted formula
of siege in the following opening words: "The chief opponent of
Germany in this war is England. Her most vulnerable point is commerce at sea. The war at sea against England, militarily, is therefore
to be conducted as an economic war with the aim to destroy in the
shortest time England's will to resist and force her readiness for peace
[Friedensbereitschaft]." The study bore the date of 15 October 1939.

Eventually, in November 1939, Führer Directive No. 9 was
squeezed out in support, and a special staff for economic warfare
was set up in OKW. But this all turned out so much eye-wash for the
dynamic feeling that ruled in June 1940. The Germans stood on the
Channel, but what to do with it no one could say. The problem
bulked harder and bigger: with wrecked Channel ports, usable only
by small craft and perhaps a few submarines, and an appalling lack
of equipment and personnel, this seacoast promised nothing but more
trouble, particularly in defense against British incursion. The ports
were too open to enemy action, as prophesied by Reinicke in the fall
of 1939. So ran the thoughts filling the naval records, much like
the thoughts of white elephant after *Norway*. A naval posture against
Portsmouth from Cherbourg, say, to dispute Channel waters did
not enter the calculation strongly, except to recommend air action.
Due note was taken of British public apprehension over control of
this sector and fear of Invasion England. But the images thus raised
by the British failed to fire the Germans sailors' blood. They were
wedded to siege. England was ever a problem apart, awesome and
uncertain.

Besides, the early June days, filled as they were with more *Norway*
uproar, afforded little time for branching off into visionary projects
like invasion. An operation by heavy combat ships was underway
in far off north Norway to relieve the pressure on Narvik, where the
redoubtable Dietl was still under pressure. The naval operation mis-
carried, to Raeder's annoyance and Göring's joy. He got in some
nasty blows. These worries mounted when Hitler adopted Göring's
suggestion about the superliners *Bremen* and *Europa*. He ordered
them made ready to reinforce Narvik. Refitting them as troop car-

riers and installing heavy lift gear was hard enough, but to order
these fat ships up the long Norwegian coast through an uncommanded
sea was sheer lunacy.   After a while the shock of the West offensive
into France brought relief.   The Allies had to abandon Norway.
Thus freed, the German Navy sidetracked the liner project and turned
its thoughts more directly toward England; OKW planners commenced to scan the England horizon too.   Head planning assistant,
Colonel Warlimont, came to Naval Headquarters to compare notes
with the Navy planner, Rear-Admiral Fricke, on 17 June 1940.

Record of the conference appears in both Skl and OKW papers.
Fricke presented the Navy views for handling the situation.   England,
Fricke argued (in sly words that seem out of character for him and
Skl), commanded great respect in the world; it might be disadvantageous to the white race to smash her and the Empire.   To Warlimont this talk rang right from the Führer's mouth.   He could freely
confirm it so and add that, after the overthrow of France, the Führer
expected to make peace with Britain at French expense.   "With re-
respect to invasion," the Skl war diary records, "according to chief
L [Warlimont], Führer had up to now expressed no such intention
since he saw fully the extraordinary difficulties of such an undertaking.   Therefore no preliminary work or preparations had been met
in OKW."   Warlimont admitted that aside from the preliminary
work in invasion by Skl, the Luftwaffe had gone ahead with the con-
stitution of a parachute division, and General von Schell had suggested
the building of special landing craft.   But these excursions were of
minor importance; the real thing was that Hitler had not changed on
England.[9]

We should remember that the Fricke-Warlimont conference took
place toward the end of the Führer's glorious *Gröfaz* day of 17 June.
Leading up to it, tension had mounted day by day.   Who could tell
what nonsense the unstable Hitler, now emancipated by France's collapse, might conceive, what sudden orders he might issue.   Admiral
Raeder was constantly plagued with this thought.   We can guess
that he posted Fricke to put an ear to the ground by insinuating Hitler's well-known private view into conversation with Warlimont.   The

[9] The reference to von Schell denoted the officer charged with the building of
automative equipment for the Army.   In June 1940 Skl got word that he had instigated inquiries among industrial contractors for the building of assault landing boats.
About the same time advices also reached Skl that Professor Gottfried Feder, a long-
standing functionary of the Nazi party, had already in April proposed to the Army
the building of submersible tanks for assaulting England.

stratagem is given away by the fact that Fricke's leading remarks on Britain stood in direct contradiction to all previous Skl recorded effusions on the subject. Indeed, that office had pictured Britain as the villainous foe, a foe bent on nothing less than exterminating the German people. So it appears that Fricke, though personally not averse to trying a landing, took a sounding for the benefit of his Chief, who wanted no part of such an undertaking. Raeder himself planned to brace the Führer again on the question of England three days later. The intelligence that Fricke elicited indicated that the subject was a safe one, even to the point of pushing to get invasion foolishness rejected, once and for all. All seemed clear, with not a sign of hasty invasion orders from OKW in sight.

Fear of wild orders were not without foundation—the scheme of using the *Bremen* and *Europa* to throw large troop masses here and there across open seas, for instance. Shortly after the hurrah over Narvik subsided, someone in OKW thought of Iceland. A few thousand German troops on the island would make the isolation of England complete. OKW accordingly gave orders to keep on with activating the giant liners. This was worse and more of it. Shudders again crept up and down the spines of Neptune's sons in Skl. Fricke had gingerly tested that area with Warlimont, too; he assured his visitor from OKW of the Navy's readiness to shoulder any reasonable task, if only advised in advance, so that the best Navy talents could be brought to bear. The record reflects unmistakable signs of a subordinate command straining with all politeness in staff vernacular to keep the superior within bounds. It says in effect: "For God's sake, boys, be reasonable about this; you can see the thing is completely crazy. Give us a break!" Warlimont was able to reply that the Iceland project had collided with Göring's wishes; the possibilities for Air installations there were meager. Good, this killed it.

The Iceland madness, which carried the code name *Ikarus,* made another point, after England, on Raeder's check-off list for a crucial Führer Conference scheduled for 20 June 1940. Raeder's briefcase bulged with projects when he stepped into the conference room. He well appreciated the pivotal importance of the time. France was out. Hitler was in the midst of concocting armistice terms. The Germans in June 1940 stood where they had not dreamed of standing until 1943. In the sailors' minds this was the hour for striking Britain on the sea. The abnormal mass of preparatory notes the Admiral carried bore witness to intense and careful groundwork. Nor did the old gentleman lack private and very personal grievances to present his Führer. A grossly insulting telegram from Göring in reply to Raeder's proposal for retaining strong air units near the new naval base at Trondheim in Norway stuck in his craw. He raised the point early in the conference by reading aloud the rude mind-your-own-business response from Göring. Hitler evaded with the request that future suggestions for air protection be routed through OKW.

The Raeder-Göring exchange evidenced in graphic terms the bitter animosity existent between the two service heads and their staffs. Later, in August, Göring apologized, but the harm was irremediable. He never brooked interference with his aspiration to win the war, or the peace, singlehanded, and he strove to arrogate the glory of it all to himself, next after Hitler. No Foreign Office, Army, or Navy was going to dilute it. Raeder gradually came to fully apprehend Göring's wretched techniques and their selfish aim. No endeavor toward conciliation, however earnest, effected the slightest basic change; Göring's ambition, he concluded, would lead to German failure. The quarrel held grave consequences for the war on England.

The Navy thought it had turned the tables on Göring over England. It was up to him to make good. There was agreement on every hand (including Mr. Churchill's) that decision for or against invasion turned first on the outcome of the air war. The primary prerequisite stipulated in all invasion thought had been that command of the air over the Channel had to be fact before the problem could be seriously carried further. Raeder drove on this point with all force in the conference of 20 June, vigorous air attacks on British bases should start immediately, he advised. Then, as though the Navy had invasion going full blast, he reported on the naval preparations in hand: the question of mines; the shipping available; the localities for landing. But again he insisted, "control of the air is a necessary pre-condition for invasion . . . ." Next he touched on the construction of special landing craft as proposed by Schell and Feder and obtained agreement from Hitler that such craft would be developed by the Navy. Both his postconference notes and the more explicit résumé furnished by his staff affected to treat invasion as an established project. By inference his story went: The Navy is proceeding; there remains, of course, the matter of air control, with which Göring should get on; and then, also, the Army should determine the composition of its landing divisions, and what equipment could be left behind.[10]

[10] *FC,* 1940, I, 54-59.

So much glory had fallen to the Army and to the Luftwaffe in these past weeks of victory; scarcely a word for the Navy. Disgruntled rumblings came from within the Navy itself. Admiral Raeder's record of the Führer Conference of 20 June among other things implies a wish to square things for the Navy. Britain was still to be dealt with. It was time to get on with the Navy's war! Were the Air Force and Army ready? His personal and official doctrine had always been siege, but now quite casually he lapsed into mention of invasion in most logical context, despite good evidence that he was more than willing to have invasion killed. Raeder's game seems to have had the double purpose of calling the Army and Air Force to task and thereby also freeing the atmosphere of invasion folly forever. Siege, the Navy gospel, could then proceed. He succeeded in accomplishing the exact opposite; instead of impetus to siege, he furnished wholly unintended stimulus to invasion.

The Führer's naval aide who attended the conference besides Generals Keitel and Jodl recalled that Hitler's reaction, while not one of outright rejection, distinctly opposed the thought. "How can we do an operation of this sort?" he complained. "It looks completely impossible to me. Losses will be heavy and no guarantee of success. How can we take on such casualties after conquering France with none to speak of?"[11]

Hitler was far afield in another area, absorbed in armistice terms, revising them and rerevising. On the happy morrow they would be handed to the French. His thoughts dwelt on peace, and how to beguile the British into it, rather than on how to knock them down on their home island. General Jodl, however, took careful note about invasion; landing ideas had also been bruited about his planning bailiwick, where the question of What next? was a burning one.

The fact that the Navy Chief could feel secure in glibly preening himself on the Navy's feeble landing preparations hints at the depth of the dilemma facing the German military. Up to this point the high soldiery had felt confidently at home in its own element of exciting land campaigning. Now the campaigns had run out, and the campaigners looked about them somewhat at a loss. No one had finished the picture of standing on the shore of the Channel surrounded by a horde of victorious troops. Some two and a half million soldiers idle; how long could they be left unemployed? The Raeder invasion prodding provided welcome relief in the upper planning

[11] Told to me by Konteradmiral von Puttkamer (Germany, 1953).

reaches. On the troop levels, indeed, on almost all levels the world over, dynamic events had pushed the thinking far beyond the German planners. The very air of conquest and its exhilarating climate told the troops what came next. The Navy's answer, siege, seemed much too slow and prosaic.

The Army Answer—June 1940

In the early twenties Herr Fritz Siebel had given employment to a vagrant flyer from World War I, Hermann Göring, and thus tided him over a difficult period. Siebel was a man of parts who manufactured aircraft. When World War II came along, it became a case of turnabout; Göring gave employment to Siebel, not that he needed tiding over, but because Göring needed Siebel's talents in Luftwaffe plane production. In June 1940 as a major of the Luftwaffe Siebel was busy reactivating a captured French aircraft plant near Albert in northeastern France. Many visitors came by the plant, curious soldiers, party functionaries, and others. Usually, in his anxiety to get on with the plant, Siebel excused himself and gave the visitors the run of the place. But one Lieutenant Colonel, who commanded a nearby battalion of "water engineers," piqued his curiosity with a strange request. The engineer wanted access to a huge pile of empty gasoline containers alongside the plant. Siebel said he would be glad to let them go, if only the Colonel would explain what he wanted with them. The reply flabbergasted him—the empty tanks were the very thing, the engineer said, for constructing floats to ferry troops and equipment over the Channel to England.

The incident marked the genesis of the Siebel Fähre (Siebel Ferry) that later did much for German sea transport, including belated support for Rommel in the Mediterranean. The craft got their start from troop-level thinking on the problem of crossing the Channel to England. Siebel, who agreed with the engineer colonel that England had to be next on the list, became interested and undertook the development of landing craft. By the time he got through he had created a sizable Luftwaffe Navy. It was only one of many signs that evidenced the pull of the time toward invasion.[12]

[12] Herr Fritz Siebel recounted this story to me in Germany during 1953. The ferry that finally emerged presented an ingenious adaptation of materials already on hand —engineer pontoons as catamaran floats spanned by a sturdy deck on which could be mounted three 88-mm. guns plus a quad of 40's and a twin 20, or if only 20 mm's

The *Zeitgeist* was strong. It took hold among the younger idea-men in the Army planning levels as it had in the Navy. A member of the Operations section of OKH has recounted how it reached into those precincts about mid-June. This officer, Colonel Wilhelm Willemer, managed to get sprung from his headquarters desk to witness the entry of German troops into Paris on 14 June. When he returned to OKH, he found instructions to join another officer in devising an exploratory plan for landing in England. Willemer was able to fix the period and its thinking at about 19 June 1940 because of association with the unforgettable happenings just experienced in Paris. He checked his own recollections both as to time and content of work with the other participating officer, General Philippi.

The pair set to work. Much nonsense on how to get over to England flowed around them in headquarters gossip. One story made it a very simple undertaking; they would go over on the Channel bottom in submersible tanks rigged with snorkel tubes for air. Actually, something of the sort was under trial off the island of Sylt near the Danish border. Clever miracle-working schemes of this sort abounded, but of exact data and good maps, of information about enemy defenses and fighting strength, there was little. Explorers Willemer and Philippi had resource to a schoolboy geography. In two days they hammered together a presentable opus and turned it in to their superior, Colonel von Greiffenberg. It received the treatment of a purely theoretical paper meant only for internal education of the Operations Section, OKH. No special notice was taken elsewhere, though the whole subject commenced to warm up.

The exploratory plan worked out to a modest crossing in the Dover Narrows by three divisions, aimed for a landing between Ramsgate and Hastings. The tactic followed the pattern of a super river-crossing. When the water engineers were consulted they demanded more lateral elbow room for probing, and so, little by little, responding

---

were used 60 to 80 tons of cargo or troops could be transported, i.e., about two companies of infantry. For propulsion they used the power of obsolete aircraft engines at first turning air screws and later water propellers. The craft drew little water but did well in a seaway at speeds of 9 to 11 knots. It appears they offered an answer for the production of landing craft in mass in a short space of time. During the summer of 1940 Siebel got 181 assorted air-screw-driven ferries ready and also 128 air-screw-driven prahms. Production and acceptance fell into competition with the Navy, which had undertaken the production of its own landing craft, called the Marine Fährprahm (MFP). Had the practical need of landing craft been taken to heart by the planners, the invasion story might have come out differently. The final Siebel Ferry is still in operation on the Rhine. There we had the pleasure of riding one during 1953 and found her a very able little ship.

to one need after another, the frontage swelled sideways, uninhibited. The immediate object was to seize a bridgehead from which operations might be launched to conquer England. The final objective line ran from Liverpool to the Humber.[13] There is no evidence that old *Studie Nordwest* of late 1939 was consulted, but the earlier name became current for reference to invasion thought through its use by the Navy during this formative period.

Raeder's Führer Conference of 20 June added heat to the landing question. Also, the Navy agents at court seemed to have gotten wind of the latest Army study, and the *Nordwest* routine of intrigue began to repeat itself. Staff interchanges between the Navy and Army demonstrated a wish within the Army High Command to hold aloof from the landing rage; for on the day after Raeder's conference with Hitler (20 June), and perhaps because of it, the Army Operations Section went on record in these words: "OKH has not occupied itself with the question of England, execution [of a landing] considered impossible . . . 20 [defending] divisions in England [so] 40 German divisions would have to get over. Air supremacy seems unattainable. The [Army] General Staff rejects the operation." Indeed, the Commander-in-Chief of the Army officially instructed his Army Group Commanders in the field on 26 June that with the decisive success in the West the Army's tasks were completed. He added that further conduct of the war against England would rest on the Navy and Air Force. Nevertheless, OKH took care to send an officer for copies of the up-to-date Navy planning papers and charts of England.

At about this point, toward the end of June, a marked change came about in the Army attitude. The top leadership shifted its ground radically by taking a definite stand favoring invasion. Interest in that direction was roused by hints from the policy sanctum of Joachim von Ribbentrop, the Foreign Minister. The man was known to be a violent Anglophobe. Normally Ribbentrop contented himself with mimicking Hitler. He did this to Ciano on the question of peace with Britain during the prearmistice conference at Munich, ten days gone. To be peacefully inclined toward Britain was an unnatural attitude for this miniature Hitler, who bore the British a deep personal grudge. Rumors from the Foreign Office reflected his and Hitler's impatience over British disdain for peace feelers and a consequent turn toward other measures. General Halder of OKH

[13] Colonel Wilhelm Willemer (in consultation with General Alfred Philippi) to Ansel (Germany, 1953).

believes the trend might first have come to his notice on 26 June through the good offices of Hasso von Etzdorf, who liaisoned between the Foreign Ministry and the Army. At that time Halder had just returned from a grand conference of Army General Staff representatives at Versailles. The talk there had been precisely the opposite of more war; in fact, the meeting occupied itself, not too happily, with the problem of unforeseen idleness —a scaling down and reorganization of units for tasks of peace. Hasso von Etzdorf's news intimated something else might be in the air. A further demonstration of German military power could still be needed to bring Britain around.

On the following day General Halder flew to Berlin to be with family friends for his anniversary on 30 June. In Berlin he visited his old friend and confidant Ernst Freiherr von Weizsäcker, State Secretary at the Foreign Office, to take a reading of the times. It was all well and good to talk about simply shutting off the valve, about plans for scaling down and reorganizing the Army—so many divisions here, so many there, training plans, recreation plans, and what not. But would this work in a victory-happy host? The thought of this vast team of warriors unemployed did not sit well at all. This predicament—what to do after France—had not ceased to plague the Chief of the Army General Staff thirteen years later when we reviewed the 1940 situation together in conversation.

Freiherr von Weizsäcker admitted that no concrete basis for a peace existed; a vigilant watch would have to be kept on the East, where there were signs of unrest. As to England, she "will presumably be in need of one more demonstration of our military power, before she gives in and leaves us a free back [clear rear] for the East."[14] Not only had Russian restiveness grown with each German success in the West, but also, a series of signals had come in evidencing renewed Führer interest in the East. As late as 2 June (just prior to the final actions in France) Hitler addressed the assembled field commanders at Army Group A headquarters (von Rundstedt) in Charleville. It was his third and last visit of the campaign to those illustrious headquarters. As before, he affected an air of talking confidentially. He voiced hints of turning toward

[14] We trace the course of OKH's first official interest in invasion (30 June and 1 July 1940) from the *Halder Journal*, IV, 97-100, and from official German naval records. Details emerged from conversation with General Halder and correspondence with him.

Russia; now that England might well be ready for peace, he would settle accounts with the Bolsheviki.[15] These thoughts were again surprising and anything but welcome to his Army hearers. Similar Hitlerian signals multiplied, and in late June, with the West campaign completed, they still remained an unwelcome solution to the Army's unemployment problem. General Halder required something better; von Weizsäcker's remark on England opened a lead.

The General bethought himself of vague invasion talk with the Navy Operations Chief of Staff, Admiral Schniewind, prior to the French campaign. It may have been, he mused, in connection with the Navy's wanting the whole French side of the Channel up to the Atlantic. Now with this objective miraculously won, was invasion in order? Halder also probably knew of Raeder's jibe about the unclear composition of landing divisions at Führer Conference on 20 June. Perhaps the sailors had something; General Halder proceeded to ascertain firsthand. He hunted up Admiral Schniewind in his Berlin office to talk over the possibilities for continuing the war against Britain.

The Halder-Schniewind meeting of 1 July marks the first genuine effort on the part of the Army General Staff to come to grips with the problem of insular Britain and the invasion complex. The exchange is worthy of notice because out of it came the Army's enthusiastic invasion interest, based on misinterpretation of the Navy attitude and her weak landing capability. The General and the Admiral had for long enjoyed a friendly back-and-forth comparing of notes at approximately monthly intervals, though usually it was Schniewind who sought out the busy land campaigner. On this rare occasion of the contrary case, it would be natural for the Admiral to make his guest comfortable and to shove the Navy's best foot forward in landing capability, especially in view of Raeder's sanctimonious remarks at Führer Headquarters.

[15] General von Sodenstern COS, Army Group A to Ansel, December 1954: "Before the actual discussion began Hitler walked up and down in front of the building in which the officers had assembled. In this connection, i.e., more in private conversation, he bragged about Russia. 'Now that things—England being probably ready for peace—had finally gotten to this point he could begin his settling of accounts with Bolshevism! . . .' In the evening Rundstedt expressed amazement to me. He was convinced that with a campaign against Russia one could overtax the German forces." General von Sodenstern recalled no mention of Russia to the other officers, but his staffmate, General Blumentritt, thought Hitler had in passing mentioned Russian border build-up and that it would therefore be desirable to close a sensible peace with England.

Tests with landing craft on Rangsdorfer See, a lake near Berlin, to which Herr Siebel transferred his experiments. This was his so-called Kleine Fähre, the progenitor of the later design shown below. *(Courtesy General Alfred Jacob)*

Siebel Fähre of the Luftwaffe Navy. *(Courtesy Captain Walter Genz)*

General Franz Halder, Chief of the Army General Staff. *(Courtesy General Halder)*

Admiral Otto Schniewind, Chief of Staff, Naval Operations. *(Courtesy Admiral Schniewind)*

They conferred alone and, to judge from the clipped record in Halder's journal, got quickly down to cases. The well-known prerequisites of air superiority led the list. General Halder added laconically, "Then perhaps we can dispense with land warfare altogether . . . ." Next came weather. Smooth water was required; fog would interfere after mid-October. To this, Admiral Schniewind's notes added, as though echoing Halder, that this fixed the target date around mid-August, in order to allow sufficient time for the operation on land to unroll. The line of departure they accepted in talk ran from Ostend to Le Havre. It was most optimistic.

The Halder record continues with tentative conclusions on practical matters not at all justified by the desultory efforts so far pursued by the Navy. He noted: "A large number of small steamers [1,000], could be assembled . . . 100,000 men in one wave . . . ." There were actually fewer than 300 usable small steamers in all of Europe. Navy estimates of mid-June had mentioned about 15, capable of transporting 7,500 men. The Schniewind record makes no mention of steamers; as to the number of troops, it simply says that Halder estimated the strength of the first wave at about six divisions, or 100,000 men. But Halder filled out the alluring picture stroke by stroke. "Artillery cover for the second half of the run across the water and on the beaches must be furnished by the Luftwaffe. Underwater threats [from submarines] can be shut out by net barrages. Surface threats can be minimized by mines and [our own] submarines, supplementing landbased artillery and aircraft. Cliffs at Dover, Dungeness, Beachy Head, [but] rest of coast suitable for landing . . . ." And a final item: "Dr. Feder type concrete barges are now under test. Provision in sufficient numbers in July held possible." The two friends positively scudded along.

The later misunderstandings between Army and Navy stemmed in the main from this friendly but loose beginning. General Halder has said in considered writing that he recalled the Navy's landing ideas of the time as being phrased in generalities bound round with reservations about great British naval superiority, and that little enthusiasm for invasion found expression on the Navy side. He added that later outright Navy opposition grew far stronger when at every turn a new objection was brought up to plague the Army. As for opinion in OKH, which office to this point had been averse to landing, he stated: "I would like to stress however that . . . after 1 July 1940 a landing undertaking in England was, on the part of OKH, held feasible. OKH expected [therefrom] however, not a readiness for peace [*Friedensbereitschaft*] from England, but the elimination of the British island as a base for a counterattack at a later time against the German occupied Channel coast." In other words, the Army aimed at a solid military objective. The Navy and OKW, let alone the Luftwaffe, remained less clear in this regard.

The Halder reading of Skl on 1 July encouraged Army thinking and thus set the tone for a fresh approach by OKH to the invasion proposition. It was an overoptimistic tone. Later American experience was in like case. We are reminded of our own early ventures into cross-Channel thinking in the contrary direction. How full of fire our Army associates seemed to us; how we, in our sailor suits, protested and poured the coldest water on their ardor. They in turn waxed disconsolate and broke out with gibes like: "Well, if you can't put us over, the Royal Navy will." Soldiers have a zest for going.

Before leaving Naval Headquarters General Halder proffered help from Army Engineers in clearing mounting ports on the Channel. Thereupon he set sail for the Army Ordnance Office and briefed the General in Charge on the new picture. The officer protested—all along he had been told no invasion was under consideration. "I told him," recorded General Halder, "that possibilities must be examined anyhow, for if the political leadership sets a demand [for invasion], they will want everything done at top speed." The Army was on its way—landing in England.

The German Army had its answer, but significantly, the arm most needed to give it effect, and which of late years had come to regard Britain as its very own, was not directly consulted. We mean the Luftwaffe.

The Air Answer—June 1940

Air zealot Göring spent 22 July 1938 on board the smart new German destroyer *Hermann Schömann*. His purpose was not alone to look over the fine ship in her pristine freshness, but also to take a few shots at the bigwigs of the Navy and their ambitious, and to him futile, ship-building program. He had a sardonic genius for such doings when invited aboard ship. Said he to the assembled conferees, in reference to the small need for the Navy program: "From the summer of 1939 on, Germany will possess air formations that present such a threat to the British Fleet that utilization of its home ports will be rendered impossible to it."[16] By air formations Göring meant the JU-88 heavy dive bombers, which were to go into production in 1939. His boast in 1938, coupled with the more familiar one that he would "chase the English Fleet around its islands," epitomized the published Luftwaffe prewar Air gospel for the reduction of England.

England hardly came alive as a problem for the Luftwaffe until Hitler's Great Turning of 1938. It was then that he departed from his earlier course of association to one that toyed with outright challenge to armed conflict with Britain. For such trial, the Luftwaffe assured Hitler, Germany, and the world, it had the stuff, and moreover it wanted no support from the Navy. A notable protagonist was the rising young Jeschonnek, who later became Chief of the Air General Staff. He habitually took the stand that the German Navy would never be needed at all in a war against Britain. "The Luftwaffe will conquer England in a matter of months," he was prone to say to the naval liaison officer at the Air Headquarters.[17] Thus it became generally accepted that, though England traditionally had belonged to the Navy, in these modern days the Luftwaffe constituted the first line of offense against the island. From such theory, plus Hitlerian and some naval interpolations, the vague plan of siege by sea and by air from the French Channel coast eventually evolved.

With the fall of France it was time for the Luftwaffe to make good on its bombast, barring of course the supervention of peace. But already by 1939 Göring and Jeschonnek knew in their hearts that practical capabilities of the Luftwaffe could not meet their pretensions. Early actions of the war brought abundant confirmation. This knowledge, however, made little difference to *"unser* Hermann." With him (as with his Führer) it was not so much a case of what he could do, as what the British thought he could do. His wishful conviciton in June 1940 was that the Englanders had been convinced of Luftwaffe power and that soon there would come the peace necessary for enjoyment of his hunting and other lordly pursuits. So he

---

[16] Vice Admiral Hellmuth Heye to Ansel (Germany, 1953-1954). He was stationed in Plans and Operations of Skl at the time of Göring's visit. Göring said this on more than one occasion. The statement appears in the official Navy records. One variation of Göring's boast was: "I will need the Navy only as submarine weather reporting stations in the Atlantic."

[17] Told to me by Rear Admiral Wilhelm Mössel, who served as naval liaison officer at OKL (Oberkommando der Luftwaffe-High Command, Air Force) from 1937 to 1945 (Germany, 1953).

paid scant heed to staff proposals for more war in the form of invasion.

Göring's official deputy, General Erhard Milch, was among the first to raise the invasion question. This occurred on 5 June 1940, a fact that he readily established from entries in his personal diary. His exploratory suggestion to Göring led nowhere, and Milch bided his time. When the French collapse again pushed the subject forward, he once more approached his Chief, and this time (27 June 1940) with a full-blown plan. He envisioned a shattering bolt from the blue by airborne troopers on the vital air fields in the south of England. With the uproar from that blow well underway, an amphibious assault could strike across the Channel and complete the havoc. According to Milch, Hitler vetoed the plan as being too risky.[18]

The principle of the plan—crippling blows by Air Infantry— had by this time taken roots in many quarters, including London. Among German airmen the ideas diverged along two lines: one followed Milch, favoring seizure of air fields in order to deny ground bases to the RAF and at the same time provide airdromes for the Luftwaffe in England; the other line advocated airborne seizure of coastal beachheads from the landward side in order to insure successful troop landings from seaward. Unfortunately for the Germans, their foremost paratrooper, General Kurt Student, lay in a hospital suffering from operational injuries. He was unable to push any plan, though much later he seemed to profess a preference for the second tactic and seemed convinced it could have succeeded.

General Albert Kesselring, who had relieved General Felmy in command of Luftflotte 2 (Airfleet 2), would have had the job of supporting either plan. During June he completed the deployment of his squadrons along the Channel coast and sat chafing at inaction in his forward command post. It stood near Wissant just above Cap Gris Nez on the Channel. There was England, over there! He could see the shore out of the embrasure porthole and felt something should be done. "We commanders at the Front could not picture how Hitler was going to succeed in coming to terms with England, when day after day, week on week passed without a thing happening." Kesselring deplored the failure to exploit the air invasion tactic learned in the Lowlands. He believed South England's

---

[18] Generalfeldmarschall Erhard Milch to Ansel, and confirmed by extracts from his personal diary (Germany, 1953).

air fields, radar installations, and beach defense could readily be taken out by the new technique. Many shared his opinion.[19]

Judgments in this vein grew and varied with the individuals, from the highest officer at headquarters to the lowliest airman at mess. And the talk passed into common gossip in which the press on both sides of the Channel took an avid interest. London papers published pictures of German paratroopers in full kit and urged their readers to be on the lookout. The data were not hard to come by, for the Luftwaffe was making deception drops over England to this very purpose. Fake maps, instructions to agents and Fifth Columnists, air photographs of landing fields and beach defenses, plus paratrooper radio gear and other bits of equipment were being released unobtrusively under the supervision of Göring's intelligence chief.[20]

As for Britain's sole outright superiority, that on the sea, there was a minimum of comment in the beguiling gabble. Naval matters were alien and remote so that action against the Royal Navy all but faded into irrelevance. Göring appeared at the Bruly Führer Headquarters during the late June period with a typical proposal. The RAF had startled the Germans with sporadic night bombing attacks against German cities far inland. Like a boy talking gang tactics, Göring proposed retaliation on English cities *"mit ver-x-fachter Kraft"* (with power raised to the nth degree). General Warlimont related how Hitler took instant exception, and then how he explained that "the Englander probably has lost his head somewhat over France's overthrow. That's how I explain these senseless bombings . . . which the RAF might be undertaking on its own . . . . In any case I want to look this over extensively before we reach for the same measures." Göring, content to take his cue from the Führer, offered nothing further on this point. Nor had he offered anything on reducing Britain's power at sea. If the Führer felt no need, neither did he.

Orthodox members of the Air General Staff held no illusions about the situation; they realized that the new circumstances called

[19] Kesselring, *op. cit.*, p. 84. Opportunity occurred to discuss the problem with the Field Marshal and his Chief of Staff, General Wilhelm Speidel, during 1953.

[20] General Schmid, the Air Intelligence Chief, has explained and substantiated to me in detail a description of the deception drops and their use, as organized by him. The packets of material were exhibited to Göring on more than one occasion, and he reported on them to Hitler. The Führer showed himself so pleased that Göring complimented Schmid at mess on the scheme. The drops were made in June before the fall of France, in August, and as late as September 1940 (Germany 1953 and 1954).

for a "new look." The Army presumably had run out of targets, the Navy could continue to plug away at its old ones, but the Luftwaffe faced a changed and challenging picture. Though not completely unanticipated, the heavy new responsibility had arrived too soon. Sober Jeschonnek took the burden to heart and set about producing a directive to deal with it along doctrinaire lines. It issued over Göring's signature on 30 June in a much watered-down version of the signer's habitual hyperbole. The prevailing tone was one of bafflement about how to fill the period of redeployment toward the Channel with a due amount of action. In time, when all was ready, Commander-in-Chief Göring would order planned Air action on selected group targets in England to accord with the general war situation, the directive said, and until such time, action was to be confined to: weak harassing attacks on British industry and aircraft plants; familiarizing flights to probe enemy opposition; attacks on Channel sea traffic. He ordered Fliegerkorps VIII, of *Dunkirk* fame, to take on the Channel job. The resulting operation was later known as the *Kanalkampf* (the Channel fight). No vestige of thought about co-ordinating action with the Navy appeared in the directive, nor was more than passing reference made to the Royal Navy, either at sea or in bases.

The plain truth was that the Air Force was even further adrift about Problem England than were the other two services. All three had a right to look toward OKW for a beacon light to show the way.

The OKW Answer—June 1940

The one mind that could frame an answer on England and make it stick remained relatively serene and unhurried. Hitler turned his thoughts toward relaxation; he wanted his turn at liberty too. The headquarters were being shifted to the Schwarzwald region; while this was in progress he would take his ease. There were scores from World War I to make up. Two comrades from that war joined him to help share memories of 1914-1918 battles while they cruised over the old front. The party left Bruly by car on 25 June, the day all gunfire ceased in France, and made a roundabout way to the new Führer Headquarters, called Tannenberg, in the Black Forest, by the 29th. The Führer relaxed. Between excursions into nearby Alsace and even to Paris, he monologued ideas for his upcoming Reichstag speech. This speech, he frankly advertised, would point for his private plan of settlement with Britain. Meanwhile, OKW planners had set themselves the task of exploring the opposite view of continued war.

Under the stimulus of active warfare and consequent mounting demands, OKW had expanded, as these empires always do; it more than doubled over the original modest skeleton of some dozen officers. The forward echelon of Colonel Warlimont's planning section alone numbered twenty-five officers by 1940. Of these, four represented Army operations, three Air, and the same solitary Lieutenant Commander spoke for naval operations. He was Wolf Junge; his Army running-mate was Lieutenant Colonel Bernhard von Lossberg. For the most part the Warlimont section worked things out on paper for General Jodl. It assembled reference data, advisory information from services, and drafted Führer Directives; but it exercised very little initiative in command planning. Nevertheless, being zealous young people, the officers were far from backward about offering professional opinions, which the Dietl and *Dunkirk* incidents demonstrated. In harmony with the changing situation or the demands of their own services they spoke their pieces; and this proved likewise the case for invasion.

In OKW, more than in other headquarters, the official plan of siege faded into irrelevance after France. Siege, that phantom reality, seemed much too long and laborious and had to make way for the more exciting solution attune to the times. The same pull of the times that moved the planners of the Army took hold in L section of OKW. Of this phenomenon General von Lossberg wrote later:

As our troops stood around Calais after the victory . . . they saw before them the chalk cliffs of Dover on the other side of the Channel. In the exaltation of the past success these German soldiers and their leaders, came to believe themselves capable of things that no one even dared to think of before the West Offensive. Thus, more out of the mood at the front than from the sober evaluation of the Armed Forces Leadership, the thought was born to land in England.[21]

We can establish that invasion talk fired up in the L section immediately after *Dunkirk*. Both Warlimont and Junge recalled conversations about landing during late May, and Junge included von

[21] Von Lossberg, *op. cit.,* p. 89.

Lossberg as partner in their pursuit. Nothing came of them. Shortly after their arrival at the new headquarters, Tannenberg, on 25 June the Young Turks raised the subject again. General Warlimont recalled this too when he wrote:

Very soon after the Armistice with France there once more turned up the idea within my section that an Invasion of England would not be beyond the reach of the victorious German Army, and that it would much sooner lead to an early and definite peace than air and sea warfare alone. At this time, i.e., in the last days of June, I reported to Jodl orally on the subject and found him, at first, thinking on the same lines. He then took up the matter with Hitler and told me that this one showed himself as very reluctant. I had to repeat my inquiries and suggestions several times before Jodl advised me that Hitler would give his consent only to the sharply restricted planning directive of 2 July [1940].[22]

Clearly, General Jodl could not have laid any proposal before Hitler until after the latter's arrival at Tannenberg on 29 June. In the interim it would have been but natural for the conscientious Jodl, now being jogged from below, to put pencil to paper and commence ordering his own thoughts on the war's continuation. By 30 June he had gathered together on six pages the interplay of his own cogitations with those often heard from Hitler. Now Germany and Hitler sat on top, he began, and would dispose. That set the tone of Jodl's summation.[23]

The document reflects the exposure of Jodl, as apart from the L section, to the Führer's private hopes and his plan of action if these failed him. Jodl strove hard to reconcile the whole with the fresh practicalities of the times. General Warlimont surmised as much when he remarked further: "I should think that Jodl's estimate of the situation, which I do not recall in particular, had already been influenced by Hitler's declining attitude [toward invasion] but that it was all the same drawn up by Jodl in order to obtain Hitler's permission at least for [invasion] planning activities." Soldier Jodl could not ignore the fact that the strongest foe remained unvanquished and dangerous; he attempted to meliorate these misgivings wih his Führer's extravagant hopes. He staunchly labeled his summation "The Continuation of the War against England" and launched forth on the old theme of Britain's will to resist: "If

[22] Warlimont to Ansel (Germany, 1953).
[23] The Jodl summation of 30 June 1940 is *IMT* doc. 1776-PS. It faithfully reflected the Hitlerian feeling of the time and at the same time forecast the course of German efforts to resolve Problem England in 1940.

political measures do not lead to the goal, England's will to resist must be broken by force." Two possibilities presented themselves, he thought: direct attack on the English homeland; and extension of the war to Britain's periphery. Under the first he saw three plausible courses of action: siege; psychological warfare through terror attacks on population centers; and landing assault with the object of occupation.

In brief discussion Jodl then fell back on a by-product of Hitlerian vexation at the Great Turning during late 1938. This was that the British thenceforth had to come to him; we perceive in it the very nub of Hitler's posture toward the British at this time and with its help can explain much of the to-and-fro of that summer, 1940. Hitler was intent on making the British eat humble pie. In June 1940 he believed that the situation created by him left the British no alternative. Had he not killed every prospect of action by them on the Continent? What booted it them to continue? Indeed, what could they do but sue for peace? The little man could not get over the immensity of his own deeds. "The final German victory," Hitler/Jodl continued, "including victory over England, is thenceforth only a question of time. Enemy attack operations on a grand scale are no longer possible. Germany can therefore choose a course of action that spares her strength and avoids risks."

This done, a shift was made to the defensive. Hitler wanted merely to hold the status quo of the picture and gradually intensify it by paralyzing England, if necessary, from the air. Again he would cast stones from afar, if need be, but not venture to the boundary line and slug it out. The fight against the RAF stood naturally in the first rank for such tactic, with the added defensive reason of minimizing air dangers to German war economy. Jodl's paper prophesied progress toward wiping out war industries in south England by fighting down the RAF. If the London-Birmingham aircraft industries could be destroyed, there would be no replacements, and with that England must lose all capability of action against Germany. This first and all-important objective should be augmented by war on food stores, imports and exports. Tied in with all would com propaganda and occasional terror attacks. The increasing inroads on supplies would *"paralyze and finally break the will of the people to resist and thereby force their government to capitulate."* (The italics are Jodl's.) The arrogant cocksureness reeks of Hitler and his master strokes of finality.

But surely the British would see the light and make overture. Invasion? Jodl's soldier sense induced him to wring a concession for such finale from his Führer. He proceeded:

A landing in England can be taken into view only if the command of the air has been gained by the German Air Force. A landing should therefore not be undertaken for the purpose of overthrowing England *militarily,* which can practically be achieved through the Air Force and the Navy, but only to deal the death stroke, if still necessary, to an economically paralyzed and in the air impotent England. It is not expected this state will come to pass before the end of August or early September; . . . nevertheless the landing must be prepared in all details as *ultima ratio.*

He finished off the courses of action with a brief, uninspired consideration of peripheral warfare. Thereupon the Hitler/Jodl piece returned to gratifying dream of peace in these concluding words: "Since England no longer fights for victory but only to retain its possessions and its position in the world, there is every expectation she will be inclined toward peace if she learns that this objective can still be gotten relatively cheaply . . . ."

The manifest motif was peace, plus a hedge for the possible need of its encouragement by force in the unhappy, unexpected event Britain should remain recalcitrant. This was the best Hitler's military advisers could get out of him, despite the impatient pull of the times to get along, do something—*etwas veranlassen,* as one heard on the Channel shore, in the troop billets, and even on the street. The leaderhip was not up to it. We think back to *Dunkirk.*

In L section Jodl's fire-eaters set about softening the tone of the planning instructions that they had used to heckle him. He finally approved their revised efforts, and Keitel got around to signing them into the Führer Directive of 2 July. Its chief interest centers around the fact that this paper was the first Hitlerian directive that concerned itself directly and exclusively with landing in England; and as such, it set a mild pace of invasion thinking. The gist of it ran as follows: The Führer and Supreme Commander has decided" that under certain preconditions, of which winning air supremacy is the most important, "*landing in* England *can* come into question." The time, for the present, remains open. Preparations for execution at the earliest possible time are to be initiated. Supporting planning data therefore are desired from the services at the earliest. *Army:* Estimate of British Army strength and capability in the next few months. Judgment on artillery fire and effect from the Continent to augment protection of shipping against British sea forces (in co-operation with the Navy). *Navy:* Judgment on possibility of landing strong army forces (25-40 divisions) in south England in the face of British sea and land forces. Determination of sea areas and means by which troops and supply in this strength can be transported in adequate security. In this connection, landing on a broad front will facilitate a breakthrough by the Army. The kind and amount of transport space available and the time needed to make it ready. *Air Force:* Estimate of whether and when decisive air superiority can be achieved. In what strength can the crossing be supported by airborne landings?

The directive closed with the singular admonition that all preparatory work "must take account of the fact that a plan to land in England has by no means taken firm form and that it is only a question of *preparation for a possible eventuality.*" Who but a peacebemused Hitler could have hung such a deflating caution on the end of an official directive? The paper was of such little consequence to him that he left it for Keitel to sign. Let it go if you must! It was all the answer that OKW could muster up for the problem of England—a weak answer of straddle.

Peace was in the air! June was clearly too soon for working up a storm of any kind, even against Britain.

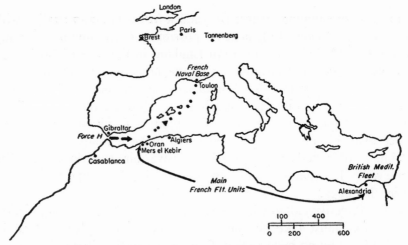

The French Fleet at Mers el Kebir: July 1940.

2 July: British *Force H* (1 carrier, 3 battleships, cruisers, destroyers), under Vice Admiral Somerville, sets out from Gibraltar toward Mers el Kebir to effect the neutralization of the French naval forces there.

3 July: Somerville lies off Mers el Kebir while his officer envoy negotiates with Admiral Gensoul, commanding the French ships berthed behind the breakwater (4 battleships, 3 cruisers, destroyers, submarines).

After several exchanges with Gensoul, none of which brings agreement on how to keep the French ships from the Germans, Somerville opens fire on the French force.

The British fire puts all heavy ships out of action except the new fast battleship *Strasbourg.* Accompanied by assorted small craft she escapes to the home port of Toulon.

French naval units based at Alexandria reached agreement with Admiral Cunningham, commanding British Mediterranean Fleet.

The news of the action at Mers el Kebir bursts in on Hitler at his Headquarters, *Tannenberg,* like a thunderclap.

6. *July Stand By*

The French Fleet

At Compiègne Hitler had called out over the heads of the French to Britain, acknowledging Rule Britannia and pledging to respect that sea realm. "Germany will reduce to a minimum the occupation of the western coast after the cessation of hostilities with Great Britain . . . ," the armistice terms stated. "The French fleet shall be collected in ports . . . demobilized and disarmed . . . . The German government solemnly declare that they have no intention of using the French fleet for their own purposes during the war . . . ." From that day in June forward Hitler's expectation of overture from Britain took on the old assurance of the gospel of association. Nothing else counted; no other outcome was tenable or could scarcely be discussed at Führer Headquarters. A message came from Japan offering immediate entry into the war on the Axis side; Hitler replied, *"Erntehilfe unerwünscht"* (Harvest help not desired).[1] Apparently Hitler meant to take immediate and forthright notice of any British overture in a Reichstag speech. He wanted to prepare a concrete detailed basis of settlement that he would make in response. But the

---

[1] Von Lossberg, *op. cit.*, p. 87, and in conversation. He wrote: "He [Hitler] was firmly convinced that England in a short time would be *friedensbereit* [ripe for peace]. 'The Englanders have lost the war, they have just not noted it yet; one must give them time, they will come around all right,' thus Jodl repeated Hitler's evaluation to us." Hitler's conviction was evidently very strong. It is possible he was deluded by favorable misinformation from England.

British had to make the first move.   Plans for triumphal entry into
Berlin and Reichstag convocation proceeded under the Führer's close
personal supervision.

In such happy anticipation a few pleasant days at Tannenberg in
the Schwarzwald saw June pass into July; Hitler entertained dignitaries and expounded the peace theme on picnics in the beautiful
countryside.   One of the house guests, State Secretary Otto Meissner,
reported an instructive contemporary picture.   He wrote:

> Hitler spoke repeatedly in his table conversations of this, that he saw the
> time had arrived . . . for making a peace proposal on a grand and gen-
> erous scale to Great Britain.   He would therefore, in a Reichstag speech,
> make an offer of a covenanted peace with precise detailed proposals, which
> would accordingly set forth the basis for a peace treaty; he hoped that the
> English people themselves, if their government still resisted, would concur
> with his proposal and thereby exert pressure on the warmonger-led cab-
> inet.[2]

Hitler meant Churchill and Company, but chiefly Churchill himself.   Personal animosity whetted his appetite.   He wanted him
thrown out like Reynaud, in the Continental parliamentary manner,
and he firmly believed this not only probable, but virtually inevitable.
German propaganda drummed on signs of disunion within the British
cabinet.   In London, where invasion fear was mounting, the effect
proved sufficiently dangerous for Messrs. Churchill, Chamberlain,
and Attlee to turn the rumors back on their originator in rousing
speeches of refutation.   The speeches were scarcely necessary, for
the British in turn thought of personalities, and the object of their
scorn was Adolf Hitler.   That he stubbornly disbelieved in the
genuineness of this deep antipathy was one of the remarkable things
about the man.   Some inkling of British irreconcilability came home
to him however on 3 July 1940 when British ships fired on the French
fleet at Mers el Kebir on the North African coast.

On the evening of 2 July the French Navy directed the resumption of normal radio communication; orders implementing the armistice terms commenced to flow out to French ships and units far and
wide.   The terms included the recall of ships to designated ports for
immobilization.   Important French fleet units were based at Mers
el Kebir near Oran, Algeria, where it had been settled that they
would deactivate.   On this same evening of 2 July Force H, the

---

[2] Otto Meissner, *Staatssekretär unter Ebert, Hindenburg, Hitler* (Hamburg, 1950),
p. 448.

British naval striking force at Gibraltar, sortied in strength and headed eastward into the Mediterranean. It consisted of a carrier, three battleships, several cruisers, and the usual destroyers. German intelligence agents in Spain immediately alerted Skl in Berlin to the abnormal move, and all through the day hints of trouble brewing persisted. Word arrived from Wiesbaden, where the Armistice Commission sat, of French concern for their ships. If any headed for France, would not the British intervene? Two French battleships, two cruisers, and sundry small craft awaited the turn of events in British home ports, and there occurred the first confirmatory reaction. Boarding parties from the Royal Navy seized the ships at dawn on 3 July with only one minor scuffle. At Mers el Kebir things took a different turn.

Force H appeared off that French base in the forenoon of this memorable day. Berthed behind the breakwater lay some of France's most powerful naval vessels—four "heavies," including the new fast battleships *Strasbourg* and *Dunkerque,* and three cruisers, plus a number of destroyers and submarines. Several exchanges between the British and French commanders via officer emissary followed. Vice Admiral Somerville, commanding Force H, wanted his French counterpart, Admiral Gensoul, to accept any one of several proposals, cut naturally to the British interest for keeping the French units out of German hands. Somerville was charged with obtaining settlement, and he had to have it this day. Time wore on in polite futilities; no common ground developed. The French ships made ready to defend themselves. Minutes passed into hours, and the end of the day approached. Nothing remained in Somerville's book but settlement by force. At length, in the failing afternoon light he opened fire on the French ships. The ensuing short engagement put most of the heavy ships out of action. The *Strasbourg* alone, with a few destroyers and small craft, escaped and made for the home port of Toulon.

The shots of this dispiriting action—brother-in-arms against brother—echoed round the world, though with little jubilation and even less understanding—understanding of their true import, especially for Germany and her Führer. They struck into Hitler's Tannenberg headquarters like a thunderclap. His naval adjutant well remembered the uproar occasioned. He was not present at the delivery of the news to Hitler but readily recalled the general consternation and the succeeding gloom. The little-realized truth was that the Hitlerian gospel had been dealt a mortal blow. That cardinal tenet of his personal mythology, union with Britain, nursed so carefully in private and to this moment almost realized, was suddenly thrown into doubt. The whole mythological contrivance shook to its roots. Not that he comprehended fully, and certainly not that he lost heart. Far from it. Only the wisdom of postknowledge marks Mers el Kebir for us as Adolf Hitler's first psychological defeat of the war, and thus another turning point. Much of this war was fought more in psychology than in shells and bombs, notably between Hitler and Churchill. The leaders of Britain here punctuated a point in history with the unequivocal force of shellfire. They demonstrated that they would not deal. Realization of this commenced to gnaw at Hitler.[3]

Viewed practically, it took no inspired thinker to recognize this British meaning. If they could go to these lengths against brothers, what would they not muster up for Hitler? They had torn up his solemn promise called out at Compiègne and tossed it aside like a bad check. Though the great self could scarcely admit error, he took pause. He stormed and raged, but beneath, he grew less sure. Perplexity over the British, begun even before their action off Mers el Kebir, was evidenced by various straws, Foreign Office hints to Halder on 30 June, expressions to Italy's Ambassador on 1 July, and grudging approval of Jodl's invasion planning.[4] Mers el Kebir thus gave the final forceful push into an abyss of indecision that found no relief until late July. Confidence dribbled out of the Führer's know-it-all conviction of early *Verständigung* (coming to an understanding), and his wishful private plan began to lose authority.

Self-debate began again. Was this after all a propitious time for making a noble gesture of peace in Reichstag speech? The climate was reminiscent of post-Munich 1938. The short promenade with

[3] An attempt has been made to portray the effect on Hitler of British defiance. Viewed at home, the British action at Mers el Kebir was not dictated by rugged defiance alone, but also by fear of invasion. In some quarters the threat of invasion had already by this time worked up near-panic reactions. Immediately, on 3 July, Hitler in recognition of "the French fleet's outstanding performance" ordered the armistice commision to examine the lifting of certain conditions of the armistice agreement. "The stand of the French fleet," he vouched, "would be taken into account in concluding the peace." From the W. D. Skl, 3 July 1940.

[4] Hitler's expressions to the Italians must always be treated with caution because he often used them as a sounding board to London. He could not, however, obliterate the pattern developed gradually in Ciano's interpretations. Ciano, *op. cit.*, pp. 271-73, shows that both Alfieri, the Italian Ambassador, and Ciano were aware of Hitler's perplexity.

the gospel, begun at Dunkirk and confirmed at Compiègne, was over. Hitler whipped up press and radio. A torrent of anti-British, anti-Churchill abuse spewed from Nazi propaganda organs in confirmation of his discomfiture. Emphasis was personal in the extreme; a soldier's word had been befouled; Churchill was "the greatest criminal in all history . . . . It would not surprise us if the English people . . . were to hang Winston Churchill on a scaffold opposite Nelson's statue in Trafalgar Square." The previous turn, begun in 1938, produced the cry, "England is to blame!" Now with the start of a new cycle, Churchill was to blame. Plans for a grand re-entry into Berlin and a Reichstag speech were already well along when Mers el Kebir broke. The arrangements were speeded for the sixth of July, for Churchill bade fair to steal the international stage.

In a melancholy yet moving report about Mers el Kebir before the House of Commons on 4 July 1940 Britain's Prime Minister said: "Any idea of that [negotiation], should be completely swept away by the very drastic and grievous action we have felt ourselves compelled to take . . . . We shall on the contrary prosecute the war with utmost vigor . . . ." His hearers responded with what the London *Times* called "a remarkable demonstration" of support.[5]

Hitler received the plaudits of Berlin crowds on the afternoon of 6 July. He entered the city at roomy old Anhalter Bahnhof at 1500. On the festooned platform stood a VVIP assortment of ministers, Party functionaries, and the military all backed by a guard of honor from each of the services. As the loudspeakers blared, *"Der Führer kommt,"* a reserved Hitler descended and greeted the dignitaries briefly but not without leveling a shaft at Herr Schacht, the gloomy Minister of Economics. *"Ja, Herr Schact, was sagen Sie nun?"* (Well, Mister Schacht, what do you say now?), he shot out; then into his car and on for triumphal progress through the cheering multitudes toward the Reichskanzlei. Arrived there he gained a balcony and let the crowd cut loose.

Meanwhile the commanders-in-chief stood ignored in an anteroom until Hitler had had his fill. The happy conqueror pose was counterfeit. His true mood burst forth when he turned belatedly to the waiting officers; he ranted about Britain's intransigence almost as though

[5] New York *Times,* 5 July 1940; *Völkischer Beobachter,* 1-8 July 1940; *Times,* Weekly Edition (London), 3, 10 July 1940. See also Maxime Mourin, *Les Tentatives de Paix dans la Seconde Guerre Mondiale 1930-45* (Paris, 1949), pp. 84-87. The course of events was faithfully recorded in W.D. Skl, 4 July 1940.

they had caused it.   General Halder still remembers his own superior's account of the frosty treatment accorded him and how it contrasted with the Party's jubilation.   Hitler's angry mood found no balm in the discouraging Foreign Office reports in Berlin; they confirmed Churchill's villainy.   It was no time for Reichstag convocation.   Soon word circulated that the session had been postponed, "because of a probable reshuffle of the British Cabinet."

Actually it was in Hitler's head that the reshuffle was taking place; he needed time to think through this worst of all dilemmas. Berlin's high German atmosphere was no place for this; its alien spirit had never brought him inspiration.   He picked up and virtually fled to his beloved Berghof below Munich, where genius found freedom and brightness could flow into his soul.   Before flight Hitler received Ciano, who had come up from Rome for the expected Reichstag pronouncement.   Mussolini's emissary confided to his journal on 7 July: "He [Hitler] is rather inclined to continue the struggle and to unleash a storm of wrath and of steel upon the English.   But the final decision has not been reached, and it is for this reason he is delaying his speech, of which, as he himself puts it, he wants to weigh every word."

Doldrums—July 1940

It is a curious thing.   There stood Hitler, at his peak, unassailable, the alpha and omega of Germany, even of Europe.   Yet he was at painful odds with the course of events.   They seemed to be taking a turn different from that he had reckoned on.   The climate of the times and pressure of events would as always exert strong influence from without, but the controlling force in what happened, or did not happen, would in the end arise from the independent and privately formed inner convictions of Adolf Hitler.   Time was when he puzzled over what he wanted.   Now the decision hinged not so much on what, as on how.   He thought he knew well enough what he wanted— settlement with Britain.   The hitch came in figuring how he would come by it.   But that was no longer the whole of it, for now a more bothersome question intruded: whether settlement was necessary, or indeed, wanted at this time.   So badly had Mers el Kebir shaken the private design.

He escaped to the quiet and tranquillity of his chalet on the Obersalzberg and let himself go. "When I go to Obersalzberg," he said, ". . . I feel myself far from petty things and my imagination is stimulated . . . . by night at the Berghof, I often remain for hours with my eyes open, contemplating from my bed the mountains lit up by the moon. It's at such moments that brightness enters my mind . . . . All my great decisions were taken at Obersalzberg. That's where I conceived the offensive of May 1940 and the attack on Russia . . . ." So spoke the self-confessed genius after the evening meal on bleak 2 January 1942. Then again, with the offensive into Russia bogged down, he had need of the Berghof to encourage genius out of that prodigious and inscrutable self that lay at the root of things both in victory—decision—and in failure—indecision.

The doldrums of indecision, that was where he now lounged in carefree Austrian *Schlamperei*. We are in the second week of July 1940. No bustle and hurry, no compelling call to action presses. The Führer seemed content to drift in the apparent security of the moment. Jodl had agreed, there was time to burn and a wide choice of action stood open. Let the situation, and the British in particular, come to him! So ran the prevailing tone as we make it out from contemporary observers and his own utterances.

In essence two courses were open: intensified war on Britain; or intensified peace. But how could one intensify peace, let alone work up a front over it? There was nothing to smash, nothing to rant and storm about. Peace was an abstraction not susceptible to frontal treatment. For subjective effect it could only be invoked reflectively to mirror the glories that might crown it. One could dream of vast projects to be undertaken during peace, of a Continent to be reorganized and netted with a system of *Autobahnen,* but to wage a blitz offensive of peace, how could that be done? The quip "when peace breaks out" nevertheless betrays the dynamism underlying German/Hitlerian thought. The glories would come after mastery of the Continent was realized. Then peace must assert itself, for there was nothing else. Hitler indulged in dreams of this kind to his heart's content. Admiral Raeder found him in a reflective mood on 11 July at Führer Conference.

Only Keitel and von Puttkamer audited this meeting at the Berghof. The Admiral's mood expressed that of the German world generally, as inspired from above. It was a confident mood, almost expansive, and far from reality. He came armed with several papers as

usual, among them one on postwar ship-building plans. They pre-
supposed German mastery of the Continent, supported by a far-flung
Middle African colonial empire and numerous interconnecting naval
bases. Fantastic ideas, we call them, almost puerile in their naïveté,
yet these were the inordinate fancies besetting a suddenly freed powerhouse of eighty-million Germans. They had all gone Hitler. But
Raeder wisely left his maverick ideas for the last; first he brought up
the question of bases nearer at hand, those in Norway. This set Hitler
off to reveal what strange delusions he was feeding on. Raeder's cryp-
tic notes report these remarks: "The most beautiful German city shall
arise apart from Trondheim on the fiord; the city need have no connection with the ship-yards . . . . Reichsautobahn–Lübeck–Fehmarn-
belt–bridge–Szelland–Helsingör–bridge–Sweden–Trondheim . . . .
For use of Swedish territory Sweden gets railroad to Narvik. A road
Trondheim–Kirkenes will be built (partially blasted into the rocks;
10-15 years work)." We can smile at these sallies today, but we
might not have in July 1940 when world-wide anxiety admitted conjectures equally excessive.

Passing lightly over U-boat war, auxiliary cruisers, and Baltic
defenses, Raeder took a tack into reality and elicited a curious query
from Hitler. Raeder proposed that a formal state of siege be declared
against Britain with the expected commencement of intensified action.
Hitler nodded assent, adverting at once, however, to his own plan
to bring Britain around by Reichstag speech. Did the Admiral believe such a speech held promise of success? Whether Hitler thought
that the sea might have given the Navy a deeper insight into British
character or what, it was most extraordinary that he should seek advice in his own forte, the power of the spoken word, from an outsider.
It may give a hint of the depth of his perplexity. Raeder replied
cautiously that the content of the speech had to reach the British
people and then launched into a Douhet-Göring air exposition, far
afield from sailorman doctrine. The British people must be made to
feel the war in their persons through two courses of action: strangulation of sea imports; and heavy air attacks on principal centers.
Attacks at many points were only pinpricks. An early concentrated
attack on Liverpool, for example, was needed to let all the people feel
the war. There was the point of whether these blows should precede
or follow the speech. He favored blows first. London itself was of
great importance, he thought, with its mass of people who could not
be evacuated; the Thames ought to be blocked with mines. Accord-

ing to the Admiral's record, Hitler agreed with these brutal actions; yet one senses an offhandedness and preoccupation with words of peace and not bombs. He was weighing every word of his speech so carefully; the question for him was, were the British people ripe for any such generosity?[6]

Raeder followed his bloodthirsty sermon with a series of heavy salvos against invasion, as though to sink a project believed already badly wounded. We can recall his probing at the last Führer Conference on 20 June when he brought out the suggestion of landing attack as a sort of target to be torpedoed. Since then OKW had issued its planning directive of 2 July, and to it the Admiral now reacted. From a long list he studiously ticked off each item, submitting substantiating papers on each main one. Finally, in Jodl's language he relegated landing attack to the "*last* resort for making England ripe for peace." Strangulation and air attack on centers could achieve the same result alone; thereupon he fired his heaviest personal shot. "The Commander-in-Chief Navy can therefore *not* urge landing in England *for his part,* as he did landing in Norway." He reiterated the now well-worn prerequisites of complete air command and mine-free disembarkation areas. Because of the heavy commitments demanded by these tasks, he said, "preparation should not be ordered until the decision to land has been made." Raeder had used his strongest words and believed that they had scored. He recorded that the Führer likewise regarded "landing as a *last* resort," and that he considered air command indispensable. But this was far from the whole story. Hitler had also shown an unhealthy interest in long-

---

[6] Raeder's out-of-character urging of terror on England can be charged to several influences. He evidently intended a slur at Göring's mismanagement of air warfare, but the overrriding wish was probably to bring an expeditious end to the war, which this moment appeared to offer. The carnival of peace just around the corner had made inroads on the sober Raeder and his staff too. Supporting this view was Raeder's generally negative reply to a second question posed by Hitler at this conference. It was: Should the French Navy be permitted to take part in the war against Britain, say with submarines in the Atlantic? It was the first direct conversation between the two men on the subject of the French fleet since Mers el Kebir. In the interim, the picture had reversed itself. Instead of the Germans driving the French fleet into British hands, the British were now driving the French into the arms of the Germans—who no longer wanted them. French naval aircraft bombed British ships at Gibraltar; the British again attacked the wounded *Dunkerque* at Mers el Kebir, and only two days before they attacked the new battleship *Richelieu* at Dakar and skirmished off Casablanca. The French Navy went white hot. "Let us fight!" the leadership importuned. The German naval leaders reacted haltingly: it was a political question; the French wanted merely to gain bargaining power for the peace terms, and so on. The thought was apparently that peace was close and could be better gained without Frenchmen.

range Channel artillery, which could only mean that he had been con-
niving with Jodl and Keitel on invasion. After a few more points
of expansive agreement by the Führer, the Navy Chief went away
from the meeting confirmed in the happy belief that invasion was as
good as sunk and, in particular, that no physical preparatory measures
would be ordered until the basic decision to invade was fact. These
glad tidings he spread among his associates in Berlin. It was another
of many misreadings of Hitler made by this earnest officer. He had
been duped.

Jodl and staff had been busy making the first outline strokes of an
invasion directive, of which Hitler could hardly have been unaware.
Indeed, the signs are that he had taken a hand. Yet he refrained from
calling Jodl in when Raeder started talking landing attack and let
the Admiral have his say in peace. It was far easier in this enticing
but dubious overwater game to let the Navy carry the negative side.
He betrayed his own invasion plotting, however, by calling Raeder's
attention to the need of speeding the emplacement of coastal artillery
on the Channel. Artillery could protect embarkation ports and also
command the Channel waters during crossing. Much space was devoted to this subject in Jodl's deliberations, and Keitel had isssued a
special covering directive the previous day, 10 July. This action was
the first and, during the doldrum period, the only practical measure
instituted against the island kingdom, but that it in truth owed its inspiration to invasion thought alone is open to doubt. Rather it was
a concomitant of Hitler's defensive posture against everything outside
the European Continent, especially England. It was his *Festung* complex.[7] By the planning directive of 2 July the Army was merely to
render judgment on the efficacy of coastal artillery against British sea
force in the Channel. Much had happened since that day, so that

---

[7] Defense, physical as well as spiritual, possessed Hitler first. This may have
led to his singular fascination for fortresses, big guns, and the like. Every detail
of the Siegfried Line opposite France had received his personal attention, and
when it came to ships he had to have the biggest and strongest battleships in the
world like the *Bismarck* and the *Tirpitz*. The coast of Norway had to be made
impregnable with guns and more guns. Now the guns on the Channel would be a
start on the Atlantic wall toward *Festung Europa*, secure and self-contained. Under
a transparent excuse of providing protection to transports, Hitler indulged his need
to be safe from England, and his wish to hurl shells at her. The Navy Chief of
Staff for Operations, Admiral Schniewind, explained that the extraordinary pressure
exerted from above on the project, from as early as 20 June 1940, indicated it enjoyed Führer priority. Army had been alerted even earlier. On 30 May 1940, OKH
asked Navy to select military targets to a range of 120 km. into England from
Calais. Navy complied with a chart designating twenty-six targets from Harwich to
Beachy Head.

Kietel's follow-up of the tenth ordered, at Führer behest, the actual emplacement of heavy batteries from Calais to Boulogne under Navy direction. The subject apparently fitted in with the planning endeavors of Jodl and staff on invasion.

In talking things over with the staff Jodl started with the remark, "We must set the thing up as an enlarged river crossing," as Navy representative Junge later explained. When thereupon he had reminded his superior that the Royal Navy still enjoyed the freedom of this river, Jodl readily conceded the point, but his words and thoughts continued to course along the line of forcing a bridge over a stream for a fight on the other bank. Or were they Hitler's thoughts? Both were soldiers and this was how soldiers did it. Artillery was needed on the near shore. In this vein the first OKW paper about Invasion England went into production. It must have been underway before the Raeder conference, since it carried the date of only a day later, 12 July 1940. Jodl or Hitler assigned the code name *Löwe* (Lion), perhaps because the job entailed twisting the Lion's tail.

Löwe began in deep pessimism, bewailing the monstrous difficulties before him. *"Die Landung ist schwierig"* (The landing will be hard). Britain commands the sea, Jodl reasoned, and therefore landing is only possible on the south Channel coast where the way is short and we can redress sea command by air power; recognition of this circumstance in England has brought about the massing of her ground forces so they can readily concentrate toward the point of attack; mounting preparations are hardly to be hidden, which makes strategic surprise unattainable. There seemed to be nothing for it but frontal assault; a clever stroke to foil both defenders and circumstances eluded him. So be it, frontal assault across a water hazard, but this assault would be a mighty one. And Jodl set down his general plan in these power-words: "The landing must therefore be effected in the form of a mighty river-crossing on a broad front, where the air force takes the role of artillery; the first wave of crossing forces must be very strong, and . . . bridge building will be replaced by the creations of a sea transport road [*Seetransportstrasse*], completely secure against attack from sea, in the Dover Narrows." Poor Jodl and poor *Lion*. To fight across the sea was a specialty, not just an extraordinary game of cops and robbers.[8]

We miss the normal Army General Staff format about *Lion*; no statement of the problem, no operational objective nor listing of

[8] Löwe is *IMT* doc. 1781-PS.

assumptions. We forget that Jodl worked for Hitler and that the two of them had covered these ground factors in their summation of 30 June, when landing figured solely as coup de grâce. The basics remained, but the circumstances had tightened in the meantime. We detect in this writing heightened landing interest on Hitler's part, as we trace the line of thought. It followed the natural order in which questions might occur to a man of his make-up rather than a prescribed professional sequence. After exalting decision for mighty river-crossing (*gewaltsamen Flussübergang*), what could be more natural than to think of command next. Who would—who could—command Grand Invasion England? Who else but the Führer himself, *natürlich!* Under him each commander-in-chief, the paper specified, was to direct his own forces, the Army to charge an Army Group Commander, directly under the Führer, with the conduct of the operations on the English mainland, as was done for *Norway*. The three commanders-in-chief must pitch their camps close by the Führer Headquarters, and Jodl named exact locations: Army at Giessen; Air near Ziegenberg, which was also to be Hitler's spot; and Navy in Wildungen. Minutiae of this sort divulge the Hitlerian touch.

Next came Preparations, and first among them was how to get over the water. Landing craft must be provided and by the Navy. This question automatically raised another as to the number of bodies to be accommodated and how they would be brought into action. An outline of the crossing and landing attack thus took shape. "It will be necessary," wrote Jodl, "to land the assault elements of seven divisions simultaneously at seven separate places between Dover and Bournemouth . . . ." This stretch, Dover to Bournemouth, was broad-front with a vengeance, some 160 miles, which was well over three times the breadth of the Allied Normandy landings four years later. A conflict of concepts appeared in Jodl's planning. A sea road at Dover Narrows could not serve a front stretching 160 miles westward; apparently he therefore broadened his road westward (to conform to the front) as far as Alderney-Portland, which he gave as the location of a western mine barrier. Thus the river-crossing concept, with its secure sea road in place of bridging, broke down early. We recall the earlier experience of Willemer and Philippi in OKH. The Navy he charged with the determination of embarkation ports, and moreover, landing points, in co-operation with the Army according to sea and tactical considerations. He added punch to this unusual concession to the

Navy from a soldier by saying the sea demands would govern in the end. Junge had got in some licks. Or maybe Hitler was going Navy. We find the succeeding instructions, devoted to the Hitlerian obsession of coastal artillery, insisting that fire control be vested in the Navy, no matter who furnished or manned the batteries. The Army was to retain only batteries K 5 and K 12, which were specially fitted for bombarding deep into England. Further artillery provisions betrayed direct Führer interest again when they emphasized a massing of guns to "command the straits of Dover under all circumstances for prolonged duration." In fact, the Jodl plan continued a notable slant favorable to naval considerations throughout. Having now done with the preparatory steps, he attempted to visualize the runoff of the undertaking.

Yet the thing was not ready to go! There were operational preconditions to be fulfilled, which went beyond mere preparatory measures. We are back with the fatal prerequisites designed to make the operation safe and presage Britain's collapse. Jodl listed five: (1) the moral and actual defeat of the British Air Force to the point where the opponent no longer exhibited any spirit of attack against the crossing worthy of mention; (2) the destruction or dispersal of all British naval forces stationed on the south coast of England; (3) the creation of mine-free crossing routes; (4) the protection of the flanks by mine barriers; (5) operations to nail down British naval forces in the North Sea, as well as those in the Mediterranean by the Italians. The obstacles thus melted away before the wishful imaginings, and nothing was left before the invading troops but the British soldiery. The extravagant preliminaries had disposed of everything except a successful field campaign against Britain's Army; and this the German Army would deal with in short order. This was the end object, the nub of the Jodl/Hitler planning effort, to set the stage for a push-over Army campaign. It grew all the more evident on the following day when Hitler heard and quickly approved the Army plan presented by Generals von Brauchitsch and Halder. But as in his mind's eye he commenced the crossing, one item, Hitler found, had been omitted— the weather. Jodl hastily added favorable weather for boating, flying, and paratrooping as "the prerequisite for success." Now *Lion* was ready to roll.[9]

[9] We labor the prerequisites because they formed a key stumbling block to genuine amphibious thought on the German side. They were taken for granted from superficial early invasion thinking, and their validity was never adequately proofed. Similar preconceptions among the Allies had to be overcome for the Normandy landings.

Lion achieved the peak of fighting *élan* with the words "Mighty River-Crossing" at the beginning and thereupon petered out. He failed to develop the erstwhile crescendo lift, stroke on stroke, toward victory. This characteristic Hitlerian spirit was not present when pitted against England. All these tentative strokes turned into safety devices to assure something never clearly expressed. So it went too with the brief anticlimactic inventory of the actual execution near the end of Jodl's paper. The list was an operational extension of the safety insured by the already accomplished prerequisites. "Passage over and disembarkation," wrote Jodl, will take place *"under the protection of the entire Air Force . . . ," "the mine barriers . . . ."* and "the long range coastal artillery . . . ." He enumerated the considerable tasks falling to the Luftwaffe as follows: to prevent interference by enemy air force and attack enemy naval forces while yet far off from the crossing points; to reduce coastal fortifications that could operate against the landing points, break the resistance of enemy ground forces, and annihilate oncoming reserves; to destroy the principal routes of reinforcement. Even for Hermann these tricks must have made a handful; the words were flat and lifeless. Doubtless the high tide of action would already have been reached for him during the preceding air operations in which he was destined to bring about "the moral and actual defeat" of the RAF. *Lion* held only the one early bolt in his locker. Though he failed to rouse up a Hitlerian Front, he formed a step in a more complex evolution.

The thoughts about *Lion* were the uncomfortable, discordant notes on landing in England that the pull of the times had drawn out of the doldrums on the Berghof. The thinking presented an elaboration of the Hitler/Jodl invasion thesis of 30 June, which had been accepted as *ultima ratio,* but which was now forcing a way into the realm of actable conduct. Every day since June, Britain had revealed herself far from ripe for peace; carnival palled and the German populace wondered what, then, if not peace. News and radio delightedly belabored the arrogant English.

England has a little war!
Aber fern von der Gefahr [But from danger very far]
Sitzen Tom und Fred und Bess
Ganz vergnügt und pitiless [All beguiled and pitiless]
Essen toast und trinken tea
Oh, the little war on Sea! (Ludwig Thoma, quoted in *Völkischer Beobachter.*)

Gone were the stirring reports on military campaigning to rivet attention, to demand restraint and sacrifice. Like many idle soldiers, the populace grew bored and restive. The people and the leadership were falling out of tune, and sensitive politician Hitler began to feel this.

No end was in sight. Doubt and doldrum mood held on; yet inaction would hardly do while public anticipation and professional planning moved invasion adventure from backstage into the footlights. The initiative was slipping away and something had to be done. But what? At Army Headquarters in Fontainebleau landing enthusiasm had pursued the exuberant pace set in early July. Now on the day after Jodl's *Lion* appeared, Hitler prepared to hear the Army chieftains' report. For that conference *Lion* had furnished valuable advance briefing.

The Strength of an Idea Whose Time Has Come

The times pulled, and the Army had to go somewhere. Because this was so, it alone of the services produced a strategical answer to Problem England. We recur to the early July days when the Army General Staff first gave landing ideas official sanction and pronounced the project feasible. By mid-July, invasion din at OKH had become deafening and reverberated along the Channel. The time had come!

When General Halder, Chief of the Army General Staff, returned from Berlin on 2 July with intriguing hints of what the future might hold, his Commander-in-Chief, General von Brauchitsch, took off for his own turn at the capital scuttlebutt. Before he departed, he asked General Halder to initiate some operational thinking on the Russian problem. The request might well have been sparked by Halder's own report that a free hand was desired for Germany in the East. On 3 July in compliance General Halder issued instructions to the Chief of Operations. His journal records the gist: "In the foreground of operational questions stand the question of England, which is to be dealt with separately, and the question of the East. The latter, one must regard from the standpoint of how a military blow against Russia is to be executed to induce her to recognize the dominant role of Germany in Europe."[10] We note the endeavor to keep Britain apart

[10] Information about General von Brauchitsch's direction to General Halder to initiate planning on Russia comes from a footnote of the Lissance translation of the *Halder Journal*. The gist of his instruction to "Operations" is taken from the original German edition.

and to push Russia provisionally into the background. OKH staff sections were reorganized accordingly; two working subsections set up shop in adjacent rooms, one for England and one for Russia. Official Invasion England planning started in earnest. It quickly fastened interest and took the center of the stage between the two plan leaders, Lieutenant Colonel Pistorius with E for England, and his neighbor, Lieutenant Colonel Feierabend for Russia.

Work in E section boomed. Pistorius received first-class support, not only from the Operations section in general but from Halder with his far-reaching resources as head of the Army General Staff. Not a day went by without entry of new invasion items for checking off in his journal or for recording the solution of some puzzling invasion riddle. With naïve astonishment the soldiers discovered one old problem after another in the alien field of amphibious warfare, usually giving little heed to corresponding problems of the sister service, the Navy. Starting with the modest unofficial Operations section survey made in the latter half of June, the new plan expanded swiftly to an assault of six full divisions and more, each backed by armored battalions. The Continental coast from Ostend to Cherbourg would mount the attack on England from the Thames to Lyme Bay. The appointed hour would fall in August, target the fifteenth, for later fog interfered, so they had read. Many technical problems bobbed up. The submersible tanks: could the Channel perhaps be negotiated on the bottom? What of rocket projectors and smoke-laying gear? How out-fit the *Sturmboote* (assault boats of the water engineers)? Rhine river barges: in what way should they be converted, and how would heavy machines be loaded and unloaded? The many questions engulfed the planners, yet things began rolling and at a truly dizzy pace. The practical problems were turned over to a special experiment staff under General Hans Reinhardt, who was to work them out at Putlos on an old firing range in Kiel bight. No better man could probably have been found than tough tankman Reinhardt, who commanded the XXXXI Corps before Dunkirk and who had urged pushing forward at that time. By 11 July, when the Navy believed invasion had been squelched forever at the Berghof, a greatly inflated Army plan rounded into shape.

Navy Headquarters, Berlin, felt only occasional reverberations from the distant Army clamor and shrugged them off. To most blue-water sailors amphibious warfare has always been a dirty stepchild, and the German seamen proved no exception. To them Invasion

England was assuming the guise of an unwanted Army child, and in consequence naval tasks took on a convenient ancillary character completely free of command responsibilities. The Skl war diary of 9 July stated: "Undertaking essentially to be regarded as a transport problem." On the following day the diarist added, "Skl does not believe it would serve a useful purpose to strive for conduct of the combined operation through the Navy." It amounted to abdication on the part of the Navy. Skl strove to evade the inevitable by temporizing, and at length became by this tactic the eternal objector. American evolution of landing power, later in the war, followed a similar course; stimulus came from Army demands and incitement, rather than from Navy foresight and co-operation.

General von Brauchitsch and his assistants early became aware of this countercurrent from Navy. He called in his Chief of Engineers, General Alfred Jacob, and told him what was up—landing in England. He wanted to do something about it and explained that he felt the Navy might let him down.[11] Jacob and his engineers were to get behind the material and technical requirements and push them. What Brauchitsch in effect demanded was a private Navy so he could do without the Kriegsmarine, should that become necessary. General Jacob got busy, and soon the working levels of the Navy fell in line; he encountered but few blocks. Army water engineers and Navy sailors grew interchangeable and together learned to perform veritable amphibious miracles. This usually happens on the praxis levels.

Planning held back at Navy. Not until 9 July did the brethren of the sea at Berlin get around to talking about a special staff to look into this tremendous undertaking, and then they were kicked into it by a visit from General Reinhardt, in search of personnel and co-operation for his technical experiments. High time. Fricke detailed Reinicke to act as wheelhorse of a group that took its name from the old 1939 Army study; it was called *Sonderstab Nordwest* (Special Staff Northwest). The first paper put out seemed to accept the Army concept of expanded river-crossing by suggesting a front that corresponded to Fricke's Area Red of late May. It reached from longitude 1°30′ East, the vicinity of Margate on Thames mouth, to 1°30′ West, near the Isle of Wight. That stretch met the Army's desideratum. Then followed a list of questions designed to keep the Army planners occupied, but it also advertised a rebellious Navy attitude: what troop units are to be embarked? How are they to be allocated

---

[11] Told to me by General Alfred Jacob (Germany, February 1953).

to waves? What equipment, munitions, and fuels accompany the troops? Where does the Army General Staff wish to load? Where land? And so on, and on, and on. The paper closed with a plaint about the disproportionate work load heaped upon the Navy and a sanctimonious cheer for the cautions it had urged six months earlier at the time of *Studie Nordwest*. Not a very helpful piece of writing, this start at earnest invasion planning. General Halder recorded an unsympathetic reception for the Skl questions and the centralization of planning they implied. The Army was in the saddle and figured on staying there by force of precedent, plus the help of a few more naval liaison officers, then urgently demanded. These problems cannot be solved by liaison channels. Naval representatives were desired only for expert testimony and to be told what to demand of the Navy. No one mentioned the need of strengthening Army representation at Navy. These things are always two-sided, as both services would learn again.

What the poor little shallop of a German Navy had less of than anything else were sailormen to liaison for, or run, such a stupendous job. Navy was beset from every side and commenced to feel the warming curiosity about England, even from the unworried and free-wheeling Luftwaffe. To this point not a sign of interest had emanated from that quarter. The flyers had been enjoying something of a lull while regrouping closer to the Channel. On the same day that General Reinhardt looked in on Skl to ask about personnel for landing experiments, the Chief of the Air General Staff, General Jeschonnek, appeared with ideas on expanded air operations. He wanted to pry the naval air squadrons away from the Navy for the coming conquest of England. Skl had its own thoughts about employment for the naval air groups, and Göring's groups as well. Support for siege still stood to the fore, but that growing absorption, invasion, needed air support also.

The inner circle of Skl met as usual with Admiral Raeder in the forenoon of 12 July. The Chief gave a fill-in on the Führer Conference of the preceding day at the Berghof; his recital favored the view that the Führer and he were in agreement, but despite his brushing off invasion as *"das letzte Mittel"* (the last means), talk swung toward landing questions, and seemingly with fresh confidence and interest. Captain Loycke, liaisoning at OKH for the Navy, had forwarded an outline of Army ideas, and Keitel's directive from OKW about accelerating emplacement of coastal artillery near Calais was on hand.

Out of the ensuing discussion came the following skeleton estimate as entered by the Skl diarist:

The British can interfere with mounting preparations, crossing and landing in the Straits of Dover, by air, by naval forces of all kinds, and by coast defenses.

Own opposing possibilities are:

(1) Gaining air command in the sea area and coastal zone, a task for C-in-C Air.
(2) Exercising sea command of the crossing lanes by barring ingress with coastal artillery and mine barrages. The barriers to run: on the north flank, from Rytingen (off Dunkirk) to Thames mouth; on the south flank, from Boulogne to the vicinity of Dungeness.
(3) Destroying British coastal and ground defenses by German artillery and air attack.

Thus, useful thought for the project was being provoked on the Navy side, yet pitifully little. While the discussion was still in progress, the head of naval ordnance joined in to advise that the performance expected from the coastal artillery was not justified. Knowing Hitler's predilection for the monster guns, he recommended that the true lesser capabilities be made plain to the Führer.

Navy and Army each labored under the delusion that it had the inside track with the Supreme Commander. The origin of the Loycke outline of Army planning, which Skl was discussing, is obscure. It bore the date of 11 July and the label *Studie Nordwest*; its provisions carried the hallmark of the late June unofficial OKH thinking in that it proposed a thrust on either side of Dover. Otherwise the demands were relatively modest and the tone, conciliatory. This outline may have been a sop thrown to Loycke to quiet the Navy, and to this extent it succeeded. The Navy, already having been reassured by its Chief, was now doubly misled by an apparent Army blind. For this reason and another the Loycke version is worthy of notice. The second reason is that among the early conjectures this one came closest to the plan finally worked out. Four action phases were projected: first, seizure of a sixty-mile beachhead from Margate to Hastings; second, expansion to obtain elbow room, from Hastings to Portsmouth; third, operations against south England to gain a line from Maldon in the East to Severn mouth in the West; and finally, occupation of all England. Six reinforced infantry divisions were to carry the beachhead; two additional ones, plus two motorized with armored units, were allocated for the second task. From there on new estimates would be required. Navy saw in this collection some hopeful tangibles for comparison. The differences did not appear irreconcilable: a thirty-mile beachhead on the Navy side against one of sixty miles for the Army; six assault divisions sounded much better than the staggering twenty-five and up that had been hinted. Yet the small common ground between Army and Navy failed of exploitation; each service went its own way along the route of its own jealous pride. Navy furtively hoped for reprieve by Führer halt order, while Army joyously expanded on a do-it-yourself basis. It was to prove a dangerous division.

The plan Army presented for Hitler's approval two days later, swiftly sanctioned by him, differed radically from the one slipped to Loycke. Generals von Brauchitsch and Halder arrived at the Berghof at 1100, 13 July, with their preview of Invasion England at finger-tip readiness. In a few pithy lines of record General Halder revealed his strong grasp of the job to be done and how to go about it. One notes a marked contrast to Jodl's rambling unschooled *Lion*.

Introductory remarks on over-all objectives of Armed Forces. Task of Army. Basis for attainment. Time factors. Strength.
Conduct of the attack:

I. *Enemy:* Ground forces, coastal defenses, distribution and expected actions.
II. *Own Deployment:* Coast, terrain England, mounting base, disposition and strength estimate at hop-off. Further actions.
III. *Own Task Organizations:* and technical preparations.
IV. *Own Scheme:* River-crossing, landing, development of attack—strength estimates and organization.
V. *Summary of Proposals:* and demands on other arms.
VI. *Time Schedule:* and preparations initiated by now.

We grow aware of the prodigious growth the plan had undergone; if noticed by Hitler, this elicited no discussion worthy of Halder's record. In fact, whatever the exchanges with the Führer, they could not have been of any great content or heat, for General Halder entered simply: "Recommendations are accepted as a basis for practical preparations. Order for practical preparations, which are to start immediately, given." Apparently there had been little or no back-and-forth discussion, only a suggestion on the Führer's part about possibly raiding the Isle of Wight, and his familiar anxiety about coastal artillery. Nothing but harmony and complete agreement with the Army planning, plus a gratifying order to commence preparing at once. But how astounding!

For the second time we have caught Hitler rising to crisis by apparently deciding a far-reaching action extemporaneously, almost casually. The outcome of the war was this time truly in the balance, and he tipped the scales as coolly as if he had been dealing out a pound of sausage. No pause for more data: no queries. This constituted the first formal exchange with the Army on this totally alien subject—but no dither or procrastinating over the huge price, no weighing of alternatives, only simple, forthright approval, and what is more, implementation by order. Hitler took no notice of the shift from all previous utterances, nor did the Army representatives, who had their desired answer. The answer is just as hard to square with habitual Hitlerian performance as was his pat affirmative answer to Göring on 23 May when the German tanks had the BEF at their mercy in the Dunkirk pocket. The patterns of the two instances correspond closely; in the former instance the Army was left out; now it would be the Navy. The truth in both cases was that predecision was already formed and needed only to be uttered in an affectation of quiet finality. The way is clear for judging what this latest predecision may have been made of.

The entire Brauchitsch-Halder visit lasted scarcely two hours, yet time remained after invasion presentation for canvassing the politico-military situation. Hitler dropped some significant hints of things to come. He suggested that, rather than deactivating thirty-five divisions as planned, the troops of twenty be merely furloughed so as to keep them readily available for recall. Prospect of peace seemed on the wane. The Führer breezed on confidently, as with Raeder, to touch upon Spain and getting her into the game to complete Britain's isolation; on Russia's interest in restricting German expansion; on redrawing boundaries in the Balkans; and on to Africa, where he was reserving the coast, as well as the French and Belgian Congo, for Germany. Through it all Halder noted, however, his recurring primary preoccupation with Britain and why she was unwilling "to go the way of peace." "He sees," wrote Halder, "as we do, the answer in British hope of Russia. He reckons therefore on having to compel England by force to make peace. But he does this sort of thing reluctantly. Reason: If we smash England militarily, the British world empire falls in pieces. From that Germany gets nothing. German blood would have gained something for the good of Japan, America, and others."

He was losing faith in petition from England and painfully was laboring through a decision to use force against the island kingdom. Hitler's perplexity had not left him, nor had the times ceased their call for action.

The nature of the force to be invoked would be of a peculiar Hitlerian brand, as we shall see, but force it remained. The hour had struck long since; gradually its pull crept up on Hitler, and he perceived that he must respond. With Jodl he moved invasion from the background of last resort into the foreground and attempted feebly to beat up a Front over *Lion*. The more he beat, the weaker and less aggressive the beast got; inspiration failed. And as usual in such circumstance Hitler took the easier option of straddle. Preparing to strike could not hurt him mortally; let practical preparations come into view. They could always become useful. So, Hitler gave in to the strength of an idea he could not withstand, but with his own twists of meaning and intent. We shall discover more and more of them as the story unfolds. There were many ingredients in this tentative move toward war, in place of longed-for-peace.

An unpredictable force was being loosed, one that could readily get out of hand. Political operator Hitler may have reckoned without his host. Once one is committed to an operation of these proportions, holding back is fraught with complications. Walking the cat back can be harder and more harmful than urging her on. The thing gathers its own momentum and rolls of itself. The Führer of the Germans did not know it on 13 July 1940, but on that day, when he coolly sanctioned the Army plan, he surrendered a substantial part of his erstwhile freedom of action. He committed his initiative to a gigantic military undertaking on which he had made no decision, and with him were committed the Germans, their Fatherland, and all its resources, as well as those of all Europe.

Lion *Becomes* Sea Lion

After the perfunctory Führer approval of the Army plan on 13 July, Jodl's quaking *Lion* took heart and began swift transmigration into the skin of a blustering *Sea Lion*. That is the name and character fastened on Invasion England 1940 when, on 16 July, Hitler signed Directive No. 16, which ordered initiation of physical preparations for the undertaking. In the Warlimont staff of OKW, General Jodl, who usually affixed such code designators, was noted for selecting names far too suggestive of the true operation. That surely was the case in this instance. According to Junge, the name *Sea Lion* floated about OKW for some days and by usage at length gained legality. In German the name is *Seelöwe,* and to most Germans any of the comical seals in the excellent and numerous German zoos pass for sea lions. In true identity sea lions are overgrown seals who inhabit the shores of the North Pacific. In America they frolic on beaches and rocks off California. They grow to size like true Californians, and the bulls of one variety reach a ton in weight. Says an authority: "Sea lions pride themselves on a loud roar, the cows have a raucous growl. The pups howl. In fact, all seem to try to make noise continuously." This German *Sea Lion* of summer 1940 ran true to form.[12]

Hitler lost no time in setting him a-bellowing. On the very day of the beast's birth he despatched a long letter to Mussolini, telling him of the impending attack on England. This counted in OKW as a direct message to London. The Führer's intention to make a generous proffer of peace had likewise been repeatedly advertised through these same Italian channels; only the day before the Italian Ambassador, Alfieri, telephoned Rome from Germany that the Reichstag speech was still under consideration. It is not unlikely that a Churchillian salute of consolation to France for Bastille Day had helped stir the lion in Hitler.

Even to us in America Churchill's call rang through the tumult of Democrats in convention at Chicago and the question of a third-term president. Over there, the old warrior took a new "no quarter" stand against invasion; he had set the pace in June, quickened it on 4 July after Mers el Kebir, and returned to the charge on the evening of Sunday, 14 July. We rehear him loose one defiant salvo after another and our pulse still quickens. "We shall seek no terms, we shall tolerate no parley. We may show mercy, but we shall ask none . . . . But Hitler has not yet been withstood by a great nation with a will power the equal of his own. . . . in our island we are in good health and in good heart. . . . let all strive without failing in faith or in duty, and the dark curse of Hitler will be lifted from our age." Bitter medicine was this for that Austrian master of oratory on the Berghof. About this time he decided to summon the Reichstag

[12] Hitler entertained a fondness for the word "lion." He often quipped, "On land I am [a] lion, but with the water, I don't know where to begin."

into session at Berlin for the nineteenth of July. His guns had been all but spiked.

We descend from the lofty heights to trace the reaction the *Sea Lion* directive encountered on the levels below. Army's OKH hardly had need to await the arrival of the printed word, the Chiefs having been assured by the Führer personally that they might go ahead. General Halder wasted no time. Immediately on his return from the Berghof to Fontainebleau he called a conference of staff section heads. Troop build-up along the Channel took shape on paper and so did a new command organization; a map maneuver was set in train to test the Pistorius operational beginnings. By the seventeenth Halder recorded that invasion arrangements *"can now be officially started,"* and accordingly he alerted the field forces by wire. Attack Group Calais, AOK 16 (AOK abbreviates Armeeoberkommando, that is, Army Command), would issue from the region between Ostend and the Somme to assault the English coast from Margate to Hastings; Attack Group Le Havre, AOK 9, from the Dieppe–Caen area, would assault the opposite coast between Brighton and Portsmouth; and Attack Group Cherbourg, AOK 6, was to be held ready to hit on either side of Weymouth. It would be Rundstedt again, this time commanding the main effort as a *Generalfeldmarschall*. The operations mushroomed in forces and scope along these lines with rising invasion fever about the halls of OKH. There are always more heads and hands to go around in army establishments. Navy's reception of *Sea Lion* in Berlin was far less happy.

The news broke in on Skl by telephone on 15 July: Practical preparations for invasion ordered to begin at once. It was unbelievable! Twice, frantic phone calls were made to OKW requesting verification. But there it was. Admiral Raeder's worst fears seemed realized— precipitate order for invasion, no time to prepare, and certainly no conception of what was involved. We can see the sailor heads shaking; they still refused to believe it fully and hoped for some mistake to show up shortly. The blow struck with double force, for the sons of Neptune were far at sea in a dream world of their own, checking off prospective German naval bases in Africa—Dakar, Freetown, along to Fernando Po, off-lying St. Helena and Ascension, around to Zanzibar, Mombasa, the Seychelles. These absurdities are a matter of record in the Skl war diary. Think of the havoc that the reality of *Sea Lion* order could wreak on such fancies and on other bona fide plans closer to home—siege, for instance. What was

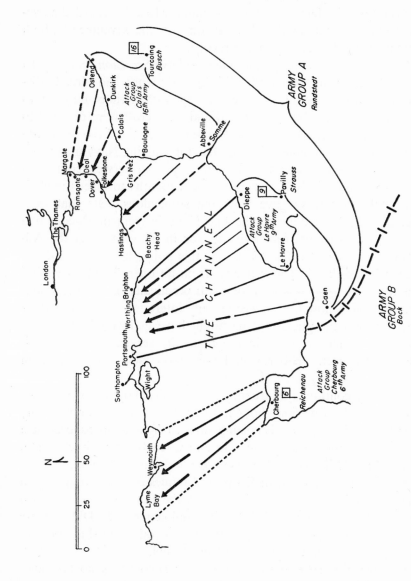

Army (OKH) invasion plan of mid-July 1940. This plan persisted as the basic
Army concept.

to become of it? Should the Navy speak out or hold its peace? Raeder resolved to stick by his guns, which meant oppose invasion, and to speak as required. Diarist Heinz Assmann on 15 July recorded a five-page evaluation and another lengthy one on the seventeenth, both made with meticulous care for the record.

Most alarming was the requirement to have *Sea Lion* ready by 15 August, a scant four weeks off. Exploratory work had already disclosed immense material problems along with serious dangers to Germany's internal economy if canal and river craft were diverted to invasion use. Aside from all this, the seamen doubted the feasibility of such a gigantic sea undertaking. The top-ranking Navy men never freed themselves of these initial doubts, yet no service contended harder and more faithfully during the next months to meet the challenge. All other tasks gave way; the stupendous feats that were accomplished were tribute to the fine Navy instrument Raeder had created. But different from *Norway,* for in his own heart the Admiral had no place for *Sea Lion.* At this point, however, he drove to meet the deadline. Theoretically, from an operational viewpoint, that date, 15 August, was well founded; practically, it was utter nonsense. Knowing how little invasion truly interested Hitler, von Puttkamer ventured the guess that he might have deliberately made the preparatory period so short in the hope the services would find it impossible to meet. Hitler would thereupon have gained freedom to continue only a byplay to keep up appearances.

The Navy continued its truancy from reality, hoping for reprieve, and confining its invasion thought to transport space for so many soldier bodies instead of visualizing how to fight them ashore on a hostile beach. On 17 July came an end when Führer Directive No. 16 arrived at Skl in print. Up rose a fresh chorus of lament. Fricke took up his role of fixer with OKW and requested final confirmation of the Führer intention in writing. Was the Führer aware that *Sea Lion* preparations would wreck the internal economy? Did he truly want this? And so on in staff language: Do you mean this, no fooling? He got an affirmative answer from Keitel.

Directive No. 16 that so disturbed the sailors was no profound piece of writing; not a sign of genius relieved its singularly ignorant and inept passages. Instead of clarion call to battle, the preamble opened its subject with apology: "Since England, despite her hopeless military situation, still shows no sign of readiness to come to an understanding, I have decided to prepare a landing operation against England and if necessary to carry it out." The old iffiness of Jodl's summations lent a provisional flavor to all that followed. The Army had got a strategic objective (missing from *Lion*) inserted next: "Purpose of the operation is to eliminate the English homeland as a base for the continuation of the war against Germany, and if required, to occupy it completely." In fact, as was to be expected, Führer Directive No. 16 combined Jodl's *Lion* and the Army plan of 13 July, and thus pushed *fait accompli* over on the Navy.[13] A Navy ear immediately apprehends a predominating ring of Army about the language and a conspicuous silence of Navy tones. True, Navy had shied off and abandoned its basic invasion interest; yet once invasion was ordered, only ships and craft of the Navy could put the troops over. It could have been that OKW deliberately excluded authoritative naval participation in the final development of the directive to avoid unanswerable objections and to force acceptance on the reluctant sailors with signed order. This suspicion gains strength by the heavy Army flavor of the General Plan in the next paragraph. It followed the pompous words, "For this purpose I order the following": "1) The landing must run off in the form of a surprise crossing on a broad front . . . [of some 160 miles] . . . whereby elements of the Air Force will play the role of artillery, and elements of the Navy the role of Engineers." This was pure Army river-crossing lingo, with only the word "river" omitted. Jodl's substitute bridge of a sea transport road at Dover Straits had been erased, and the Navy had been amalgamated with the Army Engineers. After suggesting advance seizure of the Isle of Wight and Cornwall, the General Plan closed with the bombshell of deadline date: "The preparations for the whole operation must be closed off by mid-August." Naturally, the Army would experience little trouble in moving troops to embarkation points by 15 August, but what would the troops embark in? The game was all Army, in doctrinaire field operating fashion—roll up the trains at rail heads and load them.

Lion prerequisites—a defeated RAF, the use of mine-free routes, the laying of flank mine barriers, the readiness of coastal artillery, a neutralized Royal Navy—filled paragraph 2 of the order; and again like *Lion,* little action would remain for *Sea Lion,* except to swim across and take over. For that high moment Hitler made command provision in the succeeding paragraph, "under my Command and according to my general directives the Commanders-in-Chief will lead

[13] Führer Directive No. 16 appears as *IMT* doc. 442-PS.

those elements of their forces committed." He named his own command post as Ziegenberg and required the service command staffs to set up by 1 August within a radius of thirty miles.

What this galaxy could not have done with a show the like of *Sea Lion!* Our imagination flashes ahead to S Day and a bang-up circus performance, rich in Dietl and Dunkirk explosions, a whole chain series of them. Imaginary though it be, our flight nevertheless underlines the jeopardy in which the faulty command structure placed *Sea Lion* from birth. It constituted his gravest weakness. There was only Hitler from whom the soul of a plan could issue; he had appointed no accountable professional clothed with authority or responsibility for getting *Sea Lion* ready and going. As a result, instead of a natural flourishing growth under an interested sponsor, as problems were surmounted, each one uncovered condemned *Sea Lion* further to an unremitting three-cornered wrangle. The three arms went separate ways along the tasks prescribed.

The Army tasks required but small space in the order: produce an operation plan for the first wave; allocate the transport craft (mind you) to the troops; and determine with the Navy the points of embarkation and debarkation. Purely naval assignments were equally brief: provide the means of crossing; assemble the craft at embarking ports desired by the Army. Aside from the over-all protection to be provided by the Air Force, the Navy had the responsibility for guarding the flanks of the crossing. Well over twice as much writing was given over to assigning the Navy the nonnaval engrossment with coastal artillery. (V-1 and V-2 must have been the final product of this strange complex.)

Direct command during crossing was left a deferred question. Presumably the operation plan to be produced by the Army concerned the land fight; but *Sea Lion* was a shore-to-shore landing fight that began at departure from the friendly near shore. His highest hazards rose from the water, and there was where contol was missing. Serious misapprehensions befogged the German invasion thinking.

The Luftwaffe tasks bore out the preposterous assignments made in *Lion*: prevent interference by enemy air forces; neutralize beach defenses; break the resistance of defending troops; and interdict movement of reinforcements. There was more. The order lumped the Royal Navy with mobile land reserves in the following language: "Further [the Air] will destroy important roads for the movement of enemy reserves and will attack approaching enemy naval forces far from the crossing points." Hitler and many Germans believed the Luftwaffe actually possessed powers equal to these prodigies.

The beleaguered order-writer's delight, the catch-all paragraph in which all things forgotten and those thought of at the last moment can be included, constituted the final one, paragraph 5, for *Sea Lion,* too. Full advantage was taken of its license with ten assorted items. We mention only the last, which recurred to the order's grave weakness on the question of command. The Navy had abdicated; the Army had settled for control by indirection; the Air was not interested. General Reinhardt from Putlos, with only short experience in the problems of loading and unloading landing craft, pled for a "high ranking staff charged with all preparations, and a commander unreservedly empowered to act." But Hitler had to consider that with a top professional command *Sea Lion* could prosper too well and thus get out of hand. General Warlimont of OKW wrote in 1953 in reply to a query about the loose command structure: ". . . a proposal to set up a special commander would certainly have been refuted by Hitler, also for the further reason that, as he saw it, political issues of the utmost importance were constantly involved in every step of the military preparations for this action." The same problem had occurred before *Dunkirk,* where we found Hitler jealously insuring exclusive control for himself when pitted against the British alone. Political and psychological overtones were always present to drown out solid strategical aims. Conceivably he saw safer gains in *Sea Lion* toward his devious private plans if the project developed in several directions at once under his own general guidance. *Sea Lion* did just that.

Peace and Reichstag Circus—July 1940

So Hitler had chosen war. At any rate he fostered a climate of renewed storm in his immediate surroundings from mid-July onward, by demeanor, order, and actions. The climate lacked authority, for at the same time he seemed loath to abandon thoughts of peace; neither had that hope died in Britain, in France, and in the world generally. The trouble came in defining what peace was to mean. To Hitler and Company it meant hegemony over the European Continent, while to the world it signified surcease from Hitlerism and a return to ante bellum days, with perhaps a few adjustments. Peace plots, great and small, direct and crooked, had to play themselves out, but the one among the many that never reached finale was Hitler's own peace play. It proved the most devious of all, likewise the most instructive.

Schemes for ending the war abounded both in and out of Germany. They alone make more than a story, and among them the so-called Resistance Movement (against Hitler) ranks foremost. It has no place here, especially so because Hitler was not party to it, for the good reason that his removal, as a precondition of peace, was included. The movement against Hitler established excellent connections with high places in Britain and elsewhere. The British moved warily. Grave risks faced the German participants. Sympathetic Germans still feel the movement did not receive the trust and co-operation deserved. We shall confine ourselves to Hitler's own peace offensive and a serious endeavor of a Dutch citizen that paralleled Hitler's of this time in July 1940. He was Dr. Albert Plesman.

By July 1940 Hitler had exhausted all channels but one for relaying his peaceful sentiments to England; the remaining one was his speech. In his earlier tenders he had not neglected the American press. On 11 June, with France tottering, he granted U.S. newsman Karl von Wiegand an interview, the first such in years. He assured Wiegand that he was innocent of designs on the Western Hemisphere and furthermore that he had never wanted the destruction of the British Empire, and thereupon suggested the replacement of warmonger Churchill. A week late, Ribbentrop parroted similar assurances to Ciano ostensibly for transmission to London: no destruction of the British Empire; Britain need only recognize the *fait accompli* and renounce a few of her possessions. If she chose peace on these terms, the Führer would be happy to collaborate; if war, it would be total destruction. Both parties, German and British, nibbled toward negotiation through agents. Nothing at all concrete developed, for the agents were merely gathering intelligence, yet either from his own eager image of these flimsy bits, or from undercover maneuvers that he may have instigated privately, Hitler grew so confident of what-will-you-settle-for feeling in Britain that he cut loose from the subtle approaches and turned his mind toward going directly to the British people. He took up the composition of his peace speech, it may have been, with the bizarre idea of pushing the British over and unseating Churchill at one stroke.[14]

[14] New York *Times,* 15 June 1940 and *Times,* Weekly Edition (London), 19 June

Came the shock of Mers el Kebir to drive him into doldrum re-appraisal. Time and again however the old longing for association reasserted itself in monologue and table talk. "I must not give up; the English will eventually see it my way," his naval aide used to hear the hard-dying hope burst forth. The spiritual weather, though cheerful enough, grew fitful and unpredictable, like that of Godesberg in 1938. But things were so changed now; Germany and Britain were locked in a death struggle, and time was wasting. How could he bring Britain around? Or need he?

Perhaps it would be better for his Continental aims merely to keep Britain prostrate. That was the dirty thought. Peace carnival was skidding out of control, and peace might not do at all, certainly not if the English refused to concede German predominance in Europe and could rise again to threaten the German rear. It began to dawn on him that accession to compromise spelled defeat to the British just as plainly as overthrow on the field of battle. Compromise would mean a complete reversal of policy, and besides, Britons preferred trial by arms when it came to Hitler. This attitude had remained obscure to moral-bankrupt Hitler, and to most of the victory-surfeited Germans. Yet something had to be done. In the slow realization that took shape, he prepared to accept military neutralization of England in place of peace; at least he was done with generous proffer. Perhaps union need no longer come first.

To say that Hitler came to a hard and fast conclusion to postpone peace would be saying too much. Fond hope of a break, bringing settlement, never let him get that clear on England. Exactly this had been the content of doldrums and continued dilemma. However, peace as the one and only solution lost stature, and markedly so between the eighth and nineteenth of July. Events of this span support a gradual shift, which not only admitted doing without settlement, but sought support for such a departure. Amid Berlin fanfare of 6–8 July Hitler abruptly postponed his Reichstag speech with its touted peace message. On 9 July he abandoned Berlin for his beloved Berghof. He showed himself in Munich on the tenth. On the eleventh at the Berghof he dreamed of Germania with Raeder, but also asked advice on Britain and the effect of his speech-to-be on her. Raeder counseled more force before a peace proffer. Meanwhile

---

1940. *Ciano Diplomatic Papers* (London, 1948), pp. 373, 378. Hesse, *op. cit.*, pp. 103-106. *The Memoirs of Cordell Hull* (New York, 1948), I, 844, 845; Weizsäcker, *op. cit.*, pp. 294, 295; von Hassell, *op. cit.*, p. 145.

Jodl worked on invasion plan *Lion,* whose outlines revealed Hitlerian touches.   On 13 July Hitler approved the Army invasion plan, yet confessed puzzlement over British intransigence to von Brauchitsch and Halder.   The next day Churchill told him and the world in a broadcast that Britain would "seek no terms . . . tolerate no parley." On the fifteenth Hitler responded with a long letter to Mussolini, apprising him of decision to invade; on the sixteenth he signed Führer Directive No. 16 into action; on the seventeenth he returned to Berlin for fevered revision of his speech; on the eighteenth he presided at a victory parade at Brandenburg Tor, and on the nineteenth he spoke for one hour and thirty-five minutes in the Kroll Opera House at Reichstag session, not to the British public, but to the German people, whom he wanted to unite for more war.   Two words characterized the beginning and end of this progression from peace to war, *Gross-zügig,* or grandly generous, which expressed Hitler's overflowing cup of victory in the West, and *Vernunft,* or reason, to which he attempted return after facing a recalcitrant Britain.   At Kroll Opera House he used the word "reason" to frame his proffer of peace.

The Nazi delegates were all in their appointed places on the main floor, ring upon ring of them.   In the center of the first balcony glittered the regalia of Germany's military, and from the flanking boxes amid drapery of red-white-black peered favored diplomats and Party notables.   Presiding under a mammoth swastika hulked Göring at the speaker's desk.   In front of him a calm and uncommonly low-speaking Führer proceeded with an accounting.

Skilfully he re-enacted the war's miracles and led the expectant audience step by step naturally to the summit of victory.   He detailed the feats, beyond all credibility, of the past ten months in measured tones, bringing them to a high point of pride in achievement.   Here came pause to bestow promotions on doers of these deeds, amid thunderous prolonged applause.   Göring clapped happily, and gesticulated toward his Milch and Kesselring as they were raised to *General-feldmarschälle.*   But his own accession to *Reichsmarschall,* of which there was not one other, furnished the true climax of the happy circus. Hitler passed on with a shift toward the enemy; he went into a derisory attack on the British leadership.   In bitter, spiteful words Churchill got the brunt.   He taunted him on rumored plans to remove the seat of government to Canada (a real fear in Hitler's own heart) and then adverted to British connivance with Russia, assuring the audience of its futility.   He had other assurance; he had never intended even to injure the British Empire, whose doom he forecast if war continued. The great moment of so much preparation and so much fanfare had arrived. In fifty-seven colorless words Hitler voiced his empty bid for peace: "In this hour I feel duty bound before my conscience once again to direct an appeal to reason even in England. I believe I am enabled to do this because I do not plead for something, as one who has been conquered, but as the victor [alone can] speak only for reason. I see no ground that should force the continuation of this struggle." He ran on in sorrow over suffering to come despite the ardor of German manhood for a reckoning, wives and mothers giving their all; and ended with a final fixing jab at Churchill. So passed the great moment. Not a stir, not a sound, only tense spontaneous silence within the opera house, and without around millions of radios; joined together again the Germans were, come what may. Their Führer had put it up to Britain, cried the public advices. In truth he had put it up to them.[15]

An end was made of carnival and a free hand assured for continuing the war. It is not true that Britain could have had peace for the asking during July 1940. She could have had an uneasy *pax Hitlerana* at the expense of the Continent, had she petitioned. This she would not do, and Hitler came to realize it shortly before 19 July. Thereafter any tender from London had to be tantamount to surrender. No evidence offers better proof of this fact than the course of a peace offensive waged at this time through Göring by Dr. Albert Plesman. He was the founder of the world's oldest airline, KLM, Royal Dutch Airlines, and in July 1940 served as its active head at The Hague.

Dr. Plesman arrived in Berlin from Holland on the nineteenth in the middle of the uproar over the Reichstag session and the Führer's speech. He was determined to open exchanges between Berlin and London somehow. The fostering of international co-operation had long engrossed Plesman, and his skill had ripened in the world-wide business of KLM. Like many people, he reacted to the fall of France by speculating on peace. He discussed ways and means with highly

---

[15] William L. Shirer witnessed the grand spectacle and wrote prophetically the same day: "As a maneuver to rally them [the Germans] for the fight against Britain [or anyone else] it was a masterpiece," *Berlin Diary* (New York, 1941), p. 452. Hitler's interpreter Paul Schmidt transmitted his translation of the speech as Hitler uttered it to the world by radio. Shirer expressed his amazement of the emptiness of the peace passage after the build-up he had heard from Hitler on occasions in the preceding weeks.

placed friends of the Netherlands Foreign Ministry and experienced diplomatists. Plans took form, but how to establish the first contact, that was the problem. Plesman felt sure of his connections in London; in Berlin the matter would take some doing. Göring's repute as a man of peace centered attention on him, and also a possible approach existed through a KLM pilot who was a nephew of Göring's first wife. Plesman decided he must make the attempt. He concentrated his efforts on producing talk between the belligerents. The chief difficulty lay in creating an innocent channel of communication, but Dr. Plesman was a man of ideas. If both governments, for instance, permitted a KLM plane grounded in England to fly to Holland and there pick up Plesman for liaison flight to London as initial contact, "the ice might be broken." His bright blue eyes lit up with a friendly but dedicated light when he thought back to those exciting summer days of 1940. Said he finally, "Don't make too much of it. It turned out a broken egg, but we tried." That he had, with great resource and fine resolution, as the record reveals.[16]

The nineteenth of July 1940 was a Friday; with the hurrah of Führer in town it proved hard for Dr. Plesman to make contact with anyone in authority. Not until Monday the twenty-second did he succeed in entering preliminary exchanges with Göring's Chief of Intelligence, Colonel Schmid, and Dr. Böttger of the Air Ministry. Plesman impressed Schmid with his passionate sincerity, his breadth of outlook, and his concept of settlement on the basis of Anglo-German co-operation. After a three-hour conference Schmid called Karinhall and told General Bodenschatz that Göring "must see this man." They arranged a meeting for Wednesday the twenty-fourth.

Precious moments of a crucial time were passing. From London, Halifax had rejected Hitler's appeal to "reason" of the nineteenth. Germany still hoped, while speculation on air offensive against England dominated talk of the day in Berlin. Dr. Plesman appreciated the great urgency of the moment, and as he alighted at Karinhall

[16] After our conversation (at The Hague in May 1953) Dr. Plesman was kind enough to make the records of his peace endeavors available. These records have been summarized by Dr. Heinrich Uhlig for the *Institut für Zeitgeschichte* (Munich). The Plesman efforts are also recorded in Enquête-Commissie Regeringsbeleid, 1940-1945, *Verslag houdende de uitkomsten van het onderzoek* ('s Gravenhage: Staatsdrukkerijen Uitgererijbedrijf, 1949-), Deel 2, A en B, pp. 179-184. We are in substantial agreement that this effort for peace was among the most purposeful and energetically driven. Generalleutnant Josef Schmid, former Luftwaffe Intelligence chief, first brought the Plesman endeavor to my attention. His recollections and those of others have entered into this writing.

in the forenoon of 24 July he realized he must convince Göring at this meeting. Acting his happiest role of squire, the host suggested a stroll in nature's out of doors while they conversed. Many guests had exchanged views with Göring in this setting and invariably found him surprisingly candid and reasonable, and this was likewise the experience of Dr. Plesman. From the start his burly good-natured host seemed to fall in with the ideas Plesman so earnestly and carefully elucidated and promised to take them up with the Führer on the following day when he would return to Berlin from the south.

Plesman proposed a long-range scheme for lasting peace through international co-operation, founded on mutual trust. In the main, he wanted to link Britain and Germany, with the possible addition of the United States, in a frame of common effort to preserve peace. If needed, spheres of influence could take the following form: Britain would have her Empire; Germany, the Continent; and the United States, Latin America. In Europe the existing Russo-German relationship was to be encouraged to expand toward more complete exchange. Africa offered an area for initial practical action.

How logical it all must have sounded to host Göring, who so often had heard his Führer expound a comparable balance: Britain and Germany together, "the land for us, the sea for England." His guest took away a strong impression of Germany's willingness to co-operate on such a basis. In a summary made a day or so later, Plesman recorded Göring's pleased reaction, adding that almost all important areas of international politics and economics had been discussed. He became convinced of the wish on the part of the German leadership for an understanding that ruled out further conflict. ("Der Wunsch um eine Verständigung . . . sehr gewiss vorhanden, . . . Sinne . . . verbeugung weitere Konflikte . . . .") As to specific conditions for conversations, Plesman on the twenty-seventh recorded his recollection of them as voiced by Göring and repeated them in extended form on the thirtieth, in a confirmatory memorandum to Göring, as follows:

1. No surrender of [British] fleet units will take place.
2. Former German colonies will be given back; for the rest Germany will raise no territorial demands.
3. Powers who are to hold colonial possessions in Africa shall work in close co-operation there.
4. Gold will to a certain extent be reactivated, above all in the restocking of Europe immediately after peace.
5. Poland and Czechoslovakia will not be disturbed in their national development. The appropriate regulation of these countries must be left

to Germany. Although Germany will be accountable for the development of these people, a mixing-in in this matter on the part of other
powers cannot be permitted.
6. Norway, Denmark, Netherlands, Belgium, and France remain free in
their choice of government and organization so that fruitful co-operation
with Germany rather than against her, is insured . . . .
7. Germany will withdraw her occupation of Norway, Denmark, Netherlands, Belgium and France, and will bring no military demands to bear
in these countries.

In total content here was little new in these refurbished slogans. A
few showed Plesman's influence, but for the most part Hitler had
voiced their sense often, and Göring could have had no trouble in
reeling them off in perfect order. Only the fact that, at this point in
time, these words may have constituted an elaboration of Hitler's peace
bid, lent them extra significance.

The fleet item spoke for Hitlerian political theory about sea power
as related to empire, and it certified his willingness to forego both.
He and Göring had utilized the clumsy presumption—no surrender
of fleet units—as a touchstone of reassurance to Britain. It always
popped out first, as at Compiègne. Nothing could epitomize more
strikingly the German misconception of Britain and the sea. Colonies
were always good for idle talk, and so also was Africa, which Plesman
might have injected. Poland and Czechoslovakia would be safe under
German political hegemony, as would the others, through their economy. Reactivating gold could have come from businessman Plesman.
The item on withdrawal of occupation forces caused trouble for
Göring later, which could have meant that he acceded to it at the
time. Long or short, if these points contained the substance of the
"grandly generous" proffer of peace, which had so demandingly occupied Hitler's mind, he had fretted in vain. There was in reality little
peace substance to them, or in any that he could offer, and the odds
are that he himself had come to realize this.

In one particular Göring and Plesman were far out of phase with
Hitler; this was in advocating co-operation between Germany and
Russia. This misconception, if nothing else, could have wrecked
their efforts. Knowing nothing of this, Dr. Plesman set earnestly to
work and contrived a roundabout exchange of innocent messages to
serve as the initial breakthrough. He nearly succeeded in getting the
first word on the wires, but in the end he failed. He tried other means
and methods with the strongest perseverance and ingenuity and suc-

ceeded belatedly (August) in getting the plan transmitted to London via Stockholm. It was too late for any talk. The pivotal moment for talk was far gone down the road of history.[17]

The season of peace was over; now the thing was massive air offensive and invasion.

Sea Lion *Travail—July 1940*

It was not hard for a delusion of cheap and ready victory by massive air offense to displace the worn-out delusion of peace. Yet sober thinkers recoiled from this jangling wishful clamor; they knew something more solid and basic was required, if the war was truly to be carried to England. *Sea Lion* stood on the public books, for all to see as never before in any operation.

So ran the feeling at Army Headquarters, where invasion thought was flourishing. We pick up the roseate picture at OKH. Navy Captain Loycke had been serving there as the lone seagoing adviser to

[17] Plesman's breakthrough scheme contemplated dispatch of a message to London via Baron van Nagell, Netherlands Minister in Stockholm. It was to request British "permission that Plesman . . . flies to London to discuss matter of greatest international importance . . . Dutch plane [grounded in London] and Dutch crew to fly from England to Schipol aerodrome to bring him to London." The hitch came in getting this message out of Berlin. Plesman received word on 25 July from the Reichskanzlei that this message could go. The Swedish Embassy, Berlin, enciphered it and needed only final transmission release by the German Foreign Office. That office withheld release without explanation. Could it have been a change of heart by the Führer, by Göring, or had Ribbentrop, always jealous of Foreign Office prerogatives, interfered? The message missed by only a hair, and there went the last chance before the German Air Force cast the die of finish fight. Nothing having come of his efforts, on 12 August Plesman flew to Stockholm and induced van Nagell to forward his plan to the Dutch government in exile, London. On 27 August Lord Halifax, British Foreign Secretary, acknowledged study of the Plesman papers "with much interest," in returning them to Foreign Minister van Kleffens of the Dutch government in exile. Van Kleffens replied to Halifax the same day to say he had wired Stockholm, where Plesman waited, "to the effect that the documents he sent have been studied here with interest . . . but that I cannot attach great importance to what he related, considering, inter alia, the withdrawal of permission on the part of the Germans to dispatch the telegram Mr. Plesman suggested . . . on 25 July, and the space of time which has elapsed since that date . . . ." On 29 August Halifax wrote van Kleffens, "I think that the message which you have telegraphed your Minister in Stockholm [re: Plesman] is entirely on the right lines." Göring and Plesman met again at The Hague at the end of August, and Göring again promised to see Hitler, but on the fifteenth of September, in a long letter, he took issue with Plesman on his record of their first conversation and subsequent events. He was at pains to disassociate himself from the Plesman project and to make an end of it. In May 1941 Gestapo searchers found the peace papers in Plesman's home, arrested him, and held him prisoner for eleven months without explanation.

the soldiers, now suddenly turned enthusiastic sailormen. A contemporary vignette presented Loycke plodding about the confines of Fontainebleau, mournfully shaking his head. "Kinder, Kinder!" he warned, "you don't know what you've got a hold of." About mid-July Commander Alfred Schulze-Hinrichs joined him to help beef-up the Navy side. He recounted recollections of happy invasion-fired Army planners, envoys from already alerted fighting units scouting the planning ground, broad outlines for the crossing nearing completion, and other high headquarters G2 bits and pieces. A firm plan had not yet issued, but the scouts were assured it would follow the lines of a river-crossing. If this was the only comprehensible language, let it go. But the naval officers wondered if the deeps of Fontainebleau forest furnished the environment for learning about the river. So water education was undertaken in week-end excursions to the fine Channel beach resorts for acquaintance with wave, tide, and wind. Transport craft were studied, models whittled out and maneuvered over imaginary seas. Tidal eccentricities amazed the soldiers. A general northeasterly tending current, helped by a prevailing breeze from southwest, could easily sweep a poorly powered invasion fleet up into the North Sea. These were damaging premonitions of disaster. Philip's Armada suffered that inglorious fate in 1588 while the Duke of Parma waited and wondered on shore, and over 1,600 years earlier Caesar had barely escaped it. A wiseacre found favorable comparison between Caesar's sail- and oar-powered vessels and the awkward tug-towing-barge arrangement currently proposed. Not all was in jest either. Caesar's commentaries were assiduously combed for ideas. He having succeeded, his advice was favored. What could better attest the Army's zeal and, at the same time, the paucity of fresh aspects or any true understanding of the problem than these oddments of planning that were drunk in and gossiped over?

Moreover, the realization dawned that the sea hazards all had to be weathered before a single foot tested England's shore in front of formidable beach defenses. Aerial photo studies showed strength growing day on day; these works would be no push-over. Estimates of casualties touched frightening figures. The Army never wavered; armor and shellfire and superior leadership would break a way. The naval representatives stood cheerfully by, losing none of their skepticism. Schulze-Hinrichs recollected a quip of late July: "If peace ever comes, we ought to really try this trick to see if it could have worked."

While the OKH planners acquired some vicarious taste for the sea, the soldier who learned most, and all on the practical side, was General Georg Hans Reinhardt, who directed technical experiments at Putlos and Sylt. Whatever fictions may have deluded others, he remained unaffected. On 14 July, aware of the great urgency, he put together the impressions gained so far and submitted them in an excellent report to his superiors. By that day, he reported, not a single tank had been successfully unloaded from ship to beach. The heavy reliance placed on submersible tanks that were to rise from the Channel deeps and overrun British beach defenses seemed rash to him. Reinhardt recommended against going overboard on a single miracle weapon like the U (for *unterwasser*) tank and urged plans that could succeed without these gimcracks. Americans would note a curious, though inevitable, parallel between the course and sequence of the problems confronting the Germans and their own later experience. But we were blessed with more time and unlimited resources. The interested Germans contended against threefold odds—time, meager resources, and opposition in the home camp, including their Führer.

In contrast to the Navy, Reinhardt instinctively differentiated *Sea Lion* from a *Norway*-like overseas movement. He immediately grasped the primacy of landing craft, because he recognized the job for what it was, *assault from the sea on a beach position.* That pointed directly at assault craft of shallow draft that could pour strong infantry units over the beaches. Far down on a Navy inventory of craft appeared 2,000 river and canal barges. Each might handle two to four vehicles or some 150 troops in a draft of only a little over a meter. Unfortunately, lack of enough built-in power for seagoing use imposed towing; also, the barge bows required alteration to permit beach unloading, and the hulls needed strengthening against the rigors of the Channel waters. Time-consuming, all of this; but there was yet more. Allowance of time had to be made for commandeering and manning the craft, for squeezing them through war-damaged canals and locks, and for assembling them in mounting ports. These labors added up to appalling delays; but how else? Reinhardt went to work with a will and ranged far beyond the scope of his original ticket in the readying of landing craft. With the Navy he settled on a routine for seizure and alteration of barges and for the clearing of canals and ports. Army engineers filled the failing number of Navy hands; things got done. Several hundred fishing vessels and assorted motor boats were inventoried, and, finally, there were the engineer sturmboats (river-crossing boats). These were the only beach assault craft available. Some way would have to be found to ferry them cross-Channel and to launch them onto the landing beaches.

Totting up, General Reinhardt reached the practical conclusion that an assault wave of only four infantry divisions and two of armor might be managed with the craft in prospect. He advised his superiors that in view of the shortness of time the Army cut the initial wave to this figure. The unwelcome truth was available, but it could hardly find a favorable reaction in the expansive feeling that ruled OKH. Two eminently sound recommendations closed the Reinhardt report: (1) Every day was precious. To meet the deadline, unequivocal orders requiring action on the preparatory tasks had to go out to all services. (2) A high-ranking staff, charged with the preparation of all arms, had to be designated, and a commander of such staff unreservedly empowered to act, even to intervening in matters of war economy. In many places, General Reinhart had apparently found a reluctance to get on with the job; he and his staff had come a long way in a short ten days. What he had learned was fundamental but none too acceptable at OKH, nor at Navy.

The Navy we left groaning over Directive No. 16 as the inner circle debated its provisions in conference with Admiral Raeder on 17 July. The conferees found nothing but gloom to record: a critical shortage of landing craft; the dubiousness of absolute air command; equal doubt over the mine barriers; the total unfamiliarity with landing operations; and, most disconcerting of all, the glowering British fleet. Admiral Raeder picked up and departed for a meeting with the head of the Army, General von Brauchitsch. Incredibly, it was their first contact on this subject so vital to them and their country.

The meeting proved unproductive, except to convince von Brauchitsch that he could expect little from the Navy. The Army's beachhead, so incomprehensibly broadened, worried the sailors. Raeder refused any guarantee whatever for the security of a crossing stretching from Ramsgate to the Isle of Wight. Also, he charged the Army with commissioning its own Navy; signs of this had been accumulating. Then he tried to sober his Army colleague with warnings of disaster. The Army, Raeder surmised, failed to recognize the grave difficulties and hazards; total loss of all troops committed had to enter into reckoning. Brauchitsch gave no sign of weakening. He shared his staff's opinion of a reluctant Navy. Army gossip had it that

Navy had started this thing and now was getting "cold feet," just as in *Norway*. The jeer was still current in 1953.

Innuendo of this kind could only hurt the cause. It tended to make the Navy the goat. She found herself crowded on every hand. The Führer wanted "report whether the Navy can meet the 15 August" deadline, despite the fact that Navy had not yet received a definitive Army troop list. The circumstances favor a presumption that the information had been deliberately withheld until the Führer's stamp of approval made commitment to an Army brand of *Sea Lion* fact. "Even now," wrote the Skl diarist on 18 July, "one can see that the degree and kind of preparations in no wise permit an undertaking on 15 August . . . ." The arrival on 18 July of Army troop data finally afforded opportunity for an extensive review of the situation, which the special invasion staff furnished on 19 July. It was a carping report that was to serve also as preamble for the first Navy instructions to subordinate commands. The report held that the tasks assigned the Navy bore no relationship to her true capabilities and were grossly disproportionate to the jobs of the Army and Air Force. Whereas Army had simply to reallocate troops available, and Air merely to fill out its long-touted air offensive against Britain, Navy faced a top-to-bottom reorganization for executing a huge enterprise, completely alien and unfamiliar. But try as they might to shift the onus to more deserving shoulders, the brethren of the sea failed to free themselves of blame. A stain of reluctance about *Sea Lion* never left them.[18]

The landsman misapprehension is understandable; it harks back to soldier boredom. The appearance is that they wish merely to get on with the business; their resources in planners, men, material, and time are limitless. They simply overwhelm you, the Navy, because they are in a lull and you are not. You can handle not another damn thing; they can handle anything. The Army operates by mass in a sporadic game of pitched offensives; often the mass is spoiling for something to do. On the other hand, the Navy must operate a unified unsimple mechanism continuously and concentrate on keeping it going, battle or no. Thus time for reflection releases the soldiers, and

[18] Hitler remarked in the hearing of his naval adjutant in 1943 to the effect, "I should never have allowed the Navy to talk me out of *Sea Lion*." The jibe caused a stir at Navy so that by March 1944 the Navy had a documented history of its *Sea Lion* record under production by its historian, Vice Admiral Kurt Assmann. Later he published it in substantial part in his book, *Deutsche Schicksalsjahre* (Wiesbaden, 1951). Army sources corroborate Hitler's feeling that Navy was the villain in *Sea Lion*.

lack of it binds the sailors, and from this difficulty comes the sailor repute of arbitrary mien and lack of pliancy. Nowadays the trouble is mitigated somewhat by working together on common amphibious force staffs. The Germans depended on staff liaison representatives, who labored against dual allegiance.

One further observation about the Skl *Sea Lion* review of 19 July merits mention. The sailors at long last faced the dirty business of beaching on an open coast. The job of deliberately crashing vessels aground goes against the seaman grain; it refutes all tradition and training. But in just that capability, to pour assault troops onto the beaches, lives the very sling and stone of amphibious power. The German seaman took to the new departure in ship-handling as unwillingly as any seamen and added that mental hurdle to the material problem of making their craft fit for beaching. The bows of all landing barges had to be altered and fitted with ramps. The time delay, Reinhardt had already said, would be costly, nearly prohibitive. Navy plowed ahead, slow and disconsolate, while Army sailed happily along pretty much on her own.

By now, 20 July, the grand Army plan firmed into the fantastic arrangement already foreshadowed: Five grand waves were to flood out of the French ports from Dunkirk to Cherbourg and inundate England's open coast from Thames' mouth—ever further westward—to Lyme Bay, a frightening total breadth of 237 miles. The total strength reached equally grand figures: 30 infantry divisions, 6 of armor, and 4 motorized. Out of these came the initial beach assault by 13 divisions plus advanced armored elements. Two regimental combat teams from each of the 13 landing divisions constituted the core of assault; thus 26 such teams, working in pairs, constituted the first grand wave. As the beguiling landlubber picture had it, a continuous shore-to-shore landing craft shuttle service would go into effect as soon as the assault wave had crashed ashore. "Hitlerian" is the only word that can do justice to this devastating production; and on its unfettered tenets the Army and Hitler took an unnatural stand together.

The next event of moment for *Sea Lion* was a full-scale Führer Conference with the Commanders-in-Chief on 21 July in Berlin. Some of the Navy misgivings had rung through to Hitler, as the meeting quickly disclosed. He used the saturnine Navy view to buttress a nagging perplexity that still hung on. Opposing camps of Army and Navy squared off for trial, their attending commanders armed with literature and backed by aides. But they might as well have left the ammunition at home, for Hitler did the talking in this most revealing of all the famed Führer briefings. It was the first such on *Sea Lion*.

Ostensibly, for the final turn, Britain had been offered peace. A complete answer was not yet in hand on that Sunday, 21 July 1940, when Hitler addressed his chiefs. British press reaction and the lack of prompt official response portended rejection; yet this struck no fire. His listeners heard no transported Führer tear them along with the vigor of his words toward action and victory over England. Rather, he lapsed into the puzzled doldrum mood, speculated about a new British Cabinet under Lloyd George, and asked: What hope could England still have for continuing the war? A week earlier von Brauchitsch and Halder had experienced the same bemused air after presenting their invasion plan on the Berghof. The briefing of the twenty-first continued the pattern in monologue form. We follow the Navy recording as corroborated by Army notes.[19] "The decision of the war has fallen," Hitler declared; "either Britain has not yet recognized this or she sees some prospect of changing her fate. For the continuation of the war Britain can hope for a change in America . . . or a change in position by Russia . . . ." He allowed his thoughts to drift on in self-debate. Both possibilities required evaluation. An early ending of the war was, of course, in the interest of the German people but hardly urgent. Time would bring no improvement to Britain, whereas Germany was well situated for a long war. And thereupon Adolf Hitler faced invasion squarely in these cogent words (as edited by Raeder):

Despite this favorable situation, a speedy ending of the war should be striven for with all means to exploit as quickly as possible our favorable military and political situation. As the most effective means herefor, execution of the operation *Sea Lion* comes into question. Thorough examination is necessary [to determine] whether and in what time a direct operation can force England down. At the same time diplomatic measures must be undertaken toward Spain, Russia and Japan. These measures are however difficult as long as the world awaits a new miracle and such has not yet put in an appearance.

[19] Three records of the conference are available: (1) that recorded in his usual practice by Admiral Raeder; (2) that entered in the Skl war diary, which elaborated on the first a little; (3) that recorded by General Halder, as reported to him by his Commander-in-Chief on the following day. The third is in agreement with the other two, though it is not as complete on Britain as they are. It adds, however, thoughts about Russia that von Brauchitsch must have received direct from Hitler.

He seemed to be aware of the immense initiative at stake. Yet, as the master thus hinted at propaganda having outrun his powers, he took refuge in a negative attitude.

An unwonted Hitler spate of sailor talk followed—all negative in feeling. Plowing through British waves was something far beyond the compass of this man's spirit. His monologue justified his own fears and pushed the burden of *Sea Lion* toward the Kriegsmarine. The way might be short, he asserted, yet it would be no mere river-crossing but a movement over a sea commanded by the adversary, no one-way trip, as was *Norway*. (How proud of Führer education Admiral Raeder must have felt.) There would be not a chance at surprise. An utterly determined foe stood on guard and commanded the sea; logistic support would be the hardest problem. (Was Raeder's record embellishing the Führer's words?) He launched into the familiar face-saving prerequisites: complete air command; coastal artillery and flanking mine barriers; and weather, to boot, which, especially for the Luftwaffe, demanded that the main operation be completed in the good weather period before 15 September. As he felt the need "to gain a clearer picture of the possibilities at the earliest," his build-up toward some critical posers became plain. Hitler pointed his questions all at the Navy: (a) When can the Navy be in the clear about technical preparations? (b) When will the emplacement of artillery be finished [a Navy task]? (c) To what extent can the Navy actively and passively protect the crossing?" In these words Hitler hung *Sea Lion* around the dejected Navy neck of Admiral Raeder.

Poor Raeder was in bad company. He replied that he hoped for a firm answer within four days on the technical matters; the operational questions could not yet be judged, he said, and added the dig that the Navy could really begin practical preparations only after air command was a fact. Undoubtedly, the Führer's omission of questions to Army and Air had struck him, as it does us. For example, in how many days would air command be established, or how long would the Army require to take London? The answer to the latter question would set the scale of logistics on a critical or manageable level. Brauchitsch spoke up of his own volition and evidenced a strong liking for *Sea Lion*; by Navy standards, however, he seemed none too clear on the magnitude of the practical difficulties nor the power of enemy counteraction. Göring had not bothered to attend. Jeschonnek was present to carry the word for him, and he did this without taking a stand on *Sea Lion.* All he wanted, he averred, when Hitler mentioned fair weather for the Luftwaffe, was a free hand to start the great air offensive. Hitler made him no answer. He returned to the luckless Chief of the Navy with the request that renewed report be made as soon as possible, "If preparations cannot with certainty be completed by the beginning of September it is necessary to consider other plans." The language may have meant more than it said. It was symptomatic of change in Hitlerian spiritual weather. But at any rate, *Sea Lion* was now up to the Navy.

A few sidelights support our feeling of change. Signs point to a huddle with von Brauchitsch after the others departed on the twenty-first. In recording his Chief's report of this Führer briefing, General Halder linked the matters discussed with thoughts of Russia so closely that they must have proceeded from von Brauchitsch's conversation with Hitler. The Halder sequence ended with:

(6) By mid-week on report by Raeder decision by Führer whether landing operation shall be carried out *this fall.* If not now, not until May next year. Clarification probably end of this week. Final decision whether sharpest form of U-boat and Air war shall be taken up probably not until beginning August. Operation E [for England] then about 25 August.

(7) Stalin is flirting with England to keep England at war and tie us down, to gain time for taking what he wants and what cannot be taken if peace breaks out . . . . But no signs of Russian activity against us are at hand.

(8) Take Russian problem in hand. Organize thinking.

To the Führer has been reported: . . . .

Included in a list following were time factors of German deployment against Russia, an outline of a campaign, political aims, strength estimates, and so on. And then came the give-away. "If we attack Russia this fall, England will be relieved, as far as Air is concerned . . . ." The foregoing certified typical Hitlerian straddle. Under pressure for decisive word on invasion, he began feeding on escape elsewhere.

Admiral Raeder, ignorant of these vagaries, stirred himself to discharge the business nearer at hand, *Sea Lion.* Meeting a new deadline of 1 September had been mercilessly pinned on him. Skl dished up a rebuttal already in the typewriter; it aimed to pass the buck straight back to the Air. An inventory of work underway apprised OKW, the Army, and the Air Force that all assigned tasks led back to the urgent need of absolute air command (which the Navy suspected, even hoped, Göring could not deliver). Nothing of consequence, Skl said, could be accomplished until command of the air was in hand. This dulling harpoon bounced back again and again, but the Navy kept hurling it. About the deadline the rebuttal said: "It must be reported that the preparations will *in no wise* be finished by mid-August." And, it continued, the ready date could only be determined when the day of Air command over the Channel was in sight. Finally Navy rose to her own responsibilities. In this summary of 22 July Raeder stated unequivocably that the command on the water would be exercised by the naval commander of the fleet: "From the moment of embarkation until after successful disembarkation on the enemy coast the direction must rest in the hands of the Navy." Some of *Sea Lion's* ambiguity left him.

The atmosphere cleared a little, and things looked up at Navy. The Todt Organization, a miracle-working species of Seabee Corps, joined to assist in harbor and canal clearance, the emplacement of coastal artillery, and other odd jobs. New hands to the number of 24,000 were inducted to man invasion craft; these and combatant ships were allocated to yards for conversion work; ships in commission were cannibalized for men and materials. Sailor hats became visible along the Channel shores as Naval Command Stations took charge of all ports from Flanders to Brittany.

The command and operation of a wide alien sea frontier of this breadth presented an appalling task, one for which no navy is ever adequately prepared. The job lies on shore, out of the navy line. While the Army plays landlord in occupied areas and lives with the local populace, which can fill many of its landbound needs, the Navy finds little help afloat. The local talent has disappeared, and one's own must be spread much too thin. So it happened with the German Navy. Each lonely Naval Station Commander found himself surrounded by numberless eager soldiers instead of pilots and seamen. Whichever way he turned, there was Heinz or Heinrich wanting to set sail (or motor) for England. Each one had his pet contraption for getting over to conquer those Englanders. Nothing much really had been done in a practical way toward cleaning up the water-front litter of damaged ships and docks. By and by, however, the station commanders found out what they had ahold of, and a few things began falling into place. Yet doubt over what in truth was intended persisted.[20]

One remote magical concept kept recurring in the talk of high places, including those of the Navy, during this period of *Sea Lion* travail. It had to do with *Grosseinsatz der Luftwaffe* (massive air offensive). This was the easy option left over from Jodl's summation of 30 June and from long-forgotten official plan of siege against England by air and by sea. Now in the revised version, the concept became all air. Arduous and exhausting labors of prolonged siege had long since faded from mind, and in their place rose a confidence in air offense alone, without anyone's knowing exactly what was meant. The Luftwaffe claimed it was ready; the Führer apparently reserved decision. He played only one card at a time of the many in his hand.

Answers made by Admiral Raeder to the critical questions put during the briefing of 21 July reflected the evolving, more favorable Navy outlook. The Admiral conferred with his Führer late on the afternoon of the twenty-fifth in Berlin. (It was the day he must also have heard about Plesman from Göring, if Göring executed his promise.) A naval ordnance expert explained the details of coastal artillery installation, thus disposing of 21 July's second question, concerning the time when this task would be finished. Hitler added a touch of his own and confirmed an abiding interest in the project by volunteering permission to "open fire as soon as ready." The date of technical readiness for Invasion, the first query, controlled the answer to the final and toughest question of all, the Navy's capacity to insure a safe crossing. Raeder explained that he hoped to have technical problems solved by the end of July, and then he could also answer the question of protecting the Channel passage. Without further ado Hitler scheduled a meeting for 31 July.

How unlike the impetuous Führer of yesteryear, or the puzzled one of four days earlier. In the face of recurring delays, his tantrum

[20] Naval Group Command West, with headquarters in Paris after July 1940, was the Navy operational control center for the theatre. Admiral Saalwächter commanded, his Chief-of-Staff was Rear Admiral Otto Ciliax. The latter confirmed to me by correspondence in December 1954 that the first *Sea Lion* directive "struck in like a bomb shell" at the Group Command Headquarters. Prior to Führer Directive No. 16, he said, he and Saalwächter had been agreed on the infeasibility of landing in England. They had been kept in the dark about landing thought higher up. All the more astonished were they when the first *Sea Lion* orders reached them "because of the utter lack of preparatory measures," and this fact raised doubt immediately about the seriousness of the landing intention. Naval command in *Sea Lion* suffered from this doubt throughout.

index remained at a cool zero. Raeder had prefaced his accounting with a renewed exposition of the internal upheaval occasioned by *Sea Lion*. Without blinking an eye, Hitler assented to topmost priority for *Sea Lion* industrial demands. Keitel later implemented this far-reaching decision in a directive. For the rest, the Führer offered no comment on air command when the Navy's chief could not omit its mention. In fact, Hitler, in sharp contrast to the twenty-first, said only enough to frame clipped, incisive agreement or approval. Puzzled before and still at odds with the situation, he now appeared at peace with the problem and himself. We experience an uncanny feeling of pattern repeated. It was 25 July 1940.

The month of July slid by, and all through its precious days Navy and Army planners remained far, far apart, in mind and in body, one grouped in Berlin, the other in Fontainebleau. At last the two bodies made contact, not alongside for mutual help but in a head-on fatal collision. By dint of *fait accompli* plan, OKH had pursued the witless obsession that troop lift could be provided on order at any time and place specified and landed according to railroad schedule. Reinhardt's advices to the contrary gave no pause. Instead the Army played out the highly theoretical plans in a map maneuver at Fontainebleau, 23 July, to complete satisfaction all around; only the assault wave needed a bit of reinforcing. The soldiers might as well have played at boats in a bathtub. In actuality the contemplated lifts could not have been approached even with the tightest cramming into the craft available. Denouement came with the arrival at OKH on 28 July of the Navy's honest solution for moving each of the five grand waves. A terrible thought smote the soldiers—that Navy proposed piecemealing the beach assault force into battle over a period of ten days. General Halder exploded: ". . . throws all previous lift calculations overboard . . . need ten days to put first [assault] echelon over . . . . If this checks out then previous advices of Navy have been nonsense and in that case a landing operation is not at all possible." He despatched General von Greiffenberg to Skl in Berlin to ascertain what could be done. Although the most ambitious amphibious operation of all time had been under prosecution by both services for over a month, this visit marked the first direct contact between top Army and Navy planners. Both sides were at fault. The incident demonstrated the positive dangers of independent theoretical planning; and for *Sea Lion,* it exacerbated the existing disruptive tendencies into an open and senseless quarrel.[21]

Greiffenberg found Navy not so bad as pictured on the specific point at issue, but even worse on other sea lore that his visit uncovered. Skl was putting finishing touches on what constituted the final studied Navy effort to sink invasion. Greiffenberg received thorough briefing and a special advance copy of the Navy's gloomy views to carry back to OKH. We share the misgivings engrossing the sailor minds as they contemplated *Sea Lion* catastrophe. In a sea and weather area as fickle and uncompromising as any in the world, a vast hodgepodge of towed and propelled barges, fishing craft, small boats, and steamers, never before at sea together, was to maneuver in darkness through a powerful enemy fleet toward the assault of a hostile shore. Surely this could only be a sailor's bad dream!

Skl expounded four cardinal problems and added its final conclusion:

1. The Army demand for a dawn landing and the seaman's need for half light by moon for maneuvering *Sea Lion* limited execution to to a short three or fours days of any month.

2. Thus S Day fell into the last days of September, a notably bad weather period, so that, though the first wave might by good luck succeed in landing, the same could not be counted on for subsequent waves.

3. Neither mine barriers nor air superiority could prevent the incursion of enemy fleet units into a crossing zone stretching from the Thames to Lyme Bay.

4. The paucity of landing craft demanded that the second grand wave could not start landing until forty-eight hours after the first, and eight to ten days would be required to get the second wave over completely, once it started.

Navy then came to the painless conclusion that *Sea Lion* should be deferred. Skl felt bound to advise against execution during 1940 and proposed to continue preparations in case "the unrestricted air

[21] Nevertheless the Army's independent attack on various technical landing problems had carried thinking well ahead of the Navy, who had lacked time and men to think that far. The Army had advanced to questions of assault boat landings, equipping of assault teams, subdivisions of barges according to tasks. General Halder's notes reveal Army thinking about the actual beach fight, while Navy thought remained bogged in battered mounting ports, loading there and trying vainly to sortie. So it often goes. (Col. von Greiffenberg had been promoted.)

offensive, together with Navy measures [siege] do not render the adversary amenable to negotiation." Execution of *Sea Lion* could then be taken up again in May 1941. Skl was trying hard to haul back to the old official plan, now all but forgotten. We note too a hint even of sailor confidence in air offensive alone.[22]

A crestfallen OKH deliberated the dispiriting news from Navy. The Commander-in-Chief joined his Chief of Staff for a long evening's discussion on the thirtieth. The talk was unproductive. They agreed that: "According to the outlook, the Navy will not get us the means necessary this fall to a successful hop-off for England. Only two possibilities remain to us . . . : defer the attack to the bad weather period . . . on the whole disadvantageous or wait until spring '41 (May). Our situation with respect to England will not improve . . . . The greatest danger of waiting lies in the fact that we will not retain the military-political initiative strongly enough in hand." We feel the Halder touch in this last; he was always alive to the initiative and the need of exploiting it, but his awareness failed to carry through. The Generals again stood at crucial crossroad of what next. They inventoried other possibilities for getting at Britain—Gibraltar, Suez, the Near and Middle East—and inevitably landed on the warming danger of British-Russian collaboration. Turning on Russia to forefend such alliance, they rejected, favoring rather the pursuit of Russian friendship for building Continental solidarity. "Then," concluded the notes, "we can confidently contemplate years of war with England." When pressed, they had reverted to outworn continentalism while precious initiative in the West dissipated into "hot air."[23]

Meanwhile, among the troops along the Channel coast, things were different, positive and decided. The soldiers had taken en masse to the water like so many ducklings only just finding their element— swimming instruction, boating, and beach sports. Who could act as

---

[22] The fifteen-page Navy document was a well-reasoned exposition, which brought out the full magnitude of the hazards from a seaman's point of view. Two hours after high tide was the optimum time for beaching in order that the barges would hold fast for unloading. They would lie for eight to twelve hours awaiting the next tide to refloat them. Army dawn landing meant a difficult approach in darkness, and unobserved approach by the Royal Navy to kill the landing also. Weather was decisive; with so many tows, a seaway of less than force two was imperative. Weather could prolong the crossing, leaving the first-landed wave stranded for weeks; so also could the British fleet isolate the first assault. Eight hours was required to get the barges of a wave out of a port, such as Boulogne, all under possible observation of enemy aircraft. Once out of port, the conglomeration of craft had to find exact locations on the opposing shore.

[23] *Halder Journal,* IV, 124.

Fahrer (driver) for the Colonel's boat? Some contented themselves with paddling about on inflated rubber mattresses or in engineer bridging pontoons. Cradled platforms, to simulate ship motion, were rigged on shore, and rifle-firing practiced from them. Major Siebel's propulsion of pontoons by air screws got underway at Fécamp. Landings were practiced wherever a few boats could be commandeered and a stretch of beach found free. All the pent-up energies, stored from the end of a campaign, burst out over the beaches. "This sailor stuff wasn't so bad; nothing to it!" The thinly spread sailors were hard put to keep up; in fact, they could not hope to.

Readiness earlier than 15 September was out of the question. But most alarming of all about Navy readiness was the question of combatant ships. Aside from minecraft, forty-eight submarines, and lesser vessels, only one heavy cruiser, the *Hipper,* four destroyers, and three torpedo boats would be fit for *Sea Lion* action. Here the paralyzing toll of *Norway* spoke out.

And still, on the highest level, the fundamental decision—was *Sea Lion* to go or not—hung in the balance. In politics and, to a lesser degree, in field operations, final decision of executing an operation can be made contingent on the success and efficiency of deployment for attack. The preliminaries can probe and test for the final act in the fullest sense. Not so with a huge amphibious operation. Mounting goes hand in hand with firm resolution to carry through, come hell or high water, to the enemy shore and beyond. There lay the root of *Sea Lion's* predicament; no one had yet said he was going. A showdown had to come soon; all signs of *Sea Lion's* prolonged travail during July in the high headquarters pointed to decision at Führer Conference on 31 July 1940.

Decision or Unabänderlicher Entschluss

Compared to the action-packed months before it, July 1940, the month of doldrums and dilemma, had been a failure. Events of this month in distant quarters, however, helped to spark a progression toward decision. In Moscow on this July's very first day, Joseph Stalin received a newly arrived negotiator from London, Sir Stafford Cripps. It was only his second day in the capital, and he had already been admitted to Stalin. The speedy getting-together made news not lost on partner Hitler. Just returned from Paris, Germany's Führer had hardly had time to accustom himself to the new surroundings and comforts of the Tannenberg headquarters in the Schwarzwald. There came conscientious Jodl with ideas of war finale with Britain. She would probably settle, but still, as *ultima ratio,* should not some preparatory steps for more war be set in train? The events in Moscow gave further pause to the old confidence in British settlement. None too happily, Hitler permitted the release of the initial invasion planning directive of 2 July 1940. What could the British in Moscow be up to?

This fresh Anglo-Russian approach toward common cause appeared in sharp contrast to similar endeavors of a year earlier. Then the Russians had let the British Ambassador and London's Russian expert, William Strang, cool their heels for days on end. The slow progress was closely watched from Führer Headquarters, and when British suggestions of military staff exchanges appeared, interest immediately picked up. But the Führer himself remained unworried. The naval liaison officer at OKW attributed his equanimity to a peculiar Hitlerian trait.

It was a marked peculiarity of Hitler to make far-reaching decisions from apparently inconsequential bits of detailed information . . . . During the Moscow negotiations of 1939 there prevailed among us [in OKW] much puzzled deliberation. The change from the political . . . to the military on the part of Strang seemed to bode ill. At this point Hitler took us completely by surprise in remarking, "They have, of course, gotten no agreement. I arranged to have Strang observed on his return arrival at Croydon. It was a homecoming typical of a beaten man."[24]

Mr. Strang's spirits at Croydon naturally constituted but one bit of evidence, an important final mosaic bit, however, and with an oddment of this character on hand the scheming Hitler could gratify wishful thinking and nudge himself toward decision. Straining to fetch the voice, as he often did, access to what he called the subconscious became easier, so that in the end self learned to fabricate its own infallible voices. We have watched the practice take hold more and more in the operational field of the war, as well as in the jumble that passed for strategy. In the earlier instance he was working up to attack Poland; now, with Cripps in Moscow, it was something else.

Another light comes from a year hence, summer 1941, when the old voices were standing trial in the Russian offensive. The Supreme Commander of the Germans then stood amidst the Armageddon of his own making. The tide of battle tended strongly in his favor; final

[24] Wolf Junge to Ansel in correspondence (Germany, 1953).

Hitler monologues to his Naval Aide on the Berghof. *(Courtesy Rear Admiral von Puttkamer)*

Festung Complex—Heavy coastal artillery embrasure Cap Gris Nez. On 10 July 1940 Hitler had a special directive issued to speed up the installation of numerous heavy batteries against England in the Gris Nez area. The heavy batteries were a manifestation of the Hitlerian Fortress Complex.

Experiments with river and canal barges (prahms) for beaching and discharging heavy equipment over bow ramps onto land. *(Courtesy Captain Erich Lehmann)*

On to England! The soldiers take to the water. Early landing exercises on the French coast, July 1940. *(Courtesy Colonel Wilhelm Willemer)*

Rifle practice from a moving cradle to simulate boat motion, on the Channel coast, summer of 1940. *(Courtesy Colonel Schuber)*

The Führer studies the situation. What shall he do? Left to right: von Puttkamer, Keitel, Deyle, Hitler, Jodl, Engel. Note the Führer's eyeglasses. (*Courtesy Rear Admiral von Puttkamer*)

Göring and his Intelligence Chief Beppo Schmid. The Commander-in-Chief of the Luftwaffe signs an Order of the Day. (*Courtesy Lieutenant General Josef Schmid*)

victory seemed only to need a few more strokes. Führer Headquarters, *Wolfschanze* (Wolf's Dugout), lay in a pine wood of East Prussia near Rastenburg. There during July 1941, Party functionary and office manager Martin Bormann, aware that the drama of Germania's creation had entered the final act, induced Hitler to permit stenographic recording of his mess talk. The official family that repaired to the rustic messroom at meal times ranged from (by that time) Generalfeldmarschall Wilhelm Keitel, through General Jodl, the adjutants, party officials, and department heads, down to the personal physician and the recorder—in all, some two dozen persons. Young Dr. Henry Picker, the second to occupy the recorder post, told how he carried on his task, how the half whispered conversations died away whenever the Führer spoke from mid-table, and how after the meal the members remained around the table. Hitler then perused the despatches brought by his orderly and gave directions or opinions on some as he dealt them out. The talk picked up, though rarely in two-way exchanges, because *he* did the talking, on topics as varied as religion and the whaling industry or Führertum and his own childhood experience. Almost always the words bubbled forth spontaneously, said Picker, but he detected a regard for "consumption" and persuading and, moreover, a repetition of unguarded remarks that traced a pattern of basic urges.

We could expect the pattern to include reference to Armageddon and how its master managed to bring it about. That was precisely what happened. A diffusive impressionistic canvas of many strokes unrolled in the record of the mess-table monologues. Its flashbacks to the problem of far-away England confirm the interdependence of Problems Russia and Britain. Hitler spoke on self-congratulatory tones of the fateful decision to turn on Russia. We have already noticed his remark over the table in the waning summer of 1941: "The spirit of decision does not mean acting at all costs. The spirit of decision consists simply in not hesitating when an inner conviction commands you to act. Last year I needed great spiritual strength to take the decision to attack Bolshevism." And then, three months later, after the eastern campaign had ground to a halt in dreadful ice and cold, he stood fast: "All my great decisions were taken on the Obersalzberg; that's where I conceived the offensive of May 1940 and the attack on Russia." There rings a bell for us.[25]

[25] The two quotations above come from *Hitler's Secret Conversations 1941-1944*. Two versions of Hitler's table talk are extant (1) *Hitler's Tischgespräche 1941-*

The master of the Russian havoc himself placed the inner conviction for that adventure in our current *Sea Lion* period and designated the Berghof as the place of origin. There is good ground for believing that decision to turn on Russia matured in Hitler between the twenty-third and twenty-fifth of July 1940 when *Sea Lion* was but a scant ten days old. We must attempt to illumine that maturing process. It proved of pivotal importance in the war.

At the bottom there was a simple fact: Adolf Hitler, like his countrymen, was a landsman through and through. On land he found a specific role; on the sea, nothing that compared. Thoughts that led beyond the rim of the Continent over the water disturbed him. We have only to recall the painful *Norway* experience. Not only did he lack a role there; he found in the sea a definite threat to his self-sufficiency. And so no genuine place existed for the sea either in practice or mythology; not for fighting forces, for bases, and, actually, not for colonies and world empire. As a result, problems related to the water started with two counts against them in the Hitlerian mind.

Now the land—that was bread and wine to Hitler! The spaces of a continent—what could they not call up in his mind? He crisscrossed them with *Autobahnen,* linking the newly created centers of the limitless Continental empire that was Germania. The image never ceased to enthrall him. It fitted into the defense concept of self, too— a fortress-like, self-sufficient land mass, controlled from within. Let the others come over the water to him. His glory would rise from the vast rolling land oceans of the European Continent. There lay his destiny!

We say again, this was the primordial substance of Hitler's road to glory. First the cause found expression in the slogan *Lebensraum,* living space for the bewildered and beleaguered German people. From *Lebensraum* to Germania was a natural evolution, helped by oddments of geopolitics that he encountered. We have observed the mixture fermenting in *Mein Kampf* and afterward. The thinker attempted to find a place for England, but willy-nilly, and in pace with

---

1942 (Bonn, 1951) from the hand of Dr. Henry Picker. He published both the notes passed on to him by his predecessor, Heinrich Heim, who recorded from July 1941 to March 1942, and his own recordings made from March 1942 to August 1942. (2) *Hitler's Secret Conversations 1941-1944.* This translation came from a document known as the *Bormann Vermerke.* How it came to publishers is unclear. The two publications authenticate each other; the latter contains a greater number of recordings for 1941 and 1942, and a few for 1943 and 1944. It appears they might have been exposed to Bormann's correction and elaboration. They nevertheless ring true Hitlerian.

his political successes, he kept on expanding the East concept. "What India has been to England, the East space will be to us."[26] And then recurred always that one devilish flaw: What about England herself? She never quite fitted in the place he made for her in his world. Whither first, East or West? That was the crux of the problem.

At first he had struck east, into Poland, and then west; yet thoughts of the East held on. They spilled out in whipping-up sessions before the military (23 November 1939), and they can be traced with precision through a number of progressive acts and private conversations. The acts stand out sharply in Russo-German naval dealings because more enduring results of co-operation could embarrass objectives to the contrary. Hitler kept Raeder in the dark, fending off the Admiral's co-operative attitude toward Russia during the fall of 1939 and early 1940. The matters covered such subjects as the purchase of submarines, the sale of half-completed German ships, the furnishing of ship plans, the sharing of bases in Norway. At one point Hitler advised the Chief of the Navy to procrastinate on deliveries to Russia with the view of tapering off to no deliveries at all. The practice became policy. He gave in reluctantly to Raeder's plan on *Norway*, but finally did, and *Norway's* eligibility as groundwork toward *Russia* cannot be ignored. The significance of a secure flank for himself in the north could not have escaped a schemer of Hitler's versatility.[27] The most convincing proof came out of Hitler's own mouth. We noted an early June instance (page 107), which occurred during the untrammeled elation over success in the West. The time and place, von Rundstedt's headquarters at Charleville, were right for encouraging confidences from this man of destiny who felt his fondest dreams coming true. Ostensibly the purpose of the meeting was to thank his Army leaders for their fine field performance and to brief them on the last strokes against France. He arrived a little ahead of schedule, and while the officers assembled he paced up and down before the hall with host Rundstedt. The talk that went on during this little promenade General von Rundstedt imparted to his Chief of Staff at the end of the day: ". . . now that things—England being probably ready for peace—had finally gotten to this point he [Hitler]

[26] Picker, *op. cit.*, p. 45.

[27] See *FC*, October 1939 through April 1940. Admiral Raeder's own evaluation *"Day of Reckoning,"* *IMT* doc. O66-C, written in January 1944, bears out progressive tightening up against Russia. Hubatsch, *op. cit.*, pp. 259-62, explored and rejected the idea that Operation *Norway* figured as preparation for later Operation *Russia*. We hold it was a case of how strongly Hitler related one to the other.

would begin settling accounts with Bolshevism!" Von Sodenstern recalled his commander's angry reaction to such madness and reassured himself with the thought that Britain would in any case not give in so easily, and a two-front war Hitler himself had always declared unthinkable. Only one angle bothered the victory-happy Führer, reported von Rundstedt: how to make a turn on Russia look right. Hitler employed the apologetic phrase, "How will I tell it to my child?" and then proceeded to indulge himself further at Russian expense. No matter, the childlike German people he had managed before. The need of the moment was to get rid of the British threat in his rear and insinuate eastern thinking into the Army ranks.

He succeeded. As more and more signals pointed toward Russia, over half of the game in the high professional circles turned to outguessing their *Gröfaz*. We recall the Foreign Office hint to General Halder and his countering plunge into invasion. The Army, while favoring action against Britain, could not afford to overlook Hitler's magnet in the East. General Gerhard Feierabend began work about mid-July on a campaign into Russia. Swapping yarns with his neighbors, as one does, he found amusement in the diversity of projects underway. He himself was deep in the East space; on one side of him, *Sea Lion* splashed and roared, while on the other flank, demobilization and peace made bustle and clamor. Directions came to hold off on deactivating so many divisions. What could be wanted with twenty extra divisions? Certainly no *Sea Lion* need existed for 350,000 extra troops. Many other unanswerable questions mystified the planners. It grew difficult to feel sure that one was working on the real thing. Could this or that project be a cover plan? At all events, by 22 July OKH had furnished Hitler a preliminary survey on the possibilities of a campaign into Russia.

Also on that day, 22 July, the British Foreign Secretary, Lord Halifax, took notice of Hitler's Reichstag speech of the nineteenth and rejected him and all his works. Public talk of peace came to an end; now it was war to the death. But just where, Hitler was not yet sure. He discussed the Army data on Russia with Keitel and Jodl and found them lukewarm. He had only himself to work on. No rousing responses from frenzied auditors. What should he do? Where could he turn? He needed help as never before, and he found it in his own peculiar fashion.

A year ago he had gone to war shortly after attending the Wagnerian festival at Bayreuth. In this year 1940 he stood on the threshold of decision for all time. On Tuesday 23 July 1940, the day after the Halifax broadcast, at approximately three in the afternoon, the opening trumpets sounded at Bayreuth, and Adolph Hitler took his special place to witness the final performance, *Die Götterdämmerung*. Indications are this event proved decisive for him.

August Kubizek, his boyhood friend, attended as Hitler's guest at both the 1939 and 1940 festival. In August of 1939 the two had enjoyed a moving visit together. Musician Kubizek lived for another meeting in 1940, and this came about. The meeting proved their last, and one that climaxed for Kubizek all that Wagner meant to him, and revived what that master likewise meant to his friend and host. He tells how Wagner transported Hitler and brought him release and redemption. "When he listened to Wagner's music he was a changed man; his violence left him . . . his own destiny became unimportant . . . . Willingly he let himself be carried away into the mystical universe which was more real to him than the actual workaday world . . . . He was transported into the blissful regions of the German[28] antiquity, that ideal world which was the lofty goal for all his endeavors." This man was capable of substituting *Götterdämmerung* for reality and identifying himself and Germania with Wagner's characters. Reproach, cleansing fire, and final lofty dedication, all promised a regenerated order to come. The heroics were made for Hitler's jumbled mosaic. Here was the fire that could shake it into order and trigger him to action. And it did. His mind made up, inner peace came to him; Hitler's farewell to Kubizek on the same day and his quiet composure before Raeder on the twenty-fifth bear witness; he had found redemption.

What could be more simple; the first task was, of course, to make Germania whole as Europa. Marriage could come later, and so he rationalized *Russia* into becoming a "detour on the way to England."

It was unroutine for General Jodl to send word that he would lunch with the planners in *Atlas,* the Warlimont staff railroad car at Reichenhall. He rarely came over from Bischofswiesen, below the

---

[28] Kubizek, *op. cit.,* 101, 191, 192, 286-95. Herr Kubizek mentions another scene of self-immolation with which Hitler identified himself, the finale of the immature Wagner's third opera, *Rienzi*. The two youths heard it together in Linz. So moved was Hitler he carried his friend to a hilltop and there under the stars, in complete ecstasy, he overwhelmed Kubizek with a torrent of words: his mandate, his mission—he would rise and lead his people, even as Rienzi, the Tribune of Rome. When Kubizek recalled the incident to Hitler on 3 August 1939 during their first meeting at Bayreuth, Hitler readily acknowledged it and assured Kubizek and Frau Wagner, "In that hour it began."

Berghof, where, with General Keitel, he held down the so-called Little Chancellery. Anticipation of an unusual event increased in *Atlas* by reason of his request to speak to the section heads before lunch. Colonel Warlimont called them together in his compartment, a representative from each of the services. They took chairs around the table. Fanned by the generous promotions at the Reichstag session on the nineteenth, gossip had been going the rounds about advancements for them too. Maybe their turn came now. Jodl in his quiet way stood in good relationship with these hand-picked officers, and it was perfectly natural that they should receive him with friendly respect and understanding. But what was their astonishment when instead of pleasantries about promotion he launched directly into a subject entirely foreign to their thoughts. Out it came, accompanied by enjoinder of highest secrecy: The Führer intends to attack Russia! Planning to that end shall start at once. His hearers, in the words of Warlimont, fell out of their chairs.

Surprises were not infrequent in that world of unpredictable weather, yet these men understood the pattern and its limits and imagined themselves pretty well in on the deepest "know." Here Jodl handed out one that knocked them flat. They refused to believe their ears. Colonel Warlimont requested repetition. Had he heard right? The others chimed in. Did not Germany stand in good rapport with Russia? Were not deliveries arriving promptly in grains, petroleums, and other stores? And their own war machine—was not the Army demobilizing divisions? What about England; what about a two-front war? The flood poured out over unhappy Jodl. He would not have come personally but for having anticipated just this, the pain of telling his children. At length he reared back from the barrage and blurted out: "Gentlemen, it is not a question for discussion but a decision of the Führer [*Entschluss des Führers*]!"

That could have meant only one thing—by 29 July 1940 opportunity for arguing with Hitler had been exhausted. The decision had by this time been sanctified into the granite character of *unabänderlicher Entschluss*. Further direct discussion was futile. Junge, the Navy representative who attended, wrote in 1953: "From [this] beginning never a doubt about the 'unalterable decision' existed." In the course of some few weeks the fact of it gradually established itself.[29]

[29] The revelation of Hitler's momentous decision is detailed in Warlimont's written account of 3 October 1945 and his interrogation for the *IMT* of 12 October 1945

The words Jodl used to expound decision for *Russia* to his assistants were palpably of Hitlerian coinage: strong evidence of a closing deal between Britain and Russia . . . can only be forestalled by eliminating the Continental party, Russia . . . which can be accomplished in a matter of weeks and then a return made to the West in redoubled strength . . . (the staff remained unconvinced and Jodl shifted his ground) . . . war with Russia was bound to come up some day anyhow . . . better have it now while Germany had the jump. He mentioned May 1941 as the target time and gave orders for the preparation of planning papers under a code name *Aufbau Ost* (*Build-up East*). It developed that Keitel and Jodl had fought down a Hitlerian inspiration to attack Russia then and there in 1940, so strong had the inner voice sounded its clarion call. They had barely succeeded in arguing him out of it through a detailed presentation of insuperable obstacles: inadequate bridging; poor road and rail nets in the East; plus the uncertainties of weather and early fall rains. By May 1941 this could all be brought into order, and as an "out" for the meantime, let intensified air action on Britain and sharpened submarine warfare see what could be achieved toward reducing the hazards of *Sea Lion*. So ran a memo signed by Keitel and seen by Warlimont on 29 July, or close thereafter.

Again we hear that pet phrase, knocking the dagger out of the opponent's hand, and again it was the *Festlanddegen,* the Continental dagger Russia, being struck from the hand of Britain. The slogan was as trite as mosaic filling and inner voice, but they all seemed to be imperishable while Hitler was talking to Germans. Back in August 1939, when Ribbentrop had brought off the new entente with Stalin, Hitler exulted with the same cry. Now a year later he twisted the sense somewhat by coining the phrase *Umweg über Russland* (*Detour over Russia*) on the way to England.[30]

The question of Britain and *Sea Lion* came to the fore immediately from his strong supporters in the Warlimont staff. Which would take precedence, Russia or England? Jodl replied with the curious excuse that, since Russia's collapse should at last incline Britain to-

---

(*Nazi Conspiracy and Aggression,* Supp. B (Washington, 1946) p. 1634). Coverage is also given by Helmuth Greiner (who served as diarist for the section), *op. cit.,* pp. 116-17, 288-90; by von Lossberg, *op. cit.,* pp. 105, 106. My understanding of the incident has been filled out in detail by consultation with Warlimont and von Lossberg, and by correspondence with General Warlimont and Captain Junge (Germany, 1953).

[30] Warlimont to Ansel (Germany, 1953).

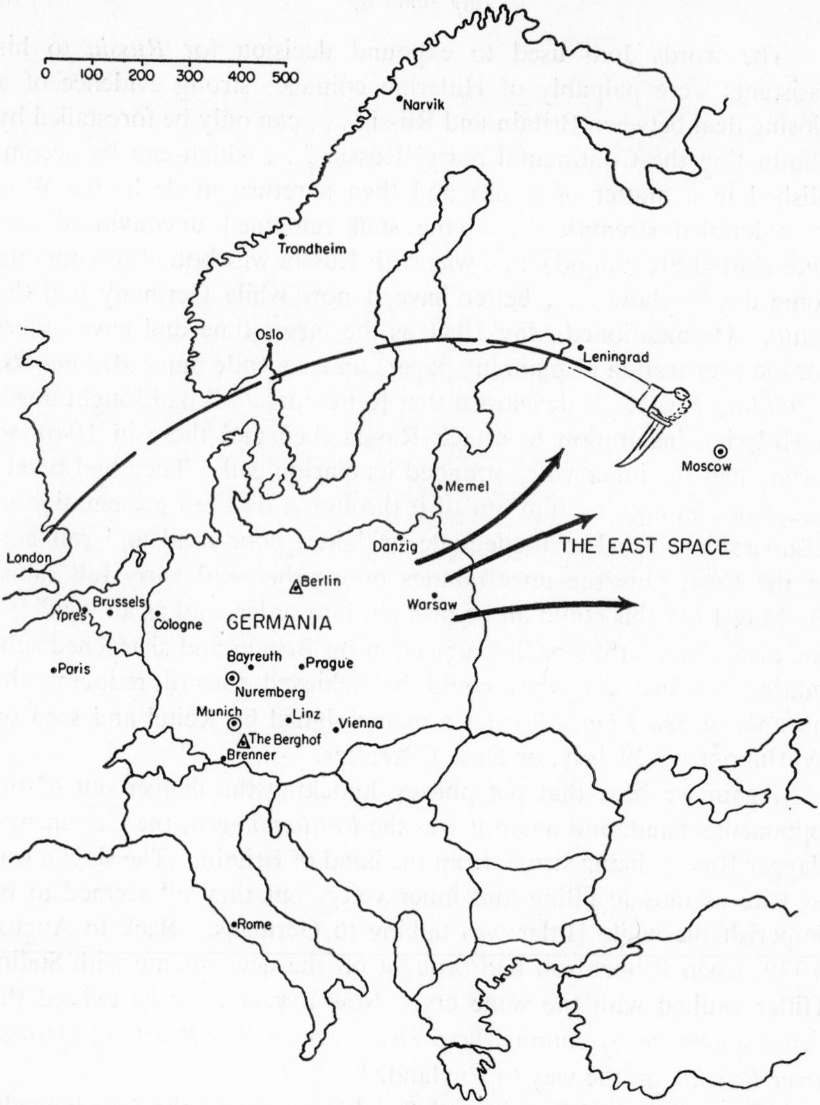
0 100 200 300 400 500
Narvik
Trondheim
Oslo
Leningrad
Moscow
Memel
Danzig
THE EAST SPACE
London
Berlin
Warsaw
Brussels
Ypres
Cologne
GERMANIA
Paris
Bayreuth
Prague
Nuremberg
Munich
Linz
Vienna
The Berghof
Brenner
Rome

Hitler's world: 31 July 1940.

ward peace anyhow, actions aimed at Russia could be carried out independently of the projected operations against England. This double talk betrayed the Hitlerian rationale in classic example. He had abandoned strategy.

The subject hardly deserves further laboring, yet justice to the German professionals demands a few more notes. Both Navy and Army representatives on Warlimont's staff submitted formal ob-

jections to Jodl in the days following the first shock of his bombshell.
They drew up their more sober reflections and appeared with them
personally.   Wrote Captain Junge:

Fully committed as I was in my own mind to *Sea Lion* and the Air
Offensive, Jodl's words had shaken me badly.   Therefore, a few days later
I presented myself with a short memorandum: Whether Russia had to be
attacked was a question for the statesman rather than the soldier; for my
part I had however to object to starting such a campaign before completing
the victory in the West and thereby freeing the rear . . . .   It seemed the
Führer's decision might be dictated by a Continental attitude, that is,
underestimation of the potential of Western sea power.   Jodl accepted my
presentation with unusual frankness . . . .   It seemed to me the business
bothered him too.   After about a week, having had extensive discussion
with Hitler, he explained that one's arguments in greater detail, exactly
in the words I later heard from Hitler's mouth.   He rejected the imputa-
tion of continentalism, saying that just because he rated sea power so
highly, had he arrived at the Russian decision.   With our [German] arms
situation, we were not at all in the position . . . to strike England decisively.
For the final battle against the West the center of gravity of armament
would have to be shifted from the Army to the Navy and Air.   But the
Army could not be weakened as long as Russia stood ready to attack us in
the rear . . . .

To counter von Lossberg's objections, Jodl ventured on a different
tack.   He said: "The Führer is afraid that the mood of the people
after a victory over England would hardly permit him to embark on
a new war against Russia."   In sum, Hitler's mind and spirit were
united on Russia, and he reached for any argument, plausible or farfetched, to turn objections back on their originators.   A little of each
facile argument he tried to believe himself, and probably did, but in
the main, he was making slick excuses.   Pertinent for *Sea Lion* was
his blanket evasion that Germany was in any event not armed to strike
a decisive blow at Britain.

We might suppose that apostasy of such dimension at the very
top would have cooled invasion ardor all along the chain of command and that a confused *Sea Lion* would have sickened and died.
Exactly the opposite happened.   In response to direct queries on the
beast's health after 29 July, the OKW planners, Warlimont, von Lossberg, and Junge, separately averred that, while they recognized Jodl's
news as a vote of no confidence in *Sea Lion* by Hitler, they for their
part spurred support of invasion all the more; they, who now knew
of the frightening Russian project, redoubled their efforts at pumping

new life and vigor into *Sea Lion* in the hope that his obvious fitness, and hoped-for preliminary successes, might blot out the eastern obsession. It was, of course, an uphill fight, for any operation that lacked Hitlerian inspirational drive had trouble getting ahead. General Feierabend, the OKH Russian planner, recalled that to him at the end of July *Sea Lion's* chance of survival looked dim. He had sensed a slackening off, and so had the junior Navy representative at Army Headquarters, Schulze-Hinrichs. Down below, however, that is to say, in the Army divisional ranks and the parallel Navy organizations, invasion feeling ran high and went higher. Steam had only just begun to build up on the job. No inkling of weak confidence or hints of abandonment had reached these enthusiastic regions. In size and multiplying demands, *Sea Lion* grew day on day. Something was going to have to be done with him.

The top leadership was well aware of the need for clarifying the ambiguous situation. The primary questions left open at the last Führer Conference on 25 July with Admiral Raeder were: (1) When could the Navy be ready? (2) What degree of protection would be guaranteed for the crossing? When Raeder said he hoped to have the answers by the end of July, Hitler had promptly scheduled a general conference for the thirty-first at the Berghof. That meeting of momentous import is now before us. The session began toward midday. In attendance were: for OKW, Keitel, Jodl, and von Puttkamer; for Army, von Brauchitsch and Halder; for Navy, Raeder. The Air Force was conspicuously absent; it developed later that Göring had already received orders privately from the Führer. Because *Sea Lion's* life was now up to him, Admiral Raeder led off.

He took an encouraging, though cautious, tone as he accounted favorable progress and thus strove to shake the onus for readiness from his shoulders. The preliminaries, he said, were proceeding with utmost pressure. Based on this experience, 15 September 1940 became the earliest ready date. Hitler broke in with a query about the weather from 15 September on. Around the twentieth it had usually been bad, Raeder admitted, and then it improved toward the last of September and in early October. He returned to proof of Navy advances by offering a brief of details from the well-reasoned Skl summary. Barge procurement and alteration were in train; manning, and deployment to mounting ports could be managed by target date (15 September) if luck held; the same applied to larger transport vessels. Mine clearance was underway, but its efficacy and that of barrier-laying depended on the achievement of air command. The diversion of water transport and personnel from inland traffic, and likewise from neighboring countries, was bound to cause major troubles in the internal economy; fisheries were also going to suffer. Raeder stressed these items once more in closing his remarks on the first question, Navy readiness. His pertinent answer came finally in the shape of a none-too-positive proposal to put off the operation until spring. And that answer he used again to the question of security during passage, which he took up next.

A feeling gains credence that, having failed to kill *Sea Lion* outright, Raeder was insinuating postponement. He devoted the rest of his recital to elucidating the hazards of executing the operation under the conditions demanded by the Army, rather than to enumerating the powers of the Navy for assuring passage. We have heard them from Skl: the tortures of a dark crossing imposed by a dawn landing; the need of beaching on an ebbing tide; the absolute requirement of a calm sea; and the probability of a prolonged interval between the assault wave and its reinforcement. Admiral Raeder explained that a reconciliation of Army-Navy differences on these points, and an attempt to meet the absolutes of tide and moonlight alone, made the problem one of timing, so that only two periods qualified: (1) from 20 to 26 August, which came too early; and (2) from 19 to 26 September, which fell in a doubtful weather period. What then? The Admiral left this to the imagination and passed on to the cardinal conflict, the Army insistence on a front that reached so far to the westward into Lyme Bay. Transports there, he claimed, would risk attack from Britain's primary naval bases while immobilized at anchor during a thirty-six-hour unloading period, and to expose them in that manner would be folly. Since widely separated landings could not be protected, the only solution he could offer was that the landing be confined to the protectable Dover Narrows. He realized, said he, that this burdened the Army with a harder task, but his wish in the first place was to insure that the Army got over. On this note of working together in the Narrows the Navy Chief ended his formal remarks, concluding that, all things considered, May or June 1941 offered the best time for carrying out *Sea Lion*. Admiral Raeder made no proposal for actions in the empty months until that time.[31]

[31] The course of the discussion has been plotted from three sources: (1) Admiral Raeder's recording, usually made shortly after the meeting, as aided by preconference notes (*FC*, 1940, vol. II); (2) W.D. Skl, which depended on (1) and on the Ad-

This was not the first time that postponement had crossed the minds of these conferees. But now the thought had been uttered openly, though lukewarmly, on behalf of the Navy. It was due for some skilful manipulation. Hitler immediately took up the word to exploit and guide the fresh possibilities. First he re-emphasized the controlling influences of weather. It was an old subject in connection with invasion to him and always a safe negative talking point. Nothing much could be done against it; force was of no avail. He ran on at length with examples of the havoc that could befall the operation. Next, there were the hazards posed by the British Army. Now it was down; in eight or ten months (of postponement) it could be reconstituted; perhaps air attack could retard British war production, but there remained the possibility of aid from Russia and America. Thereupon this master of suggestion turned contemplative as he had during the 21 July conference. He paltered over what else could be undertaken during a deferment, now seemingly accepted in his thinking. In his fishing-about on the twenty-first we perceived boredom with Britain as a problem. If nothing was to be done with her now, what else was on hand? But then decision for *Russia* had not fallen. By the thirty-first, it had. Hitler thereupon drew attention to the void of inaction that Raeder's deferment would create. The Hitler void ran until Invasion Russia, while Raeder's ran until Invasion England, an apparent coincidence of result but for widely differing reasons. Before *Dunkirk* we saw a similar confusion govern exchanges between Hitler and von Rundstedt. But in this case anything that Raeder, or the others, might accomplish against England, including perfecting invasion readiness, was bound to contribute to Invasion Russia, since Britain under prolonged threat might still give in and so free the rear for the East. For this reason Hitler could safely and with sincerity ask what else could be done in the interim. "How can we bridge the gap until May?" he asked, "Air Force, submarine

miral's verbal interpretations to the diarist; and (3) General Halder's shorthand recording on the spot. From a number of comparisons, as previously noted, a strong tendency on Admiral Raeder's part to put his best foot forward to Skl and the record can be traced. The important thing is that what he recorded, and told Skl for the diary record, make a complete exposition of what the conference results were to him, and on that understanding the Navy based its actions. General Halder's notes were necessarily briefer, and while they stressed Army points of interest, they rarely missed anything essential. They preserved the sequence of the exchanges and thus permit a reasonable reconstruction of the atmosphere.

warfare, Gibraltar?" He seldom opened himself to counsel so freely, and when he did it was a sure sign of manipulation.

Among other things, Hitler wanted the discussion to develop the only prudent course, deferment of decision on *Sea Lion,* while air attack went ahead. When the Army jumped in to propose reinforcing the Italians in North Africa, he parried and brought the focus back to direct action against Britain. "These diversionary maneuvers must be examined," he said. "Truly decisive results only through attack on England." In turning the Army off, Hitler passed the question back to the Navy, which was always good for baiting with the pretense that Britain belonged in her bailiwick. His words were both salve and challenge. They admitted the justice of Raeder's persistent preachment that Britain was the one to beat and at the same time put the riddle of how to do it up to him. It was clearly Raeder's turn again, and the Admiral was not loath to oblige. He proposed the landing of ten regimental groups in the Folkestone region and ran on warmly urging this project, but switched it to spring. He totaled up quickly the powerful additions to accrue to the Navy by May. By that time the *Bismarck* and the *Tirpitz* would have joined the fleet, also four cruisers and some destroyers, besides small craft. Hitler cut the misdirected sailor enthusiasm short with a sharp question. He obviously wanted solution for the moment, not for the following spring. What, he asked, would the relative strengths of the two navies be in the spring? Raeder was ready for this one. Oh happy thought! "That will depend on Air Force results," he shot back, and added that Britain still had her backbone of the fleet, thirteen battleships. He could not have spoken better for his Führer's design. Hitler took immediate advantage of the opening for springing his patently preconceived course of action: pin his faith on air offensive and leave *Sea Lion* dangling. He proceeded at once to pronounce that judgment.[32]

Hitler adroitly larded the statement of his verdict with a series of "ifs" and "buts" from which each service might draw some comfort, but it was mainly the Navy that he soft soaped. He covered every

---

[32] The Army by proposing action in North Africa had offered Raeder an ideal opportunity for forming a service combination and escaping from *Sea Lion.* North Africa action had found favor in Skl too. But instead of joining with the Army, Raeder leaves us with the impression of combining with his Führer against the Army, and also getting in a final dig at the Air Force. So strong ran the individual service desire for the all powerful Führer favor.

contingency that had come up and reserved for himself a wide latitude of choice. We quote in full from General Halder's record:

[There will be] increasing difficulty as things run on. Air war starts now. It will show with what relative strength we come out.
If outcome of air is not satisfactory, then [landing] preparation shall be checked.
If the impression comes, that the British are being shaken and that in due time [desired] effect is coming about, then [on] to attack.
So put up with economic derangements another 10 days. Conversion of barges can be continued during the winter in case of postponement to next year.
Diplomatic action: Spain. Question of North Africa is discussed. Führer considers [air] effect on enemy harbors. Effect on fleet? Dive bombers on armored decks.
Order: Preparations [for landing] shall be continued further; Decision in 8–10 days on actual [landing] attack. Army: Gear to target date of 15 September, broad front.[33]

There it was, the long-awaited showdown decision on invasion that decided only not yet to decide. In this regard it constituted a stall to trick Raeder into prosecuting *Sea Lion* preliminaries with renewed vigor. Hitler succeeded brilliantly. He topped off his performance with solicitous inquiry after the submarine war, granted increased materials to the submarine program, and again gave assurance of *Sea Lion* top priority, at Raeder's request.

Having spoken his piece and received some satisfaction, the Admiral made ready to go. Nothing at all of the eroding influence of the East plans was known to him. He rested content. Britain had been confirmed as the primary military target; the burden of dealing with her had been shifted somewhat toward the Luftwaffe. As for *Sea Lion,* he now possessed the highest priority, though it seemed to Raeder probable that the operation would be deferred to 1941. A

---

[33] Hitler exhibited his usual flair for graphic words, often indicators of his true feelings, in this important passage. It deserves most careful study in translation, for Hitler set forth what later guided German action (or inaction) against England. The fourth sentence summarized Hitler's invasion philosophy. It prescribes the condition under which he might have been willing to release *Sea Lion.* We interpret this condition to have been clear signs of deteriorating British morale to the point where a plea for negotiation stood in good prospect. This situation approximated that contained in Göring's comment on the late 1939 *Studie Nordwest.* He raised the thought that in such circumstance invasion would scarcely be necessary. Jodl's summation of 30 June implied the same line of thought. It comprised the confirmed invasion policy that was carried out.

mollified Navy chief went away to pass his misapprehensions, including one of a narrow front, on to his subordinates at Skl.[34]

The words of showdown decision revealed a design much deeper than mere duping of the Navy chief. They insured complete freedom of action for Adolf Hitler and laid the official groundwork for abandoning the West in favor of the East. Note how he spoke first of Air failure—almost anticipated it; yet not to evoke a remedy but only to put off *Sea Lion*. Note also how in case the Air effort should succeed he hedged *Sea Lion's* actual release with ambiguous qualifications of his own impression of Air effect on the British people and the likelihood of their giving in. Thus Hitler remained uncommitted, free to pursue redemption in the East. We turn to his discussion of it with the Army chieftains, which immediately followed Admiral Raeder's departure from the conference.

Hitler led in his secret with a show of care. He returned to *Sea Lion* and ran over the major infirmities—an operation surrounded by many technical difficulties, the hazards of weather, and enemy counteraction. "Our little Navy," he sighed, "only 15% that of the enemy's, . . . there remain: Mines (not fully reliable). Coastal artillery—good! Air Force. Decision shall always take account that we risk nothing without gain." Hitler referred to the decision that would initiate the invasion of England, and already in his mind he was building fences from a negative approach. He anticipated that Britain would not break under air attack. "Suppose," he said, "Britain made no approach [for settlement]: Eliminate the hopes that can encourage Britain still to expect a change in her situation. The war as such is won . . . ." He quickly threw out submarine action and air war as too slow and got down to cases: *"Britain's hope rests in*

[34] The established order of material priorities and changes therein during war offer a barometer of strategical thinking. War industry at home moves ponderously to meet the needs of strategy in the field so that once committed to a strategic decision a change can be made only with the greatest difficulty. Hitler exercised only a dubious understanding of these facts. The German Chief of War Economy and Armament, General Georg Thomas, understood them thoroughly, and experienced great trouble in meeting the changes ordered from above. After the war he wrote that at the end of July 1940 a Führer Directive required material "preparations for landing in England (*Sea Lion*) to be accelerated." He implemented these instructions with an economic directive of his own, which said: "The preparations for the landing in England (Operation *Sea Lion*) stand at first priority above all other measures." He recorded further that on 2 August he was informed by OKW that "the Führer viewed the general situation differently than at the close of the West campaign, and that for the year of 1941 preparations were to be met for every possible change in the political situation," and that Army strength was to be increased rather than decreased.

Russia and America," he pronounced. *"If her hope in Russia fails, America drops out too* because Russia's dropping out would enormously increase *Japan's* importance [against America] in East Asia. *Russia is the east Asian dagger of Britain and America against Japan . . . . Russia is the factor on which Britain places most reliance. Something has happened in London!"*

The British, said he, had been completely "down" but now they were again cheered up, as evidenced by intercepted telephone conversations; also Russia had been shaken by the swift development of the Western European situation. She had only to say, he explained, that she wanted no strong Germany and the British would take hope like a man on the point of drowning; thus in six or eight months the situation would be completely different (for invasion). Finally came the enchanting alternative: *"But, if Russia is smashed, then Britain's last hope is extinguished.* The master of Europe and the Balkans will then be Germany."[35]

With this climax the prospective master of all Europe dropped any pretense of interest in Britain as he launched into his heart's desire. *"Decision: In the course of this drive of setting things aright Russia must be eliminated. Spring '41."* Now he acted more the transported Führer of yore, grasping for his power words with the keenest relish: *zerschlagen,* beat to pieces, smash, filled his speech. *"The sooner we smash Russia the better.* Operation only makes sense if we smash the [Russian] state to its depths at one stroke. Mere conquest of certain land areas will not suffice." Racing ahead he inadvertently disclosed a background of prolonged scheming to justify his dream of Russia. He explained that a campaign halt during the winter of 1940-1941 would be dubious; therefore waiting until spring 1941 would be better. He even thought to drag in the crowded condition of the Baltic as further justification for eliminating Russia there. And back to the campaign: "May '41," he exulted, "5 months time for carrying the job through. This year would still have been best. But it won't go if unified execution is to be achieved. Object: The destruction of Russia's power of survival." Forgotten was the "detour on the way to England"; now it was all smash Russia.

So Hitler corroborated Jodl's news of 29 July, line, verse, and chapter; they were old, old words dug up from the deeps of the Hitlerian soul. They formed his fatal *unabänderlicher Entschluss,*

[35] The words and the course of the conference discussion are taken from the *Halder Journal* (German edition), IV, 126-29.

from which there could be no turning. How dreadfully personal this thing had gotten. Inner compulsions and limits such as surrounded Hitler are indigenous to every self, yet seldom do those of a single person so gravely affect the course of history. How many of us in summer 1940 would have dreamed that this man, out of himself, solely, had determined on Invasion Russia as his primary performance and had charged off England as an interim sideshow of small promise? That is where our investigation to this point has led us, and it comes as something of a shock.

The case is by no means complete, but we commence to see what we have been coming at for some time. Should we not stop here and cross off our fabulous beast as a monstrous fraud? Nothing came of him anyhow! The thought has plagued this reporter more than once. Is *Sea Lion's* devious course worth tracing further? Much simpler, let him die. But history is rarely simple. *Sea Lion* did have his effect. He did rouse the Germans. If we abandon him, we follow them into superficial circles of nearsighted postjudgment. To many German participants the answer to *Sea Lion* is stark simplicity itself— Hitler could not get interested. When conversing on the subject they invariably wonder at the curiosity of an outsider and with a grin get around to asking, "So why bother?" Trying to explain gets nowhere —that *Sea Lion* stood for Invasion England in our time, a point of history for any time, and for the West a ruddy moment of stress and strain, and lofty devotion. He cleansed Britons of all doubts and dedicated them to finishing the war as nothing else could have. Things that do not happen, that men render impossible, history may note more pointedly than some that did.

Then too *Sea Lion,* as none other, affords a first-hand demonstration of Adolf Hitler's decision–action machinery in operation. Not in stunning victory, but in flat failure. Thus *Sea Lion* etched on the pages of history the pattern of this man's shackled spirit.

What, indeed, is decision made of—or indecision?

Adlertag— *13 August 1940*

Sea Lion was dead! Everybody high up knew so, or thought he did. Yet these same everybodies knew this only in single isolated moments; in between they felt unsure of exactly what they knew. Included among them was Adolf Hitler. There England still was; he was not done with her, nor she with him. Could a bolt from the air produce what he could not give up? This was the question.

Since early July 1940, and before, the Luftwaffe had carried on a private small war against England, half-jokingly known as the *Kanalkampf*. The participants were dubbed *Kanalkämpfer,* canal fighters or brawlers. The fighting rose from no profound planning, but rather from the initiative of the flyers on the spot, for lack of a studied plan. Göring at Karinhall paid little heed; something had to be done, it might as well be that, while home leave, material renovation, and redeployment went forward. An odd laissez-faire attitude suffused Luftwaffe activities while time passed pleasantly in fine summer weather. Nothing was happening, not to the British fleet nor to its islands. The record shows no connection with *Sea Lion* or the remotest interest in him, either on the part of Göring or his Luftwaffe. In fact, the contrary was the case. When an air liaison officer from the L section of OKW went to Air Force Headquarters to clarify some invasion questions, the Luftwaffe spokesman astounded him with the remark, "Why, we are not doing a thing about that [*Sea Lion*]; Göring has passed the word nothing will come of it." Ill as this boded for invasion co-operation, it meant also that when and if necessary the Luftwaffe would do the British job singlehanded. Talk became current of *Grosseinsatz der Luftwaffe,* grand air offensive. Göring directed the operating forces to submit their "combat recommendations for winning air command in attack against England."[1]

There was more than a story behind grand air offensive, this exhilarating concept that now seized the popular imagination. The idea of decision over England by air action alone had, in truth, been discredited as early as 1938. General Felmy, former commander of Airfleet 2, had proofed the proposition in exhaustive map exercises and reached the explicit conclusion that a war of annihilation against England appeared beyond the capability of the means in prospect; only disruption of British life could be counted on, and whether this could crush the will to fight depended on many unassessable factors. Göring engraved his chagrin across the face of the Felmy study in his own hand: "I did not ask for a study that sets forth the possibilities and establishes our weaknesses—these I alone know best of all . . . ." Possibly he did, but he would have been the last to admit them to others and least of all to his master. Jeschonnek, who was friendly with Felmy, returned the study with a verbal message priceless for gauging Göring's personal strategy and character: "Judgments such as these make the Luftwaffe impossible! This is a slap in the face to the Field Marshal. He wants you to be told that if he commits the Luftwaffe against England in a concentration of all squadrons, then will the heavens over London grow dark."[2]

[1] The two airfleets concerned most were Airfleet 2, deployed in northeast France, the low Countries, and northeast Germany, commanded by Generalfeldmarschall Albert Kesselring, headquarters Brussels, and Airfleet 3, deployed in west and southeast France and southwest Germany, commanded by Generaloberst Sperrle, headquarters Paris. Airfleet 5 in Norway was available for diversionary operations against the British east coast and northern naval bases and the ships there. Deployment of air fleets is shown on the attached sketch. Kesselring to Ansel (Germany, 1953).

[2] Generalleutnant H. J. Rieckhoff, *Trumpf oder Bluff?* (Geneva, 1945), p. 17. General Rieckhoff was Plans and Operations officer to General Felmy, who has corroborated the Göring endorsement quoted above to me. As to the verbal message, he believed Rieckhoff may have withheld it from him, for he could not recall it, in order to spare him pain. In reputation General Felmy was among the few Air officers who understood air operations overseas and co-operation with naval forces on them. His honesty about the poor prospect of the air conquest of Britain contributed to his relief as the commander of Airfleet 2 in January of 1940.

Felmy nevertheless persisted. Backed by his younger friend Jeschonnek, who seemed to be just learning the facts of life, he conducted extensive map and game board exercises at the Braunschweig headquarters during the spring and summer of 1939. Support came also from a survey by the Luftwaffe's Intelligence Section, called *Studie Blau*. Together these two studies formed the high-level professional body of air thought with which the Luftwaffe entered the war. For Felmy the Royal Navy always constituted the primary target, yet the action radius of his bombers proved too short, and, moreover, their armament did not suit the task of ship attack. Likewise for his second priority, British overseas imports, the planes were too short-legged. Simulated daylight attacks on central England produced staggering losses, and a shift to low-visibility operation revealed techniques and training far below required standards. And so on down Felmy's well-considered list, one target after another tumbled into impossibility. His final judgment opposed the trump—terror attack on London—on which, the records reveal, the highest level had stacked its hopes from the beginning. "It is doubtful that a catastrophic effect on the capital city is in the position to reach decisive significance in the war. The probability exists much more strongly that in view of the toughness of the English mentality the national will to utmost resistance will experience an undesirable rise." The rejection of terror bombing recurs in each professional study with such frequency that it becomes clear that the German professional airmen were fighting an influence from above. They recognized it as an ill-advised and illusory method for waging war. However, they played along rather than face the full implications of standing firm.

Actually Göring's delusion of decision from the air was a practical property of no great depth. Bombast formed his stock in trade and, according to close observers, was quite undependable as an indicator of his true understanding. We know that he possessed good information and the mental capacity to apply it. But whether he would, made quite another matter. His simple problem turned about two interdependent goals: the Führer's favor, and the enemy's fear. If he could maintain or enhance the first by pumping up the second, he was made. Göring's nature did not permit disabusing his master of the Luftwaffe's invincibility, nor could this in any case have profited him. The question was not one of the air doctrine's validity as much as belief in it by the foreign powers. If they could be convinced (as indeed, they for a time were) that Nazi Germany possessed the power of decision from the air, good; the first need of the situation was met. In counter to misgivings of the careful Raeder, Göring played the tower of reassuring strength—"I can do this for you, mein Führer." Hitler had no trouble in believing what he wanted to hear. But this all made ancient history in July 1940. Then Göring seemed to be turning reluctant dragon. He procrastinated toward Hitler over attack on England, but applied the whip to the Luftwaffe.

Despite dallying and personal laziness Göring held a tight, though extended, rein on his underlings. He flicked the whip over them by telephone and conference at Karinhall. A meeting on 21 July deliberated actions until massive air offensive, which had gained general acceptance as matter of course, should start. At the conference Göring charged his commanders to have all in readiness beginning with the last week in July. For the meantime, he added to the Channel attack on commercial sea traffic the task of paralyzing "as far as possible" his Majesty's ships in home bases. From there he jumped joyfully to his stronger fascination—*Eagle Day,* or *Adlertag.* Air Fleets 2 and 3, according to plan, would hit south England, while Fleet 5 (from Norway) tied down British fighters in east and middle England. The objective was elimination of the RAF and only total *ausschaltung* (eradication) could provide the desired opportunity for deep attacks into the country. Therefore the aircraft industry came second. For *Adlertag,* he exclaimed, "I will order the time [to begin]. All fighters together in combined onslaught to knock out the bulk of the enemy fighters . . . ."[3] He was the boy, back in the heyday of pursuit squadron Richthofen of World War I as the last commander of that illustrious group, shooting out orders to this one and that one. To hell with the papers, he would tell them. The Luftwaffe's erratic performance and the dearth of reliable records bear testimony to his system. Still, the pattern of these quips and snap orders followed a conditioned course. The theoretical conditioning for Göring's Luftwaffe orders flowed from the early thirties and Colonel Wever, the first Chief of the Air General Staff.

In those formative years Wever, who was an Army General Staff product turned air enthusiast, fixed the initial course along which

[3] Vorträge und Besprechungen mit dem Reichsmarschall, 1940, 114, H 1237-1320 (MS in von Rohden Collection, National Archives, Special Collection Branch, Alexandria, Va.).

German air strategy hoped to develop. His teaching evidenced strong Douhet influence in that he emphasized an air capability for first eliminating the enemy air force, and then launching a knockout blow at the well spring of his war economy. For this decisive task Wever wanted four-engine bombers—he called them Ural bombers—and set about developing a prototype. The type never got into production.[4] In thus charting the course of the budding new weapon, Wever enjoyed the confidence of Hitler and Göring alike. What the Führer wanted most was a weapon of decision and he believed Wever could produce one. Unfortunately for the Luftwaffe this long-headed thinker died in a crash during 1936, and his concept, barely outlined and never truly proofed by himself, fell prey to his unstable sponsors.

Between them, Hitler and Göring worked up their own special air quackery in which the Hitler factor, stressing psychological effect, predominated. The vague generalized concept of decision by air fright exerted untold influence on the conduct of the war against Britain. Its thread can be discerned in almost every action. As we have said before, it produced the confidence that dared provoke war and its failure provided bewilderment leading to defeat on the European shores of the English Channel.

Some signs of invasion had already appeared along the Channel shores when Hitler on 30 July 1940 alerted the Luftwaffe for massive air offensive. The telegraphic order of that day from OKW to Göring read: "The Führer has commanded that the preparations for the Grand Attack of the German Air Force against England are to be met with greatest acceleration so that the battle may begin twelve hours after release of the [final] order by the Führer."

As we know, the decision to give Air a try had fallen. Keitel followed the conference of the thirty-first with a confirmatory summary to all the services on 1 August:

1. The preparations for *Sea Lion* are to be continued and completed by 15 September.
2. After eight or at most fourteen days, commencing with the grand (air) battle against England, which may begin about 5 August, the Führer will decide, according to the results of the

---

[4] Kesselring, *op. cit.*, pp. 32-41, 459-569, and Rieckhoff, *op. cit.*, pp. 39-61, are informative on the development of German air thought. Generalfeldmarschall Kesselring (who succeeded Wever) and General Paul Deichmann (who served under Wever and Kesselring in the Air General Staff) have remarked on the failure to produce four-engined bombers as a cardinal failure (1953 and 1954 to Ansel).

battle, whether the undertaking *Sea Lion* will take place during this year or not.

3. If the decision is *against* the execution of *Sea Lion* in September, all preparations are nevertheless to be continued but in a form so as to exclude serious injury to the economy by the paralysis of inland water traffic.

4. The operational preparations for the time being are to be continued on the currently planned broad basis in spite of the indication from the Navy that it can insure security only to a narrow [crossing] lane.

Combined in this brief summary of show-down decision were invasion and Hitler/Göring air magic in an ambiguous union, making of it all a plan within a plan within a plan to scare the British into submission. Fright motive was of course, an open secret, and as all projects do, this one acquired its distinctive label in staff vernacular, which was *angstmachen,* or make them take fright—really scare them. Despite hints to the contrary in Führer Directive No. 17 of the same day, no true operational link to invasion existed in the air reckoning. The two projects had but one thing in common, and that was to produce fright.

Directive No. 17 of 1 August 1940 furnished the awaited executive signal. Like many it belonged to the genre of official directives that constructed a plausible façade around private Hitlerian hopes. Officially it professed to be a decision culminating the siege preparations initiated so long ago in Directive No. 9 of November 1939. Herein now by No. 17 were provided the final prerequisites for Britain's immediate overthrow. What a journey, since November! Then England seemed remote to the Germans, scarcely worthy of notice. Let the Navy play with her at sea. Directive No. 9 had climaxed the Navy drive for recognition of her part in the war, Britain. It had presented a judicious mixture of siege by sea and by air in the hope of inducing Luftwaffe to join in. But how different in July from the anticipated siege. Indeed, siege had sunk into irrelevance; it was too plodding, too pedestrian. Now things had to go with a few shattering bolts from the blue. Two to three weeks at the outside should do it. "Give us two weeks of good flying weather!" the airmen cried. They had learned better long ago from Felmy, but many factors now invited them to change. The Hitler factor, the war's miraculous progress—Poland, Norway, France—all revived the earlier bombast of air invincibility. The trump card implicit in air power was about to be proved. Hitler had never wavered from that concept in his own mind since Bleriot's flight of 1909. Göring and his Chief of Staff readily agreed. Jeschonnek had his desired "Execute."

OKW staffers clothed Hitler's instructions in official words of the past in Directive No. 17, and thus lent an air of consistency and continuity to the thing. In the preamble we read the old cliché ". . . intensify air and sea war against the English mainland." The words began as of old but the tune jumped quickly to finale. Hitler dealt out six tasks, all Air except for a final lame filler granting the Navy freedom to sink everything at sea around England on sight. Summarized, the tasks ran:

1. Fight the RAF down with all forces available through attack on flight units, their ground organization, communications, aircraft industry and anti-aircraft equipment.
2. After air superiority is achieved, shift attack to ports, especially the installations serving food distribution to the interior. Spare southern ports as practicable.
3. Air attack on naval and merchant ships may thus be stepped down unless contributing to objectives of 2.
4. Remain ready to support naval operations and *Sea Lion.*
5. I reserve terror attacks in reprisal for my own ordering.
6. Intensified air war may begin 5 August at discretion of Luftwaffe. The Navy is granted freedom to begin projected intensified naval warfare.

The overriding emphasis on civilian life was clear; the British were to be made hungry but quickly, and perhaps terrorized a bit too, just as prophesied at the end of June in the Hitler/Jodl summation.[5]

While casting about in search of fresh aspects and late ideas, Göring had the Air General Staff call on the operating forces for their recommendations "in the fight to win air command during attack against England . . . ." This was the stated purpose of the first phase of action, beyond which planning hardly needed to go. Accord-

[5] In certification of exclusive emphasis on air effort, by memo of 5 August Keitel commended subsidiary tasks to support the air effort on the part of the Army and Navy. These concerned defense of own air fields, air/sea rescue work in the Channel, and increased submarine activity, which might become possible against the Royal Navy when it appeared in force under the impression the "attack of air force represented preparation for a landing."

ing to Jeschonnek, an outline of ideas from II Fliegerkorps (of Kesselring's Airfleet 2) was settled upon as framework. That outline, in common with all others (including British evaluation) seized on RAF Fighter Command as the tough nut to crack. But how; how decoy the RAF fighters aloft south of London where the short-legged German Messerschmitts could get at them? The planners were bedeviled by two interacting technical weaknesses: short-range fighters (Me 109) of inadequate number, and vulnerable bombers of deficient bomb capacity. These deficiencies, though known, were not considered fatal in the enthusiastic *Eagle* talk that pervaded early August. Perhaps the key lay in London itself, in whose defense the last British fighter would have to rise. Around a planning core of this sort—a threat to, or even attack upon inviolate London, the scheme of massive air offensive shaped up. Alongside came bombing of reachable fighter values, airfields, directing centers, and so forth, in South England. Once British fighter strength sagged, reduction would accelerate. For the rest, unescorted German bombers could thereupon knock out the air industries to make RAF air command over England irretrievable and leave it absolute in Luftwaffe hands. By thus eliminating enemy air potential in the Weverian tradition, the job was to be delivered in a simple neat package. Thence one could pursue any of a number of final strokes, including invasion. However, *Sea Lion* never actually entered the self-sufficient calculations of the Luftwaffe. Air power would do it all.[6]

The battle of the fighters carried a full flavor that huntsman-fighter-pilot Hermann could go for; in complete character he designated the forthcoming trial *Adlerangriff* (*Eagle* Onslaught), and its grand opening, *Adlertag*. On 31 July at Karinhall conference with his chiefs he reviewed the plan worked up during ten days of to-and-fro between operating forces and Air Headquarters. The minutes of the meeting record Göring's slogan-like adaptations, which emerged

[6] An examination of the outline ideas submitted by I, II, and III Fliegerkorps shows that all concentrated on the purpose of air action for command, to the absolute exclusion of invasion ideas. One outline hazarded a guess that *simulated* invasion preparations could contribute to the air purpose by attracting RAF aircraft. General Paul Deichmann, Chief of Staff at the time of II Fliegerkorps, has explained the details of the outline submitted by his Korps (Deichmann to Ansel, Germany, 1953; Annapolis, 1954, 1955). *Sea Lion* did not, he stated, enter the picture then, nor during the course of the operations, and not in Göring's conferences except for downgrading. Luftwaffe expert on English air target priority (the Chief of Intelligence, Schmid) was not consulted for recommendation of targets even related to invasion.

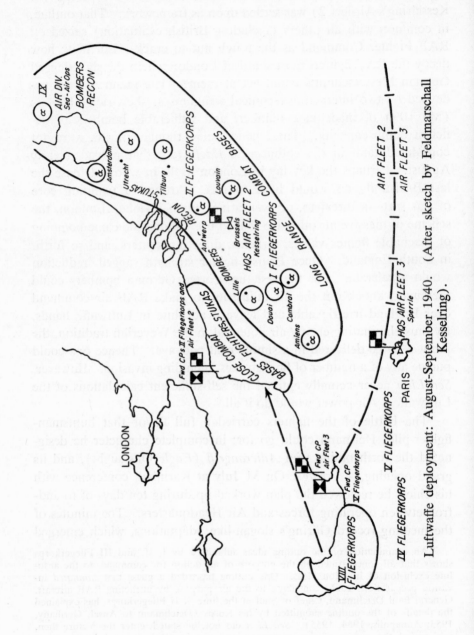

Luftwaffe deployment: August-September 1940. (After sketch by Feldmarschall Kesselring).

two days later as *Adler* directive. It aimed at RAF knockout à la Poland and France and gave no terminal date; three or four good days would suffice. He called for three successive attacks by Airfleets 2 and 3 to round out the grand opening day; Airfleet 5 from Norway would then join in on *Eagle* plus one day. Attack waves varied in allocation of fighter and bomber strength in order to confuse the enemy into committing fighters against every incursion. Attack number two repeated one, and in the early evening was to come a mighty third onslaught as clincher. Indeed the heavens were to darken over London—but only by induction. For in these early advices provision was made only for a pass or two at the city, to put the populace on edge and bring up fighters. A series of nagging oddments cluttered the conference, showing Göring's propensity to tamper and change, loss of aim, and interference, even here before action was joined. The thing had the look and feeling of improvisation and play. Most striking of all in big Hermann's monitions, written and verbal alike, was the absence of end purpose or any hint of it. Operationally therefore, this was a pure and simple contest of fighter aircraft for the right to fly. Progress was to be gauged by the estimate of total fighters left to the RAF each day. This figure had to fall below three hundred to mean victory on the way.

Conference followed conference toward the day of reckoning, each one crowded with more and more palaver. Simulated attack on London fell out, reserved for the Führer's personal order—old airman that he was. The number of specific admonitions jotted into the minutes sometimes ran to eighteen, twenty-two, or twenty-four items. On 6 August a superconclave, complete with *Eagle* toasts to consecrate *The Day* took place in Karinhall. An occasion it was, with all trimmings. Host Göring gave a whacking performance and set the date for two days hence, the eighth. Weather intervened to deflate the big build-up; as it did on the tenth, the next selected day. Hitler had descended from the mountain to be on hand for the fireworks; he fussed and fumed, by the eighth he gave up and returned disgruntled to the hill country. When Göring telephoned him late on the twelfth and reported good prospects for the thirteenth, he returned to Berlin. At long last *Eagle* took wing in anticlimax on Tuesday 13 August 1940. The preliminaries had not clicked at all well; the Luftwaffe literally stumbled into action.[7]

[7] The sequence of events and their atmosphere derive from official records, chiefly the von Rohden Collection and the war diary of OKW Operations; from

But for the flyers, *Eagle* was already on the wing the eleventh and twelfth despite Göring and weather. Fleets 2 and 3 had made forays on their own initiative against ports and ships along the length of the Channel, singling out Portland and Weymouth for extra attention. Lively fighter combat resulted over the water, giving a bag of 176 British planes, reported German Air Headquarters. Such a ridiculously high figure for the initial bag pointed to dangerous optimism that could lead to self-deception. It confirmed the lighthearted air of quick success, extant in the command precincts of invincible Luftwaffe.

On the day of days itself, 13 August 1940, fog and mist hung on and on to all but defeat the pumped-up hopes. In Airfleet 2 several formations eventually got off in advance of Göring's phoned postponement. Fleet 3 (Sperrle) farther along the coast, where breezes from the Atlantic cleared the way, fared better. It flew a substantial part of the assigned missions. The fourteenth came and went—weather and more weather; and then the fifteenth. Forecasts of both Navy and Air Force were proving unreliable. However the fifteenth did turn out a day of sorts. Toward midday, the weather permitted flying that approached *Eagle* pretensions. During the afternoon and on into the night all three air fleets, 1 and 2 over the Channel and Fleet 5 across the North Sea from Norway, entered the fray in massive co-ordinate actions. Well over 1,500 planes were committed to this first massed air onslaught in the world's experience. Göring pressed to get Operation *Lichtmeer,* or *Sea of Lights,* a planned knockout sequel to *Eagle,* into the air.[8]

By these exertions 15 August seemed to culminate *Eagle's* stumbling start in some measure, but he still fell far short of the vaunted blitz from the blue. In Britain the day was hardly distinguishable from others. It was in the Luftwaffe that mounting orders paced internal troubles and gave a delusive feeling of mounting effect. Controlling so many closely timed actions grew in com-

---

Helmuth Greiner, *op. cit.,* pp. 130-32; from Kesselring, *op. cit.,* pp. 100-109, plus consultation with him and his Chief of Staff of the time, General Wilhelm Speidel (Germany, 1953); from consultation with Generalfeldmarschall Erhard Milch, Göring's deputy; and from COS II Fliegerkorps, General Deichmann.

[8] Attack *Lichtmeer* (*Sea of Lights*) on air installations about London was planned as a follow-up blow to finish off British fighters. The sea of lights to be kindled around London was to convince the British time was up. The operation suffered postponements just as all other planned climaxes. The attacks of 18 August eventually approximated *Lichtmeer* intentions. Sharp RAF reaction shocked the Luftwaffe.

plexity. How different from operating over France, where each leader could confidently scan terra firma below and enjoy the freedom of a wide choice of action. Here against England a five-minute delay in arrival at bomber–fighter rendezvous near the Channel could ruin the strike before it was really underway. Communication between fighter and bomber had to be established in minutes just before entering combat; failures there and in control procedures heightened the hazards of intervening clouds and the strangeness of flying over water for the pilots. They might themselves soon be struggling in that very water. Short endurance was a constant worry. Operating out of Norway swiftly lost popularity while the rest of the bumpy performance vented some sharp complaints. German losses mounted to figures far from negligible, and England stood as tight and secure as ever. But not in the Hitler–Göring view.[9]

Earnest airmen wondered why they were still as late as 15 August peddling fake paratroop kits and counterfeit invasion literature onto England in lieu of bombs. The truth was that the top leadership continued to indulge its incredible fancies. Göring fumed about the weather and ordered the outfitting of a weather ship for the Atlantic that would do better than the Navy had, and then he took pains to explain the situation to an eager but impatient Führer. British fighter strength was down, Göring could safely report from Air General Staff evaluations. But try as he might, Chief of Staff Jeschonnek could not coax either him or the Führer to the scene of action on the coast. Both hovered over the nerve center of political intelligence in Berlin. Political fireworks in London was what these two avidly encouraged each other to believe in. The air demonstration could go on without them. For a final punch Hitler declared England under total blockade. He seized on the air show of the fifteenth as convincing proof of this and loosed a blast of verbal bombs to certify it. Then he departed for the mountains and let Goebbels spread himself in news releases carrying the most extravagant nonsense: "The beleagured fortress is no longer Germany but the British Island Kingdom. Germany will now oppose the unsuccessful British hunger blockade against German women and children by a total blockade of the

---

[9] The bulk of the German bombers took off from their bases without fighter cover, flew toward the Channel and there, over fighter bases on the coast, picked up their fighter escorts. The rendezvous had to be closely timed both to save fighter endurance and bomber navigation. Establishment of fighter/bomber communication had to click on the dot, and a chance cloud interposing at joining up could complicate the business immeasurably.

British Isles that is herewith declared . . . . The war at sea about England has burst into full flame . . . the whole region is contaminated by mines. Aircraft are attacking every ship . . . ." Hitler awaited the effect on the Berghof, and it was not long in coming. The British replied almost immediately with stepped-up bombing of Germany, ranging nightly in 100-plane sorties far and wide over Europe, even as far south as Munich. Nervously Germany's Führer ordered anti-aircraft guns redoubled in strength all over the Fatherland from war booty stocks. The wind had gone out of his verbal bombs and Göring's name was Meier several times over.[10]

What atrocious weather! Nothing much got done on the sixteenth with attack *Lichtmeer* to build on the effect of the day before, and less on the seventeenth. Then came a break. During the eighteenth flight conditions improved and offered opportunity for the second big day. The Luftwaffe swarmed over ground installations below London, some by mistake got in as far as Croydon, and others hit Portsmouth repeatedly. The reaction from RAF fighters was sharp and fierce. They wisely concentrated on the vulnerable German bombers who found themselves pursued well out over the Channel on the way home. One Spitfire rammed a lumbering Do 17. Luftwaffe fighters were at a loss, and the bombers, particularly that Continental workhorse, the Stuka, took a severe beating. The twin-engine Messerschmitt (Me 110) was no match for the Spitfire; not only that, the Spits easily held their own with the single-engine Me 109. In effective fighter strength, Spitfire against Me 109, the two air forces therefore might approach equality. By degrees the German miscalculations came home on the operating levels as the ferocity of the actions mounted. Yet despite uneven results, the Air General Staff felt enough encouraged to record a generally optimistic judgment: ". . . the large British commitment of fighters for defense confirms evaluations . . . and the necessity of beating the enemy fighters in the air before extending the air war . . . . The [German] units report combat zeal by enemy fighters has fallen off but not stubbornness of attack on bombers and their pursuit after attack . . . . Air Operations Staff

[10] Göring often boasted that if any enemy planes got into Germany his name was Meier. Navy leadership took strong exception in the Skl war diary to the paper blockade declaration. The claims, Skl knew, ran so far beyond well-known German capabilities as to discredit the maneuver in its own words. The sailors took no action but took comfort that over the Atlantic in America the blast might have a deterrent effect. They knew that the Hitler/Goebbels claims were so absurd as to discredit themselves in the British view.

sticks by continuation of the battle against enemy fighters under all circumstances . . . ." It was 18 August. Weather barred continuation in significant power until the twenty-fourth. The respite came as a godsend to hard-pressed Fighter Command in England.[11]

Operating level or Air General Staff, neither place was where this first pure air war was going to be won or lost. On the face of things *Eagle* had failed his publicity. Almost a week was gone now, and he had wrought no wonders, raised no apocalypse, or even raised a thrilling turn through incredible feat of arms as, say, in well-remembered 10 to 18 May past. Then the exciting news ran from one ecstacy to a greater one on the morrow. It was now Göring's war, and he needed to recapture the old mood for himself and his Führer, fretting on the Berghof. Göring summoned his leaders for a noonday check on the eighteenth. He opened the meeting with sarcasm, "attack air industries, not the lightship off Dover," and proceeded to deal out some eighteen further complaints: keep closer touch with me; try to outmaneuver the weather; and so on and on. Disgruntled leaders bided their time and returned to their hard-working, busy commands. The attacks of the eighteenth had taken place in their absence. That big baboon, spouting about lightships. What does he know? He has not been near the front.

Both Fleets 2 and 3 were able to renew attacks against ground installations on 24 August. Fleet 2 hit targets southeast of London while Fleet 3 took care of those around Portsmouth. Only feeble response met the Portsmouth attackers, but about London surprisingly sharp reaction met Kesselring's fighters and developed extensive air combat. The official reckoning came up with a guess of some two hundred defending fighters still active around London alone, a figure which was altogether contrary to expectation, and most disappointing. The picture remained hazy and unfinished as before. How many RAF fighters were there actually and where did the renewed strength come from? Was the time ripe for the next phase of deep attacks on industry, or what? The Luftwaffe command never really gained an insight of sufficient exactitude. One day's experience failed to mesh with that of the next or any other; there were too many variables and no one gauge read true. These were the new mysteries of pure air

[11] The quotation above comes from the Skl war diary. The Naval liaison officer at the Luftwaffe Headquarters made daily detailed reports to the Navy on the air war. The reports form an excellent record of the air war from the German side.

war in which physical certification of results was lacking, and where tricks of God and man compounded the imponderables.

On the firing line the going got heavier perceptibly; spirits held high generally, but here a word and there a sign of tension and uncertainty. The field commanders stuck fast by the aim to extinguish Fighter Command despite some ordered digressions brought on by continued unfavorable weather. A second five-day period of poor flying weather descended (25 to 30 August), and Luftwaffe bomb emphasis shifted to night drops on deeper-lying industrial cities like Birmingham, Coventry, Hull, and then to Manchester, Liverpool, and Birkenhead. Shipping had been spotted glutting the docks of the latter ports. For several succeeding nights upwards of 140 German planes were over them. Air mining of the Thames was increased also and at its head, Tilbury was heavily hit. But no stratagem to decoy RAF fighters aloft for combat was omitted—still without definitive success. The fighter bags varied from forty to a doubtful seventy. On the thirtieth and thirty-first this figure took a decided jump—better weather had arrived.

"August you must"—on each of its final two days over 1,200 German fighters took the air to strike final blows against Fighter Command. They were the only days, of the long and grueling stretch, since *Eagle* Day, in which cumulative effect could have been hoped for. Luftwaffe intelligence estimated 100 RAF planes downed on each, and even with a 30 per cent discount, which was the going rate, the figures were impressive. It seemed that only the last little way remained and that the tide at last was turning in Luftwaffe favor. Recalling that situation in 1952, the Chief of Air intelligence wrote: "The position of Fighter Command at end of August . . . was judged as highly critical by Commander in Chief Air [Göring]. The total strength of British fighters at this time was estimated as some 300 operational planes . . . . The German Air Force had achieved temporary command over the air in the southern part of the British island, though it had not succeeded in wiping out the British fighter units . . . ." But was it enough?

No cry of enough had come out of England, no sign of collapse on the way, no populace in revolt, no political fireworks, only sour, thick smoke and defiance. Things seemed not changed at all in political feeling. In fact, nothing was different about Problem England, except that the will to resist among Englishmen had been tempered into the toughest steel. *Eagle* remained something of a buzzard, valiantly though young German airmen had fought to make him over. They were not yet done; presently they roared directly over London in the final trial. While they regrouped for that adventure, we can catch up on *Eagle's* running mate, *Sea Lion*. Rather than wriggling himself out of sight, he had been growing day on day, and without the least help from the air war.

Broad versus Narrow Front—August 1940

Army and Navy did in truth prosecute *Sea Lion's* readying in dead earnest during August. Interest ran high and went higher as *Eagle* faltered. The volume of papers issuing on a subject is always a fair index of what goes on, and how strongly. As to *Sea Lion,* his interest could be gauged by the weight of papers alone. In August this figure took on heavily and nearly doubled the output of July.[12] But not alone in office and typewriter did things warm up. The waterfront had never seen such stir and agitation, or such a mixture of soldiers and sailors rushing here and there. A bird's-eye view was, however, deceptive, for the courses of the two services diverged day by day toward wholly different objectives. Theorizing apart in an alien field had led to irreconcilable preconceptions.

Admiral Raeder departed the Führer Conference of 31 July after stating his *Sea Lion* case, while the Army representatives remained behind. Raeder's theme turned about those eternal disrupters of amphibious harmony—time of landing (daylight or dark) and breadth of landing (broad or narrow front). On the first he appeared to have consoled himself with pushing *Sea Lion* into a bad weather period, for he disposed of the Army's insistence on a dawn landing by simply stating that under those conditions the operation was executable only in the narrow time span from 19 to 26 September. The second, the Army's desire to spread its beach assaults over 235 miles of coastline, Raeder rejected altogether as irresponsible. No one joined issue with him at the conference. Though this in no wise justified an assumption that his point had carried, Raeder gave that

---

[12] No operation can rival an amphibious attack in paper production. A captain of a U.S. cruiser became aware of this early in the Normandy landing and kept accurate weight tally of the pertinent papers reaching his ship. His total by D Day had climbed to 236 pounds.

interpretation to Skl on his return there—that is, the assault would be restricted to the Dover Narrows.[13]

In actuality, after Raeder departed, Hitler heard the Army and approved exactly the opposite; he directed that preparations continue on the broad basis. Keitel made this clear in his summary of the decisions for that day. Hitler added an undeliberated and naïve straddle to his decision; that if necessary, the operation could be narrowed in the course of execution. The Army chieftains registered no objection to this wild notion. They were content, having scored again by Führer decision. As on 13 July, they had maneuvered approval of their own hard and fast invasion plan. Now, with broad front in the bag, they could fetch a sigh to relieve the gloom spread by von Greiffenberg's discouraging Navy news of the previous day (page 169 above). The intestine struggle was not yet over. We trace its course, for out of the wrangle eventually emerged the final plan for Invasion England, 1940.[14]

At Navy, Skl fetched its own sigh, and set diligently and thriftily about intensifying preparations for the narrow front. On this basis renewed guides and directions went out to effectuate an ingenious scheme as follows. So far, sorting out the Army's landing-wave requirements in terms of ship space by the Navy had led to serious time-robbing misunderstandings. The soldiers innocently thought to array grand attack waves on the open sea off the mounting ports. All

---

[13] The Navy mentioned no figure of 235 miles but did mention figures in the neighborhood of 60 miles. From North Foreland to Lyme Bay tots up some 235 statute miles, and this was the Army front that the Navy would have been compelled to protect on the sea. It may be that shorter Navy estimates of frontage came from totaling of individual assault areas.

[14] Draft entries in War Diary Defense Branch Wehrmacht Operations (MS, Office of Chief of Military History, Washington, D.C.: hereinafter cited as the W.D. OKW Ops) recorded for 1 August 1940: "After the report of C-in-C Army on the state of preparations for Operation Sea Lion the Führer has decided that planning for a landing on a broad front should be continued. Necessary restrictions could take place in the course of the operation." Keitel's summary of the Führer's decisions, though dated 1 August, did not issue until after 2 August and was not commented on in the Skl war diary until 5 August. During this lag Navy planning and dispositions for a narrow front (based on Admiral Raeder's misapprehension that broad front had been discarded at Führer Conference 31 July) gathered headway. Keitel's summary of Hitler's decisions were recorded in the Skl war diary, 5 August, as follows: "a) Preparations for Sea Lion are to be continued and to be completed, also by Army and Air Force by 15 Sept. b) Führer will decide after 8-14 days after beginning of massive air offensive if Sea Lion will still take place this year. c) Even if decision *against* execution in Sept. falls, all preparations are to continue but in such a manner that serious injury to the economy is avoided. d) The operational preparations are to continue on the *broad basis* in spite of Navy notice that it can guarantee only a narrow lane."

their imagination and exercises with models would not dissuade them nor bring out the tribulation of loading in shell-torn ports and sortie-ing thence through imperfectly cleared channels to wave stations off an open coast. The Army's primary wish, Navy figured, was to throw troops in the strength of three divisions upon the hostile shore simul-taneously and have them fight for a beachhead. Good! This, Navy could do, but only in the Narrows; and so Navy proposed centering effort on the creation of a tight, secure crossing lane there, through which landing craft could stream in a closed circuit from shore to shore. Thus would be constituted a continuous-flow pipeline, as originally imagined by Jodl. The northern boundary of the pipe ran from Ostend to North Foreland, the southern, from Le Touquet to Beachy Head, the diameter in the neighborhood of sixty land miles. After further consideration, the landing frontage on the English shore narrowed to a strip from Folkestone to Beachy Head. The concep-tion of a secure continuous flow lane (which seems today as good as the landing equipment and the circumstances afforded) became the core of the latest Navy plan. Even this greatly reduced plan would demand herculean feats in making usable the devastated mounting ports of Ostend, Dunkirk, Calais, and Boulogne, as well as satellite ports and inland approach canals. But to the Navy there was in the plan the distinct advantage of at last knowing where things stood. The sailors could accurately estimate the ports' mounting capacity and cut their craft requirements to that cloth. Getting the limits established is a point of progress in every landing venture. Admiral Raeder ordered another all-out effort to meet the changed require-ments on this basis, while Skl despatched the newly arrived Army liaison officer, Colonel von Witzleben, to squeeze concurrence out of OKH. Said the Skl diarist on 2 August, "Skl fears that the [Army] General Staff will not depart from its demand for an operation on a broad basis."

The next few days, 2 to 5 August, produced a lull in the Army-Navy contest because the leading players were absent from their teams. They were off visiting test demonstrations of amphibious assault gear. On the island of Sylt, off the Danish border, Field Marshal (since 19 July) von Brauchitsch and General Halder fore-gathered at the Reinhardt experimental base to witness river-barge beach-unloading, beachfire from barges, and sundry tank demonstrations. Admiral Raeder represented the Navy, and he closed at once with von Brauchitsch for their second *Sea Lion* discussion. It was now 2 August 1940 with tentative S Day but six weeks off.

That distinguished day-to-be came under discussion at the outset, apparently at the Army's instance. Intelligence had been received at Army that Navy might steal a march by reporting ready earlier than anticipated, even by late August. The Chief of Army Engineers, who worked with the Navy in providing landing craft, was directed to "oppose the earlier date . . . . Possibly a maneuver of Navy to have entire plan dropped by showing the Army could not hold up its end."[15] So, naturally, von Brauchitsch eagerly sounded Raeder; they agreed that the provisional September hop-off date the fifteenth must stand. Amphibious tanks, their transport and launching, another favorite with the Army Commander-in-Chief, came under discussion; also, something on command responsibilities, and on the tactical particulars of crossing. Raeder proffered training courses at Emden for commanding officers. All seemed harmony, but the vital question of broad or narrow front was ignored, and for the good reasons that both parties wanted to avoid muddying the waters; each felt safe with Führer backing for his own view. They met again in direct collision over this point on 5 August in Berlin.

The experimentation centers, Army at Sylt under General Reinhardt, Navy at Emden under Fregattenkapitän Heinrich Bartels and Air Force at Rangsdorfer See under Colonel Siebel, were paying off handsomely. Reinhardt and Bartels worked closely together. The practical realities of amphibious assault bore in on the mutual understanding stronger day on day. The approach to the landing beach and the firing of guns from the water to cover this critical stage, the dire lack of true landing craft, disembarkation and beach fighting, the muddle of bridging from prahm (barge) to firm beach to unload tanks and trucks, the hazards of broaching, the cumber of prahm towing, all of these disturbing problems plus the unfamiliar sea techniques involved and the prodigious labors they called forth, were discovered and worked over with notable logic and excellent results. However, the number of soldiers and sailors exposed to the teachings remained pitifully small. Troop units along the coast began just now to get at the nub of their appalling tasks. Each strove man-

---

[15] *Halder Journal* (Lissance), VIII, IV 9. For the record of the conference, see IV, 147 a.

fully to devise its own unique solution. Much was being learned
and a great deal accomplished but at the cost of irreplaceable time.[16]

Herr Fritz Siebel's interest in landing craft had prospered and
blossomed finally into a *Sonderkommando* (special command) to
improvise Luftwaffe invasion craft, and test them on Rangsdorfer
See, a lake near Berlin. Everyone for himself, with a private navy,
seemed the order of the day. Siebel had by now evolved his *kleine
Fähre* (small ferry), which consisted of two bridging pontoons in
catamarran arrangement, spanned by a trusswork that carried aircraft
engines with air propellers. On the quiet Rangsdorf lake the contrivance turned out great noise but only about four knots through the
water. To watch this and pass judgment, the high Army party arrived
from Sylt. Its members professed interest, but their final verdict was
unfavorable; General Halder entered simply, "Nothing new, may not
stand up in surf." Remarks to the Siebel command brought out that
the Army talent not only questioned seaworthiness but also the ability
of troops to withstand the rigors of crossing in the flimsy craft; they
would arrive on the hostile shore unfit for combat. It may have been
a hasty judgment, for when fitted with water screws later, they proved
themselves. All the materials were on hand, pontoons were far
more plentiful and handier than barges, and their novel utilization
implied a means of solving the critical landing craft shortage. The
record shows no attendance by Navy at this test. Army turned the
project down.

In the following days the battle of *Sea Lion* frontage—was it
to be broad or narrow—resumed. The Skl's diarist had read the signs
right; the Navy's proposed continuous-flow lane received a dour recep-

---

[16] The efficacy of the experimentation centers is evident from the reports of their
commanders, fortified, in the case of the Navy, by talks with Captain Bartels (who
later in 1940 commanded at Dunkirk's contribution to *Sea Lion*), and in the case
of Air Force by conversations and correspondence with Herr Siebel and his close
associate Dr. Justus Koch. Reinhardt made a meaty report to his superiors at the
end of July and in response to it came the visit from von Brauchitsch and Raeder.
In his report Reinhardt ticked off the course of his discoveries. He invited attention
to the fact that a much smaller number of suitable canal barges than anticipated
would become available. The barges were called by various names, the inclusive
term being *Prahm*. The beaching and ramp unloading of *Prähme* (plural, rendered
herein by prahms) had not been solved. Firing guns from sea had been practiced
with mediocre success; beach assault from small river-crossing boats and towed
floats had gone better. Submersible tanks bulked as the trump card; tests were progressing. The importance attached to these juggernauts becomes clear from Reinhardt's recommendation that the Luftwaffe refrain from dropping bombs in the
shallows of landing beaches to leave the bottom clear for submersible tank movement
onto the beach.

tion in OKH.   Jodl from OKW informed Navy that Raeder had misinterpreted the Führer's words, but Keitel on 5 August left the question hanging when Raeder pressed for clarification.   He had failed to budge von Brauchitsch from the broad front during a prolonged session on that same day.   At the end Raeder proposed that the chiefs of staff of the two services once more review the whole business and settle it.   We perceive the Chief of the Army General Staff getting his wind up when he remarked, "What would be the good of it since we have no common ground for discussion?"   He was correct in more ways than the one he had in mind—the lack of a common operational basis.   More than mere operational differences lay at the root of this grand impasse.   Each service had so long gone its private way, outguessing and outmaneuvering the other, that making any common cause at this late hour went far beyond human capacity.   At any rate the cards at last were down; make of them what they could.

We have a stake in the result, for it affords vivid demonstration of how the prolonged pursuit of parochialism and self-interest can lead otherwise devoted services into a dead end.   Late on 7 August the conferees boarded a staff railroad train outward bound from OKH at Fontainebleau for the Channel coast, where the Chief of the Army General Staff wanted to gather first-hand impressions of the invasion theater and its training hubbub.   Admiral Schniewind, assisted by Fricke and Reinicke, stood in for the Navy; General Halder spoke for the Army.   Face up, the cards did have a strictly operational look, but if we remember their history, suspicions and chicanery clouded their meaning.   The Navy's reluctant approach to invasion and dubious hopes of quashing it altogether that ended in proposal to confine the landings to the Dover Narrows stood against the Army's suddenly roused interest through "unemployment" problem, and the adroitly maneuvered preapproval of a monstrously infeasible broad-front invasion.

With each side wedded to its own preconceptions the first truly authoritative efforts at mutual instruction and compromise began.   They were to make a common plan, but this fact was poorly understood.   In defense of his plan General Halder set a friendly tone to the proceedings by explaining the land fight reasons that rendered a narrow front unacceptable.   He reasoned well that the Navy proposal meant the frontal assault of a bastion headland (Folkestone to Beachy Head) from a marshy foreshore that excluded all opportunity of outflanking the high ground.   Twelve British divisions could sit secure

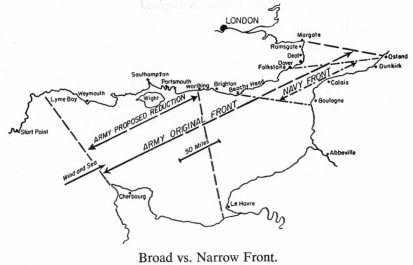

Broad vs. Narrow Front.

---

on the heights back of the marshes and, when ready, could turn it into a graveyard for the floundering attackers, who would have neither tank nor artillery support. He pictured a grim fate for the three divisions that the Navy wanted to throw ashore on this narrow frontage in the first strike. Some way had to be found to get at the flanks of the position, and thereupon the General brought out the minimum conditions that would meet Army needs—a flank landing at Brighton in the west. Lyme Bay still further west would fall out. And the need for flank action applied equally in the east. For that purpose a complementary landing was required at Deal, above Dover. The Halder case for this reduced front, Deal to Brighton, was eminently sound fom the land fight view. With Lyme Bay gone, the Army had given up close to half of the original demand frontage, which was no trivial concession. But would it do from the sea view? Could the troops be gotten ashore for even this shrunken front by the meager sea-going hardware on hand? The land fight against the landing fight— here the two arms parted company, as is commonly the case, the sailors straining to make sure of a landing at all, while the soldiers concentrated just as hard on winning the ground fight that must follow. In reconciling these two fundamentals in one attack plan lay the nub of joint amphibious planning.

The Navy representatives objected to the Deal proposal at once on the grounds of a poor sea approach and exposure to artillery fire from shore. Nothing daunted, General Halder sailed on to express confidence in the advantage of tactical surprise by the landings. Navy had to reject that idea too and explained how far out of question surprise lay, since the eight-hour turmoil of craft sortie from jammed Channel ports could not remain hidden from the foe. This news, which actually was old, took the soldiers completely aback. They finally countered with the suggestion of diversionary movements at sea to mislead the opponents. But neither craft nor sea room existed for such byplay, and again the Navy had to refuse. It was becoming a habit and the brothers in arms were growing unhappy. It seemed there was very little the Navy could do but object and reject.

More was yet to come as the Navy team returned to the horror of the still widely spread front from Deal to Brighton. The hazards from open sea, from tide and weather, the problem of logistics all applied equally to Army's Brighton as they had to Lyme Bay; and Brighton suffered the added threat of counteraction from Royal Naval forces based at adjacent Portsmouth. On these points the sailors took their pious stand; Brighton, too, was out for them. The debate was back where it started. The futility of it all was too much for General Halder. He swiftly reaffirmed the Army position and concluded with a rejection of his own in these terms: "I reject the proposal of the Navy for executing the landing only in the narrow space Folkestone–Beachy Head in sharpest terms and designate such proceeding from the standpoint of the Army as pure suicide. I might just as well at once turn the landing troops through the meat grinder." Navy responded in kind that it in turn rejected the broad landing as not alone suicide, but as an outright sacrifice of the troops committed.

There followed a few exchanges on the countermeasures the British could really bring to bear against invasion while it was on the water. A sense of overanxiety on Navy's part seemed to be what the soldiers were baiting; but surprise smote them once again when they learned the true poverty of German naval combat strength and the limited number of suitable transports. A quick calculation showed that the landing on the broad front under the most favorable circumstances might string out for forty-two interminable days. Surprise and rejection had been worn out; there was no use of further discussion. Each side restated its case without change, and on that futile note the meeting broke up. The conferees agreed only to report disagreement to their superior so that decision ex cathedra, on this purely professional operational matter, might be sought from the Führer.[17]

[17] The war diary of Skl briefs the minutes of this important conference. The

But how was World War I's Austrian regimental runner to judge this vast overseas project? Or had his stature in this new age of miracles truly achieved these proportions? Here was unequivocal proof that it had. This group of high-minded, well-equipped men relinquished to Hitler the solution of a purely professional problem, which lay wholly within their own competence. The incident provides a most singular historical fact.

The two arms continued their physical *Sea Lion* preparations along independent lines, each according to its own persuasion, while the third engaged in a private enterprise to reduce England from the air. We need to catch up on the waterfront and the separate plans and activities of Navy and Army there.

The sailors were well along on the righteous road of narrow front by the 10th day of August 1940. They divided the Channel into mounting areas A and B. Area A encompassed the gray French nose jutting toward England; its ports were from east to west, Ostend-Dunkirk-Calais-Boulogne. Area B, auxiliary to A, adjoined it at either end, east and west. Thus Rotterdam and Antwerp in the east, and Le Havre and Cherbourg on the far west, were to ready craft and feed them into A, whose ports, satellites, and inland canal nets constituted the heart of the invasion complex. So the Navy cut her cloth to achieve balance between craft available and capacity of the complex to accommodate them. Army requirements, Navy decided, would have to conform.

The chain of naval command placed an officer over each main port and adjuncts, naming him Naval Station Commander Ostend, or Dunkirk and so on. His numerous tasks included seizure of likely craft, barges, tugs, and motor boats in his bailiwick, readying the ports for loading and hop-off, and reconciling this work with interested Army authorities, who were, of course, preparing a wide landing. Over the whole water labyrinth two higher Navy commands held sway from headquarters in Paris; over general Navy shore administration and control of inland waterways stood the Commanding Admiral France, while over sea operations, and their general direction, was the Naval Group Commander West. Under him came the Fleet Commander who actually carried out the sea operations. *Sea Lion* thus became the specific affliction of Vizeadmiral Lütjens of later *Bismarck* fame. He planned to establish himself at once-fashionable

---

Halder Journal, IV, 136 agrees, as does the information gathered from officers present.

Trouville near Le Havre; neither his command post, nor other Navy command posts, began normal functioning until August was well along. An important lesser post was the mine command, because nothing could move until the minesweepers cleared a way, and no crossing lane could approach usefulness until flanking mine barriers were laid to impede Royal Navy ingress. Commodore Ruge regulated these matters; he set up shop alongside the Fleet Command near Trouville.

None of this shore basing by sea commands came easy. Getting established ashore, setting up communications, the quartering, messing, and policing were troublesome chores. Sailor skill at piracy notwithstanding, they have never understood fully how to go about the shore business—how to stake out a claim, or what its limits should be, or how to come by the essential paraphernalia through hook or crook from the neighborhood, and how to get the whole encampment functioning. Sailors do much better on a vessel afloat, any old hulk or station ship in which control can be direct and positive, and sustaining life can lose its many worries. Like most young men would, the German seamen responded to the tasks and learned the shore game, but it took time.

Navy problems in men and material multiplied. The amphibious desideratum eternal, adequate landing craft, had early given promise of easy solution. On paper the resources of Germany, the Lowlands, Scandinavia, and France in floating equipment seemed ample. An estimated requirement of 1,800 canal or river barges, 500 tugs, 150 steamships, and 1200 motorboats, it was thought, could be met from vessels scattered throughout the Continent. But, then came the practical rubs of physical seizure, manning and assembly at repair yards; of strengthening and fitting for beaching; and finally, of deploying swarms of these floating misfits to mounting ports through war-damaged inland waterways. To do these wonders the Navy overnight created a totally new force manned by 24,000 bewildered landsmen. Finding qualified crewmen pinched even harder than finding craft for them. The assignment of a sprinkling from the regular Navy, the release of soldiers and airmen, impressment of fisherfolk and rivermen, went on apace, and, as ever, not without its humors.

The German word for inland waterman is *Binnenschiffer*—a man in great demand in these days—and for beekeeper is *Bienenzüchter*; not too far apart for a good punster. "All right, my man," said the press gang leader, deep in south Germany, to a vagrant just picked up, "what do you do?" *"Bienenzüchter,"* came the broad southern reply. *"Binnenschiffer?* Good! You're just the man we want. Here is your ticket. Report to Motorprahm 682 at Mannheim by noon tomorrow." Many such stories enlivened the waterfront. The Chief of the Army Engineers, General Alfred Jacob, recounted one from his own family, on the mixing of Army and Navy personnel. He encountered his nephew on the street in a strange sailor uniform. "But I thought you were an engineer?" queried the uncle. "Yes, sir, I am, but now I'm taking my second training in the Navy."

No cocksure deciding, no action however resolute, could dispel practical problems of these proportions. Only time and training shakes out the bugs and eventually brings order, and of either there was the least in *Sea Lion's* charged atmosphere of "get going," "do something." Up the great home rivers, and especially the Rhine, went the Navy to contest the indefeasible right of landlord Army to everything in the hinterland. Press gangs swept craft and their crews wholesale down the river. Boat and shipyards along the river banks undertook conversion work as the barges or prahms lumbered down toward the estuaries. For France and the Lowlands a reckless character who went by the title of Transport Chief Paris, stepped high, wide, and handsome in his new-found glory. He did an extravagant plenty of commandeering, converting, and ordering, to the point where no one knew what craft were on hand or where. Something was being done, often too much. Stolid waterfolk broke into smiles of wonderment and disbelief. What would they think of next?

It was madness, said these old hands, to think of taking maimed barges to sea in the winds and tides of the Channel. Even should they succeed in stemming the currents (at four or five knots), the bow wave would wash over into the holds and sink the lot. The land soldiers found the conjectures discomforting. Gossip and stories grew, while deliveries of craft to troop units fell far short of initial promise. Experiment and training centers, mounting ports, and troop leaders, everyone along the coast, set up a yammer for practice craft. Admiral Raeder made a flying inspection through his dizzy new kingdom and issued renewed instruction of great length. Hard-pressed Navy could do little about relieving the shortages.

However, the craft were sifting out into loose-type categories according to their prospective uses. The canal or river barge (prahm) remained from first to last, the do-all work horse of the German amphibious remuda.   It attained ubiquity akin to that of the Allied LST. Beach assault needs came to light later when the Germans came to grips with the landing fight and realized how sharply it differed from land combat.   The prahms had capacities ranging from two to seven hundred tons; about one third were to be powered, the re- mainder towed; all required degaussing against mines, most required hull stiffening and changes to the bow.   The majority for troop and vehicle transport received the type designation A; other letters (AS, AF, B, and C) differentiated those fitted for such specialized tasks as landing submersible tanks and waterproofed vehicles.   By mid-August the number of type A prahms seized in Germany and Holland tallied 1,728, but of these only 230 were fit for towing to their mounting ports.   Four weeks later those ports would be so over- stuffed that a bomb could not fail to hit one.   Said one Port Com- mander, "I walked for miles from prahm to prahm; a patch of open water was hard to find."   So thick were the work horses in their stables.

The prahms had company.   Inland and coastal waters were like- wise denuded of ship and boat population to fill other invasion de- mands.   Included were 156 steamers, 274 tugs, 137 trawlers, 1586 motorboats, 127 motor coasters.   Twenty-seven of the last were destined to carry artillery to furnish gunfire in support of landing. They were in the same feeble state of readiness as all others, but their designation for gunfire support marked the progress of thinking toward the beach fight.   Provision of logistics for the huge landing fleet had only just begun.   In aggregate, the Navy's physical prepara- tions by mid-August totted up to a dispiriting 12 per cent ready for S Day, one month off.

Broad versus Narrow Front had at least stirred and leavened the vague ideas of how, after all, the toe hold was to be wrested from the defenders.   Soldier concern for the beach fight pushed forward in mind: How would prahms be protected and formed while approaching the beach?   And then beaching, that was a trick in itself.   How could the defenses be neutralized during the critical leap from craft to shore? What would keep the defenders down?   Sketches of boat formations appeared in the records, with emphatic marks on vessels capable of delivering beach fire; notes about air support by bombs and smoke, about getting tanks into the assault wave.   Perhaps the prahms could carry tanks, but for the assault infantry those hulks were too cumber- some.   A new scheme unfolded.   At Emden Army and Navy working together devised a means of skidding *Sturmboote* (engineer river-crossing boats, hereinafter sturmboats), into the sea stern first from cradles hung on the sides of trawlers or minesweepers. The boats were light, fast, and maneuverable with outboard power; each could accommodate a small six-to-eight-man squad. Two hundred trawlers, forty minecraft, and a large number of tugs were immediately ordered outfitted with these cradles and boats. Troops could thus be poured on the beach in shuttle relays from the mother trawlers, who would approach the beach in line abreast. With this development a mighty stride forward had been negotiated. The beach assault began to make sense.

A storm of papers descended from OKH on amphibious combat, as figured by the training section, and as developed by Reinhardt at Sylt and by Bartels at Emden. Troops were to exercise in sturmboats to get the hang of things, life jackets were to be worn, the rudiments of fighting off hostile small craft with hand weapons were to be drilled. Generalfeldmarschall Brauchitsch directly charged the three Army commanders with a drill program that coursed the full gauntlet of all landing hardships and included loading at mounting ports, beaching of prahms and laborious unloading over steep ramps, vehicle-driving in sand, evasion of beach obstacles, and the hustling of weapons forward to the front. Termination of this rugged stint he set for 10 September.

The Army commands, we recall, were the 16th Army in the Calais region, the 9th about Le Havre, and the 6th at Cherbourg; to each belonged four to five divisions of infantry and two to three of armor, plus special reinforcements for the peculiar *Sea Lion* tasks before them. As they got into the swing their zeal for fresh adventure grew loud and eager, in contrast to the doubting attitude of their Army Group Commander, Generalfeldmarschal von Rundstedt. He never believed in *Sea Lion,* and the functioning of his Group A headquarters in the deluxe environs of St. Germain showed it. Rundstedt held aloof and delegated much of the operational planning and training to AOK 16, Generaloberst Ernst Busch at Tourcoing near Lille.

Sea Lion thus entered the actable phase of development in which the wide divergence of aim between broad and narrow front in a very short time exercised a confused and debilitating influence. Command linkages between Army and Navy for planning purposes established themselves in the following order: Army Group A (von Rundstedt, St. Germain) dealt with Naval Group Command West (Saalwächter, Paris); 16th Army (Busch, Tourcoing) with Fleet Command (Lütjens, Trouville); 9th Army (Strauss) and the 6th (Reichenau) entered into interservice high planning only a little. Corps and divisions commands along the coast dealt with Transport Fleet and Naval Stations Commands in mounting ports. The sole level at which proximity could ameliorate inevitable differences was the lowest, where, in the end, mutual trust would count the most.

Army commands based their invasion acts on guides produced by a grand caucus of chieftains at OKH during July. Even then they figured on confining the landing to the strip between Thames mouth and Brighton. The twenty-two-page record of the meeting provides a conspectus of amphibious warfare doctrine as comprehended by the German Army with respect to the specific task of invading England; in a word, this writing represented the current invasion Bible. Naturally the main concern was the land conquest of England, and for that goal the planning had concluded that decision must fall in a battle for England's southern quarter about London. The scheme therefore went little beyond fighting north from the Channel to a line running from Maldon in the east across the island to the Severn estuary on the west. To win that objective drives were to lash out from a bridgehead boundary stringing from the Thames to Southampton, which line had in turn been gained by expanding initial lodgements along the coast from Ramsgate to the westward of Brighton. Trickery and bargaining over a Lyme Bay side show was not yet done, but its dubious character had long been recognized. Off there 180 miles outside of support it posed an eccentric move resembling Narvik. The idea had originally come from Hitler and Jodl amid thoughts of cutting off Cornwall. The Army fooled around with it, considered a combination of sea and air landings, and in the end retained it merely for talking purposes. The papers indicate that early in the game private planning of the soldiers regarded Brighton as the westernmost limit; nevertheless the original turgid ideas prevailed.

From Brighton eastward the invasion was to unfold in four successive tides of men and steel, called *Treffen*. We can render the sense best by the word "strike." Strike One, made up of thirteen selected and specially outfitted infantry Landing Divisions, plus advance elements from nine Mobile Divisions (armored and motorized), comprised the spearhead. Each Landing Division was subdivided into a first and second Transport Echelon; the first was to land in assault to seize a beach toe hold and be followed closely by the second echelon, which would push through and secure a tactical beachhead

Basic Army engrossment, the land fight, August 1940.

running from Ramsgate to Portsmouth. All this was to be achieved by S plus 3, that is, during the initial three days of invasion. Strike Two comprised the remaining bulk of the Mobile Divisions. It was to land close on the heels of Strike One and expand the tactical beachhead into an operational bridgehead as far as the Thames–Southampton Line. Strikes Three and Four contained reserves who were to land later and finish the land fight forward from that operational bridgehead.

Plainly, Strikes One and Two together were the powerhouse of this invasion. Their power was to insure bridgehead seizure, and thus victory over England. With the Thames Line in hand, the German soldiers felt that superior field leadership must carry the day. These elating thoughts of field operating evidently formed the starting point for soldier imagery, for the sequence of problems seemed to work back from that final land fight toward the water. There on the shore, both soldier and sailor imagination arrived belated and ignorant.　By nature the two arms approached the landing crux from opposite ends; the Army worked back from the field fight, while Navy labored out of the mounting ports.　Thirteen infantry and nine armored divisions approximated the forces engaged in the Flanders fight during May.　But how different here!　Instead of stealthy breakthrough at Sedan and miraculous roll-up here, before England, it could only be forthright frontal assault over water, first to gain lodgement at all, and then to hold on for life and tactical elbowroom.　The power house designated could swing it, if ever it got ashore.

That was the Navy's sorrow—getting the machine ashore, and in England.　The sailor mind labored a hard way out of battered French ports.　In the offing the mobs of barges and boats had to assume formation stations and then on signal maneuver through crowded routes, or fall into hopeless chaos.　Meanwhile the Royal Navy would hardly stand idle, nor the RAF, during an eighty-mile invasion trek from Le Havre to Brighton or while another movement made out from Calais toward Dungeness.　Battered by these thoughts and those of wind and tide, the Navy felt an imagined course through mine hazards toward England.　There the problem opened into finding the right beach.　It is among the most ticklish of problems in the entire amphibious frame.　The Army Bible summarily dismissed it with the words: "Responsible for the point of landing, the Army officer [embarked]; the naval officer, for the technical execution."　Avast with such nonsense!　Some of it, exercises along the coast had already deflated, as the two arms approached that great common ground of beach assault.　Fruitless bickering began to fade.　Data on the character of England's shores filtered in; Navy distributed excellent enlargements of beaches and reliefs of the foreshore.　The peculiarities of each beach revealed themselves.　Here one could land and fight his way inland, there, obviously not.　Here a prahm-tow could get in to launch tanks, but not at all over there.　Obstacles along there would require special treatment.　Every beach possessed its individual countenance and character that called for an individual scheme and for united genius to master it.

Adjustments such as these usually begin when the arms get down to cases together, but on this Channel waterfront it was hard to do, for no one knew for sure where he was going.　Was it Brighton (for the 9th Army) or to Eastbourne, to Deal (for the 16th Army) or to Folkestone?　Would the 9th mount at Boulogne or Le Havre?　Who would use Calais, who Dunkirk, or Ostend?　To what ports and in what strength should the distracted Naval Transport Office distribute the craft? These questions, controversy over broad-against-narrow-front still kept open. Generalfeldmarschall von Brauchitsch submitted his final review of the Army position to OKW (Warlimont) on 10 August; on the same day Skl armed Admiral Raeder with notes in rebuttal for Führer colloquy and at once made written response to the Army exposition.

The background "whys" of the two postures we know. Their fresh restatement suggested no softening or loophole; in fact, the impolitic tone of von Brauchitsch roused the Navy further. He made demands, and this was no time for demanding. Four points, of which the third carried the key, wound up the Army case:

1. A landing confined to the strip Folkestone–Beachy Head cannot be answered for by the Army.
2. A simultaneous landing at Brighton cannot be given up. An early landing at Deal is necessary for winning the heights north of Dover.
3. Sufficient lift must be readied to permit landing the first and second echelons of ten divisions in a span of four days between Ramsgate and Brighton.
4. The idea of landing in Lyme Bay should be retained if at all possible.

Some ground the Army had given: landing thirteen divisions in three days had subsided to ten divisions in four days. Deal landing waned, but to Brighton the soldiers held grimly fast. Yet even this version, the Skl diarist recorded on 12 August, the Navy simply could not meet for lack of troop-lift alone. Admiral Raeder declared himself in complete accord with his staff, and so he intended reporting to the Führer on the following day, 13 August.[18]

Alas, *Gröfaz* must decide. This is the sad but momentous note that distinguishes the episode; not what he decides, or what he does not decide, but that he may decide, and that German genius has ebbed so low. Hitler emerged from the West Campaign as infallible war lord, and after a little while he designated himself to command the war's greatest venture. *Sea Lion* became the victim of the man's

[18] Admiral Raeder held exhaustive discussion with his planners on 10 and 12 August; he proofed the status of craft, ports, canals, mining and coastal artillery, as well as Broad vs. Narrow Front from A to Z, and braced himself for report to Hitler on 13 August.

enhanced stature in Führer Directive No. 16 of 16 July: "Under my command and according to my general directives, the commanders in chief will lead elements of their forces committed." But he had done nothing about commanding. Now at crucial operational conjuncture on 13 August 1940 he was to step in and render omniscient judgment.

Adlertag had brought the Führer to Berlin at noon on that important Tuesday of 13 August. Raeder and Schniewind were admitted for conference at 1730. Present were Keitel, Jodl, and von Puttkamer; Warlimont had prepared the meeting ground well, even hinted to Jodl by telephone at a possible compromise over Brighton by means of an unsupported motorboat landing there from Le Havre. But first, Raeder was to have one more say. His bedraggled tale varied not a bit. He granted the justice of the Army stand, but dearth of craft, tidal differences, and exposure to enemy action and weather forbade all thought of a landing at Brighton, and all the more in Lyme Bay. Early decision, he urged, was needed to prevent impairment of readiness. He summarized "that in view of the limited number of naval and other sea transport means at our disposal Operation *Sea Lion* could only be carried out as '*ultima ratio*' if England could not be forced into peace by any other approach."[19] Jodl's old phrase, *ultima ratio,* from Raeder's lips gave Hitler a cue—the danger of failure. He dwelt on its implications this day and the next.

Hitler repeated his performance of the 31 July showdown. He expressed himself "in complete agreement with these [Raeder] arguments . . . ." Said the OKW Operations diary, should the landing fail "the British would gain immensely in prestige." But he temporized over No or Yes; it would be best to await the effect of the intensified air war just beginning. Meanwhile the Commander-in-Chief of the Army could be heard, and then—decision. That disposed of the crises no better than 31 July; the identical points had been raised, and similarly disposed, yet now with more blandishment for the Navy by wholehearted agreement. We scent a fish thrown to Raeder in a following abrupt switch by Hitler toward Norway. The Navy should strengthen the north flank in Norway to fend off possible Russian interest, and "in order to create a basis for occupying the port of Petsamo." His mind had been busy with heart's desire, Russia, not with troublesome *Sea Lion*. Raeder's counterrequest for more submarine torpedo materials Hitler approved with fulsome praise and

[19] W.D. OKW Ops, p. 38.

directed Keitel to see to it. Raeder went off, smeared with the same duping salve.

An echo of the Hitlerian swindle came from his chief war counsellor, General Jodl. The broad-narrow dispute had long since reached the gravity of requiring his arbitration. Now he took a tardy hand, not however to compose the differences so that *Sea Lion* could get going, but to render the unfortunate beast impossible. Jodl re-estimated *Sea Lion's* chances after receipt of von Brauchitsch's latest demands and handed the result to his planning staff on the fourteenth. "The planned operation must under no circumstances miscarry," he said, "since the political consequences would far exceed the military ones . . . . To avoid failure, he [Jodl] in agreement with the Army, deemed it necessary to get a foothold . . . from Folkestone to Brighton and that in this sector 10 divisions be thrown ashore within 4 days, followed by 3 full divisions in another 4 days via the Straits of Dover . . . ." He believed further that the Luftwaffe could deny the south English coast to British naval vessels and could also practically eliminate RAF counteraction, but if the Navy could not fulfil the broad landing requirements, then a "landing would be an act of sheer desperation for a desperate situation" that was not Germany's. He saw other means of forcing Britain to her knees: intensify the air war with Axis co-operation and destroy the economy of south England; the same by submarine warfare from French ports; or, seize Egypt and Gibraltar. Victory over Britain was the goal of the moment, and Britain's will to resist had to be broken by spring, if not by landing, then by all other means. "All powers, submarine and air, must be brought to bear in the decisive direction against the British homeland." The General seemed about to join the Navy! He had joined his Führer unreservedly long ago and demonstrated it here again in most transparent terms. The two were casting about for a safe and contributive way to fill the interregnum until Russia. The best contribution was, of course, the collapse of England, but without invasion, if at all possible. Though *Sea Lion* crowded them, Jodl/Hitler returned at each crisis to their anchor-thoughts, as expressed in the summation of 30 June.[20]

Jodl let the secret a little further out of the bag to Fricke when he admitted the justice of the Navy attitude and granted that the con-

[20] See Helmuth Greiner, *op. cit.*, p. 125, and W.D. OKW Ops, pp. 44, 45. About this time, mid-August, OKW started planning seizure of Gibraltar as a step toward ousting Britain from the Mediterranean.

ditions permitted only a narrow, militarily inadequate, landing. Agent Fricke had his man. He quickly spotted the weakness of Jodl's position and returned to the attack the following day, after catching wind of a confirmatory Führer admission while bestowing batons on fourteen field marshals, promoted in that dim past of 19 July.

Adolf Hitler was never more carefree and candid than while dispensing largess. In that mood, amid glitter and fine array, and mindful of glorious victory, he explained to his assembled field marshals that he did not "intend to carry through an operation, the risk of which is too high, since he held the view that the aim of Britain's overthrow is not dependent on landing *alone,* but can also be achieved by other means. [Massive Air Offensive had already begun.] Independent of the eventual decision, the Führer wants that the *threat* of invasion be maintained against England in every way. The preparations must therefore proceed, however the decision may fall." Most of his hearers felt relieved about *Sea Lion.*[21] So Hitler and Jodl had switched to Navy, and of all things, here came the freshly batonned Reichsmarschall Göring to join up, clutching his bauble in hand. Admiral Raeder drew him out, after hearing the Führer, somewhat as Fricke had Jodl. In reply, mellow Göring "seconded the view of Chief Skl [Raeder] profusely." Hitler's views and those of his two most faithful reflectors, Göring and Jodl, thus coincided perfectly. Unwittingly, Raeder was in the same company. None of these gentlemen favored *Sea Lion;* on the contrary, each was figuring how to get around him without shame.[22]

Fricke wanted to proof his impression. He returned to Jodl with the open secret couched in a series of propositons, designed to smoke out the truth about *Sea Lion*:

[21] From the W.D. Skl, 15 August 1940. Generalfeldmarschall von Bock was one of the guests who received his baton at this ceremony. The account in his private diary agrees substantially with that of Raeder above (extract from W.D. Skl). Von Bock added that the Führer also dilated upon the situation in the East and the need of restraining Russia.

[22] W.D. Skl, 15 August 1940. Raeder thought Göring and he were off to a new start. Two days earlier he had received a fulsome letter of apology from Göring for his rude mind-your-own-business communication of mid-June. The apology was tardy, and altogether out of character for Göring. It was very likely inspired by a desire to mollify Raeder at this time, possibly over *Sea Lion*. We may be sure Hitler knew of the apology. The Admiral took pains to apprise his Skl staff of Göring's change of heart, called an end to all the quarrels; all was to be sweetness and light. It lasted not very long. Göring was soon up to his old tricks. In January 1943 when Raeder took his departure from Hitler on leaving the post of Commander-in-Chief of the Navy, his last words were, according to his own testimony, "Will you please protect the Navy and my successors from Göring . . ." (*Nazi Conspiracy and Aggression*, VIII, 713).

1) In case the Führer is privately determined not to carry out Operation Sea Lion, yet wants the *fiction* of an invasion maintained: *Proposal, Sound Retreat* on Sea Lion in order to relieve the economy. Set up deception operations to maintain the threat against the adversary.

2) In case the Führer holds to the execution of the operation: *Proposal,* Restriction of the landing to the narrow basis, nevertheless setting up the preparations on a broad basis.

3) Rejection [in any case] of landing strong troop units at Brighton . . . for a continuing supply and reenforcement in that area is *not* possible.

"General Jodl," recorded the Skl diarist, "agreed basically with these thought processes." Jodl saw he could muster up no valid counters to Fricke's penetrating questions, and therefore he merely gave in to their justice without specific replies. *Sea Lion* was left hanging somewhere between threat and possible execution. Hitler, Jodl knew, had not made up his mind, save on Russia.

Perhaps things had gone too far. Jodl found opportunity to consult his Führer in more sober surroundings after the guests departed and the effusions of the baton ceremony had died away. Fricke's searching interpellation was still with him. Together with Hitler he settled on what was to be disseminated in print, and passed it on to Warlimont that evening. Two days later (16 August) the determinations issued as Führer decisions. They were that: preparations should hew to the stipulated deadline (15 September); decision as to execution was reserved pending development of the general situation; Lyme Bay landing was to be abandoned but mounting must still cover the length of the coast from Ostend to Le Havre in order to effect dispersion of landing craft and deceive the enemy. The preparations were to be set up so that a crossing on a narrow front was not excluded, provided eight days' notice was given, and the execution of one lightly equipped landing near Brighton should remain possible. This was the best that Warlimont could make of the Hitler-Jodl jumble. Warlimont and staff labored on undismayed to keep *Sea Lion* alive through an Army-Navy compromise on the last-mentioned possibility—a light landing at Brighton. Landing near Deal on the other flank had dropped out.[23]

[23] The Hitler determinations as received by Warlimont are given in the W.D., OKW Ops, pp. 45, 46, 47. What he worked out and was able to get approved for distribution we have given above. There are other lights in the diary that illuminate Hitler's casting about, far removed from invasion. The plan for capture of Gibraltar was advancing, as were plans for the capture of Atlantic Islands such as the Azores and the Canaries. Meanwhile the position against Russia (*Aufbau Ost,* or *Build-up East*), was progressing; the Army was being increased; Hitler had

From *Sea Lion's* inception, von Lossberg and Junge of the planning staff rated as stalwart boosters. They thought he provided a
means of ending the war soon, whereas ideas of Russian adventure
struck them as dubious. They inspired redoubled efforts in *Sea Lion's*
behalf. Under Warlimont's guidance the two young men had gone to
work on resolving the Brighton impasse to infuse hope and purpose
into *Sea Lion*. Colonel Witzleben joined in from Skl, where he liaisoned, with difficulty, for Army. The forces out of Le Havre were now
being called the Green Move, while the main effort out of Boulogne
and ports to the north and east became the Blue Move. The Navy
expressed a willingness to deal on a first draft compromise that ran as
follows: (a) Cross direct from Le Havre to Brighton with two regimental groups in 500 motor boats, the groups each to total 2,100 and
include howitzer and antitank units; (b) Simultaneously, drop two
regimental groups by air on the South Downs back of the Brighton
beach assault area; (c) Reinforce and maintain the whole by air
drops; (d) in the begnning the Luftwaffe, acting as artillery, would
have to smash any forces approaching across the line Southampton–
London. "In this connection an all-out air attack on London might
prove promising, . . . as it would undoubtedly result on a mass exodus
. . . blocking roads and having a demoralizing effect."[24] The proposal had already been passed to Jodl and service planning agencies
on 13 August.

Neither Army nor Navy could raise a passion over compromise
under the clouding effect of Hitler's apparent switch to "threat" on the
fourteenth. Threat of invasion already existed; besides, great things
were eagerly anticipated from Massive Air Offensive. In consequence, at this critical point, when intensified effort was needed, a
Sea Lion planning hiatus set in for about ten days between the two
services. We have time to turn our eyes and ears toward the other
side of the Channel with the Germans to follow their avid search for
signs of breakup.

It was curious; one side peered hopefully, and full of excitement,
awaiting air decision to obviate invasion, while the other fixed on
Hitler and stolidly endured air punishment, convinced that the worst,

---

ordered General von Falkenhorst down from Norway to discuss the same subject as
touched on with Raeder, the strengthening of the northern flank, toward the east.
Göring was ordered to prepare an air base in northern Norway. The stumbling
start of the air offensive against England was an irritant that added to Hitlerian
impatience for action.

[24] W.D., OKW Ops, pp. 39, 40.

invasion, was yet to come, and almost hoped it would, and soon. "Do you think Hitler is coming, sir?" a miner and home guardsman queried his Commander in the North on inspection (General Sir Ronald Adam), and continued, "It will be an awful pity if he doesn't." Singling Hitler out grew in common usage. Among the people a challenge fixed on "him," in a direct and personal way: "Let *him* come!"—that contemptible upstart. To grapple him to earth with bare hands and get a grip around his throat became the lust of Englishmen, and with that, any German ever setting foot on English soil was a Hitler. Rumors are still current of an order directing that no quarter be granted invaders. There is no question that this was the public and official mood. Britain was aroused.[25]

The personalized animosity dug Hitler where it hurt; he was inordinately sensitive to contempt and personal hostility. All the more so in this instance because the British had turned the tables; he ascribed the hatred to propaganda alone, his very own forte. Goebbels and Fritzsche held old orders to convict warmonger Churchill. During August 1940 the pillory redoubled its pressure; Churchill's publicity curve on German media mounted to an all-time high with the crescendo of Massive Air Offensive. Invasion talk gave way to decision by air. "The great German victories of today" have made "it quite clear to the English people that this war is essentially to be decided by the Air Force," summed up the common theme of the radio announcer, often followed by the calming assurance, "Everything will be done at the right time." But there was little calm. Announcers heaped crash on crash; the fury of air attack came alive through moving accounts of individual pilots, hair-raising experiences all, and always with devastating success. Each report spawned fresh superlatives about increasing frenzy in England. Then a prime piece of "heresy" clinched any argument for the Germans as to proper emphasis through the emotional appeal of song. A new jingle made

[25] The German records took uneasy note of expressions by public figures (Mr. Lloyd George) and government officials (Mr. Butler) welcoming a chance to repel invasion and thus demonstrate British hardihood. They also took outraged note of refusal to grant immunity to air-sea-rescue planes displaying the Geneva cross, while engaged in fishing downed pilots from the Channel. Churchill's unremitting challenge was bearing fruit. As early as 27 June he had cabled to General Smuts in South Africa: "Obviously, we have first to repulse any attack on Great Britain by invasion, and show ourselves able to maintain our development of air power. This can only be settled by trial. If Hitler fails to beat us here, *he will probably recoil eastward. Indeed he may do this even without trying invasion,* to find employment for his Army, and take the edge off the winter strain upon him . . . ."

its debut for signing off radio announcements. It was "Wir fliegen gegen England" in place of the old "Wir fahren gegen Engelland."[26] The pressure was meant for England but it acted more convincingly on the home folk. They were whirling along the leading edge of a fake Hitlerian emotional Front under the compelling expectation of British collapse.

Professional Navy planners did not remain immune to the frontal blasts; they ardently shared their countrymen's hopes. Yet, while one hoped, to sit idly by and accept the extravagant claims in the news just would not do at all. The Navy possessed ample evidence of deficient air command over the Channel. Skl took nervous cognizance of growing RAF activity over mounting ports, fuel storage fired in Boulogne, minecraft and prahm casualties in Ostend and Rotterdam, but deeper down, the gripping weakness at sea came home. Luftwaffe reported two British cruisers in Portland, two more, backed by a battleship, in Portsmouth, plus twenty-two destroyers that came and went on coastal surveillance from Falmouth and Plymouth. Both the OKW Operations war diary and that of Skl recorded a broadcast of mid-August in which Mr. Anthony Eden highlighted the British fleet superiority. Britain had only just begun to fight, he declared; in this long war, sea power along with growing air power, would bring victory in the end to Britain.

That overwhelming power on the sea kept Britain alive and fightings was no news to Skl. What was news, and of the most shocking kind, was to hear Goebbels officially on 17 August sabotage the carefully laid Navy plans for winning a long war of attrition. A truly effective blockade by sea and air might achieve results, a gradually tightening siege of fortress England, as the means therefor in submarines and other weapons became available. To Navy dismay these painfully nurtured plans fell victim to the Hitler-Göring-Goebbels mid-August frenzy to reduce Britain by words. They declared England under total blockade, by sea and by air, in releases by the official news

[26] Our "reading" comes from a scrutiny of DNB (German News Agency) news despatches. Kris and Speier are informative on radio. The German military records bear out the trend of the news, but also substantiate the psychological drift of the offensive. On 16 August the W.D., OKW Ops recorded, "Parachute kits, faking paratroop landings were dropped. Caused great excitement in the English press." Another type of drop, reported by the London *Times* of 7 and 14 August, caused excitement too, but of a different character. English briefs of Hitler's speech of 19 July were scattered over southern England. The brief carried the caption "A Last Appeal to Reason; by Adolf Hitler." Derisive Britons gathered them in and raffled off copies for the benefit of the Red Cross.

agency. Remarked the Skl diary: The declaration "must be regarded as a pure political propaganda measure . . . ." A paper blockade was what Hitler had proclaimed, well knowing the means for effective blockade were not on hand. The highly disturbing event may have mellowed both Navy and Army into seeking new compromise on Broad versus Narrow Front in the following days.

Meanwhile occasion had developed for testing sea control in the region of Boulogne. That port furnished AOK 16's central window toward the Channel sea, and near there General Busch centered amphibious training of troop leaders. The swank Paris Plage at Le Touquet, fifteen miles south of Boulogne, was set up as an exercise beach. It is a fine stretch of wide, gradually shoaling sand—a little too fine and too gradual. Army bigwigs from Field Marshal von Brauchitsch down assembled there to witness their first and biggest demonstration landing on 17 August 1940. Navy minecraft provided sea security and transport from Boulogne to the scene of the exercises. The enchanted soldiery crowded aboard the diminutive craft in Boulogne, snapping pictures right and left of this first exposure to sea duty. They were out on a lark. Minecraft boss Ruge stood ready for the rank with two R boats, and had another pair guarding to seaward. Away they sailed for Paris Plage, but slowly, thought General Halder; the Channel current was against them. The 16th Army put on a landing in regimental strength under simulated supporting fire from seaward. Both sea and skies remained their own clear blue without a sign of British counteraction; not a ship or plane intruded. Concern over sea or air control in this instance proved bootless.

A more specific question was the feeling generated for or against *Sea Lion* in the Army leadership by this premier performance of any size in landing attack. Local Army talent had labored hard to stage a bang-up show by well-written script, perfectly drilled troops, and ingenious facsimiles of actual combat. There was much going on and a great deal of noise. General Halder took instant exception to simulation of supporting fire from ships at sea by exploding charges planted in advance on the beach. Where were the ships to throw the shells, he wondered, to the mine commander as they watched the cumbersome prahms struggle onto the beach. Unloading went painfully slow; soft beaches, barges grounding too far out, ramp troubles, and sundry other difficulties interfered. But the water engineers were marvelous. They accomplished the impossible and got the stuff out.

All agreed that the water engineers had done well, and that progress on the problems and the ingenuity displayed was impressive. The lower ranks, who were closest to the heaving and hauling, felt encouraged that they had mastered the outworks of the tough amphibious game. At any rate a fine outing had been enjoyed. The Army Commander-in-Chief addressed his assembled commanders and expressed his confidence. He directed AOK 16 to set up a regular curriculum for continuing training. In general, *Sea Lion* benefited.[27]

The soldiers, engrossed in these *Sea Lion* chores, were oblivious to most of the air and propaganda war raging around them. They were much more concerned about the British Order of Battle for defense of their island. As usual, information on this score lacked the detailed completeness that combat commands habitually demand; for the critical sector between the Thames and Brighton the available intelligence was particularly sketchy. A general estimate granted the British thirty-nine divisions in all, of which about half were considered full strength and of first-line quality. These were believed to form a Mobile Defense Force for opposing the German main effort, when identified. To the mobile force the Germans added the only two British armored divisions and a few motorized ones. Beyond this, a cordon defense of coastal belts was anticipated, each belt varying along its length according to the dangers, and all bound together into a Coastal Defense Force. Mention occurred of the Home Guards, whom the Germans expected to find defending inland areas. An overall shortage of British artillery was noted. The order of battle so constituted was on the generous side. British counterintelligence had done well.

The Germans prosecuted measures to the same deceptive purpose vigorously. Deception schemes in *Sea Lion's* direct operational interest were extensive, ordered by OKW and painstakingly nurtured by the services. Ideas germinated early for diverting attention from the closest point of contact at the Channel; almost before *Sea Lion* himself emerged. A feint toward Ireland was always good for some talk in the Continental pattern, and after *Norway,* a faked descent on Scotland or northeast England came automatically under scrutiny. Navy led in the northern plotting, since the movement had to pass overseas,

---

[27] Impressions of the exercise have been reviewed with General Halder and Commodore Ruge, with General Edger Röricht, the OKH training officer, with General Rudolf Hofman, Chief of Staff, Army Corps XIII, and General Herbert Loch, who commanded 17th Infantry Division posted on *Sea Lion's* open right wing, close to Dover.

and because to the Navy, any diversion from its weakness in the Channel was doubly welcome. On such plans, far-sighted Admiral Carls of Naval Group Command North at Wilhelmshaven despatched detailed recommendations in early August. He proposed moving a counterfeit transport fleet of ten steamers, convoyed by cruisers, small craft, and air toward Scotland from Norwegian ports. OKW took up these hints eagerly and followed soon with a directive that projected camouflage in grand Hitlerian style. The invasion picture was to be so befogged that the Channel preparations looked like fakes in deference to the strong defenses opposite, while the specious strength on the wings should bear the mark of main effort. On the west wing in the Brest and Biscay region a landing bound for Ireland was to be represented, and on the east in the Low Countries and Scandinavia strong landings bound for east England. These measures should have added to *Sea Lion's* true stature, but it turned out otherwise.

Nothing came of the pretense against Ireland except papers. On the opposite flank the simulated operations got more encouragement; yet oddly, instead of being added as normal extensions of *Sea Lion,* they were severed from him by a separate code name *Herbstreise* (*Autumn Journey*) and by a distinctive series of directives of great length and detail. The Army version contemplated two fake operations, the lesser one to mount in Holland and land on the southeast English coast between the Wash and Harwich, and a main effort from Norway toward the coast between Edinburgh and Newcastle. The Holland job was entrusted to XXXVII Group Command, a ghost organization having commander and staff but little operational wherewithal. General von Falkenhorst received more serious substance for Norway dissimulation. His fake operation actually mounted in the Bergen–Oslo region; he was to embark troops on Navy-provided steamers and feint toward the British coast. Admiral Carl's early suggestion for an invasion fleet of some ten steamers was accepted and embellished with amphibious paraphernalia. Of more direct Navy interest, however, was a fine blue-water diversionary foray into the Atlantic. Pocket battleship *Scheer* and cruiser *Hipper,* it was planned, would break out between Scotland and Iceland well before *Sea Lion's* hop-off, and work on convoys far at sea. This was more to the sailor taste, since it afforded reasonable hope of enlarging the tonnage toll.

The sum total of invasion deception can be regarded as a complex Hitlerian extravaganza. Never had he compounded confusion so thoroughly. Remember that the central theme had been to give *Sea Lion* in the Channel the aspect of simulation. This stratagem offered the welcome excuse for regarding him so in fact; and prosecution of the designated fakes waxed so earnest that the validity of everything fell into question. Deception itself seemed to become the main purpose as *Herbstreise* and *Sea Lion* tended toward synonymy. In short, fact and fiction merged, not indistinguishably as good deception should, but in such a way that fiction seemed to be taking over. The declaration of total blockade added emphasis, so that in England the play on deception grew apparent to close observers of the German antics. In mid-August Skl's war diary had already noted: "Lively discussion in English press [on invasion] . . . . Führer may have made basic decision about a landing. German preparations far advanced, but not yet completed. Possible that German attack will only be simulated . . . ." Considering the Hitlerian vagaries, who could tell? Certainly not he himself.

The Hitler factor had indeed to be reckoned on, and more by the Germans than by the Britons. *Sea Lion* interest revived after *Eagle, Lichtmeer,* and other air efforts came and went, wanting in decisive power and failing to produce a vestige of British collapse. Total blockade produced nothing but derision. Hitler refueled at the Berghof. Out of its quiet, renewed interest for *Sea Lion* appeared; he might have to go after all. OKW got busy. Sparked by Warlimont interservice exchanges fired up again to break the Broad-versus-Narrow-Front impasse.

We recall the Green Move of 500 motorboats out of Le Havre, cooked up in compromise between Navy and OKW planners. OKH paid scant attention until 22 August when General von Greiffenberg from that office appeared at OKW to take another reading. Digesting of the compromise had gone on during the hiatus. In place of 500 motorboats for the dash to Brighton the Navy proffered 200, plus 100 coastal motorsailers, reinforced by 25 steamers. The Army wanted 70 steamers so that four divisions could be lifted (8th, 28th, 34th and 6th Mountain). Meanwhile Air acceded to committing the bulk of the 7th Paratroop Division to Brighton, but also with provision for some elements to the heights north of Dover to bolster the open right wing. In this narrowed area of differences Warlimont set about mediating. His endeavors centered on coaxing more steamers out of the Navy, stressing that the Führer would execute *Sea Lion* only under most favorable circumstances, anyhow. Risk in Green Move would thereby be lessened. Fricke at Navy understood the meaning and gave in, provided invasion got off to a favorable start. He raised the Green fleet to 50 steamers, but only half were to sail direct for Brighton, while the other half executed a detour to the northeast and joined the Blue crossing. After crossing, these would coast westward to Brighton. OKW planners felt encouraged and transmitted the hard wrung concession immediately to Jodl in Berchtesgaden. The next day, the 23rd, the L section staff train *Atlas* moved to that region too. Things looked hopeful.[28]

The hopes were short-lived; late on the twenty-fourth Army replied in forthright rejection, insisting that the four divisions, constituting the bulk of the 9th Army landing, must move out of Le Havre. (This meant seventy steamers, or nearly half of all there were.) "The Commander-in-Chief of the Army," the word came, "would clear the matter up during a personal report to the Führer." Army confidence in *Sea Lion* stood at a low ebb. Remarking on von Greiffenberg's reading at OKW General Halder recorded: "Result: on the basis of these advices attack this year has no prospect." Warlimont persevered, nonetheless, advancing the argument used to break down Fricke, but to no avail. Army wanted none of it. Thereupon he threw in his lot, and *Sea Lion's,* with the Navy; he advised Jodl that further ship increases for Le Havre (Green) could not be justified. Also he advised the Navy to proceed with its preparations on the basis of the Fricke proposition. Final decision was expected from the Führer on the twenty-sixth.

And so at last it came about early on that day. After going over a charted presentation of Green and Blue with Jodl, and after hearing von Brauchitsch object anew to tearing apart his 9th Army at Le Havre, Hitler joined the Navy unequivocally and completely. The decision was shortly disseminated to the services over Keitel's signature. The paper required Army to conform to the facts of available ship lift and the crossing hazards. It was to regroup so that Green Move comprised a streamlined assault team in small craft, crossing direct to Landing Beach E in Brighton Bay, and followed, if the situation warranted, by reinforcements in 25 steamers. Further assault elements in another 25 steamers were to proceed along the French coast, join

[28] Our accounting of proceedings to solve Broad vs. Narrow Front comes from W.D., OKW Ops, the *Halder Journal,* and W.D. Skl.

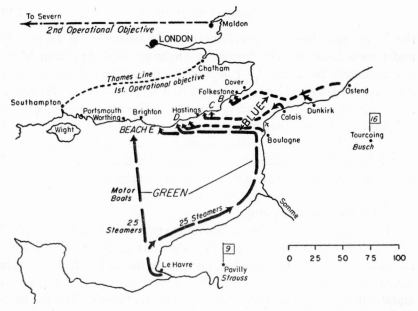

Invasion England: Broad vs. Narrow Front resolved, 26 August 1940.

Blue Move for crossing and landing at Beach D (Bexhill-New Haven). Under specially favorable circumstances these elements could proceed westward past D, to join their Green teammates at Beach E. It was an involved maze; presumably all 50 steamers would join Blue in case of serious British counter action. As a coherent command the 9th Army of Generaloberst Adolf Strauss was thus shredded into bits strewn from Boulogne to Le Havre and from Bexhill to Brighton. But *Sea Lion* was back on his flippers roaring once more.[29]

Generalfeldmarschall von Brauchitsch departed overruled but not too downhearted, because Hitler sandwiched the unwelcome *Sea Lion* determinations into a typical tour through doldrum dreams of boundless adventure. Extravagant speculations of this character always showed at Hitlerian dilemma and meant that none of what was said counted for much. He ranged over the possibilities. Spain must be brought in, as well as operations against Egypt, Cyprus, or Haifa to create a new theater against Britain. On and on he wandered; Rumania must be strengthened against Russia, also the north flank. Like a most powerful magnet, Russia drew him in at the end. The

[29] General Halder recorded on 26 August 1940 his Commander-in-Chief's news of Führer Conference: "Sea Lion stays. Interest for him seems to have mounted. . . ."

pull of it he could not evade. We recall the same puzzled, dissembling mood at 21 July Conference. Then decision *Russia* dissolved his quandary in redemption, but now interim plans were failing. What should he do until *Russia*? Where could he whip up a Front? Air was fizzling out; soon he would have to say no or yes to *Sea Lion*. That climax crept nearer day by day and brought out the Hitlerian foibles and vices in such strange light.

The prolonged Army-Navy wrangle was at last over. So freed, each arm went about bringing its orders into accord with the latest Führer directions. For Navy this entailed no radical shift; in fact, already by 20 August Reinicke's England staff had sent the final Skl plan, designated "Directive for Executive *Sea Lion*," to press. From here on Naval Group Command West in Paris, and Fleet Command at Trouville would shoulder the load. Anticipating the outcome, Skl instructed those commands to figure on landing what would become the main effort, six divisions out of area Rotterdam–Boulogne, between Dover and Beachy Head in a time span of six days via Blue Move at the Narrows and still provide for a side landing of some assault teams at Brighton in one direct (Green) strike from Le Havre. Mine clearance of prospective routes and mine barriers on either side of the Blue Move lanes were to be completed by 15 September. These flexible and timely Skl dispositions did not preclude some redistributing of the ship lift, as compromise gained strength. By the day that the Führer's favorable decision reached Skl (28 August) proper adjustments were in hand. The sailors voiced pride that Neptune's counsel had prevailed.

The bulky final Navy opus was more a reference index to accumulated planning papers and research data than a stirring call to Invasion England 1940. The covering directive referred back, erased, corrected, and solved problems through voluminous annexes. In such portfolio form the collection naturally ran to considerable length in the virgin edition. To the credit of the planners, only one-half pound more developed by way of changes. To anyone acquainted with the problems that had faced them—the tension of strife, the meagerness of resource in working staff, in experience and in material, and most of all, in the shortness of time—these men had performed veritable prodigies of amphibious warfare planning and preparation. Not much escaped their notice, and they followed each quirk with intelligence and foresight. At the end, however, the final writing leaves an impression of good riddance rather than inspired leadership. No one of rank at Navy ever took up the cudgels for *Sea Lion.* The truth was that he belonged to the Army. From first to last, Invasion England was an Army show.

On 30 August the Army Commander-in-Chief signed his basic "Instruction for Preparation of *Operation Sea Lion.*" The contrast offered by this final OKH paper to Skl's companion piece is striking. The Army urge to make something of invasion was bound to bring about a convincing difference of expression and treatment. It showed immediately in the resounding introductory phrases used to roll out the general objective of the plan: ". . . *gewaltsame* [mighty] *Landung in England* . . . , [in order to] . . . eliminate the English homeland as a base for continuing the war against Germany and, if the need develops, occupy it completely." After noting that issuance of order for execution depended on political factors, Army school phrases took over and developed the problem in delightfully simple terms and logical sequence—1, 2, 3 and a, b, c,:

Luftwaffe knocks out the English Air force . . . Navy clears minefree routes and *Army* gains local bridgeheads with specially equipped forward echelons of the First Strike. These are expanded to form a connected landing zone, the possession of which covers disembarkation of following troops . . . . As soon as sufficient forces are on hand, the attack toward the first operational objective, Thames–Heights South of London–Portsmouth, is to be launched.

Fat arrows made with a compliant grease pencil indicated direct routes of approach and development of landings in broad sweeps over an unencumbered and shoalless Channel map. It reads as pure as the statement of a Leavenworth problem, and sounds twice as inspiring.

We pass to command organization and subsidiary instructions. Field Marshal von Rundstedt, Commander Army Group A, was ordered to force a landing with Armies 16 and 9 between Folkestone in the East and Worthing in the West, and to carve out therefrom a continuous and secure coastal zone. Ports were to be readied expeditiously for unloading follow-up forces. With the seizure of the Thames–Portsmouth line, the real land campaign could begin. Thence the order contemplated a drive of fast forces (armor) west of London with the object of "tying off the center from the west and southwest" and thus facilitating further sweeps northwest toward the Watford–Swinton region.

Auxiliary Minesweeper Boulogne, showing cradle skids, for carrying sturmboat, down in trail position after launching boat. (*Courtesy Rear Admiral Werner Lindenau*)

Sturmboat carrier. (*Courtesy Captain Erich Lehmann*)

Sturmboat being recovered by carrier. Boat runs up into cradle-skid at full speed past the fulcrum of the cradle which then tips to horizontal, carrying the boat free of the water. The boat is launched stern first by releasing the after end of the cradle. (*Courtesy Herr Fritz Siebel*)

(*Below*) Sturmboats underway for beach assault exercises.

The Army goes to sea! Boulogne to Le Touquet to witness the first large scale landing exercise. *(Courtesy General Herbert Loch)*

Amphibious warfare's heterogeneity requires more than ordinary precision in detailing the tasks of subordinate commands. OKH went down through Army commands. This directive told 16th Army to mount in Rotterdam, Antwerp, Ostend, Dunkirk, and Calais, and the bulk of the 9th in Boulogne, preparing at the same time the First Echelon of three Landing Divisions for hop-off in Le Havre. The 16th Army would then strike between Folkestone and Hastings (Beaches B and C), the 9th between Bexhill and Brighton (Beaches D and E). The forward elements of the 16th Army's assault came from four landing divisions and in 9th Army from five, making a neat nine-division assault job. OKH reckoned by S plus 10 Day to have the advance elements ashore filled out to near ten complete divisions, and by S plus 16 to have five corps, commanding ten full divisions on the far shore, ready to do combat. Each interval of four days thereafter was expected to add two more divisions so that at the end of four weeks a formidable force of sixteen divisions, including armor, would be on hand.[30]

The many detailed admonitions did not obscure the effect of the truly vast canvas painted by this directive. England would be over-whelmed by four gigantic tidal waves. Lyme Bay was not given up. Army Group B was directed to stand ready for crossing from Cherbourg to Weymouth and Lyme Regis, should a favorable naval situation develop. Army operated on nothing less than the grand scale. As directives of such caliber should, this one rolled along in lofty tones of self-assurance to the von Brauchitsch signature. *Sea Lion* took another spurt.

Leaving the Near Shore and Winning the Far—Late August 1940

On the surface, the fog around *Sea Lion* cleared a little. Now he and his limits had been drawn up, approved, and prescribed in high orders. Early operational hopes had had to trim toward the

[30] For doctrinal concepts and details of beach assault OKH backed up its *Sea Lion* directive with a training section folio labeled *Küstenkampf,* or the Beach Fight. It contemplated river-crossing tactic: ". . . the fight will be conducted like an attack over a river in which protective fires from the near shore are lacking . . . ." The soldiers imagined infantry divisions afloat in line abreast, each beefed up with sub-mersible tanks. The line would push off from the near shore straight for England yonder. A permanent Shore Party of engineers would go along to assist debarkation. The independent beach fight of each landing unit to gain its compartment of the beach was stressed, as well as the need of getting weapons forward and ex-ploiting local success. Armor, paratroop landings, and air support were elaborated.

inexorable limits of material practicalities. Final measures could now proceed in greater confidence, and this they did with new-found vigor. *Sea Lion* flourished and gained daily in physical validity. We take stock of him and his actual fittings on the near shore and follow his intent toward the far one, as August, a month of must, gave way to September.

The invasion complex proper had settled to a zone stretching from Rotterdam to Le Havre along the sea, and inland, from Koblenz to Paris. This broad belt throbbed with invasion activity and rumors, which not even mounting air war could still. Invasion was next on the program, and people had come to believe in it. Visible evidence abounded. Prahms and steamers slid out of conversion yards toward assembly points; Rotterdam, Antwerp, the ports along the Rhine and its tributaries were stuffed to overflowing. Berthing space stood at a premium. The old inland traffic routes and services died, and in the Navy's own big bases of Kiel and Wilhelmshaven only two tugs stayed behind from *Sea Lion* exodus. The countryside blossomed with head-quarters, bases, and depots. Near the shore troops redoubled their training tempo of loading and unloading dummy prahms, running in and out of craft, and drilling new combat tactic. Great guns boomed out over the Channel from Cap Gris Nez at the English shore. Hither-to *Sea Lion* had been largely plan and propaganda, almost a joke; toward August's end he began really to roar, and to swell into prob-lem proportions. With each gain, he took on character and provoked new trains of interest and work. He was fixing to demand his day.

But no matter how deafening the clamor or how earnest the effort, material factors held the whip hand. As late as 20 August Hitler had personally reaffirmed that *Sea Lion* demands were to come ahead of all others; the industry and economy of the Continent turned upside down in compliance, but produced no extra invasion craft. Adequate troop lift remained the critical problem. *Sea Lion* had climbed appreciably from his alarming figure of only 12 per cent ready at mid-August, yet he was far from his goal.

Craft-accounting ranks among the most vexatious of all chores in amphibious warfare. Such a multitude of units to account for; one knows what should be, and can get it only by pencil work on paper. Weather interrupts movements, vessels break down, yard work goes uncompleted. These factors all work against accuracy and make figures unreliable. They rarely reflect the true state. Daily tallies re-ported by Skl's shipping office (A VI) proved no more reliable than has ever been the case in these circumstances. The numbers given were padded with bureaucratic optimism. On 31 August it was reported that the bulk of the larger transport ships were safely ready for business in Germany. The prahm situation was more obscure; 1,800 plus had been seized in Germany, Holland, and France, but fewer than 25 per cent had their own power, and only a little over half were ready to sail for mounting ports. While only 364 had gone forward, over 1,500 glutted the coastal waters of Holland and Germany. Towing power posed the toughest problem of all. Tugs, or their equivalent, were wanted to the number of 450. Only 360 had turned up. Unless more towing power could be found, the prahm work horse would be incapable of meeting his vital tasks. It was a worrisome question that tended to make percentage of readiness figuring illusory. A further unknown was the doubtful facility with which movement to mounting ports could be effected through crowded and damaged waterways. On the whole, it can be estimated that the landing-craft problem was little more than 40 per cent solved at the end of August.

One material item, to the credulous delight of Hitler, could boast 100 per cent readiness. This honor belonged to no other than the coastal artillery project of big rifles bristling from Pas de Calais in the center of invasion front. Not that these guns could have helped *Sea Lion* significantly, but the pressure exerted in their behalf had gained them this meaning. A sizable allotment of German war potential was fooled away on them. On 21 August the gunners fired on a Channel convoy of thirteen ships and claimed hits on three but failed to stop them or their mates. It was a case of chasing sparrows with cannon balls. Twenty-four shells were loosed at Dover, too. The Führer was anxious that these fires be synchronized with the climax of air offensive, not for their physical effect, but to tell the British how near at hand he stood and how soon he was coming over. His guns thus pinpointed the jutting center of the front from which invasion must hop-off for England.

Situated in that region, the mounting ports functioned shakily amid the litter and ruin of the past campaign—Calais in the middle, Ostend, Dunkirk on the one flank, Boulogne and Le Havre on the other. Dunkirk, the hardest hit, was having trouble freeing her locks and getting adequate berthing space cleared for the hundreds of prahms momentarily expected. Navy planned to start deployment through Rotterdam and Antwerp on 20 August. The hope had existed that by that day, the one remaining decision, not to go, would have fallen. In a little while events disclosed this to be a vain hope so that on 24 August tardy orders went out to begin scheduled movements toward the mounting ports. Hardly one of the naval port commanders felt happy about his dirty and disorganized surroundings, and the near impossible task before him.

Prahms posed the hardest operational, as well as material, problem. Their tactical organization and employment had been worked out on paper with admirable foresight and ingenuity, yet they had never been tested at sea or on beaches in volume. The standard unit, which we shall call a tow, consisted of two type A prahms (one with power and the other without) towed in tandem by a tug or trawler. Six such tows were capable of transporting a re-enforced infantry battalion and formed a tow unit. The Army called it a tow group, the Navy a tow flotilla. A flotilla could conveniently be indicated on paper by a square enclosing six tows in line abreast, or three and three. So to the Army a square meant a battalion, while to the Navy it meant six prahm tows. Soldiers are masters at this symbol and picture writing, especially German soldiers. One finds the same talent for pictography in the excellent German railroad guides, where crossed knife and fork mean diner, and a minute bed, sleeping accommodation. For *Sea Lion* they managed to portray the beach assault line-up in depth of an entire infantry division, weapons and equipment included, on a single sheet of 8 inch by 13 inch paper. But their facile diagraming took much for granted. Before beach assault came the labor of winding awkward tows out of broken mounting ports, forming them into flotillas, and steaming across Channel in some semblance of cohesive order. Responsibility for ordering the inevitable hurly-burly fell to the sea-going sailors—Admiral Lütjens and Company. Much of the job he would delegate to the escorting mine forces. Vice-Admiral Ruge, the Commander Mine Force, commented good-naturedly later, in discussing the thing, ". . . the only way it could have worked was to get them, the prahms and other landing craft, all out of port and then make one agreed upon signal, 'Formation Pigpile [Sauhaufen]. Go to England!'" From there on out his minecraft would ride herd as best they could on the flanks of the mobile pigpile and endeavor to steer it in the general direction of England.

In the neat Army sketches of the assault, the flotilla or battalion squares appeared some distance off the far shore, in a central position where one could await the shock of assault up forward to develop the situation. The squares contained the heavy power of reinforcing

From DUNKIRK			From OSTEND		
ADVANCE DET. 55th INF. REGT.	LOADING SPACE	U TANK DET. B	ADVANCE DET. 21st INF. REGT.		LOADING SPACE

3 MINESWEEPERS (LARGE)
4 TRAWLERS
4 FISHCUTTERS
2 TOWS (4 PRAHMS)

8 TOWS
DET. ENGR (16 PRAHMS)

9 MINESWEEPERS (SMALL)
8 FISHCUTTERS
2 TOWS (4 PRAHMS)

REST OF 1st ECHELON

DIV. CDR & NAVAL CDR STAFFS
2 STEAMERS

REST OF 1st ECHELON

8TH TOW GROUP REINF. II./55

55 REGT.

21 REGT.

III. Bn.   II. Bn.

III. Bn.   II. Bn.

9TH TOW GROUP REGT. STAFF 55 REINF. IV./55

3 TOWS FLAK

1ST TOW GROUP REINF. III./21

10TH TOW GROUP REST III./55

2ND TOW GROUP RGTS. STAFF 21

3RD TOW GROUP REINF. II./21

5 TOWS FLAK

M.G. 8

3 STEAMERS EACH 2 PRAHMS IN TOW

2nd ECHELON ROTTERDAM

95th INF. REGT.

LOADING SPACE:
APPROX. 14 STEAMERS

EACH 2 PRAHMS IN TOW

253

3rd ECHELON OSTEND

REST OF THE DIVISION

12 TOWS (24 PRAHMS)
IN SHUTTLESERVICE

Invasion England: combat organization, Reinforced 17th Infantry Division.

---

infantry that was to decide the battle.   Still further at sea plodded transport steamers, each towing two prahms for lightering out the steamer's load of heavy equipment, ammunition, and reserves. Ahead and inshore of the squares, motor coasters lined up to furnish landing gunfire support from their jury-rigged artillery pieces, and shoreward of them, just off the beaches were drawn up the subject of our strongest curiosity and interest—the Advance Detachments (*Vorausabteilungen*) of the First Echelon of the Landing Division. There were the sharpened spearheads that would carry the beaches.

In general terms, the assault of Advance Detachments was to pour onto the beaches in sturmboats from off-lying minelayers or trawlers in battalion size. These mother ships tended a variety of small craft and gear: engineer sturmboats; pneumatic floats; and even motorboats to rush the beach, discharge, and then return for another load, then another, in shuttle service between trawler and beach. Closely associated, sometimes integral with advance detachment, came a special prahm tow loaded with close support tanks. By these means a skirmisher's toe hold would be gained for the tow flotilla to land and expand upon with its heavy infantry power. As to beaching the prahms, at first it was planned that the powered prahm of each tow would beach itself when cast off, and its powerless mate would beach with the help of a motorboat pushing on each quarter. A better system developed in practice by which the powered prahm took the unpowered mate alongside some little distance off shore, and then beached the two together. Though by no means an impossible feat, success demanded high skill and much practice, to say nothing of favorable wind tide. We sketch a translation of the assault scheme (p. 243).

Beach assault has its moments—boats grind, bullets zing and hiss into the water. Those impious fellows who must storm out of boats in face of machine gun fire, these are the men who burn with an honest desire for naval gunfire support as hop-off day draws nigh. In *Sea Lion,* this interest developed later than customarily, particularly on the Navy's part. But when things got truly earnest during August both services spawned brain child after brain child to work fire support wonders. Troop commanders had begun early work at devising the motion of boats and practicing their men at shooting; they also tried mounting artillery pieces, mortars, and rockets on rafts and barges with great industry and resource. The Luftwaffe and Army produced the *Herbert Fähre,* relative to the Siebel craft, mounting flak pieces to furnish "fire for landing support, against sea targets and anti-tank defense." But no scheme provided the desired smothering fire on beach defenses. The Navy fitted guns on motor coasting vessels. Admiral Lütjens had still another solution. He requested Skl to proof the feasibility of committing the ancient battleships

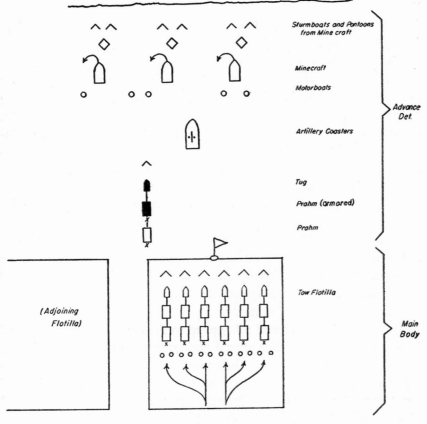

Schematic presentation of a landing.

Schlesien and *Schleswig-Holstein* to the gunfire support job. Since protecting the crossing engaged his attention first, he proposed grounding the two old battleships in the Narrows, say on Varne Shoal, or the Ridge, with the sortie of Strike One, and there let them act as anchored strong points for denying passage to enemy sea forces. He likewise mentioned their use to support beach assault. Admiral Raeder, old gunnery man, liked the idea and ranged himself strongly on Lütjens' side against expert gunnery opinion. Back and forth went the papers, but it was no use—the experts won out. They claimed that besides danger of capsizing, the battleship hulks would incur machinery failures from lack of cooling water while grounded, and if used as floating batteries off the beaches, they offered targets too vulnerable and batteries too weak for the job. The project had to be abandoned. Lack of gunfire support had come to notice too late for remedy. Nevertheless many schemes to make up for lost time kept popping up.

Another such was proposed by resourceful ferry-builder Fritz Siebel. The growing efficiency of his ferries spurred him to branch out in his invasion thinking. Invasion had to go, and he knew gun power to dominate the Channel was lacking. He and associate, Dr. Justus Koch, worked out plans with the Todt organization to construct floatable gun islands of concrete. The plan called for grounding these in the narrows off beaches in great numbers, exactly as Lütjens had suggested for the old battleships. Thus by day, Siebel thought to sew up Channel control, while by night swarms of ferries would rush troops from the near to the far shore. The scheme was pushed with confidence and vigor and acquired the name *Angriff Mückenschwarm,* gnat or mosquito swarm attack. It got no further than enthusiastic war-winning talk, and the gun islands never got off the drawing boards. They were the closest planned approach to the Allied *Mulberries* off Normandy.

But the prize wonder of all applied to the far shore, where a novel idea enjoyed wide popular appeal and gave rise to a rash of rumors. The scheme purposed to set the sea off England's beaches afire with oil as defense against landings. Research agencies on both sides of the Channel undertook experiments that soon produced practical obstacles of insuperable difficulty. First came the twin problems of getting an oil light enough to ignite readily, yet heavy enough to sustain a continuing blaze; then too, a good blaze required an extravagant amount of petroleum, even if the right combination were developed. The German Navy reached a generally negative conclusion about extensive fires off an open coast. A five-mile stretch took a prohibitive amount of oil, boosted by gasoline and fitted with specialized ignition. In isolated localities, such as marshland back of beaches, it was held, oil fires might be made to burn. The German Army went after this angle as a combat problem, while the Navy pursued the seagoing fire hazard. Both reached workable countermeasures. In the case of the Navy, special fire fighting tugs, each towing a long chain of logs, were to accompany Advance Detachments. When an oil slick or burning water was encountered off a beach, the tug was to circle the danger and enclose it in the log chain; so enclosed, the fire could be towed to sea and extinguished by materials on the tug Burning water enjoyed much wider publicity than deserved. The flood of rumors and stories about invasion attempted and repulsed, built around the scheme, all proved apocryphal.[31]

Burning water was but one of the horrors on the far shore. Scores of others disclosed themselves as *Sea Lion* toilers became familiar with the terrain. With each day's batch of photoreconnaissance reports, problems cropped up anew. A well-defined landing front, Folkestone through Brighton, had emerged from the Army-Navy bickering. Both Army and Navy intensified study of individual beaches to outwit nature and the enemy. Navy letter designators identified four assault beach areas; within them, specific stretches were favored for landing: Beach B, Folkestone to Dungeness; Beach C, Dungeness to Bexhill; Beach D, Bexhill around Beachy Head to Newhaven; Beach E, Newhaven through Brighton to Worthing. Beach F, farther along (Worthing to Selsey Bill), was mentioned occasionally. The letter designators passed themselves along to the transport fleet intended to land in the confines of the corresponding beach, that is, Transport Fleet D out of Boulogne sailed due west as part of the Blue Move and assaulted Beach D. Half of Green Move headed from Le Havre direct for Beach E, while the other half sailed along the French coast to parallel Blue from Boulogne.

Near and far shore of late August 1940 moved into sharper focus, and as each line sharpened the Germans and their Führer became more firmly committed to invasion. Hitler never visited *Sea Lion* and his near-shore hubbub.[32] The growing problems there bothered him little, but he could not avoid increasing commitments. Each solution premised itself on specific conditions, which in turn demanded commitment to action, and this snowballed invasion demands toward the day of crisis. At this point the strongest commitment came about through a statement of readiness Skl submitted at the end of August. Navy reported that 15 September could not be met and recommended that 24 September be chosen as the earliest target date. Timing, argued Skl, had to be decided to allow for laying the mine barriers, deploying submarines, and initiating diversion *Herbstreise*. Hitler

[31] The many burning water tales led to extra investigation of the subject. Admiral Schniewind (COS Ops) and Captain Reinicke (heading Staff England) separately described the experimentation and the countermeasures developed by Admiral Witzell's Ordnance Technical Office. Both recalled how Witzell first broke out the miniature chain of logs made of pencils and explained how it would function. Neither Navy nor Army suffered noteworthy casualties in the experiments.

[32] Hitler was content to let *Sea Lion* struggle alone on the shore. He stayed away from the Channel coast until Christmas 1940; his chief interest then was the big gun emplacements (von Puttkamer to Ansel, October 1954).

chose 21 September, and OKW disseminated a *Sea Lion* time table to accord with this decision in these terms:

1. Earliest time for
   a) sortie of Transport Fleets is 20.9.40
   b) S Day of the landing is 21.9.40
2. The order for initiating the operation will be given on S minus 10 days, prospectively on 11.9.40.
3. The final determination of S Day and S Time (commencement of first landing) issues at the latest on S minus 3 Days at midday.
4. All measures are to be so met that the operation can be halted 24 hours before S Time.

According to the war diary of OKW, Operations, Warlimont had reminded Jodl of the timing matter on 30 August. At that time Jodl had remarked that the Führer "does not yet consider the prerequisites for *Operation Sea Lion* fulfilled, judging from the present progress of the air war against England and he has mentioned that he will make a decision about 10 September . . . ." On this basis, and in consideration of the Navy's report, the time table was set up and approved. Therewith the time of crisis had been set. And as *Sea Lion* moved in to demand his day, all the more was a sign of British breakdown by air fright needed. Air war had faltered, and we noted changing Hitlerian weather, accompanied by fitful renewal of invasion interest. In any case, London had to signal, either to make *Sea Lion* feasible, or to render him superfluous. It was time to go after London directly from the air.

8. *September Remember*

Bombs on London

How faithfully Hitler hewed to his own fixed convictions about bringing England down! Events helped him, yet he bent them to his use and stuck fast through thick and thin by the ideas first put on paper in the Jodl summation of 30 June. At that time he made allowance for "political" measures to take effect, but should these fail, the words ran on, "This first and most important target [the RAF] will at the same time be supplemented by the fight against British food stocks . . . tied in with propaganda and *intermittent terror attacks— proclaimed as reprisal—this growing* weakening of food reserves will paralyze *the will to resist of the people and finally break it and therewith force their government to capitulate.*" Talk of direct attack on London had gone on in the Luftwaffe while working up *Eagle*; Kesselring's staff had urged it, but Hitler held back, even threatening censure for a raid that went in to Croydon on London's outskirts on 18 August. He wanted to save London as a trump card for producing the final crash. RAF attack on Berlin in late August helped in that direction by lending substance to German reprisal.

On the night of 25/26 August Berlin's outskirts were bombed lightly; on the 28th the RAF repeated in greater intensity, reaching deep into the city proper. A number of casualties resulted. Down from the mountain sped the Führer, this time to reassure his *Volk* and consult Göring about attacking London.   The desired excuse for reprisal was now in hand and whetted his impatience for a cry of uncle from cross-channel.   Göring was told to produce it.   By the last day of August *Grossangriff auf London* was common gossip.

Astonishingly though, with all the bluster no firm plan for proceeding had been settled upon.   Airfleet commanders were alerted on 29 August, the very day Hitler returned to Berlin, to submit up-to-date recommendations.   By the thirty-first preliminary orders for shifting emphasis onto London went out, and Göring called the customary rally of top leaders to meet at The Hague.   While they assembled, the air actions of September's first days followed the pattern of those before, concentrating on RAF fighters and their installations about London.   Göring's actions toward shifting to London were dilatory in the extreme.[1]   Hitler supplied his propaganda bit nevertheless.   On 4 September he took to the microphone in the Berlin Sportpalast to shout out an overture for the coming storm.   He promised reprisal for British attacks one hundredfold—"we are giving our answer night after night," he cried.   The first large-scale London attack began on the night of 5/6 September.

Counsels and spirits at The Hague had varied.   Kesselring of Fleet 2 was all optimism; for him the time was right.   Sperrle of Fleet 3 felt less sure.   Target designations provoked lively debate, but sober professional opinion prevailed and settled the primary aim on the London dock area and related food and utility plants.   Harbors of south England received secondary place, and the over-all purpose of downing fighters and erasing their bases as opportunity offered remained.   Attacks on shipping and mining of ports were to continue.   *Sea Lion* received no mention, and we note that some target designations worked directly contrary to his interest.[2]

From nine in the evening of the fifth until six the following morning the neighborhood of East London docks was for the first time of the war subjected to repeated attack by about sixty-eight bombers.   The fighter defense that met them seemed weak, the gleeful German flyers reported on return; they reported also many explosions and numerous fires left in the wake of their attacks.

---

[1] Dr. Plesman, still pursuing his peace plan, heard of impending attack on London.   He ran Göring down at The Hague rally and tried hard to dissuade him. Göring implied it was out of his hands.   The Führer had decided.   W.D. OKW Ops documents the sequence of events.

[2] Von Rohden collection: Rohden 114, H 1237-1320.

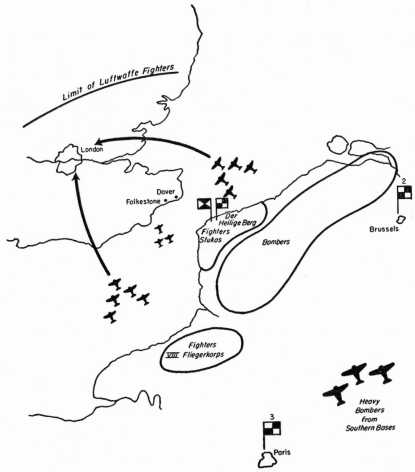

Luftwaffe deployment for attacks on London, September 1940.

Encouraged by this successful preliminary, the much advertised big attack (*der Grossangriff gegen London*) commenced during daylight late on the seventh and kept up until 0400 of the eighth. Göring was on hand to gape from the Holy Mount[3] not far from Cap Blanc Nez, chin strap cinching cap on his head as he craned to sort out the formations of black cross planes droning overhead. They could be made out well; there the first bombers, fighters joining up in good

[3] This was the forward Air Command Post of Air Fleet 2, situated on a commanding hillside near Cap Blanc Nez. It was often used by Kesselring to watch his air units form and depart for attack. Because many high personages visited the post to watch and marvel during air action it acquired the name *der heilige Berg*, or, the Holy Mount. Göring took his stance there for the Big Attack on London. It was his first appearance at the front.

order.   Fighters, in fact, were thicker than flies, yet few would get free to challenge their RAF opponents, for this was a night for bombing! In its course close to one thousand tons, dropped from some 625 bombers, would find their mark in London. Finding the target made no problem, since by nightfall the plane crews could already discern the glare of London fires on leaving France. "London docks are a sea of flame," ran the exciting advices. Göring felt in fine fettle; characteristically he dashed to the microphone and made a flamboyant broadcast report of falling London to the Germans, and incidentally to the British. "Right into the enemy's heart," the Luftwaffe had struck, he exulted.

Did he mean London docks or the spirit of Britain? Indeed, could the docks and their auxiliaries remain the sole target? That is always the problem; violence becomes indiscriminate when it gets underway in earnest. And so it went with the German flyers on 8 September when smoke and mist shrouded the designated targets. What to do with the bombs on board? Many planes returned to base as they set out, fully loaded; such a sinful waste would hardly do. During twilight of the same day, the eighth, visibility improved over London; whether this applied equally to the dock area, the official log failed to record. It did say that 21 planes "carried out an attack in excellent visibility with great success . . . . Center of effort on Kensington, Buckingham Palace and Westham . . . . In the west part of the city 15 to 20 fires . . . ." The lid was off, yet only tacitly. At the start, London bombing was meant to flush fighters up for free combat. But if no fighters responded, this purpose fell out, and now the excessive number of bombers committed required excessive fighter protection, which further diminished the chances of free fighter combat. Once they were so committed there remained at the end solely the extension of bombing. So it fell out. Though London docks, supply and utility installations, and industry remained the ordered targets, the flyers tended to lose discrimination.

Ironically, the twenty-one bombers that raised the lid with drops near Buckingham Palace belonged to Group 606, under the operational control of the Navy. Göring had disregarded the Navy and ordered the Group into combat under Airfleet 3. Navy protest against invasion of its command came to naught through Führer decision. He wanted everything to bear on London. The incident corroborated the engrossment of the highest German leadership with crash effect by bombing.

London burned and it looked to be merely a business of feeding the flames. But some semblance of order had to be maintained in the feeding; flyers were mixing routes and targets. Only weak fighter opposition had been encountered thus far. It was time to systematize the final strokes for fuller effect. Accordingly the Air General Staff arranged that Airfleet 2 take over day attacks under heavy fighter escort, while Fleet 3 handled the night sorties, presumably with fewer fighters. London town was divided into east and west target zones, designated A and B. Attacks were to roll around the clock toward total extinction of supply and dock installations in A, and the power and utility plants at B. It would be a matter of only a few more days. If this rigid scheduling was to work, however, the days had to be fair and the adversary compliant. The opposite occurred. Poor visibility made trouble in joining fighters to bombers; argument ensued between fighters and bombers over escorting techniques. Bomber crews were feeling the grind. Moreover, the RAF reacted sharply to the change of tactic, and London's morale climbed when heavy reinforcement of anti-air artillery moved in to drown out the drone of planes overhead. From the ninth till the thirteenth of September no daylight attacks of sizable power developed; the night attacks on the Thames dock area continued. Then came merciful rains to extinguish the fires. Reports from the German Air General Staff said less and less about target zones A and B and more about strikes on secondary targets and those on the sea. The system had not worked.

A week passed in this way without sign of decision. And no wonder! German bombs and bombast had given rise to a British feeling far different from the one wanted. People in England were too busy to think of giving up. There was work to be done, fires to put out, utilities to improvise, communications to rehook, and roads to clear for the final test of invasion. Not climax by air but beating off invasion, gripped English minds. That the air assault played only the prelude to a grimmer trial possessed them and thus bound Londoners and nation fast in unspoken pledge to get on and endure. The collection of landing craft cross-Channel had grown visibly. On 11 September Prime Minister Churchill warned the nation "that a full scale invasion . . . is being prepared . . . and that it may be launched at any time now . . . ." He never missed the opportunity of playing up that uglier fate. The previous day (the tenth) in its own halls of Berlin Skl had attempted a balance between air offensive and *Sea Lion*. Said the war diary:

. . . the indispensable prerequisite for the undertaking (Sea Lion) . . . has *not* been achieved, namely clear air command over the Channel . . . the shooting up of Boulogne of yesterday and today by destroyers shows the enemy is testing our defensive powers. Planned preparations for *Sea-Lion* would require the Luftwaffe now to concentrate less on London but more on Portsmouth and Dover and the (British) fleet forces . . . . However Skl does not hold it proper to come forward with such requirement to the Luftwaffe or to the Führer now since he regards the great assault on London as possibly decisive for the war and [feels] that the systematic and prolonged bombing of London can provoke an enemy attitude which might make *Sea Lion* altogether unnecessary . . . .

A queer paradox was thus presented. The soberest German professionals, who had few kind thoughts for the Luftwaffe, deferred to decision by bomb fright, while the British leapt over such picayune climax to concentrate on repelling invasion.

In the course of the thirteenth and fourteenth weather permitted renewal of the bombing in medium strength. London's beacons were rekindled, and though the city's fighter defense seemed to be weakening, patrols were encountered over the coast. September 15 proved another Big Day—reminiscent of 15 August. Then Göring had hesitated for reassessment. On this later big day he committed well over 300 planes in mediocre visibility, a sign perhaps of waxing impatience high up. They encountered surprisingly stiff opposition from fighters who clung to their bomber prey on the return run well out over the Channel and even into France. Forty-nine German planes were knocked out of the air, the highest RAF bag to that point. London suffered no fresh damage of consequence. It had been a big but bad day for Luftwaffe. Poor visibility held through the following day. The Reichsmarschall had to content himself with further reassessment and pep talk to his assembled high commanders. A change in tactic was again in order, he thought.

His farcical command system was strongly evidenced by one Schwester Christa, an important member of Göring's personal entourage. She was a nurse of many accomplishments who ministered to his aches and pains both at home and in the field, even aboard the lush railroad coach headquarters. She often "manned" his phone, received incoming messages and on occasion transmitted some to the field at her master's behest. In the course of the Air offensive on England it was not at all out of order for Jeschonnek to hear Christa on the other end of the line barking out that the Reichsmarschall wanted 300 planes over the target this night, or else. The night or day might be thick with pea-soup fog, but this was of little mind to Christa. Jeschonnek thereupon would take to his bunk with a fresh attack of ulcers. Goings-on of this sort characterized ex-fighter pilot Göring's approach to the whole thing; and they proved of enormous benefit to the British. He rarely held fast to a tactic long enough for profitable return, and the casual shifts in emphasis often came just in the nick of time to save a critical British link or sinew of defense. Actions and their planning were mixed incessantly with the hue and cry of the day and cheap overtones of publicity. His conference of 16 September like that of 18 August was no exception.

Ostensibly the meeting was called to recoup the grave losses of the day before, when the RAF had taken a toll of a half hundred Luftwaffe planes. Less obvious reasons for change might have developed from renewed assurances given the Führer in these last days. The weather, averred Göring to his chiefs, imposed a change of tactic. He explained that the erstwhile aim to get the enemy into the air for combat stood, but the lessons of the operating forces, *die Truppe,* as the Germans say, had to be taken to heart. Cannon-equipped Hurricanes must be concentrated upon; London had all the antiair artillery and most of the fighter protection. "Stick by the enemy then; in 4 or 5 days his fighters will be out! Thereafter aircraft producing centers must be eliminated . . . . Attacks on London, even if London is not destroyed, always bring response . . . ." Then came the new tactic: (a) big attack only in the very best weather and then attack with at least 300 to 400 planes; (b) during doubtful weather small heavily escorted attacks; (c) continuous attack in waves only after knocking out more RAF fighters. Target assignment in London as before. At that point he interjected a significant side remark that *"Sea-Lion must not disturb nor burden the Luftwaffe operations."* An anticlimactic Führer Conference had taken place two days earlier to ponder over almost ready, but still unhappy, *Sea Lion.* Göring did not attend, but circumstances tend to show he had stepped to the fore privately to assure his Führer that he could still handle England alone. Such assurance may indeed have led to the big commitment of planes in unfavorable visibility on the fifteenth, with such disturbing result.

A version of the new tactic, which was undoubtedly Jeschonnek's, recorded that the "Reichsmarschall believed the enemy massing of his fighters to be a welcome turn since then more could be shot down." Thereupon he summarized and reinterpreted the tasks of the airfleets:

Fleet 2 attack London in good weather with reduced bomber but heavy fighter and bomber-fighter strength in order to get at the enemy fighters. In bad weather and at night Fleets 2 and 3 make only harrassing attacks on London in the strength warranted. Fleet 3 keep after Liverpool, Southhampton, and Bristol and mining of the Thames. Both fleets retain special aircraft industrial targets. Fleet 2 remember that neutralization of enemy coastal batteries in way of *Sea Lion* belonged among its tasks. Note that there was not a word about massed attacks of 300 and 400 planes, and that *Sea Lion* support remained on the list. As reinterpreted the new tactic posed a return to the military objective of enemy fighters in lieu of dubious aim of psychological effect.

As final mention a new subject appeared: the problem of moving air units to the east frontier for possible operations in that area. Though interest in England still came first, intrusions from *East Plan* began making their mark and presaged the abandonment of air war on England. Göring's conference of 16 September registered the first signs of failure. A huddle between Hitler and Göring in the old pattern must have taken place shortly before Führer *Sea Lion* Conference of 14 September. The two expressed themselves (Hitler on the fourteenth, Göring on the sixteenth) in identical phrases, as though echoing and bolstering each other with the best possible face on things. Phrases like weather to blame, London had all the antiair, four or five days more, and so on, all bear witness to thought in common. But time and planes were running out. Even if crashing victory did not come in "four or five days" the Luftwaffe could still, with reduced commitment, certainly keep England down for a turn east. So Hitler and Göring may have consoled each other in the face of unspoken failure. For resolving a predicament into plausible terms, henchman Göring had ever been the deft counsellor.

The "four or five days more" never eventuated. After the fifteenth the German air effort on London fell off perceptibly for a number of reasons, among which weather again shouldered the brunt of the blame. There were likewise reasons internal to the Luftwaffe, where cracks in structure and confidence in the conduct of the operation began to appear. More and more the attacks drifted into the comforting cloak of night while day efforts became hit and run. Only one day, the twenty-seventh, saw a large-scale daylight attack. That was the last! The fact was the Luftwaffe had failed, and John Bull had endured in telling fashion.

England gave forthright notice to 15 September as a turning point, and so did America. U.S. General Strong returned home from sojourn in London to relate how one crisis after another had been surmounted. Churchill, too, thought the worst from the air had been weathered so that on 17 September he could counsel his countrymen that they "may await the decision of prolonged air battle with sober but increased confidence." His gift for directing shafts at vulnerable targets told. With decision in the air favorable to Britain, there could be no invasion of England, he had often averred. Nevertheless he continued to hammer on that threat as the most urgent for each day and exhorted the people to relax not a moment in work and vigilance. Invasion peril held on.

Not alone to Britons was *Sea Lion* still viable and full of promise. To many a German sailor, high and low, toiling on the shores of the Channel and in rear areas, inching him toward the water, he was alive and kicking. The beast was there for all to see in full regalia, thrashing along the beaches and estuaries. Presently we retrieve him to observe his full readiness. Before we do, a final summary note is warranted on the over-all contribution toward success of invasion made by the air effort.

On that count the score works out very close to zero, unless we lapse into the familiar delusion of air zealots that mass destruction works for all. What the Luftwaffe accomplished for invasion was more coincidental than intended. No air action was ordered or accomplished for the specific purpose of preparing *Sea Lion's* way; indeed some attacks on south England shores heightened his hazards. Thought of a teamed effort seems to have been the last to enter the air mind, a fact that was duly noted and discussed in the OKW planning staff. Recall Göring's caution against *Sea Lion* and Jeschonnek's effort to mitigate this injunction. No air plan or single order made mention of bombardment in *Sea Lion's* interest until well into September. Then in September's third week came a change. Air commands made an all too obvious show of establishing liaison with the invasion forces. The move said in effect, The air war is over; we are now free for other things. What do you have? Orders for support of invasion issued from Airfleet 2 and Air Corps 1 in the period 17-19 September, long after the expected day of crisis, the 11th. Had Hitler on that day given *Sea Lion* the nod, there was litttle on record to guide the Luftwaffe. From beginning to end the air offensive remained a single service project of conquest by its power alone. This conclusion of faulty strategical thinking, or better, the total absence of combined strategy, cannot be evaded. Of course, had RAF been beaten to earth the game might have been open to a number of endings, invasion among them. But this is not strategy; it is gambling. Hitler and his Germans gambled on a quick and easy solution of Problem England by air fright, and the play failed.

Now he turned once again and grasped at *Sea Lion.*

Final Dispositions—September 1940

"*Sea Lion,* rubbish!" was old soldier Rundstedt's counter whenever the invasion question came before him; even now during September 1940 when along the near shore and the far, anxiety pulsed ever higher, sending its tension world-wide. Tension and urge to action stayed at a feeble minimum in his Army Group A field headquarters at St. Germain. Rundstedt acted no Parma going ably about readying his troops for onslaught against England, but instead indulged his original skeptical feeling of the undertaking. He delegated most of *Sea Lion's* detailed drudgery to Generaloberst Busch, commanding 16th Army. In fact, it was Busch who on 14 September signed the Army Group A Order No. 1 for executing *Sea Lion* rather than Rundstedt, who had brushed it off as more rubbish.[4]

On the same 14 September Admiral Lütjens, Fleet Commander and Navy running mate of General Busch, also signed his Order No. 1 for *Sea Lion.* We ease down the chains of Army and Navy command via Busch and Lütjens to fix the character and spirit of final invasion dispositions. German amphibious thought had come a long way in some places.

Actually, the delegation of final Army dispositions to General Busch turned out well. His 16th Army was to carry the main landing effort, and not only was the General strong for *Sea Lion,* he also knew the most about him. His learning, which stemmed from training and experimentation at Le Touquet, he now embodied in his Order No. 1. It defined the initial Group A task as seizure of a con-

---

[4] Field Marshal von Rundstedt expressed his skepticism openly. His staff officers were of the opinion that their commander had gained his attitude from remarks by Hitler to him personally during late July or August (von Sodenstern, COS Army Gp A, to Ansel, 1953). Remember Hitler's confidences to Rundstedt of Dunkirk time and that if OKH was strong for certain action (as was the case for invasion) von Rundstedt was apt to be against it. The Group A war diary confirms the casual attitude of its leader by the dearth of invasion entries.

tinuous beachhead twelve to eighteen miles deep from Folkestone to Worthing, splitting the eighty-mile landing front almost equally between the 16th on the right and Strauss' 9th Army on the left, at St. Leonards (Hastings). Beachhead in hand, it was purposed to launch a co-ordinated field attack for gaining the "Thames Line" (Thames to Portsmouth), and from there the land fight could continue toward the final operational objective line, Maldon to Severn.

Our interest clings to the crucial stage where the arms are together during crossing and forcing the first lodgements on England's shore and then battling to extend them into a beachhead. Busch estimated that, counting redeployment, this initial struggle would consume a full week, most of it tough infighting by small units. Indeed, he devoted several passages of the Group A order and an annex to these actions, so important were they to him. The Luftwaffe, in the role of artillery, was to support the leap from sea to shore and clear the way for landing at first light on S Day. Individual and small unit combat would be the rule of that day of crisis; mortars, artillery, and tanks to be pushed forward at utmost speed no matter where they landed or to whom they belonged. Confusion of organization and mixing of units was conceded, and as remedy Busch reached down to the divisional level by appointing the division commanders to controlling power in the anticipated jumble. He directed that the ground under attack be divided into divisional stripes running straight inland from the water and told off each stripe to the province of a particular division commander. All forces landing or chancing within a stripe fell automatically under orders of the division commander who owned that stripe. The highest field command by this means attempted to insure a firm grasp on a handful of England's soil to every soldier landed. It was a sage idea.

Doctrine of this imaginative character was old stuff to General Busch, for he had urged the same line in his own series of meticulous though tentative orders for 16th Army. They began appearing as early as 3 September. He urged flexibility of organization and independent responsibility of the man on the spot to hold, and push on. The cogent and forceful soldier words gauge the progress of German soldiery in amphibious warfare thinking:

The first requisite is to join battle . . . Each ship or prahm is to be so loaded that men, weapons, equipment and munitions together make up a self-contained combat unit . . . . The governing principle is: There is no formalized scheme . . . every piece of bureaucracy must be beaten down . . . . Command authority and responsibility for loading and crossing lies in the hands of the naval command; intrusion therein on the part of army commands can breed confusion and injury to the project as a whole . . . . Comprehensive co-operation is only possible through the closest personal relationship . . . the tactical troop commander and naval commander for each unit, convoy, tow or transport fleet must be embarked on the same vessel.

These instructions went to the heart of landing combat.

The General may have been thinking of his own opposite in the Navy, Admiral Lütjens, Fleet Commander at distant Trouville.[5] We must try to keep the two together, for their fighting would be done as a team. Lütjens' rounded his final *Sea Lion* order into shape during these days. Despite the separation between Army and Navy field headquarters the linkage seems to have been good. A flavor of the sea can be smelled in the papers, and though the soldiers still preferred to talk of "bridgeheads" and not "beachheads," we note the 16th Army's use of Navy designators in England and bits of salty terminology about landing craft and their loading. Troops and staffs hewed out enthusiastic solutions for every conceivable contingency. Both Warlimont and von Lossberg of OKW commented favorably after visiting the Busch invasion ferment on the coast. Busch signed his final 16th Army "Preliminary Directive for Carrying out Operation 'Sea Lion' " on 9 September, five days before signing the similar Group A order in place of Rundstedt. General Busch's interest and energy made a good job of *Sea Lion*.

The inland limit of the main effort beachhead ran from Canterbury, along the river Great Stour to Ashford and on to Tenterden and Etchingham, there beyond the beachhead of another day (Hastings and Battle of 1066), it linked with the 9th Army. Thence the line continued westward for the 9th Army's supporting effort to Storrington. No re-enforcement of consequence, Busch told his fighters, could be expected for eight days; the job was to take the beachhead as best they could, and for it he made available four Landing Divisions to be deployed as follows:

[5] About 10 September Admiral Lütjens shifted his headquarters closer to the 16th Army near Boulogne. The mine command shifted with him.

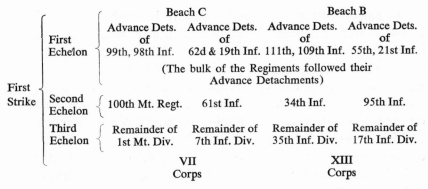

			Beach C		Beach B	
First Strike	First Echelon		Advance Dets. of 99th, 98th Inf.	Advance Dets. of 62d & 19th Inf.	Advance Dets. of 111th, 109th Inf.	Advance Dets. of 55th, 21st Inf.
			(The bulk of the Regiments followed their Advance Detachments)			
	Second Echelon		100th Mt. Regt.	61st Inf.	34th Inf.	95th Inf.
	Third Echelon		Remainder of 1st Mt. Div.	Remainder of 7th Inf. Div.	Remainder of 35th Inf. Div.	Remainder of 17th Inf. Div.
			VII Corps		XIII Corps	

On the extreme right, headed for Hythe and Folkestone, stood *Sturm-bock* (battering ram) Infantry Division 17; it would have the arduous task of keeping the open right wing secure. We shall hear more of that fine fighting outfit.

With Navy concurrence, Busch allowed eight hours for clearing port and forming up, and another ten for crossing. Both estimates were highly optimistic. Assuming that the first sturmboat touched down on England at daybreak of S Day, he figured that the forward two echelons of Strike One, about 60,000 troops, could be got ashore by evening of the second day, and the rest of that strike during the course of the third day. So, three days' time would see Strike One, totaling 110,167 troops and 24,528 horses, ashore and fighting.[6] Then came the slow-up of turn-around so incomprehensible to the soldier; by noon of S plus 8, only one additional infantry division and one of armor would have gained England, and further reinforcement could flow only at the same trickling rate. The second strike, and the third, equaled the first so that the Main Effort of *Sea Lion*, confided to able General Busch, numbered in all some 330,000 men. The complete operation ran to staggering figures of men, animals, and machinery, and reminds us that, well as German soldiers had learned their landing ABC's, they could not leave their field campaigning. Their hopes rested in the blitz technique of forcing the decisions on land by arriving first in overwhelming strength at crucial points of the bridgehead's inner boundary. Grease pencil sweeps on the planning maps brought out this point with emphatic clarity.[7]

[6] The German Army still depended on horses for mass movement. Much of the Artillery was horse drawn.

[7] The German planning and ordering seemed to have been weak and slow in attention to the use of English ports, once landing on the open shore had become the rage. There were few good ports on England's south coast, but, such as they were, they deserved a higher combat priority than is given in the orders.

In amphibious attack orders a picture is worth far more than a thousand words; it is worth ten thousand, and pounds upon pounds of paper, for it offers vital clarity of understanding. This is especially true for naval planning. Assembly and routing of ships, concentration and deployment for attack of forces leap from a chart in answer to questions that words could not clear. We have remarked on the soldier talent for pictography and how it presented a complete division deployed for attack. But deployment presented a static condition of one moment. When the soldiers got loose with their arrows to indicate movement over water, the picture, though it retained much of its charm, lost reality. *Sea Lion* attack demanded precise calculation and plotting to include tide, navigation of swept channels, avoidance of hazards, and above all, noninterference between adjoining forces. These were the factors upon which Admiral Lütjens concentrated in his Operation Order No. 1 of 14 September. Would Tow Flotilla 3 clear channel entrance X before the arrival of steamer convoy 4? What were the points where conflict was likely and how could tangles be avoided? A good picture series can stimulate answers to such questions, bringing timely decision to fend off irretrievable chaos. Admiral Lütjens endeavored to place this information on one chart backed up by a verbal description in his order.[8]

From the first a distasteful thought of auxiliary troop-lift service to the Army had clouded Navy invasion thinking. Original exploration fastened on a Navy role of simply transporting bodies rather than attack from the sea, a misconception which grew all the stronger as the lack of proper ships and craft became apparent and the operational hazards asserted themselves. Admiral Lütjens testified in his Operation Order No. 1 to this mistaken image of a *Sea Lion* owned by the Army for whom the Air Force would have to clear an impeccable way. He titled his order, Execution of Transport for Operation Sea-Lion, and stressed the thought again in a short fourteen-word statement of this principal task: "Transfer of the 9th and 16th Army over from the north-French [coast] to the English coast." Starting then

[8] When U.S. Forces first combined with the British in landing operations much obscure talk issued from our friends about the "Mickey Mouse." Meeting at this or that point, clearing this force from another, or moving out at the right moment would all become clear from the "Mickey Mouse." But what was it? The Mickey Mouse? It turned out to be a series of timed sketches in a near Disney vernacular, showing the expected positioning of forces at certain crucial moments. They were invaluable. Between thumb and forefinger the sheaf of sketches could be made to ripple past in an approximation of a motion picture.

with Rotterdam and ending at Le Havre, he set down detailed instructions for the sortie, forming, navigating and protecting of the transport craft from each port to their landing areas. Each transport fleet component of prahm tow formation or steamer convoy had an escort of minecraft assigned to help along toward the goal. Transport Fleet B, comprised of prahms out of Ostend and Dunkirk and steamers from Rotterdam, was to proceed via route 1 to Beach B; Fleet C with prahms from Calais and steamers from Antwerp was destined for Beach C over route 2; and so on, Fleet D from Boulogne over route 3; and finally Fleet E from Le Havre with a choice of two routes to Brighton. It was mainly a business of close navigation and lifting Army bodies.

The distribution of the meager combatant forces available in submarines, destroyers, and torpedo boats enlivened one short paragraph. Much loose talk had gone on about the effect of submarines in connection with invasion. The restricted Channel waters with their strong currents and many shoals were markedly unsuited for submarine operating. Lütjens ordered three groups of five boats each to operate in the western approaches of the Channel, outside the mine barriers, and two groups of three each to work to the eastward of the Narrows (total twenty-one boats). About ten destroyers and double that number of torpedo boats were to work out of Le Havre and Cherbourg against the Royal Navy; S boats, or motortorpedo craft, were similarly assigned to the eastern Channel approaches.

Direct protection and support of the Transport Fleets fell to Commodore Ruge's minecraft. The allotted tasks of this force were as hard and nearly as plentiful as those assigned Luftwaffe. They included:

1. Aided by destroyers and torpedo boats, laying mine barriers against British naval interference;

    a. Fields *Caesar* off Goodwin Sands against ingress from the east,

    b. Fields *Bruno* and *Anton* on either flank of crossing route 4 (Le Havre to Brighton),

    c. Fields *Dora* off Start Point against British ships from Plymouth;

2. Sweeping four crossing routes and approaches, clearing them of both British and German mines;

3. Escorting the Transport Fleets to the landing beaches, marking the routes as they went and fending off naval attacks;

4. Embarking Advance Detachments, launching them by sturm-boats onto the beaches;

5. Laying protective smoke screens off beaches and furnishing landing gunfire support.

In all, close to two hundred mine and picket vessels were engaged on these diverse operations. Ruge believed there would have been no trouble in laying the barriers and clearing the routes (tasks 1 and 2). They were what mineforces were for, he said, and added confidently, "We could have done it but it could not have stopped all British ships. Some always get through." Over the task of getting *Sea Lion* hodge-podge underway and moving toward England, he shook his head and had recourse to that apt remark—"Formation Pigpile, Go to England." Except for vessels engaged in the barrier jobs, the minecraft were told off to the hard-pressed Transport Fleet Commanders, whose growing troubles the Lord alone could have cured.[9]

Often one finds the operational meat of orders in the annexes where helpful detail can flourish comparatively free of censorship higher up and thus work toward clarification of the manifold inter-locking actions. Lütjens' annexes did this for the leap from ship to shore in vivid terms. Someone had gone to the trouble of putting himself into the shoes of a Transport Fleet Commander and had plotted out his grim picture of the long train of hulks approaching England. Arrived at the end of a swept route some ten miles off the coast in column, the trick was to get the Tow Flotillas to go 'by the right flank' toward the shore. It was to be attempted by a simul-

[9] Admiral Ruge's remarks are of special value, because, as against the planners, he had seen *Sea Lion* grow on the waterfront and understood his limitations. He set no great store by him for two main reasons: the prolonged period required for the landing fleet to clear the mounting ports and form, and the small margin of power available to the prahms over tide and weather of the Channel. He readily granted that the barriers could never be 100 per cent effective; breaches could be expected to develop. The barrier laying jobs make a story in themselves. They were to be executed at night, starting about S minus 8 Day, by mixed organizations of destroyers, torpedo boats, and converted minelayers from Cherbourg, Le Havre, Ostend, and Antwerp. Naval Group Commander West, Admiral Saalwächter, in Paris, kept control of these critical and widespread operations himself. He issued a governing Operations Order with a specific annex for laying each field. A Dover barrier in the tradition of World War I but in extended form had received high German attention. There were crackpot ideas for winning the war among Nazi bigwigs (notably by Hess) with mines alone. Mines laid by air drops were to isolate Britain from the world. Göring and Milch entertained similar notions.

taneous 90-degree turn of tows landward, on signal by radio, by blinking green lights, and by megaphone shouts. Imagine turning one hundred tandem barge tows, three or four abreast, from column into line off a hostile shore in the dark of the night, with a raging power of three or four knots at your command! The tows were to steam shoreward in line abreast while Advance Detachments dashed ahead to the attack, carrying the Transport Fleet Commander along in their middle. Two hours it would take the prahms to catch up. Dawn would break, and with it gun flashes along the dim shore. Was this all of the Advance Detachment ahead; could this be the right spot? A flood of images and questions are called up. But a basic plan to start from there had to be, the highly theoretical, almost impracticable, one devised on a chart by the Germans was probably the best their circumstances permitted. Transport Fleet Commanders had ended up as the unhappy goats.

For lighthearted abandon, Transport Fleet E's stint on the left wing took the prize. It qualified as *Himmelfahrtskommando,* or a command whose dangers in the jocular vernacular automatically guaranteed a ride to heaven. Yet Navy Captain Scheuerlen, the Commander, carried on undismayed. His route 4 from Le Havre to Brighton stuck out there in the west by itself, except for flanking mine barriers to right and left, which might have become as much of a hazard to Scheuerlen as to the British. He was to race up this 85 mile slot at 7 knots, leading 200 motorboats and 100 motorsailors formed into a rectangle, 20 boats wide and 15 long. Numerous motor mine sweepers and picket boats were to screen all sides. Multiplicity of targets Scheuerlen surely could have provided for the Royal Navy out of Portsmouth and bases farther west. If his run, blessed with great luck, had succeeded, Convoy No. 4 under Captain Brocksien with 25 steamers, prahms, and tugs was to follow by the same route. It might well have come about that Scheuerlen and Brocksien would draw off the brunt of British naval counteraction and thus enhance the chances of the crossings in the Narrows. But at best the left wing venture was an eccentric move from which *Sea Lion* ashore in England could have gained no important troop strength, although Scheuerlen's small craft could lift two regimental groups.

It was now far too late to recognize the left wing effort for what it was, and only could be, a sacrificial play of small hope, and make it over into a bona fide diversion strike of speed and prospect. Army too long had insisted on a heavy lift out of Le Havre. This became so because of an original faulty deployment on the near shore; the mistake was basic to all the bickering. As a result neither the desired lift nor a useful effort was obtained. Ninth Army ended scattered among several widely separated bases. The first echelons of three of her divisions were still to issue from Le Havre and the remainder, in all eight divisions, through Boulogne and other ports. Flexibility and vision all around could have produced a sounder final plan. It is likely that the feeble interest of 9th Army Command and staff rose from their ambiguous role. Their army had been saddled with an ill-starred subsidiary effort.

Orders draw pictures, and we are at the end of those outlined by the high Army and Navy orders. The German invasion of England had gravitated down to a reasonable front of near 60 miles. We have noted the forces engaged, their general deployment, plan of crossing and assault by a main effort of four Landing Divisions from the 16th Army on the right, supported by two of the 9th Army on the left. Both Navy and Army orders had stressed complete dependence on air command and close air support over the invasion area for the operation to begin.[10] The operating people, immersed in last-minute preparations, were less concerned about the air preliminaries. For a final look at those men closest of all to *Sea Lion* we turn to the open right wing, where the 17th Infantry Division gathered in a task no less interesting and equally as dangerous as that heaven-bent group on the left wing.

The Open Right Wing

All the ordained brethren know that the first private objective in any landing operation, if you are up forward, is to seize the finest villa, seraglio, cottage, nipashack, dugout, or foxhole for your boss, before a rival service or ally gets there; to hold it, and much later pridefully show it off to the "Old Man," as you recount what great deeds its capture entailed. You make a tourist map guide reconnaissance of the situation beforehand, pick out a likely looking target, run for it like

[10] General Busch's order outlined the allocation of support expected from the Luftwaffe, most of it from Air Fleet 2. Fliegerkorps II (Lörzer) with heavy bombers, Stukas and reconnaissance planes, and VIII Korps (von Richthofen) with close support planes were available. Richthofen was to concentrate attack just

Billy be damned and nail it down, post a marine or blue jacket at each entrance and go about your business of winning the war. Three hours or three days later you return to find that the sheer bulk of the friendly opposition has moved your command post out into the street, and you are faced with the job of doing it all over again, sometimes not in a "nice way."

Had this reporter been under the necessity of carrying out the foregoing routine with the *Vorausabteilung* of the 17th Infantry Division in September 1940 his choice of command post for the Division Commander, Generalmajor der Artillerie Herbert Loch, could have fallen on no better location than that comfortable beach hotel where he sat in May 1953, trying to picture from the veranda the chances of the 17th in storming the beach below. The pebbly beach fronted Hythe, a seaside town of England just southwest of Folkestone. Perhaps the spot was a little exposed for a command post, but the hotel provided a good vantage point, with fine field of vision up and down the shingly beach and also inland toward Lympne Cliffs, the first divisional objective. That eminence rose beyond the Royal Military Canal, a water hazard that had been pushed westward from Hythe when Napoleon had threatened to land. Yes, it would make a tolerable command post, but what about the beach? We went down to test it and to chat with an ancient native who was painting an ancient name on the stern of a careened fishing boat. "It was just this time thirteen years ago, it was Dunkirk Day" the old man said. "All day and all night, over and over—rain, yes, but quiet water just as today." He skilfully curved the letters "Cinque Ports" on the stern of the plump, high and dry fisherman. There must be a tidal range of over fourteen feet here, we mused, as he resumed:

We could see the smoke of fires on the other side; that life boat station there was working then; a fine motor boat, but neither crew nor the skipper wanted to go. [He spat.] So the Navy took her and lost her. They ran her on the beach at Dunkirk, they did, and she wouldn't come off—why wouldn't they lie off—the men were already wet—I dunno. But we got them off and Jerry, he didn't come. He stayed away except for his planes. Kesselring he was for coming over, and he could have done it.

---

prior to landing on Folkestone and then shift emphasis westward to Beach B. Lörzer was to cover embarkation, the crossing and landing, then take under fire inland reserves and communications. The assignments were obviously too numerous and too heavy, which both Field Marshal Kesselring and his Chief of Staff General Wilhelm Speidel readily conceded.

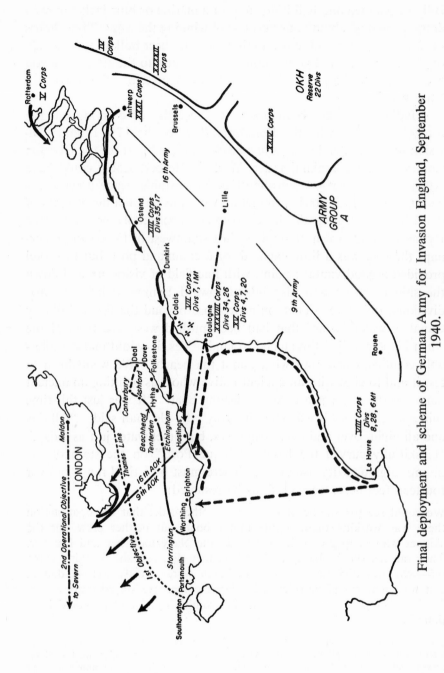

Final deployment and scheme of German Army for Invasion England, September 1940.

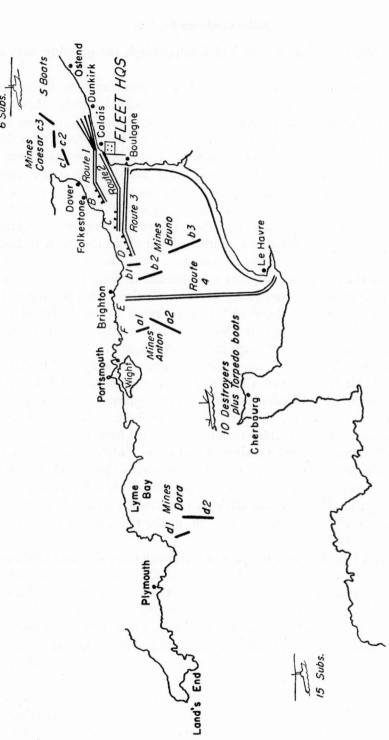

Final dispositions, German Navy, for Invasion England, September 1940.

So spoke an old man who had lived through the gripping days of invasion.

Hythe bore both more venerable and more modern distinction. One of the original Cinque Ports, along with Romney, Hastings, Dover, and Sandwich, the strong northeast-tending tidal stream has sanded it up. Only Dover survived, but from the Norman days that gave them their name down to the time of Elizabeth and the Armada, this defensive federation of Channel ports furnished the core of ships and sailors caring for control of the Narrows and all that meant to communication with the Continent or its severance. They cradled Britain's infant sea power, and their import has not been forgotten today. Only recently, Sir Winston Churchill, the present Lord Warden of the Cinque Ports, remarked on a matter of administration in the area, and said that if he needed to get this done, he had but to exercise his prerogative of Lord Warden. In 1945 the V-1's gave the region the name of "Hellfire Corner"; over 2,010 missiles thudded in to its triangular confines. From nearby Lympne airfield, RAF fighters rose to intercept the "doodlebugs."

Lympne's ancient name came into mention during the Luftwaffe's Grand Air Offensive of 1940, and for the invasion this field stood first on the 17th Division's priority list of capture. It stands high on a plateau atop of the sharp rise that starts back of Hythe and tends westward. A milder ridge runs northeastward from Lympne through Sandling Park toward Etchinghill and on to Paddlesworth, landward of Folkestone. The ridge line, Paddlesworth–Etchinghill–Sandling Park–Lympne, defined the first operational objective of the 17th Division landing. As the Division Commander said, "The situation was normal; I had objectives ahead, to the right, to the left, up and down."

The 17th had won its spurs in the Polish campaign and kept them well sharpened at Fortress Longwy and Chateau Porcien in France. His *Sturmbock,* or battering-ram, the former army superior had affectionately dubbed General Loch's command during this early campaigning and now the Division was going to have to prove itself all over again to another Army leader, General Busch, by securing his right flank in the war's most dangerous undertaking. A division posted on the open right wing of the assault on England in the Dover Narrows could be no ordinary outfit—it had to be a tried and reliable fighting force. That, this Division was. The end of the French campaign found the 17th near Dijon; from there it started a march toward

The Luftwaffe Navy! Prahms rigged with airscrew propulsion for crossing the Channel during invasion. *(Courtesy Dr. Justus Koch)*

Looking seaward from the ridge behind Folkestone along the prospective route of the 17th Division's advance.

Looking to seaward from high ground back of Hythe. The 17th Division would have had to gain this ridge.

Hythe's shingled beach, Martello towers over balustrade, Grand Redoubt in the distance.

Along Hythe Beach, Martello tower from Napoleonic Invasion scare.

Grand Redoubt's moat would still offer a problem to the attacker.

Beach obstacles adjoining Grand Redoubt.

General Herbert Loch, Commander 17th Infantry Division. *(Courtesy General Loch)*

(Below, left) Captain Erich Lehmann, Commander Naval Station Ostend. *(Courtesy Captain Lehmann)*

(Below, right) Captain Heinrich Bartels, Commander Naval Station Dunkirk *(Courtesy Captain Bartels)*

Landing exercises 17th Division, summer 1940.

(Top) A prahm beaches too far out. *(Courtesy Colonel Schuber)*

(Center) Loading and unloading was a constant drill. An armored vehicle tests a ramp. Note horses: much of 17th Division artillery was horse drawn. *(Courtesy Colonel Blumentritt)*

(Bottom) Light tanks take to the water. *(Courtesy Colonel Schuber)*

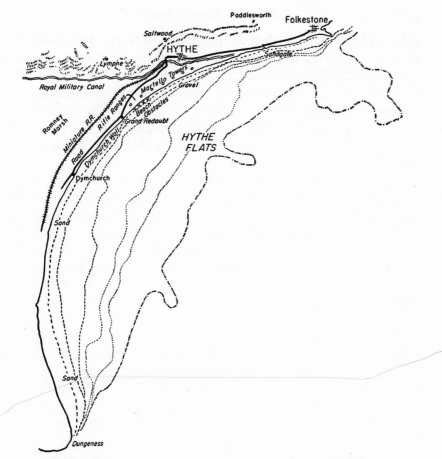

Hythe to Dungeness, attack sector, 17th Infantry Division.

the Channel, arriving in bivouac in the region of Ghent-Brugge in the first days of August. Headquarters were established at Bellem near Ghent, and the various units billeted in the surrounding countryside, whose people seemed not at all unfriendly. General Loch ruefully remarked to his journal that great difficulties beset the accomplishment of the newly announced task in *Sea Lion*. The time available was so short, and a leave program for 20 percent of the troops had to continue.

He at once instituted a reconnaissance of the seashore for landing exercise sites and settled on the region of Breskens on the south bank of the Scheldt estuary. Natural soldier skepticism over timely arrival of allocated landing craft from the Navy inspired scouting expeditions into local waters and soon produced several tugs, canal barges, and fishing trawlers as a nucleus for the division's Navy. This manifestation is peculiar to landing preparation—every soldier takes to the water, quickly becomes expert, and then sets up a private Navy. The crew for the craft come from the truck company. These lads exult in their new-found element by cutting white circles in the waters of the harbors. The "Old Man" himself might even go out for a spin, maybe a swim down the coast. "Nothing to this Navy business; it's a cinch."

By early September the shore from Breskens in Holland southwest along the coast through Ostend, to Dunkirk and beyond, throbbed with invasion fever. Few seamen met the eye; the figures were mostly soldiers storming fake beach defenses or manhauling awkward canal barges from one loading pier to another or shooting rifles from queer undulating cradles on shore. The Navy seemed almost as slow as the Air in reporting for *Sea Lion* duty. There were simply not enough sailors to go around. A thin sprinkling commenced drifting in. It was almost 1 September before General Loch made contact with his nearest naval adviser, Captain Lehmann at Ostend, who commanded the *Kriegsmarinedienststelle* (KMD), or Naval Station, there. Ostend and Dunkirk were to mount the advance elements of the 17th Division and Rotterdam its follow-up.

Papers, said the General, descended in a storm of order and counterorder to create great disorder. But parent Corps XIII near Ypres, and the Division itself, could record accomplishments showing through the confusion of map exercises, combat drills, special schools and special beach tests. The scene was the familiar one engendered by a terrifying press of time, totally new techniques and paltry resources. The floodgates opened to local improvisers, but worse, to cranks and war-winners from staffs higher up. Strange Army attachments piled in on the Division, each with his own allegiance and orders. So came the water engineers, extra artillerymen, extra quartermasters and communicators, the submersible tankmen, but without their tanks. "The side-channeled orders of these experts" from out-of-town, complained Loch's war diary, "work up fresh difficulties increasingly and make nothing but confusion." Even the combat mission of the Division fell into dispute. Not until 10 September did some sense start to shake out of the tumult, so that by the thirteenth the tentative XIII Korps directive could be issued.

The directive settled that "the Division fights thenceforth on the open right wing and that paratroops will be committed in the Division sector." General Loch and his staff were able to turn-to on their own order for carrying this heavy burden. Together they worked out a basic operation order for their attack on the English coast (*Divisions-befehl für den Angriff auf die englische Küste*), which order served as a pattern of divisional actions at a *Planspiel* set up by XIII Korps on 16 September. It would constitute the final dry run before fateful hop-off, standing close before them.

Stirring adventure and great labor contributed to the production of that basic operation order. One of the knottiest problems recurring day on day, was the calculation and planning of lift space in pace with incessantly changing combat plans and craft availability. Early in September a stream of landing craft began to flow westward past Ostend and Dunkirk. These two ports situated at the head of the line hoped for an early allotment of craft, but these passed them by. Precedence had rightly been assigned to the harbors at the far end of the line. The Navy's monstrous task was illustrated by Calais's record of arrivals. By 5 September that port could report but three local prahms available. Six days later 140 choked its basins to overflowing, and 45 were still to come; Dunkirk and Ostend experienced the same famine and feast. The waterfront chores of tending, servicing, and organizing the craft, manned by green unruly crews, were unending. Came more practice loading and unloading, recalculating and finally, training for sortie. Army engineers beefed up the Navy hands to achieve the impossible. The 17th Division was fortunate in having a pair of experienced sailormen to guide and co-ordinate these labors, Captain Lehmann at Ostend and Captain Heinrich Bartels at Dunkirk.

Heinrich Bartels presented the stocky blue-eyed salt from the old school, thoroughly practiced in the ways of the sea and how to court her. Moreover, he was an amphibious sailorman who had lived with the stuff from the beginning. He led the Navy experimentation at Emden and went from there to command the Naval Station (KMD) Dunkirk. From his talk and astonishingly accurate *Sea Lion* recollections, one quickly gathered that he had relished his work keenly. Much of it he expended on *Sea Lion* and a great deal more later on Crete and in Crimea.[11]

By 10 September 1940 Dunkirk was full of prahms. The stuffed

[11] Captain Bartels set forth his *Sea Lion* experience in correspondence before we met in company with Captain Lehmann (Ostend) at Bremerhaven in May 1953. At that time we reviewed the *Sea Lion* participation of both officers and reduced it to record. These officers worked out many challenging landing problems and drilled their tow flotillas and other craft in execution.

basins posed a critical problem because of damaged locks. A restricted capacity of the two locks that worked demanded at least two days for moving the 180 prahms assembled out into the open harbor for sortie. Thus on the day before *Sea Lion* sortie, half of them had to be hauled into the outer harbor and there loaded, a piece of intelligence impossible to hide from the British. The remaining 90 prahms had then to be moved out fully loaded during a one-and-one-half hour period of good water on sortie day. If they missed, a wait of twelve hours till the next high tide would ensue. It was enough to wreck the 17th's first echelon and the neighboring 35th Division's also. This tender factor governed operations of Dunkirk as a mounting port. It badgered Bartels constantly but failed to dishearten him. He would make it.

He organized his tows into the standard six Tow Flotillas (six tugs, twelve prahms), and designated a young Navy lieutenant to lead each Flotilla in a motorboat. Each prahm prided itself on a petty officer captain and five or six hands; the vessels varied in capacity from 200 to 600 tons. Each was catalogued according to lift space so that casualties from RAF or other cause could be remedied quickly by hauling in an equivalent reserve vessel. The average load approximated seventy troops plus four vehicles (or tanks) and their prime movers. In many cases the movers were horses, for amazingly, neither the 17th nor 35th division was fully motorized. Captured motor equipment was pressed into service, but horses could not be done without. With such curious assortment Bartels' Tow Flotillas carried out exercises on adjoining beaches through several full tidal cycles and, he thought, reached a tolerable degree of proficiency. He tried to enliven the killing pace during the early stages by music from a sound truck that circled the beach and port area. "Englandlied" alerted his men from the truck in the dawn hours of each day, blaring out: "Wir fahren gegen Engelland!"

But the gag wore bare, explained Bartels; and even in his own spirit. Whereas in August his invasion verve had run high with that of the uninitiated soldiery, later as the staggering material and training lacks unfolded and added themselves to the troubles of tide, sea, weather, and enemy, his confidence oozed lower. The men began to show signs of boredom with interminable changes and waiting, and it grew harder and harder to liven them. He told of an inspection trip by Admiral Raeder. The Admiral, impressed by Bartels' buoyant recital of how things were going, interjected, "Well, how do you really expect to get over to England?" Taken aback, Bartels gaped in wonderment at his superior, who thereupon continued, "Of course, you are an optimist." "Jawohl," he felt compelled to reply, "in this game one must be an optimist." That was doubly true in Bartels' case because his assignment included leading the *Vorausabteilung* of the 17th to the beach assault, west of Hythe, in a motorboat.

Steady, quiet-spoken Captain Lehmann of Ostend retained confidence in *Sea Lion* to the end. "We would have gotten over," he said in a final verdict in 1953. One gathered that the tone in Ostend was quieter, easier; for the reason that the lesser damaged city and harbor provided ample and better living generally. Ostend lay close to Bellem, the 17th Division headquarters, yet no really close tie with the troop command resulted. Lehmann, however, found the link adequate. He told of understandable Army propensity for bringing forth one chimera on another, as acquaintance with devil sea grew, then at high conference, the proposing of utterly impracticable solution. Soldier thinking at times hung up on piffling complaints of little substance. One such was the old fear that the bow wave of a prahm, towed faster than three knots, would roll in over its remnant prow and swamp it. This apprehension had been proved utterly groundless, but the soldiers could not get it out of their heads. Another Army requirement, dictated by the land fight, encountered Navy hostility in every quarter. It was insistence that the steamers of the Second Echelon anchor close off the beaches and commence unloading at S plus 4 hours. In speaking of this hasty plan, Captain Lehmann made the sole practical mention of an artificial harbor that came to notice. He proposed sinking medium-sized steamers, whose peak and stern tanks had been reinforced, off the beaches to form breakwaters. The naval constructors gave his plan short shrift; they had already worked through the brainstorm to ground the old battleships off shore for gunfire support and wanted no more of these fancies. Fanciful or not, the leadership of tried seamen like Bartels and Lehmann was what the Germans had too little of.

Once over, the Germans felt dead sure of victory in the field. But the question—Will we get over?—sprouted horns that grew with each day of drill and test. All along the coast the discoveries followed a related pattern. General Loch's amiable modesty did not hide the thorough-going soldier of wide experience and high capacity. The immense practical handicaps of this undertaking did not elude him. So it often goes before hop-off, while at the same time one knows the thing must go. Not every uncertainty can be fathomed out and eliminated. Orders are prepared. Like all other army commands, General Loch had to work out directions for his go at England on the assumption that the crossing was behind him. "The 17th Division, on the open right Army wing, will break through the enemy coastal defenses between Hythe and Dymchurch," began his statement of divisional task on 12 September 1940, and continued: "will gain the heights just north of the Military Canal, in order from there . . . over the high ground—Postling and Etchinghill, to attack Paddlesworth, and at the same time, via Saltwood, to seize the fortified sections of Sandgate and Folkestone from the west."[12] "Later intention," the order went on, "is to move out toward the Great Stour and Ashford, and with mobile forces to take Dover and Deal in cooperation with paratroop detachments." The 17th Division war diary evidenced a paucity of exact information on what the paratroop detachments from the 7th *Fliegerdivision* would contribute.

It is an old story. Air supporting units the world over have a curious faculty for coming in last with their contributing plans. By that late hour such plans take on the force of demands—"take it or leave it." Not until 4 October, three weeks later, did General Loch obtain sufficient Air information to round out his attack map and order. The interim saw frequent changes of paratroop strength and intentions and ended with the commitment of nearly the whole 7th *Fliegerdivision,* to insure the early capture of Folkestone and Dover. Parts of 22d Airlanding Division may also have been involved. This heavy paratroop commitment testified to belated recognition of the open right wing dangers, and the primary need of unloading ports on the far shore.[13]

[12] Diagram 1 on page 275 gives the map presentation of the 17th Division attack. We follow its lines in our inventory of these final dispositions.

[13] Defense against paratroop attack of the kind demonstrated in the Lowlands became a forward thought in British anti-invasion thinking. On the German side employment of air landings remained in a state of flux for a prolonged period. Some of the early thinking we have already noticed. With the onset of *Sea Lion* the ideas gradually settled down to support of landings from the sea at two points, back of Dungeness, or back of Folkestone. It appears Folkestone finally won out for the bulk of the airborne support. By August's end the 7th *Fliegerdivision* (paratroop) and 22d *Luftlandeddivision* (airlanding division), constituting XI Fliegerkorps, had based at Lille and Lyon, had refreshed and made good losses in men and material. Estimates of transport available ran to over 700 planes plus 150 gliders (*Halder Journal* and Generalmajor Fritz Morzick, commanding Transport Squadron 1, to Ansel, 1953). The airborne leaders were not enthusiastic; they conceded that support and facilitation of landing from sea at one point, as Folkestone, might have succeeded.

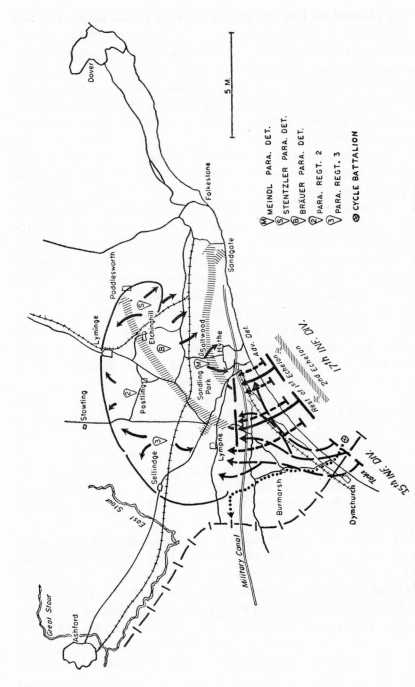

The 17th Division Attack Plan. (After sketch by General Herbert Loch.)

MEINDL PARA. DET.
STENTZLER PARA. DET.
BRÄUER PARA. DET.
PARA. REGT. 2
PARA. REGT. 3
CYCLE BATTALION

The planned air landings unfold from the attack map. The two detachments Meindl and Stentzler, each of two reinforced battalions, were to lead off with descents at S hour: Meindl to drop between Hythe and Sandling Park, push prongs south either side of Hythe, seize crossings over the Military Canal and prevent enemy flanking attacks from the east against the amphibious landing on the shore below; Stentzler to drop between Paddlesworth and Etchinghill, secure those heights and push southeast for the purpose of pinning down British forces in Sandgate. Thus in this modern day air power would at once outflank the Napoleonic Military Canal line from overhead and protect the tender right flank of the beach landing. A second wave was to drop at S plus sixty-five minutes to clinch the initial divisional perimeter: Bräuer Detachment, containing the rest of Paratroop Regiment 1, would land alongside of Stentzler and with him post Paddlesworth and go on to take Sandgate. Paratroop Regiment 2 would land north of Postling to hold that sector against counterattack from the north; and Paratroop Regiment 3 was to do the same farther on around the perimeter in the northwest sector. The capture of old friend Lympne airfield was included in its tasks. It seemed that little beyond walking ashore was left for the 17th Division to do on the ground. The paratroop plans sounded simple, almost commonplace, if it were not for a sinister cloud of "ifs" that enveloped them. Air drops supporting amphibious operations suffer from hazards similar to those of landings from sea but multiplied many fold in number and degree. In air landings open questions are bigger and more numerous, so that support from that quarter is proverbially figured as a provisional supplement, which, if all goes well, one accepts as a god-send. So the matter stood also in the 17th Division's sector. To the division the tangibles of the beach assault from boats remained much more meaningful.

We return to the shingle beach of Hythe and our painter acquaintance at work on the dried-out fisherman. High and dry like a china duck! So also would the invasion barges have to lie between tides while these pebbles took flight at each exploding shell. A long ordeal to wait-out under shell fire, as though hung up in wire on the wrong side of a trench. Prayers might go up for artillery cover, but in the *Sea Lion* sally little assault artillery could answer these agonized calls.[14] Defensive wire was plentifully strung along formidable beach

---

[14] The fixed batteries about Cap Gris Nez were augmented by Army railroad batteries which had been brought up to the coast and were ready to furnish fire.

obstacles sunk in the sand. One can still find these forbidding works in unfrequented stretches of the beach. The natural character changed from shingle to fine firm sand as the shore bent southwestward from Hythe to the pleasant village of Dymchurch, hard by its own Dymchurch Wall. This dike-like embankment fronted the sea for several miles to bulwark the shore against sea and foe, and to hold Romney Marsh intact on its landward side. The sector to be carried by the 17th Division lay here between Hythe and Dymchurch Wall; about seven thousand yards of fair landing beach.

A rich lore of song and story linked the area with landing operations of other days and other kinds that ranged from smuggling for lucre to invading for conquest. The techniques of the two have much in common; that is, get in stealthily and swiftly, get the "stuff" out, get forward under cover, and reorganize. The principles applied to forces of Bonaparte and Hitler alike. Here was a good beach with cover beyond in Romney Marsh. Defenders had to catch any would-be lander either off shore or on the narrow beach before he gained the marsh. In the old days cannon fire from Martello Towers served this purpose. These round structures of red brick had enjoyed the confidence of the early 1800's, and as silent witnesses of that era still squatted along the beach in 1940. Beginning at Hythe the towers strung beyond Dymchurch at about five-hundred-yard intervals. They were posted with machine guns in 1940 to back up the immediate beach defense works of mines, obstacles, and pillboxes. Close to the 17th Division's western junction with the 35th Division stood a monster Martello Tower named Dymchurch Tower, or Grand Redoubt. Inshore of the towers ran the coastal road from Dymchurch toward Hythe and crossed that other relic of the Napoleonic invasion scare, the Royal Military Canal, close by the town center. A miniature railroad paralleled the road on the landward side.[15]

On 17 September 1940 General Loch settled on the following shoots with the railroad artillery commander, according to the Division Diary (Office of Chief of Military History, Washington, D.C.):

"(a) Preceding *Stuka* attack concentrate all batteries on Sandgate. Neutralize batteries there.

(b) After *Stuka* attack, train on Folkestone . . .

(c) Later neutralize batteries about Dover. . . ."

Fire of the railroad batteries was, of course, not available on call to assaulting infantry. No prearranged fires for the Navy manned batteries of Cap Gris Nez appear in the Division records. Liaison officers from VIII Fliegerkorps, furnishing air support, and from Rail Artillery Command reported to the Division Commander.

[15] Reference to getting "the stuff" out brings to point the excellent solution the

Against this English seashore General Loch was to launch his tried and true infantry regiments, the 21st, 55th and 95th. He designated the 21st and the 55th to lead the assault and kept the 95th in reserve with the Second Echelon. The Advance Detachment of the 21st Infantry he ordered to land on the right near Hythe; and that of the 55th Infantry near Grand Redoubt on the left. In wake of the 55th, but closer to Dymchurch, where firm sand and gradient were better, the elusive submersible tanks were to crawl up from the sea onto Dymchurch Wall and strike across Romney Marsh for the Military Canal. That slight water hazard, tending west and then southwest to Rye Bay on the sea, made an island of the marsh area. The defenders were willing to give it back to the sea. Decisive combat was expected along the Military Canal.

News of plans to flood Romney Marsh, as had been contemplated in September 1804, filtered back to the Germans in 1940. But they believed that the amphibious tanks of this day would be equal to the strategem and likewise to oil fires, which were expected to be set on the surface of the Marsh waters. Like the air landing assurances, General Loch had to accept the tank performance as advertised, for not one reported for duty, and his staff concentrated on the more tangible matters of his advance elements. Practical troubles abounded there too.

Much thought and invention was expended on the crucial jobs of the Advance Detachments, for they too merited the designation of *Himmelfahrtskommando*. They needed all the comfort their Division Commander could offer. He did his best; supporting naval thought and action hardly got beyond talk and promises. Mother ship trawlers for practice with sturmboats never put in appearance, so that the cleansing experience of dress rehearsal on an open seacoast never came to pass. It may have been that mine tasks pre-empted the trawlers, but Lütjens' *Sea Lion* order gave another reason, and a weak one—lack of berthing space in the mounting ports. By 18

Germans had reached for this problem at the high water mark where a natural cleavage between Navy and Army can work to ruin an operation. The Germans avoided trouble by bringing large numbers of engineers into the amphibious scenery at an early date. The ordered statements of tasks of these engineer groups read: "Support the troops in loading. . . . Operate *Sturmboote* of initial landing, motor boats and pontoons; support disembarkation of men, vehicles and horses . . . clear beaches of obstacles and mines . . . . Back up the infantry in attack and maintain forces and equipment in *readiness for defense* of the beachhead at the water." No better list of dirty but vital jobs could have been devised, and all under one command.

September General Loch could wait no longer; he issued Advance Detachment instructions punctuated by many blank spaces and question marks. The composition of the detachments, and thus their combat power, hung in the balance to the last for lack of craft or even knowledge of what could be furnished. A welding of troop and sailor spirit into a team failed of consummation. The Division's best guess reckoned each Detachment would total 1,250 bodies. The fighting core consisted of two reinforced rifle companies, to which were added combat engineers, assault light artillery pieces, flame and smoke throwers, gas detectors, communicators, and a few sailors. Major Schuler commanded the 21st Infantry's Detachment out of Ostend; Major Panwitz that of the 55th Infantry from Dunkirk. The hoped-for disposition of one of them, say Schuler's, in approaching England appears below.

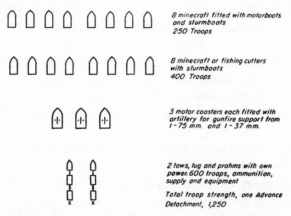

8 minecraft fitted with motorboats
and sturmboats
250 Troops

8 minecraft or fishing cutters
with sturmboats
400 Troops

3 motor coasters each fitted with
artillery for gunfire support from
1 - 75 mm. and 1 - 37 mm.

2 tows, tug and prahms with own
power. 600 troops, ammunition,
supply and equipment

Total troop strength, one Advance
Detachment, 1,250

One hope was that the vanguard assault would be made in motorboats capable of beaching high and dry to disgorge their fighters direct into combat. The succeeding wave was then to land from the minesweepers in a shuttle service of sturmboats to the beach. Jury-mounted pieces of the artillery coasters would take up fire toward the flanks and center, while the four heavy prahms beached and unloaded more troops, heavy weapons, special attachments, and some supply. The watch word was: Clear the beach and drive for the heights— target Lympne, high above there! The order granted only one point for closing up and reorganization on the edge of the marsh along the bed of the miniature railroad line connecting Hythe to Dymchurch. Only a naked outline of stupendous fighting tasks comes out of the matter-of-fact wording of the order. From the tiny railroad tracks, it was to be, over the Canal and up the ridge, and hold on there for the main body. The day would have been won.[16]

Yet only if back on the beach, a rigidly controlled parade of craft maintained its schedule. Grand marshaling the parade of craft toward the beaches of England, that is, joining up the invasion elements in proper sequence for assault after leaving diverse ports, would have been hard. The Advance Detachment of the 21st Infantry, for instance, from Ostend, had to be married at sea to that of the 55th, issuing from Dunkirk; the main bodies of both regiments, embarked in endless Tow Flotillas, had to team up astern of their spearheads, not to forget that two steamers, one carrying General Loch and the other his alternate, had to fit in just ahead. Then would come the Second Echelon packed into fourteen steamers, four hours astern from still another port, Rotterdam. The diagram shows both Advance Detachments and the First Echelon afloat, as set forth in the diary of the Division. A Mickey Mouse would have helped immeasurably. (See diagrams pages 241 and 281).

So went the novel game of landing operations, sometimes exciting, always interesting, but now near S Day, painfully exacting and burdened with many open questions. That the scheduling on which all depended would click, made but another item to be taken on faith by the soldiers, high and low. Think too of the lowliest amphibian, battened down below in the stale hold of an ex-Rhine grain barge. He might have gulped his seasick pills hours ago. His life jacket and the straps of sundry impedimenta binds him round in crouching-room-only company of 69 companions. There are yet hours to go; he may grip his piece and think, once over, all will be well! Did he but know.

Forward from the dawn landing of Schuler and Panwitz, the action swept smoothly along on the division operations map. We follow its intended course and the landmarks enumerated. The First Echelon would complete the landing of the regimental main bodies who were to close on their spearheads and gain the far side of the Military Canal. Meanwhile the 17th Cycle Battalion would have followed in the wake of the submarine tanks and struck out to guard the left flank against intrusion from the region of Aldington. Arrived on the heights above the Canal, the rifle regiments were to reform and

---

[16] At S Hour (first landing(dive bombers of Fliegerkorps VIII were to smother batteries in the vicinity of Sandgate and defense installations on the rise toward Lympne. Air thereafter was to smoke those installations. The Romney, Hythe, Dymchurch Railway runs on a track of 15-inch gauge. The line serves the area for passengers and small freight.

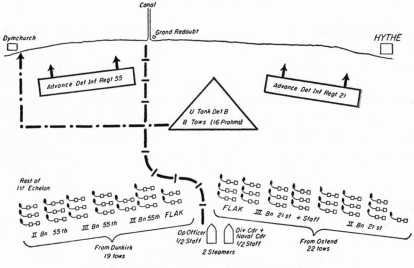

17th Division beach assault by First Echelon.

wheel right, the 55th swinging wide for Postling and beyond, the 21st
sharply round for Sandgate via Saltwood.   By this time the Second
Echelon should have commenced lightering ashore from the fourteen
steamers, its Commander prodding the left-overs of the assault regiments and artillery forward to join their comrades.   Infantry Regiment 95 would debark and move up to assemble around overworked
Lympne.   S Day's work might so have churned to an end.   By nightfall, it was hoped, the initial drive would have carried the line, Paddlesworth–Postling–Selinge, an advance of three hard miles into England.

How glibly these English names seemed to fall from the lines of
a German invasion order.   The next day would include action against
Dover on the right hand, and toward Ashford on the left.   The Division order closed on regrouping instructions for these actions.

The utmost had in this wise been done within the limits of time
and power on the Open Right Wing.   The 17th Division would
hold that flank secure if any could.   General Loch's verdict from a
field force view was that the Army had finally sifted out an acceptable
plan, that the plan had been reduced to paper in clear and succinct
terms, that it had been drilled exhaustively on map and game board,
and that preparations to the last limit of available time and material
had been met.   He felt the field forces were ready.

Ready, but without the eager gusto for hop-off that pervaded the
ranks during July.   The exposed mounting ports, stuffed with barges

and combustibles, made naked targets. From 11 September forward, stabs by RAF planes in small groups stepped up, and naval action too. On 18 September a 900-ton ammunition dump at Dunkirk went up in an horrendous blast that scattered men and materiel far and wide. Casualties from bombing occurred among barges and mine craft at Calais. Navy advices took a dim view of the tightening situation. Skl made fruitless representations to Göring for more air cover. The VII Corps diary noted the increased tempo of British counterstrokes, yet took comforting note that damage had "not yet reached serious proportion." And yet not a prahm had moved from her moorings. Invasion was losing much of its savor.

Would the final word to move be given? On 14 September troop commanders commenced final deployment for embarkation; from the nineteenth on, daily status reports were required from all commands; on the twentieth a pass word, common to all arms, ruled throughout *Sea Lion* territory of poised Army, worried Navy, and preoccupied Air Force. Last loading tables had been totted up and handed in. *Sea Lion* was as ready as he ever would be! Wretched lion that he had turned out to be, he waited from one day to the next, and the next.

Predecision

A crowded and amazing Year of War was ended, and the comparative lull of the first few September days afforded opportunity for inventory. All the world took part. In America we drew closer to the British cause; President Roosevelt announced a lend-lease loan of fifty old destroyers. London's *Times* Weekly Edition reviewed the grave crisis weathered during the year and took heart that the tide was turning. Mr. Lloyd George voiced less comforting opinion; he held that the year had ended to German advantage, and with final decision still much in doubt. One of Germany's better papers, the *Frankfurter Zeitung,* in contrast to the blatant tones heard elsewhere wrote: "We realize we are now fighting England, the toughest opponent . . . the majority of the people believe in the righteousness of their cause and stand united to their flag in their hour of danger . . . ." This had been one true result of the first year of war. Many thinking Germans knew they had no righteous cause, and all yearned for peace rather than clear cut decision. Enough had been done, they thought, nothing had happened for months, except now British bombs were falling nightly on Berlin. But their Führer preferred to fight on, or so he declared.

On 4 September Hitler made the unannounced speech, previously noted, at the Sportpalast in Berlin, ostensibly to initiate the annual Winter Help drive. For audience the party packed in women nurses and social workers by the thousands. Their idol took quick advantage of the feminine heart strings laid bare before him. He denounced the "piratical" attacks of RAF planes on innocent civilians in his capital and guaranteed reprisal, one hundred fold! The women rose, screaming approval; it grew louder and louder as Hitler heaped invective and boast one on another. He brought musclebound *Sea Lion* into the open. "In England," he rasped, "they're filled with curiosity and keep asking, 'Why doesn't he come?' . . . Be calm," he counseled, "He's coming! He's coming! *I now prefer to fight until a clear decision is finally reached.*" The ladies virtually rolled on the floor in ecstasy.[17] It was time for something, Hitler realized; time to break the lull, but how? He wanted to rouse both himself and his people, but most, to heighten anxiety in Britain. The speech played an unmistakable prelude to Bombs on London and backed it with an oversure threat to invade. To close observers, it was an empty threat.

Sea Lion timetable was on the books. Skl War Diary had entered it in the following terms on 2 September. They are helpful to refix the forecasted action:

Earliest S Day	21 September
Thus, earliest sortie day	20 September
Release of initiating warning order, S minus 10 [The bracket of ten days permitted the Navy to lay flanking mine barriers.]	11 September
[Definitive] Confirmation of S Day and S Hour, on S minus 3 at noon. All preparatory measures are to be taken so that the operation can be called off 24 hours before S hour.	[18 September]

By this sequence, Wednesday 11 September 1940 looked like the coming day.

[17] Noteworthy was that official military records made none of the customary references to Hitler's speech.

Thus while one day ticked off after another, one could expect the tone of things to sharpen. Such proved not at all the case. The high functionaries of Nazi Germany went about their routine tasks calmly and unruffled. *Sea Lion* found only perfunctory notice in the daily record of events. The reason was obvious. Hitler had long since taken the starch out of him. Decision on invasion had so often been evaded in the presence of the highest officers that the drill became commonplace. On the waterfront, we know well that *Sea Lion* was far from a myth, but in high headquarters he eked out a provisional existence somewhere between fact and fiction.

In place of invasion, high-level talk speculated on what to do before winter closed in. Ulrich von Hassell made a swing around his circuit of Resistance leaders during early September and remarked to his journal, "The blustering bravado and certainty of victory demonstrated by the government, the Party, and the Air Force have recently . . . yielded to the feeling that victory before winter . . . has become doubtful . . . ."[18] The top Army leadership had relegated *Sea Lion* to the status of an occupation measure; this OKH had stressed to Jodl and he had agreed. An operation on the narrow scale contemplated, the Army held, could, "only aim at administering an enemy, defeated by air warfare, the *coup de grace* . . . ."[19] Navy chimed in. Admiral Raeder called at the Reichskanzlei in Berlin for penultimate *Sea Lion* conference with his Führer on 6 September. Ideas in case of *Sea Lion's* demise had been quickened for the Admiral during the course of his personal inspection of landing craft and mounting ports, just now completed. What to do before winter occupied the minds of many, as September edged toward well-publicized crisis.

There face to face, now sat the two men in this world who could do the most about invasion. One of them could say, Ready to go; and the other could reply. Go then! Neither had ever been strong for going. Four months earlier at Felsennest the one had gingerly broached the subject, and the other had diffidently turned it off. So they continued, never far apart, to this very eve of crisis meeting. Yet there was no hint of such. What would the Führer's wishes be, asked Raeder casually, in the event *Sea Lion* did not go. He struck the tone of the conference. The question from the Admiral was

[18] Von Hassell, *op. cit.,* p. 149. The information gathered by the Resistance Movement, to which von Hassell was party, proved amazingly accurate. Much of it reached England.

[19] W.D., OKW Ops, p. 71.

neither dramatic, nor one shocking to Hitler, as it might well have been. To him Raeder's lukewarm attitude had become a comfort that he counted upon.

Not a climax but another turning point was what Admiral Raeder felt he had before him, and in his familiar Führer Conference method he led up to his query through a carefully phrased status report, ending with a detailed chart presentation of *Sea Lion* on the harried Channel coast. He recapitulated that if air command continued to prosper, the deadline could be met—crossing remained very difficult, Army divisions would suffer loss of unity—but, "Execution of *Sea Lion* appears possible, if favorable conditions as to air command, weather, and so on, stand in good prospect." This crowning judgment was the strongest Raeder ever managed on invasion. Instead of standing by it, it appears from his own record, he lapsed into subtle suggestion of *Sea Lion's* decline. He insinuated a better solution at this newest of turning points. It was to seize the Mediterranean via Gibraltar and Suez, meanwhile maintaining a fiction of landing against England. Hitler, who had heard some of the same from Jodl for some time, showed interest; he even directed Keitel to start actual preparations for the capture of Gibraltar, said Raeder, "in order that they be accomplished before interference from USA." Having freed themselves of *Sea Lion* and embarked on real adventure, the Admiral and his Führer zoomed on like children at play. Before their eyes danced the occupation of Atlantic islands, including as a start, the swift capture of the Canaries. Scandinavia they incorporated into a Germanic sphere. The mood was reminiscent of 11 July when they had soared together just before the surprising decision to initiate *Sea Lion*. On that occasion Reader had left, confident he had squelched invasion. It was always so with Hitlerian turning. He himself knew least of all what it might bring.[20]

Before he took wing Hitler had evidently expressed himself more fully on *Sea Lion* than Raeder entered in his hand-written record at the time. On the following day at a meeting of the inner circle in Skl the Admiral elaborated the Führer's views as follows:

[20] The attack against Gibraltar bore the code name *Felix*. Ground work of planning had gotten well along during August. Included were surprise attack by Luftwaffe to destroy the port and drive out British naval vessels; the capture of the Rock from the land side, with possibly some assistance from the sea. The physical preparations for these plans Hitler now on 6 September implemented at his conference with Raeder.

Decision of the Führer to land in England is by no means yet firm since the Führer has the conviction that the forcing down of England will be achieved even without landing. Landing is however, now as before, regarded by the Führer as the means by which, according to every prospect, an immediate, crashing end can be made of the war. Yet the Führer has no thought of executing the landing if the *risk* of the operation is too high. A failure of the operation must in so far as possible be excluded. In no way shall a miscarriage of Operation Sea Lion be permitted to lead to a decisive gain of prestige on the part of *England*.

A sensational blitz finale to war with England was what he wanted, but he recoiled from the hazards imposed by *Sea Lion*. Jodl echoed identical Hitlerian expression, and he experienced trouble in making its fuzziness clear to his staff. The most plausible explanation lay in an overshrewd design, shot through with spiritual cowardice.[21]

Fuzzy as the picture was, Warlimont and his brave little band held fast to climax with *Sea Lion*. The initiating final order for Invasion England, due 11 September, got underway. This document bore the designation, Führer Directive No. 18. Maps and other properties for commanding in chief by Hitler were collected and schemes to link the top service headquarters with that of Supreme Command at Ziegenberg proceeded. In exchanges on these matters with Warlimont, Jodl still exhibited strong interest. He approved the promulgation of a timetable forecasting the desired co-ordination among the services. It clocked off the actuating orders and the resultant action expected of each Arm, that is, at S minus 10:

Führer Decision "Initiation Operation Sea Lion."—
(OKW) Issuance of order for execution of operation. [Führer Directive 18]
(Army) a. Begin loading . . . b . . . . c . . . .
(Navy) a. Begin loading. b. Begin submarine sortie. c. Lay flanking mine barriers.
(Air) a. Begin loading. b. Regroup Air units. c. Assemble FLAK.

The table ran down the full sequence of prospective actions, arriving finally at: "S Tag, S Zeit, Beginn der Landung." Oh happy day! The timetable appeared under date of 7 September, four days before fateful eleventh and caused a mild tremor to ripple through the receiving headquarters. Was he going after all? Everyone tried to act as though this were the case—Army, Navy; and now Air, though busy with London, showed heightened *Sea Lion* interest.

[21] The Führer Conference of 6 September 1940 is reconstructed from *FC*, 1940, II, 17-21; the W.D. Skl and Helmuth Greiner's Operation *Felix*.

But Hitler's true means of blitz finale had been Air War, and still was, something neither he nor Raeder had needed to touch upon because it was so well understood. Raeder provided for the event of Air failure, and Hitler knew it. His trump card that could obviate invasion was already in play, and he was able to contemplate what might come after with no great concern.

The climate of serenity, inspired from on high, was deceptive, for in reality it betokened a waiting for something too slow in coming. Navy revealed the undercurrent clearly on 10 September. On that day, only one removed from fateful eleventh, Skl commenced striking a balance on prospective *Sea Lion* weather. It had a dark look: the normal steady high pressure for this season over England had given away to a succession of weak highs, punctuated by a series of deep lows. Both prahm distribution and mine tasks had suffered from the attendant bad weather. Navy nevertheless was able to assure OKW that the 21 September deadline would be met. Thereupon the sailors unmasked a far more telling balance, reflecting the tension of standing-by for climax of Bombs on London. We have already noticed the feeling expressed in the Skl war diary of 10 September. It is worth repeating: Preparation for *Sea Lion* requires at this point that Luftwaffe concentrate on Portsmouth and Dover and the British fleet forces rather than on London. However, it is deemed improper to press such demands on the Luftwaffe or the Führer, since he regards the Grand Attack on London as possibly decisive for the war; that is, prolonged bombing of London could provoke a British attitude "which might make the *Sea Lion* operation wholly unnecessary . . . ." In other words, by now almost every one had become so intent on this single possibility of decision by Air, that all others faded into irrelevance.

The soldiers, on the other hand, sounded the bugles of advance. The highest Army leadership stayed on the job, making last-minute checks of invasion readiness. Field Marshal von Brauchitsch and his Chief of Staff made a final swing around the invasion circuit on September 10. First they looked in on Army Group A at St. Germain only to find von Rundstedt off on leave. With his staff and top Navy talent present the completed hop-off dispositions were proofed to the last battalion, prahm, and mine sweeper. Ninth Army was found badly handicapped in mounting space; it would take five times as long as 16th Army to get its First Strike over. The high party passed on to 9th and 16th Army headquarters.

Adjustment was attempted between the two armies to ameliorate the obvious dangers to the position of the 9th as the flank guard on the left wing. There was more push to go on the part of the soldiery. To the last they strove to fit *Sea Lion* for hop-off.

At OKW the strangest byplay of all ran its destined course. In the late afternoon of the day before the day, 10 September, during his routine briefing to Warlimont, Jodl off-handedly informed his assistant that "the Führer, while hearing the report of the Chief of the Wehrmacht High Command [Keitel] decided not to make use of the earliest possible deadline for issuing the order to start Operation *Sea Lion* [11 September] as the results of the intensified air warfare against England could not yet be fully gaged . . . ." Therewith brave 11 September flattened out into just another day. Jodl ran on with extenuating reasons of shifty Hitlerian flavor: not the earliest day (21 September) but the most favorable (the twenty-fourth, originally recommended by Navy) should be chosen; better to postpone the warning order now than the confirming order on S minus 3 Day, and thereby preclude enemy sweeping of mine barriers; also the Luftwaffe's flak would be spared concentration until the last moment. These excuses were too pat. Warlimont sensed *Sea Lion's* death knell, for he thereupon tested Jodl on the decisive order of business, Führer Directive No. 18. It was *Sea Lion's* last province of strength, the push button that could set him off. Warlimont presented for approval the final draft of this basic actuating directive, worked out so carefully by his staff in agreement with the High Command of each Arm. Quietly Jodl took the "hot" paper and let it cool; he simply withheld it. The record hinted his reaction when it stated that "on account of the postponement [to the 24th] of the warning order [all directives] are [to be] kept for the time being by the Chief of the Wehrmacht Operations Staff." This was General Jodl.[22]

[22] Although the office file numbers are available, the draft copies of this Führer Directive No. 18 to execute *Sea Lion*, have not been found. One bearing the same number (18) issued in November 1940, had nothing to with with *Sea Lion's* execution. The missing draft would have rounded out the documentation of *Sea Lion* story. Its disappearance is, however, more in keeping with *Sea Lion's* lingering, anticlimactic death. We have dredged up substantial evidence of the order's make-up and content and the feeling toward it from close participants. The order was short and to the point, all on one page, and in effect, simply gave the "executive" signal to the preparatory order and scheduling already issued. After the co-ordinating table of 7 September (p. 286) *Sea Lion* required only a few words in Führer Directive 18 to set him loose.

The fact that such final order was drafted and submitted and pressed for approval is the important point to be remembered. That fact established the existence among the soldiers of sound strategical thinking and pointed up the difficulty of bringing such thought to fruition. It also evidenced a sustained drive to push *Sea Lion* over. Among the reasons may have been a wish to keep Hitler committed in the West, or even to compromise him there in a grand welter of invasion melee. We have only to think of Hitlerian *Norway* tantrum, expanded one hundred fold! Hitler might have lost control.

These were the doings on the eve of 11 September. In the Hitlerian menage the eve always proved more meaningful than any great day itself (and there were many), for when the day came the thing was already done. Had it been a true crisis, nervous anticipator Hitler would have been working himself up—formulating, weighing, consulting, excusing, countering, and rehearsing—for revelation on the morrow. We find record of such drill in nearly every authentic case, and whenever we do the pattern stands forth irrefutable. For 11 September no such working up took place or was required. Hitler had only to justify himself to compliant Keitel with a reconsidered choice of the more favorable twenty-fourth in place of the twenty-first. Automatically he thereby set up the fourteenth in place of the eleventh as decision day. The intervening days grant us a few more clues of denouement on the way. Early word of decision postponement got out to all commands and took the edge off. Skl coined an apt designator for the failing warning order, calling it *Vorentscheidung*, pre- or ante-decision. Whatever the signification intended, the feeling of the word falls perfectly into the Hitlerian atmosphere of this decision eve.

Eleven September came and went, an empty false alarm. But not on the far shore where the day had gained its own notoriety and raised anxious moments that stretched into interminable hours. Zero hour took over in England as doughty Churchill applied invasion pressure. He missed no opportunity to dramatize and enliven Britain's no-quarter stand, visiting bomb-damaged quarters, poking craters, inspecting defense forces and lashing out in speech. On the eleventh he made that most climactic invasion broadcast of all, painted his canvas with fine accuracy, and reassured his fellow countrymen, and the world, with inspiring eloquence:

Therefore we must regard the next week or so as a very important week for us in our history. It ranks with the days when the Spanish Armada was approaching the Channel and Drake was finishing his game of bowls, or when Nelson stood between us and Napoleon's Grand Army at Boulogne . . . . Every man and woman will therefore prepare to do his duty, whatever it may be, with special pride and care . . . . It is with devout but sure confidence that I say, 'Let God defend the right.'

As all knew, and Churchill had explained, the season for invasion was running out. He had struck home on the very first of the dates on *Sea Lion's* calendar.

". . . auf unbestimmte Zeit.

Admiral Raeder felt free enough on 12 September to take himself off to Kiel where the big-ship sailors assembled to hear him review the first year of war. He sharply criticized the big-ship performance of the year and promised more action in the days ahead. At heart he remained a battleship man with dreams of decisive actions on the blue water. He alluded also to invasion and its tremendous risks but with little enthusiasm. *Sea Lion* would go with utmost energy, he said, if the Führer so ordered.[23]

Navy worried along. The encouraging picture of craft distribution and Navy readiness, forecast to Hitler by Raeder on the sixth, lagged far behind fulfilment. Boulogne at the end of the line, which should have been full up by 8 September, still lacked many prahms on the twelfth. This threat to readiness for the fourteenth started a fresh wave of nervous tremors along the command lines. There lurked ever the fearsome thought that Hitler could execute. Navy had miscalculated the practicalities of distributing the craft. Glaring bits of overoptimism came to light daily, and sailor uneasiness grew all the more. A variety of vicissitudes contributed: British Air and destroyer action; mining off Channel ports; ship breakdowns; and above all the unseasonable weather, day in and out. At the root lay unadmitted miscalculation in the unfamiliar amphibious field. Yet Skl heaped all the blame on Luftwaffe in an irritable outburst about "absolute Air War." It was a nervy outcry that nevertheless marked a wholesome switch back to honest landing thought, from former reluctance to disturb decision by Air. On 12 September Skl war diary

---

[23] Admiral Raeder enlarged on *Sea Lion's* great difficulties in this speech. He also fixed the time of first invasion thought in November 1939 in connection with *Norway*.

spoke out: "The air war is being conducted independently of requirements of the war at sea, as 'absolute Air War' . . . and the fact is that execution of the landing operation has *up to now* been unaffected by the development of the intensified Air War and therefore for operational military reasons [landing] does not yet come into question." At the other extreme, the special *Sea Lion* staff felt safe in drawing up detailed procedures for a camouflage "maintenance of a fiction of landing intent." Still another headquarter's group drew up an "Organization England" for digesting and administering the vast naval affairs over there. Such discursive planning had perhaps to be done, if in these last few minutes all contingencies were to be provided against, but hardly if the leadership felt sure of its Führer. This was far from the case.

Much of the dither could be charged to normal hop-off jitters. Final self-scrutiny and self-examination before the day always uncovers a host of trivialities overlooked. Tension of hop-off inflates their importance. After the event the last-minute remedies often seem laughable. So also with some German *Sea Lion* soul-searching. One originated in OKH on 12 September. The paper directed attention to language difficulties that could bring confusion of direction on English soil. Therefore, once over in England, the order required that English place names be pronounced in German phonetics. What Heinz und Heinrich might have made out of Brighton, or say, Pulburough and Hythe, would be hard to say. Desperately serious, this landing business had gotten.

Friday has immemorially been a day of taboo for waterfolk, fish, and seals; perhaps even for sea lions. The second eve of second *Sea Lion* crisis, besides being a Friday, was also the thirteenth. We discover a few token clues of Hitler's spirit on that day, the strongest being that he took counsel of Göring. We recognize it as an old predecision signal and may moreover confidently infer that the two men dealt with the current situation. Some of the conclusions emerged in Göring's subsequent conference (the sixteenth) with his Airfleet Commanders, for he parroted identical words Hitler used at grand decision conclave on the fourteenth which Göring did not attend. Jeschonnek stood in for him as on previous occasions when the matter at issue had already been put to rest. We must try to correlate these conferences and measure their fidelity to the patterns of Hitlerian behavior established in earlier dilemmas.

For lunch on the thirteenth Hitler invited his Colonel Generals. It was their turn to dress up in their new rank and pay ceremonious respects to their Führer. Hitler repeated the gala occasion of baton presentation of 14 August, a month gone. Then as now he held forth in a genial, bounty-bestowing mood that reached back to the valor of the past and led his guests up to the current problems. General Halder attended and logged 20 *Generalobersten* (Colonel Generals) present, plus Keitel, Jodl, von Brauchitsch, Göring, and his second, Milch. The last named was just now easing out from a cloud under which he had sat most of the summer, and during the Air War. About the Air situation the Führer seemed happy; he "expressed himself most optimistically, and explained that in the current favorable [air] situation he had no thought of accepting so great a risk as posed by a landing in England."[24] Who had boomed up the air picture?

Such disarmingly frank talk could have been intended to reassure Generals Busch (AOK 16) and Strauss (AOK 9), whom Hitler drew out in conversation about the course of their adventures with *Sea Lion*. Actually he was reiterating very nearly verbatim his own words of 14 August to the new Field Marshals. At that time Grand Air Offensive, for which Göring had promised great things, had just started. Shortly after the baton ceremony, Hitler, at Jodl's instance, reconsidered and allowed him to reinvigorate *Sea Lion* by an "on-again" version in Führer decision. The "off-again-on-again" play became familiar and found re-enactment here on 13-14 September. Jodl on 13 September again felt what he heard at lunch to be "off-again," and so strong, he thought it final. By the fourteenth Hitler had reversed himself, and Jodl told Warlimont "that the Führer apparently decided on 13 September to drop *Sea Lion* utterly but that now [on the 14th] he has decided after all upon mere postponement . . . ." Thus the best even Jodl could make of the shifting wind was "on-again." Hitler was spinning in a final quandary.

But let us probe a little. What could have impelled Hitler to voice "off-again" so frankly to this large group of soldiers, who alone could make or break *Sea Lion,* and whence came his optimism about Air War? After 9 September rains had shut out daylight attacks of any size on London, the fires of dissolution died out, and Luftwaffe enthusiasm sank. Late on the twelfth the weather broke and promised a spell of fine flying. Thus the thirteenth saw resumption of Bombs

[24] Record of Situation Evaluations Defense Branch OKW (MS, Office Chief of Military History, Washington, D. C.)

on London under prospects favorable for prolongation to decisive result. Indeed, Luftwaffe attackers were streaming cross-Channel at the very moment the pleasantries at luncheon were being exchanged in the Reichskanzlei, Berlin. Bolstered by Göring talk, the newest prospect could have raised Hitler's spiirts the same way the start of Air Offensive did on 13 August at the baton ceremony. Redoubtable breach-filler Hermann had done it again. His glowing advices about current air prospects made his Führer happy, and momentarily sprung him from *Sea Lion* quandary.

The fact of quandary was implicit in the situation: time was at an end. The resources of Europe had been drained to the bottom to produce *Sea Lion,* whose sheer bulk and publicity now demanded satisfaction. Soldiers and sailors had swarmed over his troubled body and exhausted themselves in the firm faith that he would end the war. Führer face had to make good on these physical aspects as well as on the propaganda they had inspired. But propaganda had likewise nurtured a false belief that Air was clearing the way, when in reality Air War and *Sea Lion* were miles apart. Air War, going its separate way, had failed to produce decision and to attempt at this late hour to integrate it with invasion seemed utterly unthinkable. Recall the Skl remark in this regard. Should invasion now fly in the teeth of Air failure, or must both projects be abandoned? What of the precious military initiative, preached so incessantly? How could Hitler hang on to it, or was it indeed, still his? Would he still be able to go East?

At the root of all lay the ancient problem of England, and Hitler was entering the final stages of his turn at the wheel to resolve it. He had embarked on a gospel of inevitable association but ended by having to force it with a spurious compound of Air fright and invasion threat. The former has been sufficiently belabored here; the latter, with which he now played "off-again-on-again," had possessed its own unvarying philosophy from the beginning. The Colonel Generals heard it only in part; Raeder on 6 September heard it more fully to the effect that decisive results could come quickest by landing in England, but the risk might be prohibitively high. He would not risk failure, for failure would mean unacceptable prestige gains for Britain. Landing threat was to be maintained in any case.[25]

[25] Hitler in his own utterances repeatedly confirmed this invasion philosophy as the summer of 1940 advanced. Its combination with Air Fright was summarized most effectively on paper by Jodl, first at the very beginning, 30 June 1940, and toward the end, 13 August 1940. Admiral Raeder recorded it in the Skl war diary

Onus for decision over Britain rested at last where it belonged, squarely on the shoulders of Hermann Göring. At Führer Conference of 21 July, just after his abortive proffer of peace to Britain, Hitler had hung *Sea Lion* around Admiral Raeder's Navy neck. The burden for readiness to invade and the implied responsibility for decision over Britain were piled up on Navy. The disease of impossible expectation from Air War did not take full hold until late July had brought *unabänderlicher Entschluss* for Russia, and this heightened the urgency of settling Problem England. Emphasis redoubled on decision by Air. There followed the uneven efforts to wipe out RAF Fighter Command, capped by impatient Bombs on London. Many moments of grave danger came and went, but none brought decision. By 13 September time was running out. What to do?

He turned to Göring, who recognized his Führer's quandary, and took up his favorite role of blandishing, relieving, and brushing away those troubles by brave "ice cold" jump-into-the-breach. Never again would Göring have opportunity to play the part with such zest and such wide latitude. Yet we can visualize it as a dual performance, for Hitler quickly joined in as his henchman reached the master's vulnerable predilections. Together they quickly reinventoried the situation: air attacks are underway for today (the thirteenth) in good strength; the prospects are excellent. So far our attacks on London have been cursed with abominable weather, but just now meteorologists assure a spell of fine flying days. Give us four to five days, and the English fighters will surely be out. Large-scale attacks are beset with many difficulties, but there is a good chance of bringing England down. We know the Briton is already badly hurt; effect has been terrific, people nervous. All antiaircraft is concentrated around London—an enormous expenditure of ammunition. Even if it takes ten or twelve days more air action, that would be better than landing attack. Landing is in fact not necessary anyhow. Why should we take that risk? Our Ju 88 program is coming along; soon in full production. I can knock out his fleet, and cut off England. In any event, the landing does not have to be called off at this particular moment. "I can keep the English down for any length of time you wish, my Führer!" Calling off *Sea Lion* cannot be kept secret, and he may be useful when Air success comes. Why should

---

on 7 September from Führer Conference of the sixth. It is to be noted that such narrow development as the Hitlerian invasion philosophy underwent followed the line pointed out to him by Admiral Raeder.

we not just postpone *Sea Lion,* keeping the pressure of landing threat to heighten the general tension?[26]

As to what can be nailed down specifically for the Hitler side of the colloquy, there was the significant fact that he made prominent mention of Russia at decision conference the next day. Russia occupied a forward place in his thoughts on the fourteenth and probably had also on the thirteenth. If we pursue our thesis all the way, we can surmise that Göring's advices took advantage of the East plan's compulsion to make Hitler feel not only secure in that plan, but actually benefited, by the Göring assurances. As already hinted by Hitler, England need not come tumbling down just now. If she were held prostrate until after Russia, all the better. The initiative would still be his.

In such wise may have gone preparation to outwit the day of decision. We have refined the lines of resurging quandary over Problem England and the interplay of air fright and invasion to resolve that problem; we have identified the salients of probable exchanges with Göring. Hitler happily disavowed *Sea Lion* before a group of high officers at luncheon, which Göring attended. There remained yet a pronouncement to the Commanders-in-Chief. How would he tell these older children?

For master dissembler Hitler this posed no great problem. He simply took up the cudgels for *Sea Lion* and acted the role of his sole defender. He inveighed against *Sea Lion* call-off as though call-off, and not hop-off, had been the issue all along. Beyond this, Hitler's lengthy pronouncement before the Commanders-in-Chief on the fourteenth filled out its affiliation to preparatory conditioning of the day before. What came out is of sufficient import to warrant treatment in full from General Halder's on-the-spot record.

Halder's notes indicate that generalities came first. Hitler linked together Problems Russia and England all of a piece, making by implication the question one of, Which came first, Russia or England? He talked around the twin problems with the word "enemy" so confusedly that whether he meant England or Russia was up to his hearers. The one thing he made clear was that Russia stood in the forefront of his thinking.

[26] Of course we have no paper documenation for the words put in the conspiratorial mouths. The words appear in what both men said later, Hitler on the fourteenth, Göring on the sixteenth. They fit the situation for the thirteenth. Evidence that Hitler exhibited relief about this time and that Göring was the reliever comes from four highly placed persons of the three Arms.

"Occupation" of England, he remarked, would put an expeditious end to the war but the necessity did not exist "of landing by a definite time under all circumstances . . . ." Prolongation of the war [was] fraught with political dangers, for stability can never be counted on in politics [apparently he referred to combination of Britain and Russia against Germany]. "It would be clear to the enemy that conditions desired by him have not been fulfilled. Our bleeding to death, expected by Russia did not come about . . . . " The "enemy" must re-estimate the situation. Moscow's calculations went wrong. "In any event no long range security exists. Swift change is possible (witness Norway)." America's rearmament cannot become effective until 1945. Long war is undesirable. We have achieved those aims of practical value to us. Politically and economically the base [we have] won suffices.

Having thus ended his introduction on a reasonably sensible note, Hitler launched into the more gripping details.

"Quickest conclusion would be landing in England." Navy has fully met its prerequisites. The arming of the coast [artillery] has been finished. Action of the Luftwaffe is above all praise. "Four to five days of good weather needed, in order to reach decisive results." All-out air action over enemy territory carries great difficulties. "Chance to bring the British down completely, good. Effect so far terrific, but total effect, which is dependent on 4–5 good days, has not been reached. Every pause is advantageous to the enemy . . . ." London has drawn all antiair defenses, expenditure of ammunition enormous. Complete elimination of enemy fighters not yet achieved. In any case "enemy is badly hurt." "On the whole, however, despite all successes *the prerequisites for Sea Lion are not yet on hand.*"

The case was now ready for recapitulation, and for platitudinous repetition of Führer Decision:

1. Successful landing means victory, demands complete mastery of the air.
2. Until now bad weather has prevented complete air command.
3. All other factors are in order.
Therefrom, Decision:
The operation will not be called off now.

He hasted along to buttress this historic anticlimax with telltale mixture of inner rationale and Göring conditioning:

Current attacks have had terrific effect. If perhaps principally on nerves, to this effect is added the fear of landing. The pressure of landing danger must not be lifted. Even if Air success does not arrive for 10-12 days mass hysteria may break out in England. If we gain mastery of the air in certain areas in 10-12 days, then the enemy could be forced by landing to commit his destroyers against the landing. Then he will suffer losses and will not be able to protect his convoys any longer . . . . Cancellation [*Sea Lion*] won't remain secret . . . ."

The outlandish shot-in-the-dark about destroyers may have been Navy inspired, for we find Admiral Raeder stepping forward to second his Führer's nonsense fulsomely. Intensified air attack on London without regard for *Sea Lion,* Raeder argued, was the thing. Since, however, it was unlikely, he continued, that the Air situation would change before 24-27 September, those dates could be dropped from *Sea Lion* calendar and the next favorable day, 8 October, taken into prospect as S Day. If by that time the Luftwaffe had achieved complete success, it might become possible to drop *Sea Lion* altogether. The Raeder, Göring, and Hitler invasion philosophies twined themselves together indistinguishably.

The C-in-C of the Army spoke a different mind. After Hitler (for his own reasons) rejected Raeder's suggestion of delay, by insistence on 17 September as the next warning-order day, von Brauchitsch had his chance and leaped into the unknown. He sided with Hitler: Stick to the seventeenth. Thereupon old Army shot its last despairing bolt. Its Commander-in-Chief declared himself willing to land under cover of smoke, without reference to Navy dates, and we suspect he meant also, without Navy interference. Brauchitsch based his proposal on the hazards *Sea Lion* was subject to in the stuffed mounting ports during prolonged delay. Gasoline, ammunition, landing barges were blowing skyward under RAF attack, and the prospect was for more to come. For Army it was now or never. The soldiers had shown signs of wanting *Sea Lion* to go at almost any cost; and the leadership had tired of Navy hemming and hawing. Jeschonnek interjected comment about RAF attack against railroad artillery spurs on the coast. The Führer was not to be diverted. He replied to von Brauchitsch with even more confidence in air effect alone, saying, ". . . unremitting continuation of the air attacks is the decisive factor." Where have we followed such a viscid pattern before? Was it not at high conference on 31 July?

Jeschonnek's turn came next to take up the word for the Luftwaffe on another tack. "While material damage on London," said he, "had succeeded beyond expectation, no mass panic of the populace has occurred because residential sections have not been attacked and destroyed." He requested freedom to attack them. Raeder supported him strongly. But Hitler sheered off from official sanction to that extreme measure.   Granting the justice of Jeschonnek's argument, he countered with a pious preachment of principle: "attack on vital war targets is always the most important, for it destroys irreplaceable values.   So long as a target important to waging war remains one must stay on it . . . working up mass panic must be the last resort . . . ." Noteworthy is that the German Führer never got around to ordering this final hell for disintegrating England.   Directly after the conference, Hitler permitted Jodl to order some extension of the air target in London but "Terror Attacks" on housing areas he specifically excluded.   We wonder whether he was not trying to content himself, in the Göring vein, with simply keeping Britain prostrate, while he settled with Russia.

At any rate, henceforth "Fiction" ruled over *Sea Lion* to Hitler's auditors, without any question; but to him the beast retained an ambiguous viability.   This was attested by the Jodl order just mentioned; with Warlimont he settled its provisions late on the fourteenth, after the conference.   Jodl labored under the pain of explaining that the decision of the day had gone against *Sea Lion* hop-off and had come out as another vapid postponement.   "A new decision," recorded the OKW war diary, "will be made on 17 September and the preparations should continue."   Warlimont confessed his bafflement by questioning his Chief about what was truly to be expected.   In reply General Jodl, as already cited, declared that "the Führer apparently decided on 13 September to drop *Sea Lion* utterly but that now he had decided upon mere postponement."   He troubled to explain further, "This does not mean, of course, that the Führer desires to compel an execution of operation *Sea Lion* if his prerequisites are lacking, but shows, now as before, that a crossing of the Channel only comes into question, in case England, defeated by air warfare, has to be given the *coup de grace*."

Then followed Jodl's familiar refrain of vindication: Keep moral pressure on the British—withdrawal of any *Sea Lion* craft would lessen the psychological effect of the air warfare.   Besides *Sea Lion* draws RAF planes and exposes them to attack—and finally, attacks on Channel ports will decrease those on the German population. These feeble casts had all been uttered by Hitler.   Furthermore at luncheon on the thirteenth he had promised von Falkenhorst, down from Norway, additional shipping for supplies from home, and Jodl now implemented that promise by cautioning Warlimont that shipping space, "which may possibly become free [from *Sea Lion*], will have

to be placed at the disposal of *Armee-gruppe* XXI [von Falkenhorst]."
To quick-thinking Warlimont it all added up to Fiction; he gave up,
and proposed that the order of postponement also include direction
that "counter-intelligence and camouflage measures be intensified."
This was done.

Sea Lion actually heaved his last on 17 September 1940. It had
been a lingering death of frequent postponement, but a death his
master never certified. Problem England left the headlines of our
most authoritative sources after the fourteenth. General Halder
dropped the invasion subject altogether for more important business
concerning Russia. Operations Staff OKW likewise found *Sea Lion*
passé; it managed however, the release of a short teletype message to
meet 17 September's advance billing as final decision day. The message disposed of Invasion England 1940 in these five words of under-
statement: *WIRD BIS AUF WEITERES VERSCHOBEN* (Postponed until further notice). The fact that Skl alone took chronicle
notice of postponement, and found reasons therefor, implicates Navy
in having engineered the death stroke. It came at the dead of night
at two o'clock. Said Skl diary, after dilating on weather troubles,
past and future, plus lack of air command: "The Führer decides for
these reasons on *indefinite postponement of Operation Sea Lion (der
Führer entscheidet sich aus diesen Gründen für Aufschub der Operation Seeloewe auf unbestimmte Zeit.)* In forwarding this joyous word
to its subordinate commands the Navy clinched its own attitude by
adding that Operation *Hipper*—diversion in the Atlantic—was to
proceed as scheduled irrespective of *Sea Lion*. OKW's teletype
message referred to the issuance of the warning order due on S minus
10 Day. The "predecision" or warning order became the indefinitely
postponed item. Despite Navy interpellation, *Sea Lion* retained life
on paper and in Hitler's mind.

The carcass had yet to be dismembered, and in these rites Navy led
the way again, and that, contrary to Führer's wishes. Vigorous
British action against the mounting ports forced safety measures the
very next day, 18 September. Skl on its own ordered a stop to further concentration of all landing craft whatsoever and also ordered
local dispersal of supporting naval vessels. OKW confirmed the
action with a directive signed by Keitel on 19 September, though it
failed to meet the Navy's express wish for extension of the warning
period from ten to fifteen days. Hitler turned down extension; for
him, *Sea Lion* was alive and in highest possible state of readiness.

Nevertheless extension had been firmly agreed upon between Fricke and Jodl, who carried the load of convincing the Führer. In direct contravention to his wishes, Navy continued dismemberment on a fifteen-day warning basis until the job was done. It was curious that in the end who but Hitler should stand forth as *Sea Lion's* last defender. He tried hard to keep the bugles of advance sounding to cover his retreat and, too, to placate his own dogged spirit.

Sea Lion, however, lost face fast. The appellation "Fiction" verged on the unutterable, yet the fact of sham could not be disguised. It did not take the sailors along the waterfront long to react to what they saw going on all about them and what they were themselves doing. They coined a fitting name for friend *Sea Lion's* advancing paralysis, calling it *Winterschlaf* (winter's sleep, or hiberation). Army authorities, still earnestly engaged in strenuous troop training and *Kriegspiele* on invasion, were irked by this show of Navy flippancy. They stirred up sufficient gossip to reach the ears of OKW planners, who ineffectually discussed measures for combatting the down trend. It proved most difficult to shore up the waning *Sea Lion* interest, for everyone was privately willing to assist in downgrading him. A British-French move off Dakar at this time of late September under the leadership of General de Gaulle focused attention in directions away from invasion.[27]

General de Gaulle almost succeeded in uniting France and Germany. His expedition may have been devised explicitly to disrupt the invasion tide, for the numerous signs of haste that cropped up in the zany affair pointed back toward the hottest period of British invasion uproar, 11-18 September. Whatever the purpose, when it came off on 23-24 September, *Sea Lion* fell further out of notice. The explosive character of Mers el Kebir, by September almost forgotten, revived here off Dakar, and French/German feeling ran together nearly strong enough to fashion a union against Britain, not necessarily a union for invasion, but a coalescing of interest and powers that might have kept Hitler tied to the West. General Jodl, as well as Admiral Raeder, exhibited the keenest interest for influencing

---

[27] The late September efforts to shore up *Sea Lion* included a trip by General Halder to XIII Korps on the right wing, to AOK 9, and Army Group A again; also a trip by General Warlimont from OKW to AOK 16, Airfleet 2, AOK 9, and on along the coast. He reported stupendous works, yet that *Sea Lion* was still unready. Admiral Fricke from Skl visited the Channel area too but his investigations had more to do with hibernation than action. He sought to prepare for return to true Naval warfare by Navy with surface ship operations in the Atlantic from French bases.

Hitler's thought toward common cause with France, but quite aside from *Sea Lion*. Their endeavors stressed, rather, the importance of associating the French to eliminate Britain from the Mediterranean. Hitler alone held out for Russia.

He granted a long conference to his Navy chieftain about the future course of the war in the late afternoon of 26 September. In the war thus far, the Navy views had proved themselves to him, and he was ready to listen further. Knowing this, Admiral Raeder requested audience in private to pose and propose. Another "strategic moment" was at hand.

Strategic, because Raeder now suspected strongly that Hitler contemplated a radical switch in strategy. Notice had finally reached him of Hitler's *"unabänderlicher Entschluss . . .* to conduct the East campaign, despite all counter representations . . ." that England was the one to beat. Yet the Admiral required definitive confirmation from the Führer himself and moved craftily to get it. He unrolled for Hitler a Napoleonic canvas of thrilling Mediterranean adventure; it could at once eliminate Britain from that region and checkmate Russia from the south, thus making a land campaign against her in north Europe dispensable. Hitler dispelled all doubt for Raeder about his fixed intention by failing to bat an eye at this pointed mention of a campaign into Russia, a subject never before discussed with the Admiral. Poor Raeder, now he knew. He sailed on feebly from the Mediterranean to the glories that awaited them in the Indian Ocean. It was no go; his worst fears had been confirmed. Hitler's India lay in Russia. Perhaps the real dangers inherent in Northwest Africa would ring home. Prophetically, he pointed out the soft underbelly of Europe, and counseled a "going-together" with France to make that region secure first. According to Raeder's notes his fervid exposition got over to Hitler and brought a favorable response. He said he would sound out Mussolini, and also Franco, to test whether France or Spain should make the most desirable confederate. Perhaps Russia could be encouraged to find her way to the sea over Persia instead of through the Baltic. Spurred by Raeder's suggestions, Hitler let his imagination range far around the horizon. Uncompanionable thought of England and invasion receded into the dim background and was hardly worthy of further mention.[28]

[28] *IMT* doc. 066-C. In this paper of 30 January 1944 Admiral Raeder reconstructed his recollection of signs of Hitler's maturing *East* plans during the summer 1940. Raeder states that by the time of his conference with Hitler 26 September

Once again Admiral Raeder felt safe in dragging *Sea Lion* casually into the conversation for a moment of last rites. His offhand inquiries of May, long ago, had sired guilty thoughts of invasion, and now in September he would officiate at their final remission. The Navy, he reported, could not maintain *Sea Lion* readiness beyond 15 October and requested definite decision by that date on dismemberment. Hitler seems to have consented with silence, for no reply is recorded. Why bother about *Sea Lion* at this high point? The two soared on (it is the only word for it) into the future course of the war after a wondrous sailor pattern: the islands of the Atlantic; the build-up of the fleet; the virtues of ships over planes after all. It would require ships, not planes to take the Canaries, for instance, or the Azores, and hold them. *Sea Lion* was forgotten. His name caused not a ripple in the flow of their bewitching dreams.

This end treatment of momentous invasion question between Hitler and Raeder—casual, tinged with illusion, never open and above board—proved typical of the way *Sea Lion* passed into oblivion in the German high counsels. Without crisis, without ripple, he passed in anticlimax. No one knew for sure just how, or why, least of all Hitler.

1940, "The Führer had made plain his 'unalterable resolve' to conduct the *East* Campaign despite all counter presentations . . . ," and goes on to say that because of his (Raeder's) fear that the war was getting "on the wrong track" (turning away from the main danger, England), he asked for conference with the Führer "under four eyes" so that he could explain the importance of the Mediterranean and North Africa. He stated that Hitler dispelled all doubt about his firm intention of attacking Russia overland. Hitler confessed to his naval aide that Raeder impressed him, yet his own *East* ideas won out.

9. *October All Over*

> June too soon,
> July stand by.
> August you must,
> September remember,
> October all over.

By these words of caution sailormen the world over have habitually regulated security measures against typhoons or hurricanes. June came normally too soon for the "big winds" to drive up from the south, but in July, they might strike. It behooved one to stand by, and more so during August, when the storms approached their peak. In September one stood constant alert, hoping meanwhile for October, when all would be over. So it seemed to us with Invasion England from the very first. As we scanned the crests and troughs of *Sea Lion* story, the sailor jingle rang a bell of affiliation: the rise and fall of invasion pressures bespoke the typhoon season. Like those tempests, *Sea Lion* ran an uneven course—backing and filling, unpredictable, yet always dangerous—the whole summer long; and by October he blew himself out, he was all over. But unlike the storms of nature he therewith lost all potential. His spirit died too, never to revive. A fresh dilemma took over.

The totality of *Sea Lion's* quietus among German Arms was attested by the zest for schemes to supplant him. A storm of conferring, estimating, and planning raged in the high sanctums of German command. The flood of papers signaled a shift in thinking, the way rise and fall of radio traffic often presages operational change. Much was afoot and none of it about *Sea Lion*. The wordy studies dealt with Spain and Gibraltar, Italy and Greece, the Balkans, Suez, and the Atlantic Islands. Navy sealed all thought of invasion by mining the English coasts. Only from Army, struggling with the Russian puzzle, came a few feeble bleats to urge the strengthening of invasion for the future. All others eloquently certified *Sea Lion's* demise in body and soul by treating his possible resurrection with total silence. The command mind occupied itself with the question of, What now?

Hitler longed for his mountains. He hurried the signing of the Tripartite Pact and set up a Brenner Pass meeting with Mussolini to talk over the situation. From the meeting he repaired to Berchtesgaden for refueling.

Yet, existing orders insisted on *Sea Lion*. They required a double life of fact as well as fiction and the Army, like Navy, was finding the play untenable. OKH complaints were taken under consideration by General Jodl on 2 October. The arguments of Army hinted at impairment of *East* plans if something were not done to loosen the readiness orders. Jodl, who understood better than anyone the sanctity and power of those plans, readily saw the light. He approved the easing of invasion readiness on his own responsibility, pending request of the Führer for definitive "cancellation," when he should come down from the mountain. Events followed that course. Under date of 12 October 1940 an OKW directive by its effect settled *Sea Lion* forever.

The signature of a junior staff officer disposed of him in a short paper. "The Führer has decided," it read, "that preparation for the landing in England from now on until spring are to be maintained merely as measures of political and military pressure . . . ." Assurance of adequate time notice followed, should invasion again come under consideration during 1941. Freedom was granted Army to constitute new divisions for new tasks, and Navy, authority to withdraw ships and men needed in the home economy. Luftwaffe received no instruction whatever; but why should it have, never having believed in *Sea Lion* and having contributed naught to him. Significantly, of the two courses suggested by Army—extending the readiness notice with intent of reserving *Sea Lion* as death blow to a defeated Britain, or, designating him wholly political and military pressure with no intent of executing at all—Hitler chose the latter more extreme course. For the first and final time he decided about invasion. Poor *Sea Lion*: once brave thought of *Gewaltsame Landung,* now degenerated into admission of fake or something worse. "Transmigration from Lion of the Sea into tadpole," the waterfront gossip put it.[1]

Although record of desultory invasion planning and experimentation continued for a long time, the project never again rose as a factor of moment in the war with Britain. During 1941 under the names *Haifisch* and *Harpune,* invasion arose as a cover plan for dispositions against Russia. On 2 March 1942 final authority to dismantle waterfront preparation altogether was granted in a directive that placed readiness on a twelve-month notice. This meaningless stipulation signified merely that Hitler was so deeply involved in Russia that he had no time for Britain. She could wait.

Wait she did and Hitler never more got around to her. During the last months of 1940 he grieved over new dilemma. History would never forgive him, he agonized, for not using this time. October all over—and only vexation! The piping time of *Wunschkonzert* and their robust spirit of victory just around the corner . . . . Where were they now? They had faded into nothingness, leaving the fundamental question of England unresolved. Hitler's turn at the wheel was over.

Sea Lion *Capability*

We have followed Hitler through the tangle of courses he steered and know something of his methods and those of his ship. It is time to plot the circles on the chart of time and cogitate their meaning. Thinking back over the story we find no quick and easy answer; a single one, as the many questions would have it. Everyone knows *Sea Lion* did not go, but not why. So queries tend to fuse themselves into the central riddle of: Why didn't he? From there, absorbing speculations flow out about what-might-have-been. It may profit us therefore, first, to test the capability of *Sea Lion* on paper as he stood in late September 1940. Then he achieved his summit of readiness:

[1] The course of events emerge from: W.D., OKW Ops, pp. 116-28; Record of Situation Evaluations Defense Branch OKW, pp. 69-83. The records reveal a troubled Hitler. He even ordered evacuation of children from Berlin to escape RAF attacks, without consulting OKW. Jodl linked the Brenner Pass talks and Berghof with decision expressed in the directive of 12 October.

on that last decision day of 17 September 1940. What were in fact his chances?

Had Hitler instead of "Indefinite Postponement," signaled "Execute," what could have happened?

That which OKW specifically ordered postponed in the early hours of 17 September was the issuance of S minus 10 warning order to set in motion the final invasion preliminaries. Guides were prescribed for co-ordinating these steps among the three services and OKW in the timetable of 7 September. For S minus 10 Day the table led off with the all-inclusive order to commence loading materiel; additional items affected only Navy and Air. Navy was to initiate the deployment of submarines in the Channel approaches, and the laying of mine barriers on the flanks of the landing area. Air would regroup and commence the assembly of flak artillery. None of these tasks posed difficulty on 17 September, though complete loading might have been slowed because the distribution of landing craft was still underway.

Twenty-one small submarines, earmarked for invasion support, were ready and required only signaled orders to send them churning to their stations. Though the mine craft deployment promised to be far more complicated, the elements for execution rested in hand. Exploratory sweeps had been made; minecraft, mines, and assisting vessels had arrived in sortie ports along the coast. Naval Group Commander West filled his war diary with last-minute regulation for an earnest and reasonably practicable operation. He was ready; final orders for sortie awaited release.

A like probability existed for favorable execution of the initial Luftwaffe tasks. A withdrawal of flak from its current mission and its concentration toward mounting ports was well within the capability of the Luftwaffe. Regrouping of the air corps meant a shift of emphasis away from the air war on London, but it could have been done.

To return to the landing craft distribution: misgivings on meeting scheduled readiness mounted under the combined impact of British bombardments from sea, RAF attacks, and nasty weather. Yet these doubts are typical pre-hop-off worries. They make for lost time, inefficiency, and tension, but if the stuff is somewhere around it somehow gets through and surprises everyone. One constant worry was the deficiency of towing power; shortage of tugs plagued *Sea Lion* to the end. Prahm distribution suffered accordingly but not fatally. On the other hand, the prahms gave a good account of themselves in seaworthiness while en route to their bases. Available in all ports on

17 September, according to the war diary of Commanding Admiral France, were 734 prahms out of 1200 initially required, and only 86 tugs of the 422 needed. The rest were enroute. By 27 September, our figurative S Day, the picture had changed radically for the better. All ports were full up in prahms and the only deficiencies were: 25 tugs, 18 motor boats, and 5 steamers. Army authorities seemed satisfied. In general, the commands viewed the total lift status with assurance. VII Corps, commanding the center, reported for Calais, even as early as 18 September, that, "7th Division lacks [but] one, 1st Mountain Division [but] 2 prahms. Prospect of 16 more prahms available . . . ." We may therefore confidently infer that craft essential for the initial hop-off could have been in their proper ports for loading in time to meet a sortie date of 26 September, one day before S Day. Thus *Sea Lion* possessed the potential material capability of meeting an S Day of 27 September.[2]

On this favorable forecast a turn can be made to combined action's true beginning when Army and Navy team up in craft loading. Time and facility to achieve a proper working-in had been all too short for a smooth run off. But these things run on their nerve, to a point, especially early in an operation while the excitement of it holds. The chances are the job could have got done, even to loading hundreds of skittish horses. Fodder, fuel, and bullets were ready in ample dumps along the coast. So far so good.[3]

S minus 3 Day would exact the second, more binding word from the German Supreme Commander. He then had to confirm S Day and S Time, which signal meant the beginning of troop embarkation. Covertly, some troop loading would already have begun in the Low Country ports, and those loaded transports moved forward to favorable sortie positions, for the timing imposed by Hitler proved impracticable. All the foregoing lay within Sea Lion's capability. What we have recounted could have happened, and the clock could have wound on to fateful S minus 1 Day. Then, sortie had to begin, or in

---

[2] The number of vessels involved staggers one. By 27 September, 1859 prahms, 397 tugs, 68 command boats, 1000 motor boats, 100 coastal motor sailers and 159 steamers (2000 to 8000 tons) had been crammed into the Channel and Lowland ports. Casualties totaled 79 prahms, 5 tugs, 7 motor boats, 7 steamers.

[3] The fact that the lift could have been on hand is of course not the whole story. There were many grave, but hardly fatal, deficiencies within the prahms, motor boats, tugs, and steamers. A combined experience report from Transport Fleet Commanders of 23 November 1940 lists 21 technical deficiencies, 12 in commnuciation equipment and 37 other material lacks, all of which applied generally to the craft.

fact, the evening before. Hitler had reserved for that day one last opportunity to call off the operation.

At about this point, near the start of sortie, we edge out from the tangible evidence of *Sea Lion's* physical accouterment into an estimate of what he could have done with it. The answers must be extrapolated from the data already plotted by applying sailor imagination, for the troubles would rise from the sea. So far only German capability to meet the invasion requirements, as conceived, has been tested. We have only brushed the question of *Sea Lion's* true potency. Granted that in his interest the Germans dredged up all their own, and all Europe's invasion resource in an incredibly short space of time, and placed high ability and vast energies at *Sea Lion's* disposal, was it enough?

If the estimate of sortie and crossing is to make sense at all, several basic operational presumptions must be added and accepted for the sake of argument. Operable weather had to be in the prospect. Next, the integration of Luftwaffe into invasion tasks must have been effected. We assume that Luftwaffe planes would have been over the mounting ports in strength. With this shift the landing team would have been made whole with all three Arms functioning under the unified command of the Führer at Ziegenberg. Judgment on the competence of that command for the conduct of this operation we evade for the moment, and take its proficiency for granted, as we have the weather and the integration of Luftwaffe. S minus 1 is at hand.

To any seaman, the ubiquitous prahm, core of *Sea Lion,* was due for trouble. In her own bailiwick on the river at home where the smell of each bank was familiar, the feel of every current second nature, and the swinging room of each turn calculable to a hair, the Rhine river barge did marvelous execution. She had a master not so young, and a crew growing up and being schooled in her ways. Together they knew what they were about. Not so here on the coast out of her water, embroiled in mad invasion melee. The master had been succeeded by a boat club youngster from Hamburg; the crew was made up of lubbers on a lark. Her bow had been mangled, her innards poured with concrete and the wheel house cut off to get under bridges. Even her name had been changed from *Schiff* to *Prahm* with a mere number. Choked with wheels, horses, and troops, she was to go to England under tow in a complex formation. She was the German answer to the pivotal task of beaching troops and heavy equipment in quantity sufficient for a sustained land fight on England's soil. Her ponderousness and poor beaching qualities were well known. The operational hazards of crossing by the hundreds have yet to be closely examined.

The place and hour—landing beach in England at dawn, 27 September 1940—can serve as the immutable goal of a trial picture of the crossing. We backtrack from the landing beaches along Admiral Lütjen's prescribed routes toward the sortie ports, striking off points at 5 knots speed, to arrive at the German hour of sortie from each mounting port. The speed of 5 knots allowed by the Germans seems much too optimistic. Allied forces experienced a like over-optimism about untried craft. A proper discount eventually worked itself out for each type of craft, and we must apply one here to the prahm. Doubtless some tows did turn out 5 knots during trial runs or even 6 or 7, but for steaming in formation with green crews in Channel waters, 3 knots is a generous allowance; we grant 4 knots.

The tow flotillas of the eastern mounting ports faced long runs before reaching their crossing route entrance points. This made them the give-away of invasion start. Ostend lay forty-three miles to the eastward of Route 1's gate to glory, Dunkirk nineteen. Tow formations from both ports had to enter their route by 2000 of the twenty-sixth, which meant Ostend formation would make up in the forenoon of that day; while at Dunkirk, Bartels would have to shove off, with Admiral von Fischel in command of Transport Fleet B, in mid-afternoon.

Ostend had not fared badly. There had been a few bomb hits, some casualties, nothing serious. The work had gone tolerably well with the 17th Division on the job lending a hand wherever possible. Captain Lehmann preserved his quiet confidence. All things considered, it would have been no superhuman feat for Captain Hennecke, commanding Tow Formation 2, to meet his departure deadline. He might have made a get-away without important enemy molestation, for Ostend ranked among the lesser targets; yet surely his activity and that at Rotterdam and Antwerp would have been signaled to London. Steaming at the head of his straggling fifty-prahm column he could well have anticipated increased RAF interest as he hauled up toward Dunkirk.

That scarred port had suffered heavily. Captain Bartels and his scanty company wrestled with a tremendous work. Aside from obstructing wrecks (he counted 80), green hands, and the prahms themselves, his chief worry remained lockage for them from inner to outer harbor in time for sortie. In the final plan he called for beginning the operation on S minus 4, 23 September. His prahm total ran to well over 150, of which the last four flotillas (48) were to be crammed through the two operable locks in one and a half to two hours of high water during the morning of the twenty-sixth. Bartels' doubts multiplied toward this hour. There would be over 75 tows in the column departing for Route 1 on the twenty-sixth. Knowing Bartels, we grant that he would have made it.

Calais, the next port, had more room and better facilities. It mounted a tow formation of two hundred prahms under Captain Gustav Kleikamp, Transport Fleet C. He was to enter Route 2, five miles off shore, at 1800 on the twenty-sixth. Late in October 1940 he wrote in his final report, "In my opinion the belated beginning and insufficient preparations as well as a complete lack of training in craft and prahms at steaming together would have given the greatest trouble, or even might have rendered it impossible at the end of September or early October to take a transport fleet with the desired success and order . . . to the enemy shore, especially at night." But often the impossible is achieved in time of stress and strain; and we grant him a start on his way. Out of Boulogne Captain Werner Lindenau commanded Transport Fleet D. It contained the fantastic number of 330 prahms, to be funneled in tows, four abreast, into Route 3. It was hard for Lindenau to express confidence over such a piece of magic. Likewise at Le Havre Captains Scheuerlen and Brocksien found little to cheer about. Ambiguity fogged their operation by commitment to a choice of two routes after the execute signal. Recall that one route went direct to Brighton region, the other along the coast to join Boulogne traffic.

Had the execute signal then been given, 26-27 September would have shown as the critical day and night. We take stock of the remarkable picture that might have resulted: England at bay and a poorly constituted German invasion fleet thrashing its way out of port. The time would have been mid-afternoon of the 26th. Army Corps VII at mid-point of the front had entered in its journal: "Cloudy, clearing at times." Dover stood yonder, visible to the naked eye. The alarm would already have sounded: Invasion army afloat! One sure way to thwart it, an English way all Englishmen knew, was to sink it in the bottom of the sea.

We embark therefore on what had to be a one-shot affair, not a prolonged contest of many days in which cumulative effect might tell.

After 1600, four hours plus of daylight remained to the twenty-sixth for Royal Air Force to give its all, and then came a scant nine semi-dark hours for combined naval and air action. Much could have been done for and against invasion during those hours. They would make or break it.

The Channel arena was due for an immediate shift of roles in the air; the RAF going over to an all-out offense against a specific target on the water, the invasion fleet, while the Luftwaffe assumed the defense to cover that target. Such a switch was bound to reach very far in its effect, and RAF stood to gain. The plodding prahms and escorts in assembly and column forming maneuvers could present nothing but sitting-duck targets, not to be sunk outright at one stroke but to suffer seriously in morale and cohesion under repeated attack. We can think back to the faintly comparable situation during Dunkirk evacuation. There, roles were again reversed; and other dissimilar circumstances rule out comparison, except on one generality. Dunkirk evacuation succeeded through the exertions of both British air and sea power, not by one alone. In the end, power on the water became the deciding factor that uneasy air balance could not redress. And this promised also to be the case for *Sea Lion*.[4]

The Royal Navy on 26 September 1940 had deployed an over-powering array of ships and craft in home waters. According to German advices the British held available over 70 destroyers, 500 lesser craft, 20 light and 8 heavy cruisers, 3 battleships, 2 battle cruisers, and 2 carriers. Nor had the concept of employment of this bulwark, the Germans thought, changed from the days of Howard and Drake. They expected the heavier ships to assume positions in readiness while the lighter ones took up the gauge of battle. The Channel waters were best suited to fast handy vessels, and so the Germans figured that 3 or 4 light cruisers plus 20 destroyers would be committed on each flank of *Sea Lion* crossing.

Let us return to the struggling amphibians. Calais occupied the center of the stage. Captain Kleikamp's prahm tows of Fleet C would have poked their way into Route 2, three abreast. Dover batteries

---

[4] A close balancing of air strengths at this point has proved unprofitable. In the Channel arena Luftwaffe stood to gain fighter effect by easier access and freedom from some bomber escort tasks, while losing in general effect by its dispersion over numerous and widely spread *Sea Lion* tasks. RAF, whose fighters had been badly mauled, but bombers almost untouched, should have gained in fighter and bomber effect through Luftwaffe dispersion and own ability to take the offense against a single easily visible target.

may have had something to say as the columns swung southwest toward Cap Gris Nez. Twice Dover guns had straddled the locks in Calais during the week past, and immediately called forth urgent request for Luftwaffe counter action. Yet Luftwaffe could not do everything, and if English shells had splashed around him Kleikamp would have kept on, and so also the other fleet commanders. On the right wing, von Fischel, out of Dunkirk, by late afternoon would barely have straightened the van of his fleet on a westerly course. From his command ship *Weser,* the tow columns would have stretched nearly out of sight astern. Hennecke's twenty-five tows from Ostend were to join him, and where were the minecraft carrying the Advance Detachments from Ostend? Many a question far harder to answer was ready to plague these amphibians.

On the opposite flank off Boulogne, Transport Fleet D should at five in the afternoon have been entering Route 3 on course due west, thus offering the first unmistakable gesture toward England. Fleet D's commander, Captain Lindenau, planned to arrange his tows in columns four abreast. It was all he could do with so many units. He had organized and briefed his men to the last detail by exercise, word of mouth, and paper. The ship *Hela* was his command ship; Army companions aboard were to include the Commander XXXVIII Corps, General von Manstein, a strong believer in invasion for ending the war. Some of the General's troops would already have been fidgeting aboard their prahms for a day and more because of lack of loading space. But this was the least of Lindenau's worries. Boulogne had reaped the wind of confusion from Army-Navy wrangling. The quarrel had overcrowded Boulogne and its fleet with extra units. Three hundred and thirty prahms in a single formation suggests a mob scene. Even with perfect station keeping, the vast disposition had to stretch more than twelve miles athwart the Channel, and in the unschooled hands of tyro barge captains, it could straggle to fourteen or sixteen miles, over half the distance to England. What a destroyer target! There lay *Sea Lion's* deadly infirmity—the inevitability of bunched up and overextended, fragile prahm columns. "Boulogne Flotilla" of this war was the worst offender.

Natural causes also contributed to Boulogne's vulnerability. There was sea-room to get at her with light craft from the widened Channel bight to the southward. On the other hand, the invader was blessed with helpful currents that funneled northward out of this bight. An unhindered invader like Caesar found himself boosted along toward

England, though with little choice of where he might land. These features proved a double curse to the Germans, for the roomy bight improved the enemy's access, while the extra current worked against a straight westward crossing. Prahm tows in the van, struggling athwart full tide, might make bare headway, whereas their followers, less subject to its influence, would tend to bunch up. Lindenau might prudently have put his strongest tugs and ablest leaders ahead. We let them carry on while we attempt to project the outlines of the picture forward to midnight.[5]

"If peace ever comes, we should try this trick to see if it would work." That telling quip from a naval liaison officer at OKH comes more and more to point. Indeed, we deal in a quasi-peace-time picture when we advance each transport fleet on its route chart toward midnight. The discounts made, such as retardation of the tows and stretching their column length, derive solely from nature's wiles and German handicaps in craft and green personnel. There were yet other discounts, man-made ones from the far shore. We may not ignore them as we attempt to construct a basic view of *Sea Lion's* optimum situation (see following page).

Assuming that *Sea Lion's* limbs uncoiled across the Narrows over Routes 1, 2, and 3, as planned, they had to cut a figure peculiarly inviting to an attacker. The developing midnight plot was destined to take the shape of a squashed ladder of one rung, lying on its side cross-Channel with the legs extended astride Dungeness. On the north (Route 1) von Fischel would round to a southwesterly course; in the rung (Route 2) Kleikamp would be turning west; while in the south leg Lindenau, more than halfway over, would be turning southwest. Astern of the long prahm columns the route lanes would teem with double columns of worried steamers who had nowhere to go for the clutter of prahms blocking their way. Nor could they very well lie to and wait things out. Each steamer was encumbered with two prahms of her own hung astern, and the danger of mines required holding to swept routes. The hypothetical ladder had only to squash

[5] It becomes evident that, navigationally, the chances open to the Germans for crossing in 1940 were less favorable than those actually experienced by Caesar in August 55 BC. He crossed with plus or minus 98 vessels from Boulogne to Dover, between shortly before midnight and 0900 in the morning, in, say, ten hours. He was free to take advantage of both wind and tide, all his vessels were powered by sweeps, and there were not too many. Some German planners considered that Julius had all the best of it. Nelson took advantage of the Channel's conformation during his long watch off Boulogne in 1801.

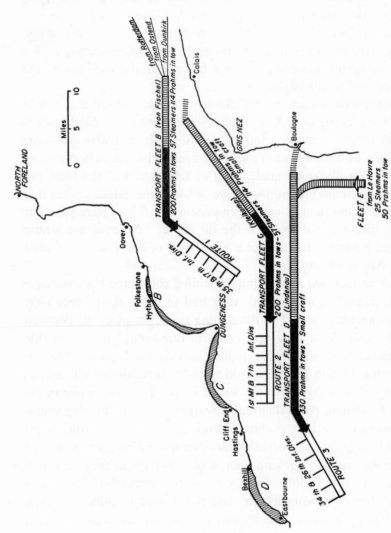

Sea Lion's optimum position, midnight, 26 September, had Hitler given the execute signal on the last possible day, 17 September, for a dawn landing in England on 27 September 1940. An extra hour was allowed at the assault line of departure for forming up.

a little more to set off a chain of disintegration that could end only in a harried bubble of men and machines crawling over each other on the bosom of the Channel. The time would have been ripe for the hungry sharks from the far shore to fall upon the bubble, if they had not already been well at it.

If Dunkirk scene of 24-26 May 1940 presented an amazing and lustful picture to German tankmen, *Sea Lion* underway on 26-27 September could have done no less for British destroyer sailors. The preliminary movements during the twenty-sixth, and before, could not have eluded evaluators in England's eager commands, ashore, afloat, and in the air. By nightfall that it was invasion had to be un-mistakable: a direct but feeble crossing from Le Havre, and a main effort of three diffused prongs in the Narrows. There was no way of hiding these facts. The counteraction that they might have called forth needs no development. To wreck invasion at sea must have been the fond hope of every destroyer. These light craft attacking in close-knits units would have held the rare advantage of open season, with every object sighted fair game and no limit on the bag. Think of tangled tows by the dozen, sitting-duck steamers, and hundreds of confused small boats! The night promised a veritable destroyer sailor's dream. Fulfilment lay easily within their capability. Dis-aster portions could have been dealt *Sea Lion* in one grand orgy, his wretched bubble whipped into a red froth on the sea.

To carry the sequence further in speculation about the actions of numerous anti-invasion patrol craft deployed closer along England's shores, or about the appearance of heavier ships in the dawn, to make sure that any landing elements who gained the shore were cut off, has small value. *Sea Lion* would already have been gutted, his vitals strewn on the waters. Execution of operation *Sea Lion* on 27 September 1940 as set up held the sole prospect of major German disaster. He could have offered no serious challenge on the field of battle in England.[6]

[6] One Transport Fleet Commander expressed himself as follows in a letter of 1953. "My present Estimate of the Situation is still the same as I wrote in my official report . . . end of October 1940. . . . In my opinion successful execution of Operation *Sea Lion* in late summer and fall 1940 was not practicable. . . ." He went on to elaborate his reasons and closed with, "The most dangerous situation for the Transport Fleet was . . . the night run where an all-out commitment of enemy light forces must have called forth incalculable troubles of a material as well as

The verdict is a devastating one. It seems to leave Invasion England 1940 not a shred of substance or authenticity. This is not so. For with correction of a few major misconceptions, the German arms could have invaded England. Who at the time was sure about these, or that correction would remain beyond the Germans? We content ourselves with mention of only one item.

Local sea control in the Channel arena could have been disputed with greater efficacy. If air and naval effort had at the outset challenged, and together concentrated against that ultimate bar to crossing, the British naval power in the Channel, a major step toward rendering *Sea Lion* feasible would have been underway. Instead, the Germans shackled themselves to an impractical air prerequisite, already muddied by psychological effect. Yes, why *Sea Lion* did not go had more to it than the question of capability. Indeed, pursuit of strictly strategical objectives based on capability was unthinkable while Hitler held Supreme Command. For him, intent, not capability, decided.

More than any other single factor, Adolf Hitler rendered invasion impossible.

---

psychological nature. . . . That I did not stand alone in my views was apparent to me from a discussion with Admiral Lütjens and his Chief of Staff during mid-October, 1940."

Sturmboats in assault exercise under smoke screen. *(Courtesy Colonel Blumentritt)*

Men who would storm the beach. *(Courtesy Colonel Schuber)*

A typical Rhine River powered barge (Motorschiff) in her own water.

A Rhine barge as converted for landing use (prahm) engaged in exercises in coastal waters. *(Courtesy Captain Erich Lehmann)*

Havoc in Dunkirk harbor, September 1940. *(Top courtesy General Kissel. Bottom courtesy Captain Heinrich Bartels)*

Captain Werner Lindenau, Commander Transport Fleet D, and aides. *(Courtesy Rear Admiral Werner Lindenau)*

Transport Fleet D exercises off Boulogne. *(Courtesy Rear Admiral Werner Lindenau)*

10. *Assessment*

Hitler's Intent

Ostensibly *Sea Lion's* writ did not extend beyond the psychological realm where his master sought so diligently to apply him. In retrospect, many Germans will have it no other way, especially men close to reflector Göring. A bluff, pure and simple, they call the landing furor. Undeniably, this in effect became *Sea Lion's* lot and, with the passage of time, the same assessment has been made of the Air effort. It must be granted that neither effort achieved strategical objectives necessary to Britain's military defeat. Hitler fought not a battle of arms but a war of nerves in which both *Eagle* and *Sea Lion* were threatening gestures lacking conviction. So it turns out today, but who could have labelled them so at the time, or would have dared to?

Post-knowledge finding of threat, or even bluff, by result, offers but a half-answer to shifty *Sea Lion,* his master and their milieu. It does not permit dismissal of invasion thought of 1940 as counterfeit, nor does it fully explain Hitlerian intent. For *Sea Lion* filled a demand inescapable and offered profits undeniable. To the times, to Englishmen generally and Germans alike, to German Army leadership and the Navy, and to the only man who could make it go, Invasion remained a vital, ineradicable and decisive course of action that would not out. Invasion had to be granted its day. Remember the por-

tentous days of *Wunschkonzert* and the pull of those times. Not to
prepare a landing would have been absurd. England understood this
and rose to defend. America worried and scraped the bottom of
her ammunition barrel, and sent the scrapings overseas. Hitler
could not escape the challenge and consented to invasion preparations much against his inner predilection for befriending Britain. *Sea
Lion* followed, and traced a strange pattern of Hitlerian insecurity
before Problem England. It wrote the story of one man's struggle
with a problem beyond him. This became the meaning of *Sea Lion*
forever to be remembered. Dictators are, like all men, in final
analysis at the mercy of their personal capacity and needs.

We retrace the threads. Dunkirk produced the first direct combat
with Britain alone. Hitler and Göring attempted to seal up the BEF
from the air to stimulate negotiation. The private formula for England was thus disclosed—invade not the island but the islanders' minds
and induce the English to talk. Recall Hitler's inner reluctance toward a slugging match with Britons—he could not gauge its consequence; recall, also, how stoutly Göring assured him the BEF would
be contained, how excuses were concocted to hold back the Army,
and how finally Hitler gave in to piece-meal release when the hostages
commenced slipping through his fingers by sea. Marked points of
correspondence to this pattern existed in *Sea Lion*. Hitler contrived
with Göring to reduce the RAF to impotence, and then to hold London hostage from the air. He procrastinated interminably on the *Sea
Lion* decision while Air effort proceeded. Stalemate ensued. But
had the British streamed out of London in panic, had the government
tottered, might he not have loosed Army *Sea Lion*, as he finally did
the tanks at Dunkirk? In his oft-expressed invasion philosophy Hitler
seemed to think of *Sea Lion* as a reserve for just such a stroke. Yet
he remained unsure, and so must we.

Throughout the summer months of 1940 General Jodl established
himself as the most reliable reflector of Hitlerian invasion thought.
The remarkable thing was that, basically, this body of thought remained fairly stable. Jodl first expressed these basic landing ideas in
his summation of 30 June. Elaborating Dunkirkian formula of Air
squeeze as a start, he went on to mention invasion as an outside
measure to be undertaken not "for the purpose of overthrowing England *militarily* . . . but only to deal the death stroke, if still necessary,
to an economically paralyzed and in the air impotent England."

"Nevertheless," he said, in response to the pull of the times, "the landing must be prepared in all details as *ultima ratio*." Hitler modified this stand only slightly and in direct proportion to mounting evidence of British intransigence. Landing attack, he finally admitted, alone offered decisive results; but then re-entered doubts followed by reassuring thoughts of still other means for eventually bringing Britain around.

Mers el Kebir shocked the complacent hope of early settlement. It brought the problem of the sea to the forefront. The incident unmasked Hitler as powerless to dispose of the French Fleet, and pointedly demonstrated German impotence to deal with Britain over the sea. The disconcerting mobility of sea power took sea-theorist Hitler aback. Though he had frequently held forth on *Seegeltung* (sea potential), and though he felt the shock of Mers el Kebir, his impatience and propensity for blitz decision drove him further along the road of victory by fright. The Royal Navy in a very practical sense lay at the crux of his problem, not alone for thwarting invasion directly, but in a broader sense as the guardian of British sovereign power. The Navy betokened Empire and Rule Britannia; if not from London, then from elsewhere. The hostages might not stay put in London any more than they had in Dunkirk; and on second thought, what good was a broken empire to him? Its pieces would only benefit others. His faultless plan for the Continent fell into jeopardy. All this, Hitler thought through and made logic of it, but he could not apply it. His indecision became apparent in the vacuous peace proffer of 19 July. The truth was the problem admitted of no direct solution by the Hitlerian method. He fell prey to his own inner urges to go the long way round, if at all, and find his redemption in Russian adventure. This he was happy to do.

Invasion Russia was his heart's desire and transcended all other dreams. The youth Hitler abandoned the slums of Vienna resolved on a career in architecture. World War I shifted that urge to political building, yet he never forgot the earlier dream and often returned to it. He depicted for himself the rebuilding of Germany, not only politically and spiritually, but physically and geographically as well. By his exacting system of self-debate he sifted out a personal and world wide solution into an obsession of granite durability. In this wise emerged the man Hitler, one of the world's strongest never-giver-uppers, wedded to his unalterable resolve to create Germania. It later produced an inner compulsion to carve out a Continental empire from the vast Russian spaces. No Hitlerian action or inaction may be treated adequately or appraised authentically without projecting it upon the screen of this controlling dream. So it went with invasion and kindred operations concerning Britain. All of them remained tributary to glorious vindication in Russia.

True decision of this character brought to Hitler the release of redemption. Two interdependent spiritual features were involved: Hitler's personal mythology; and the mechanism by which he certified and then implemented mythological tenets. Both have been observed in the course of this record. The mechanism functioned as an Estimate of the Situation through self-debate, which accumulated Drive, as it worked toward solution. The solution joined the infallible Hitlerian mythology for immediate or future use. Thus decision to act was a matter of making mythology come true; and for this reason both the decision and its execution manifested such singular personal force. Hitler's spiritual integrity depended thereon. Without Drive he could neither decide nor act.

England was a partner, not an enemy, in Hitlerian mythology. No solution by force existed, so that for *Sea Lion* the baffled Hitler was never able to generate the personal Drive requisite for getting the beast underway. What a fearsome spectacle the contrary could have offered; that is, had Hitler, primed with Frontal energies after France, set up a forward command post on the Channel, pulled out his lash and driven for the military reduction of England, as he did for the reduction of Poland and France. Speculation on such a scene still affords a rich harvest of what-might-have-beens in Europe today, so strikingly had this man's powers disclosed themselves, when a project became his very own "must"! England was never that.

But Russia was. Established in the twenties as a basic doctrine, and privately reaffirmed from time to time, this dream gave off tremendous compulsive forces. They cried out for fulfilment, no matter what; and no matter how remote Russia stood in the strategical demands of the war. The inner struggle culminated when Hitler, deep in dilemma, enacted for himself a personal brand of Götterdämmerung at the Wagnerian performance in Bayreuth on 23 July 1940. It may well have served as the final inspirational push into Russia, and with that, peace of mind about England. She could wait, a thought that brought almost the relief that a clear-cut decision would have— the old one of courtship restored, because destroying her bordered on destroying a part of himself. Air war, *Sea Lion* and related schemes took on a clear-cut and happier contributive character. The nagging dilemma was no longer what to do about England as much as it was how to speed Invasion Russia. These words frame our central finding governing Hitler's intent. His private urge to create Germania in central Europe asserted itself as the overriding force to sidetrack Problem England. The highly personalized motive at work led to the abandonment of the strategic initiative in the west, and this constituted the pivotal event of the war in Europe.

It appears we have but succeeded in coming the full circle of down-grading *Sea Lion* to inanity. The double-mindedness of his master rejects a conclusion so simple. From the rational outside the grim necessity of preserving hard-won initiative and avoiding war on two fronts persisted. Hitler pressed all the more for decision by fright; and as air prospect waned he waxed loath to give up the last tie in *Sea Lion*. All this toil and trouble could not go for naught.

Sea Lion personified Hitler discomfited; Hitler hungry for settlement with England in the West so he might go East; Hitler off-again-on-again, never quite sure, straddling to the end in the hope of a break. Invasion England failed to happen, not because Hitler willed against it, but because he could not will at all where she was concerned! Thus have we seen the German Führer struggle with a problem beyond the ken or can of his personal system. It defeated him.

Authoritarians of today are by no means free from personal fetters of the same stamp.

Let Us Study the Leaders!

Portent of failure in the war may well be the central theme of *Sea Lion* memory that history will retain, or have room for; and as such the impression will be authentic—though incomplete in many particulars. Failure before England was a manifestation of a problem rooted much deeper and wider in the phenomenon we call Hitler.

Memory is short and fickle. We have experienced a gaping difference between the reconstruction of events and the climate of the times in which they happened. It seems that history tends to want things too rational, when actually events assume that aspect only from the distance of a retrospect in possession of all factors. Today a completely rational exegesis can be readily constructed around Hit-

ler's actions, as many Germans have done. But their expositions
disclose rationalized hindsight. At the time many things were irrational. This they forget. So may history also neglect the spiritual
factors that help shape events for the leaders.

Ah, the leaders! We tire of them; most of all, we are tired of
Adolf Hitler. Yet, to come out with it is to grant him some due.
Early in this story we had hoped to fence him off in a corner of the
times, but it would not go, for he often bulked as the personifier, if
not the maker of those times. It can be that leaders only anticipate
and catalyze the forces around them. Yet Hitler seemed to do more.
Perhaps we are tired of ourselves who were also a part of his time
and failed to appraise him correctly.

Now at the end of our story we are convinced that a closer contemporary valuing of the inner Hitler might have sharpened insight
into the "why" of things and mitigated their dangers. Let us recall
the labels "official" and "private" applied to distinguish the duality
of Hitler's scheming. These terms gradually approached equality
with "rational" (or logical) on the one hand, and "irrational" (or
illogical) on the other. We have heard him debate the rational within and without; his contemporaries heard him put forth uncanny logic.
But if one knew him, one saw the "irrational" in his background,
which might likewise have been the anticipatory, increasingly claim
the day. Thus he illumined the character of his inner self—wolf and
rabbit, knave and knight—with frightening clarity, and set a pattern
for his actions. The pattern is incontestable.

It tacked this way and that, revealing many facets, but its linea-
ments held fast. They revealed a Hitler falling victim to a rare mixture of animalism and megalomania. He wove his very own design
on the simple loom of jungle law. He ignored long-established principles and disciplines of mankind for the rigid short cuts of the jungle.
In the process he began to differ markedly from other men as he
turned jungle law to universal use. It became the terrifying simplifier
that alone could see to the crux of things and remedy all ills to the
profit and exaltation of animal self. At one time art stood him in
stead as his higher allegiance, then architecture, which was succeeded
by *Volk* and Party, and eventually by Germania. She too succumbed
when self took her place. He had nowhere higher to go. No thing or
person, or symbol, deserving of his loyalty, longer existed. There

was only infallible Self, who in the end failed him too. Hitler left for our day a classic demonstration of an attempt to make animal master over man.

Dead-end in the animal kingdom becomes the sad lot of totalitarian leaders when they run out of loyalty. Usually it is possible to distinguish a lofty initial goal and trace a pattern of advance toward it. At a point they falter; the actions no longer jibe with the goal. That is the proofing point where history has seen most absolutists depart from human reality. They lose perspective and grow too big for the job. No longer do they belong to the times and express them; the times belong to them. They have lost goal and God, and there they enter the blind alley. Sober study can discover the enemy's point of departure from reality, plot his degree of divergence, and forecast within useful limits his reaction to specific events.

From Hitler's pattern we call to witness his overriding compulsion to crush Russia. It made up the ultimate sum of his intent; he had to go East. This urge, which contributed to abandonment of initiative in the West, stalemated his war in the pivotal area where history and the climate of the times demanded it be fought to conclusion. Suppose that accident had removed him in mid-summer 1940, would Invasion Russia still have prevailed over resolution of Problem England, when no *Sturm und Drang* for that eccentric East move existed, except inside Adolf Hitler? The deeper student of history can retort that the need would have developed, that is, Hitler merely anticipated and implemented the less obvious course of history. Perhaps so, but it cannot be proved, whereas the power of the Hitlerian compulsion has been. Stronger notice and accent is due these ready criteria that leaders in themselves offer. Opportunities called to notice by Hitler have not been taken advantage of.

Our investigation suggests that knowledge of the inner compulsions of men in authority can light the way of events. The definitive spiritual signals given off by Hitler were generally neglected. Of course all men emit signals on the courses to which they become committed, but the totalitarians suffer from specific weaknesses. The totality of their control makes every action or inaction a signal, and each action is circumscribed by their personal understanding. If *Sea Lion* and Hitler teach anything, it is that we must know the personal patterns of the leaders. What private compulsions impel them?

Policy Without Strategy

Reflection on the urges that incite leaders thrusts us into the realm of policy and the relation of policy to its helpmate, strategy. It was in policy that Hitler's intent expressed itself, and to the confusion of strategy. We mean by strategy, war, plus its plans and measures, for acquiring the physical objectives that will force a desired change in enemy policy. It is doubtless true that at the root of Hitler's failure lay the grandiose policy his spirit required him to adopt. But a mentality that could generate a policy so ambitious was bound by the same token to go astray in whatever strategy, political or military, it invoked to make the policy come true. This is exactly what happened. Many personal Hitlerian characteristics militated against sound military strategy, and in the forefront was a cocksure confidence in his own ability to achieve political effects without fulfilling strategical demands, or even thinking them through. His main weapon was psychological pressure, and of all examples, *Sea Lion* furnished the most convincing one. The corruption of true strategy was, however, in course long before Invasion England came into consciousness.

From the very start up his blind alley "political action," as he called it, engaged the attention of Hitler to the exclusion of all else. The connotations carried for him by this term "political" were myriad and all pleasing to his ego, for this comprised the sphere of activity in absolutes that he claimed for his own. The term lent a diffused, mysterious sense to any scheme or action, warlike or other. Indeed, he regarded war as mere intensified election brawling, on an international scale. Thus the march into the Rhineland of 1936 was touted as a political measure, which Hitler counted among his boldest decisions. The threatening scene whereby he exacted a signed request from President Hacha for "protection" of Czechoslovakia in 1939, he hailed as his cleverest political stroke. The assurances he pledged military chieftains in the fall of 1939 to justify the attack on Poland, and later the violation of the Low Countries, were all rooted in so-called "political" arrangements. He would arrange by political magic to avoid open war, or throw the blame for it on the opponents. In sum, "political" encompassed all manner of chicanery, frame-ups, pressure, and threat of violence to win an election, or to gain the ends of policy. Hitler pursued these activities with the keenest zest as he molded a political operating system, seated in deception and trickery for which military power became the principal tool. His end object was to persuade the world of overwhelming German military might. His unstrategical employment of that might led to failure.

In actual fact the sinews of German military power needful for these goings-on were simply not present, nor could they have been at the end of the short time span from 1933 to 1939. The creation of an officers' corps alone precluded it. By 1939 the active Army stood at 730,000 troops, the Luftwaffe had some 4,300 planes, the Navy 2 battleships, 3 pocket versions, 2 heavy and 6 small cruisers, 20 destroyers and 19 fleet submarines. Supplies of munitions and transport were not abundant. The assemblage constituted a tidy task force, but one capable of achieving only limited strategical objectives and thus warranting only limited goals in policy. At the time Hitler may actually have regarded his goals as limited. At any rate he kept on, and his appetite grew with eating.

For a time he succeeded. Often by catching his neighbors and their backers off balance he managed to score with a technique of political blitz, the forerunner of the military blitz. Method was the thing. It displaced true strategy with sensationalism, and miracles became the established order of the day. Technological trickery substituted for fundamental strategical thinking. Many sober minds were swept along into an unreal world of cheap, puerile superficiality.

With Hitler on their hands the professional strategists could hardly avoid thinking first of political operating, and eventually dealing directly in political matters. Differences with Hitler over the probable political reactions of the West to gambits he proposed against his smaller neighbors seduced the officers into making exaggerated political prognoses. When events proved them wrong, they took a licking. Whereupon when war came Hitler moved into the professional preserve, and to all outward appearances, repeated the performance in field operations. The soldiers (for the conflict was chiefly with that senior service, the Army) were irrevocably lost. *Gröfaz* had them.

An erosion of professional responsibility for strategy set in. While some officers had recognized the trend prior to the war, it drove in upon the leaders with a vengeance early in the hostilities. As most men would have, they attempted to co-exist with the Hitlerian usurpation, and having compromised to that extent, they were bound body and soul. The fate of the leaders was a terrible one. They found themselves forever engaged on multiple fronts: one against the war adversary, another against Hitler, a third against each other, and a tragic fourth against their own honor and integrity. Instead of honest military planning they fell into the short-sighted game of outguessing Hitler. Strategy and political operating mixed in a hopeless tangle. The corruption robbed the officers of spiritual faith in the war's aims and led to the most fateful of lacks in the operational field—the lack of a sound and worthy strategical purpose.

In due course, *Sea Lion's* floundering disclosed the truth that serious war planning had stopped short at the Channel in a confused void of random thoughts about "political" maneuvering and some oddments on air warfare. A strategical basis needful for making an end to the war with Britain had not been achieved, nor had its substance ever been thought through. This incredible failure could not be true except for the fact that it happened. Not a single orthodox military Estimate of the Situation for the circumstance is on record in the German papers; so far had strategy deteriorated.[1]

All up and down the face of German war-waging retrograde thinking left a deep scar. Its mark showed in *Sea Lion's* ambiguity but even more plainly in his companion piece of the Air. Behind the pernicious prerequisite of absolute air command over south England lurked the "private" unstrategical "political" purpose of air fright. The air effort fell between these two incompatible objectives, while ignoring any bona fide contribution toward the inevitable challenge to invade. All had been staked on evoking animal fright by grand jungle roar from on high. Under that umbrella Navy and Air took grateful refuge. Army alone stood fast for the sounder, but by then infeasible, strategy of invasion. It was far too late.

If strategy is to be preserved, and history teaches it should be even for this day, then a cure within professional confines may be in order. An essential step is professional attention to a logical derivation of strategy, followed by effective articulation to policy makers. There exists a hoary program of reasoning in professional lore called the Estimate of the Situation. It is designed to stimulate and organize mental processes while solving strategical and operational war problems.

---

[1] This is not to say there were not many papers on record to prove preconceived notions. One such was a Navy study (fall of 1939) of justification for its favorite strategy of starving England out by war on overseas commerce (*Verschärften Seekrieg gegen England*), or siege. Not this paper nor any other that has come to hand started from scratch with the circumstance of facing England crosschannel and estimated out what might be done and what could not be done.

Factors of own strength and weakness are balanced against those of the enemy and resolved into a course of action. Policy-maker Hitler ground out his own estimates vocally in monologues. They were about the only intrinsically honest ones made, and for his purposes they batted a very high average. Such other estimating as went on around him purposed mainly to palliate or defeat him, rather than produce strategy.

War colleges prescribe the Estimate for the solution of their hypothetical problems, but in actual practice of war and preparing therefor we most often dispense with the laborious drill, like children do with their books when school is out. In an effort to avoid hard-headed reasoning, we give in to intellectual laziness; or perhaps emotional forces in an actual problem overshadow those of reason; or, in dealing with politicians, higher echelons of command must push expediency and artful persuasion. "Papers" are written a-plenty, each supported by captivating charts and facile presentation. In place of a statement of the problem, we frequently start with the answer, and emerge with ammunition for its sale or with a torpedo for sinking a proposition, distasteful from the start. It is a feeble planning system, this special public pleading of likes and dislikes. Professional warriors may again be found out as the cost of strategy continues to mount, unless they return to deeper probing with honest evaluation.

If one is blessed with unlimited resources and can indulge in experimentation, the proper strategical emphasis emerges despite mistakes. One learns by doing. These days are nearing an end, and we approach the situation of the Germans, where each decision tended more and more to imply fatal commitment. The decision may have to be sound in the beginning. Infallible answers cannot be ground out by the Estimate of the Situation, any more than they can by other human processes. But objective solutions, based on logically developed thought, can provide the professional men with a sound and unifying base of strategy to strengthen them in their professional convictions. So fortified, they can efficiently and honorably discharge a meeting with policy-makers.[2]

---

[2] An Estimate of the Situation before Pearl Harbor should have developed the inevitability of Japanese naval effort to eliminate our forces sitting on their eastern flank. None worthy of the name was on hand at the time of attack. Shallow professional convictions considered such a thought fantastic. In the case of *Sea Lion,* the British professionals were armed with a good Estimate that concluded invasion was impossible. Yet Lord Alanbrooke, the commander of British Home Forces, during *Sea Lion,* recalled a dinner of 16 September 1940 and wrote of the time, "I had a

If we wonder in turn about the province of the policy-maker, we are assailed by an apparent parallel between Hitler invoking the Luftwaffe and statesmen of today calling on the nuclear bomb. Neither circumstance has marked a step forward in the refinement of war to the point of doing without it, which is strategy's ultimate mission. Hitler had policy swallow up strategy and now we seem to witness the opposite course in which A-Bomb and Company have taken over policy. The result is the same—strategy, the only viable influence for ameliorating violence, has been debased. The course of it has been simple. Technology has hurdled over tactic and strategy and has undertaken to express policy directly. It envisions an absolute policy, dictated by absolute weapons. It is so refreshingly simple and primitive that all can understand it, and its very simplicity encourages a public belief that we face an all-or-nothing alternative at each turn. Having accepted this fallacy, the laymen falls victim to the delusion of dealing in once-and-for-all settlement. There is a sophomoric ring about these notions that reminds us of Hitler, the great simplifier and his Luftwaffe or V 2. He proved those "absolutes" to be myths, yet we keep on. He proved that policy and strategy are not one. To make them so will mark a step backward toward the jungle policy of survival by simple destruction.[3]

If the present trend continues the professionals must shoulder a good share of the blame, for they have thus far failed to produce and articulate to policy-makers a sound strategy for the new weapons. Warriors long ago refined brute force into an instrument of the intellect, expressed in strategy. They thereby made an art of war, which helped mitigate its horrors. War waging became a specialty of dedicated men who acted on established principles and saved their violence for strategical results. Each new weapon found a place in the professional arsenal if it contributed to strategical effect, or it fell

---

strong conviction that we were on the eve of invasion . . ." His professional base had failed to withstand the popular hue and cry around him.

[3] It is not meant that politics and strategy can be divorced. On the contrary they must achieve a more perfect union. Yet while their interdependence is recognized and encouraged, the validity of the sphere of each must be respected. The spheres are distinguished when we say that the politican concentrates on winning the peace while the warrior devotes himself to winning the war. War gets into killing. This is the fact that sets it apart. The killing must be efficient and productive, that is, it must be strategic. Of course it is clear that Hitler committed his original sin in policy, but it is conceivable that, had he been amenable to the derivation of a sound supporting strategy, he would have discovered the fallacy in his policy. The move thereupon would have been either to change or abandon it. His wilful pursuit of policy without strategy blinded him to the policy's futility.

by the wayside. In the past evaluation of new weapons, the fuller the participation of the public, the less this principle has prevailed. Excessive public interest seems to force the use of terror weapons. In World War II the wraps were kept on gas warfare by common professional consent, not by public prohibition; while the submarine, used less discriminately and involving civilian casualties and public hue and cry, achieved a place as an accepted weapon. The same became true of the airplane and the bomb. It is the lay imagination that is today forcing preoccupation with the new weapons. The tendency is to jump over strategy in the delusion of a cheap and direct road to victory and once-and-for-all settlement. The result has been to raise the price to staggering figures. The road is two-way, open to the adversary as well as ourselves. We have arrived at a dead end that smells like Hitler's, not through a Hitler of our own but by meeting the delusive publicity of the adversary with unstrategical images of our own. It will take leadership of the highest order and integrity to banish these unstrategical cure-alls from policy, and to push the forcible measures back where they belong with the professional warriors. They are the men who must fit the new weapons into modern strategical principles, and make these speak for themselves.[4]

The natural human aspiration is to deal wholesale and eliminate the warriors and their drums altogether—do away with them and war. But reflection reveals this panacea to be as fatuous and empty as outlawing evil. What we seek on earth is not heaven, but life in the best human tradition. Life includes challenge and reply, as well as conflict, and even war, or it becomes meaningless. Building brick on brick in the tradition and experience of our human heritage offers a sounder approach to the continued way upward than radical reversion to the more primitive short cuts.

Human intellect has discovered new tools of building. The initial forcible application of nuclear power was primitive, unintelligent. Sobered by this error we should make a fresh start. History comes forward again to vouchsafe that the use of nuclear weapons for resolving human challenges will prove as ineluctable as their employ-

[4] It can be objected that Hitlerian method must be combatted with a like tactic. This answer is short on intellectual resource, and skips over true strategy. Better to ask what made the Hitlerian tactic come near succeeding. Now the "Channel" has widened to include the breadth of the Atlantic. In dealing with a threat from the far side, we seem, in the 1940 vein, to be prone to fabricate Russian capabilities that reach far beyond reality. Thus we feed the Russians' belief of their own invincibility, as was for a time the case with Hitler.

ment to meet material needs.   In practical life a restriction of eligible
targets open to warfare has proved workable and more profitable than
attempted elimination of weapons.   This may be the crux of the thing.
Nuclear weapons, unrestricted as to target eligibility, become unstrategical, and such use of them leads the world into Hitler's blind
alley.   Actually, the basic rule of limiting targets to military objectives
(which strategical employment means) has enjoyed a long and honor-
able history.   In its course some principles have been established,
and although not always observed, the urge in the right direction has
persisted.   The concept of target eligibility stands as a practical
approach toward integrating the new weapons into strategy, and
strategy can thus remain the bulwark for war's refinement rather than
its extension.

Let us look back into history and hearten ourselves with mankind's
experience; indeed we need look back only to *Sea Lion*.   Let us revive
our professional heritage, sound strategy, and bring it to the support
of our harried policy makers.

The Re-emergence of Landing Thought

We turn happily to doxologize on those *Sea Lion* signals that
emanated more strictly from professional sources.   If his experience
manifested a warning to correlate policy and strategy, it struck a
resounding blow for the need of unity in spirit among the combat
arms.   For the amphibious problem, as none other, demands that
land, sea, and air power fuse together in action toward a common military objective.   This imperative came harder to the Germans than
natural perversities warranted.

Interservice mistrust and scheming to gain the inside track with
the Führer was one factor that added yet another front to sap the
vitality and honest purposes of the German professional leadership.
Sea Lion evidenced appalling instances of self-interest and disunity.
Army and Air, having gone to glory together in the early stages of
the land campaigns, found small cause to quarrel until Dunkirk cast
a shadow.   Shortly, came Broad versus Narrow Front to muddy Army-
Navy understanding.   Between Navy and Air, Göring's arrogant can-
nibalizing of the naval air arm during the Battle of Britain fanned
a fight that was never extinguished.   All conflicts were carried to
Hitler, the omniscient, who harbored his own suspicions and designs.

The furtive method he practiced of dealing apart with each service head insured subservience, and fed personal ambition to thicken still more the general climate of jealousy and mistrust. But like all tong wars this one inherited distinctive cants from the disparate origins of the three contenders. Hitler himself epitomized the basic differences and his personal feelings, when he used to exclaim to aides on frequent occasions, "I have a reactionary Army, a Christian Navy, and a National Socialist Air Force."

The Luftwaffe, created by Hitlerian genius as a Nazi product, he could count on, safe with Göring. That one took full advantage and flew his own orbit close about the Führer on a level above the other leaders. The Luftwaffe was founded in fraud and duplicity, and Göring brought his unique position with the Führer to bear on interservice relationships. To the Army his intrigues and clownish antics made him unworthy of the highest rank of all services. The Navy he threatened with extinction from the first by air power. Overall an unhealthy climate prevailed.

The Hitlerian gibe "Christian Navy" may have been directed at Raeder's known religious principles, but it also indubitably included the holier-than-thou attitude assumed toward laymen by seamen when the imponderables of their profession are not understood. The seaman falls into the habit of invoking the mysteries of Neptune. The German sailors did their full share of this and more. Not alone that, the problem facing them defied the ordinary solutions of Neptune. Germany was hemmed in geographically so that a big-ship Navy became an artificial contrivance for which a plausible war function was hard to devise. World War I had proved this so with the failure of the risk concept.[5] Double error took over. The German sailors could not be won away from a dream of stalking the wide blue waters in British sea boots instead of slogging about coastal waters in wooden sabots, which was their lot. They nurtured an illusion of absolute naval war. It was as wide of the mark as that of absolute air war; but not to men struggling for a place in Hitlerian sun. The Navy prospered on a bigoted conception of a private war for each service, and hers would be siege by sea against England,

[5] In speaking of the faulty Tirpitz risk Concept, we should remember that Hitler's Luftwaffe and its use against England represented a similar demonstration of fallacious theorizing. It is pertinent to ask whether we are falling into the pitfalls of another *Risiko gedanke* when we propose to prevent war by postulating massive retaliation.

the chief foe.   From such heroic but uncomfortable strategic plan it seemed natural to level shafts at the more spectacular feats going on in the other private wars.   The Navy flailed about in its own tight circle with little regard for what the land objectives should be except in so far as they contributed to *Seekrieg*.   The point missed was that naval warfare offers no end in itself.   It is conducted to insure and facilitate the decisive extension of power (military and civil) on land where the final decision must fall.

There on land lay Germany's chief instrument of force—the Army —forged long ago and tempered by ceaseless land warfare into an incomparably fine weapon.   Neither on the naval side nor on that of the Army did it but fleetingly occur to the thinkers that, lacking decisive naval superiority, they might still have a chance against Britain in this day of restricted fleet action through amphibious operations within narrow, controllable waters.[6]

Land warfare never had a beginning for Germans; it had always been with them.   The natural handicap imposed by geography was surely a contributory factor, but not necessarily the determining one for a race so puissant and vigorous.   Events of history contrived to turn the Germans in on the Continent.   A small sea tradition bequeathed by the Hanseatic League lost itself in the limbo of the Thirty Years' War and a further procession of Continental conflicts.   Germany grew into a nation of soldiers in tradition and thinking; the land warriors Frederick, Blücher, Gneisenau and Moltke were the heroes of song and story, while the sailors of the coastwise commerce and fishing fleets along the drizzled uninviting northern waterfront stayed unsung and forgotten.   In the mid-twenties a disturbed Wolfgang Wegener wrote: "We are the heirs of our Continental past . . . . We all through tradition and instinct are more or less land-soldiers."

---

[6] Theoretical writing on sea power led the Old World to a concept of command of the sea as the ultimate and efficacious expression of sea power.   It encouraged a belief that a superior battle fleet implied command of the sea, and this could only be wrested from the supposed holder by challenging to fleet battle and winning it. In actual practice the modern trend is away from fleet actions toward local control or dispute of a sea area vital to a specific operations.   A convoy escorted overseas is an example.   The sea and air escort provides control in a secure bubble around, above, and below the convoy.   A landing attack is a further example; witness Guadalcanal.   Local sea control is estabilshed not by prior destruction of the enemy battle fleet but by enclosing the attack area in a bubble secure enough for the landing operation.   It is conceivable that, if German Luftwaffe and Navy could have worked together, local sea control adequate for *Sea Lion* might have been established by them in the Dover Narrows.

So the Army was landlord historically and actually; and wielded power accordingly. It was the potent force that Hitler recognized as basically opposed to him, and therefore, to him "reactionary." He used to lament that the Army held one lodge in its General Staff, that he unfortunately, had neglected to dissolve. From its commanding position nothing was more natural than that the Army felt little need for the other services except as auxiliaries. This was particularly the case with respect to that curious sailors' club, the Navy. Record of combined work is very scanty. There was the Boxer Rebellion in 1900; and the Ösel Islands of October 1917, some work together in Finland in the spring of 1918, but otherwise except for some minor communication exercises, nothing more until England was in sight cross-Channel.

These were the sterile service backgrounds upon which unhappy *Sea Lion* was superimposed. Unity of spirit or team work faced immense obstacles. Yet in practice amazing progress toward common cause resulted. *Sea Lion* proved a mighty leveler. This influence worked from the bottom up. One has only to read the concluding reports of the various commanders along the Channel coast to feel the mellowing power of everybody-in-the-same-boat. The soldiers had to go; the sailors had to get them there, with the help of the flyers. It was a revelation to discover this indivisible power of Land-Sea and Air in combat together. Here began true amphibious thought in our time. The landing spirit did not burst upon the world in a single flash; in fact, its genuine significance has not today been fully explored or digested.

When we harp on German failures connected with Invasion England, we should in fairness ask if any nation in 1940 thought well of assault from the sea or even had any clear notion of it. In Europe at that time such bizarre ideas, if not trapped in the shadows of Gallipoli, had been dissolved by the advent of air power, aided and abetted by modern mining, coastal smallcraft, and artillery. That is why Britons and Germans alike at once placed overriding emphasis on air supremacy. Invasion proposed to them an intellectual reversal, and especially so to the German Navy.

Yet there stood the water barrier; the eyes and ears of the world fixed on it. Something had to be done, that was plain. The all too tidy, but manifest, answer of invasion asserted itself because the astonished world became convinced of the possibility, even probability, in dismay over France's collapse and fear of German invincibility. For a full year and more the invasion incubus plagued Britain and transmitted its sinister warning over the world to produce a fresh awareness of landing operations and their potentialities. Our own professional thought and effort on the subject took a notable rise. Grudgingly Americans commenced tinkering with the production of landing craft, and were forced yet further along the line. Thus men grew landing conscious through *Sea Lion's* unconscious publicity, and by the time his season had ended, amphibious operations had become established as the major professional challenge of World War II. *Sea Lion* has need of no greater renown than this. He set the pace.

At the time, the far reaching implications of *Sea Lion's* teachings failed to affect German topmost professional thought significantly. Indeed, he had become something of a *bête noire* there, but elsewhere he percolated through strong and full. His practical lessons and their progression were unavoidable. German Army and Navy together learned a great deal about landing operations by the winter of 1940. Their experiences, compressed into a much shorter time span than that of the United States, foreshadowed our experience in every particular, and in about the same order: procurement of landing craft and training of crews, broad or narrow landing, day or dark, finding the designated beach, minesweeping and gunfire support, smoke screens, assault to carry the beach, timing and co-ordination, loading and unloading equipment, the beach and shore party, small unit combat, command afloat and ashore; the follow-up and the land fight. These problems were identified, and though not all solved to complete satisfaction, they first got on the books of professional thinking in dead earnest with *Sea Lion*—or in his rebuttal.

These hurdles of assault from the sea, at first formidable hazards, grew commonplace or even trite in the course of the war. Fighting men together surmounted the obstacles by making common cause. The inescapable truth broke through that among humans the ultimate decision falls on land, not in the air nor on the sea, but where men walk and live, on the good earth. That is where men give up. And to get at them, if they are beyond the seas, the sea must be crossed and the shore stormed to wrest the decision on land. One trouble in making common cause in any operation is that warriors distort the size of their own contribution toward victory. In amphibious action, however, where they struggle shoulder-to-shoulder to gain a common and visible objective, disruptive tendencies melt away. The fighters commence to realize the indivisability of their teamed efforts. In this call to team work lies the refreshing revelation and the redeeming virtue of Landing Operations. It comes to all who have toiled against the insuperable obstacles of the problem, and vindicates all travail. The rediscovery must not be lost.

Today, as never before, common cause among the combat arms cries out for fulfilment. The difficult human problem posed in the first place, and accentuated by the seductions of new weapons, can still be mastered if we have recourse to the landing experience. Out of it emerged the reality of a codified though flexible common doctrine, bearing forceful testimony of successful team work. The secret lay in physically and visibly "doing together." These are the main stays of teamwork whose climate can be made to pervade all undertakings if "doing together" grows to be more of a habit, especially in the upper echelons. The teaching offered by Hitler's failure, and his stimulation to landing doctrine, have not yet been taken to heart.

In evaluating the amphibious experience of the war a new term gained currency. We hear of "Amphibious Power" as something apart, and novel, it seems, by way of certifying a coming-of-age of assault from the sea. Yet this scheme of exerting force came of age, ages ago. Landing attack is therefore under revaluing not as something new but as a forgotten mode of operation that startled the world by re-emergence on a scale never before dreamt of and bearing decision in its hand. This event deserves added attention because of its evident strategical implications.

For America, Hitler and geography dictated the need, and the blessings of unlimited resources provided the tools. By the end of the war we had evolved the power to impose force across oceans on the point where it would do the most good: on the island of Japan, in the Mediterranean, or on the French Channel coast. America's boundaries had virtually swelled over the seas westward and eastward, to meet again, and with their expansion went her vast national potential. The key to this epochal *Völkerwanderung* resided in a highly versatile capability, evolved almost automatically out of nature's endowments, to land on a hostile shore and stay there till decision. We call this versatility Landing Power. In peace and war it personifies the initiative.

The vital strategical commodity, initiative, was what the Germans relinquished on the shores of the English Channel. The immense operational momentum rolled up against the West welled high during the summer of 1940 and threatened to sweep all before it. Then inexplicably the tide slowly receded. "The race to the sea" the Germans had won, but there they halted perplexed; not knowing what to do with it. They invoked air power only to have the Channel waters sound a Marne-like warning of stalemate. *Sea Lion* puffed and grunted, unequal to the symbolism. A stalemate by Air ensued; capability of maneuver had been lost for lack of Landing Power. From this blow to its initiative the German war machine never recovered. We say again, this was the pivotal event of the war and one in history.

Service Maritime entre la France et l'Angleterre

LANDING TICKET

delivered *gratuitously*

in exchange for a 1st class Ticket-Coupon

CALAIS to DOVER

Notice. — Passengers are warned, that no money can be claimed from them without a receipt being given out of a book with counterfoil for the amount paid.

Index

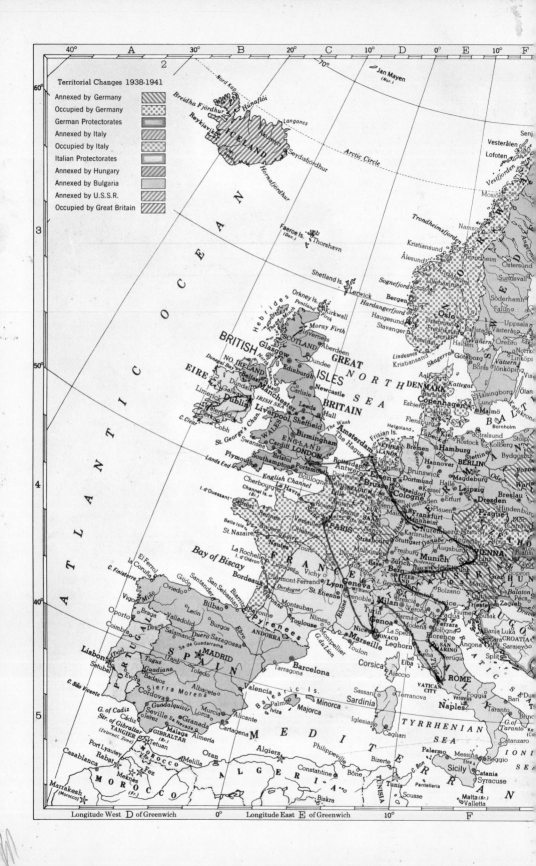

Territorial Changes 1938-1941

Annexed by Germany
Occupied by Germany
German Protectorates
Annexed by Italy
Occupied by Italy
Italian Protectorates
Annexed by Hungary
Annexed by Bulgaria
Annexed by U.S.S.R.
Occupied by Great Britain

ATLANTIC OCEAN

Arctic Circle

Jan Mayen (Nor.)

Nord Kap

Breidha Fjördhur
Reykjavik
ICELAND
Seydisfjördhur
Húnaflói
Langanes

Faeroe Is. (Dan.)
Thorshavn

Shetland Is.
Lerwick

NORWAY

Senj
Vesterålen
Lofoten
Vestfjorden
Mosjöen

Trondheimsfjorden
Namsos
Kristiansund
Ålesund
Trondheim
Östersund
Sundsvall
Söderhamn
Faluno
Uppsala

Orkney Is.
Kirkwall
Pentland Firth
Moray Firth
Inverness
Aberdeen
Dundee

Hebrides

BRITISH
ISLES

GREAT
BRITAIN

NORTH
SEA

Sognefjord
Bergen
Hardangerfjord
Haugesund
Stavanger

Oslo
Drammen
Fredrikstad

Lindesnes
Kristiansand
Skagerrak

Göteborg
Borås
Jönköping

Vänern
Vättern

Örebro
Norrkö
Visby

Glasgow
SCOTLAND
Edinburgh
Carlisle
Newcastle

The Minch

DENMARK
Aalborg
Esbjerg
Copenhagen

Kattegat
Halsingborg
Lund
Malmö

Öland

BALTIC

Bornholm

NO. IRELAND
Belfast
Donegal Bay
Galway
EIRE
Dublin
Limerick
Waterford
Cork
Cobh
C. Clear

IRISH SEA
Manchester
Liverpool
Leeds
Sheffield
ENGLAND
Birmingham
Cardiff
WALES
LONDON

Hull
The Wash

Helgoland
Frisian Is.
NETHERLANDS
Amsterdam
The Hague
Rotterdam
Antwerp
BELGIUM
Brussels

Flensburg
Lübeck
Kiel
Rostock
Hamburg
Bremen
Hannover
Münster
Dortmund
Essen
Düsseldorf
Cologne

Stralsund
Kolberg
Stettin
Oder
BERLIN
Magdeburg
Leipzig
Dresden
Breslau

Stolp
Bydgoszcz
Warszawa
Hindenburg

ATLANTIC OCEAN

St. George's Chan.
Swansea
Bristol
Southampton
Portsmouth
Plymouth
Lands End

English Channel
Cherbourg
Havre
Channel Is. (Br.)
Boulogne
Lille
Rennes
Brest
Belle Isle
St. Nazaire

FRANCE

Frankfurt
Mainz
Koblenz
Wiesbaden
Kassel
Halle
Plauen
Nuremberg
Karlsruhe
Stuttgart
Augsburg
Munich

Prague
CZECHO
Regens
VIENNA
Linz
AUSTRIA
Salzburg
Innsbruck
Bolzano

Bratislava
Györ
HUNG
Balaton
Pécs

Bay of Biscay
La Rochelle
I. d'Oléron
Bordeaux
Bayonne
Biarritz
San Sebastian

PARIS
Versailles
Orléans
Tours
Nantes
Loire
Dijon
Vichy
Clermont-Ferrand
Dordogne
St. Etienne

Strasbourg
Basel
Freiburg
Zürich
SWITZERLAND
Bern
Geneva
Mt. Blanc
Grenoble

Danube

Bodensee
Milan
Brescia
Verona
Bolzano
Turin
Padua
Venice
Trieste
Fiume
Susak
Zagreb

C. Finisterre
La Coruña
El Ferrol
Vigo
Miño
Oviedo
Gijón
Oporto
Braga
Coimbra
Douro

Santander
Bilbao
León
Valladolid
Burgos
Saragossa
Ebro

Montauban
Toulouse
Nimes
Montpellier
G. du Lion

Rhône

Lyon
Marseille
Nice
MONACO
Genoa
La Spezia
Leghorn
Parma
Modena
Bologna
Ferrara
Florence
Ancona
Perugia

YUGO
Banja Luka
CROATIA
Zara
Sarajevo
Split
ADRIATIC

SPAIN
MADRID
Salamanca
Duero
Sa de Guadarrama
ANDORRA
Pyrenees

PORTUGAL
Lisbon
Tagus (Tejo)
Setúbal
Evora
Guadiana
Badajoz
C. São Vicente

Valencia
Barcelona
Tarragona
Balearic Is.
Minorca
Majorca
Iviza
Palma

Corsica
Ajaccio
Elba

Siena
VATICAN
CITY
ROME
Naples
Vesuvius

SAN
MARINO

Foggia
Bari

Tagus
Albacete
Cordova
Guadalquivir
Seville
Jerez
Granada
Sa Nevada
Málaga
Almería
Murcia
Cartagena
Alicante

Sierra Morena
Toledo

TYRRHENIAN
SEA
Sassari
Terranova
Sardinia
Cagliari
Iglesias

Taranto
G. of
Taranto
Brinc

G. of Cadiz
Cádiz
Str. of Gibraltar
GIBRALTAR (Br.)
TANGIER (Internat. Zone)
Tetuan
Melilla
Oran

Algiers
Philippeville
Bône
Bizerte
C. Bon
Tunis
Pantelleria
TUNISIA

Palermo
Messina
Reggio
Sicily
Catania
Syracuse
Etna
Malta (Br.)
Valletta

IONI
SEA
Catanzaro

Casablanca
Rabat
Port Lyautey
MOROCCO
Fez
Meknès
Marrakesh (Morocco)

ALGERIA (Fr.)
Constantine
Biskra
Sousse
Sfax

Longitude West D of Greenwich   0°   Longitude East E of Greenwich   10°   F